About This Book

Why is this topic important?

In today's turbulent environment, both corporate and government organizations are seeking proven ways to compress cycle time, improve quality, and reduce costs. But for many, the practice of successfully implementing both dramatic *and* sustainable improvement remains elusive. One reason is that many improvement efforts take a narrow perspective. Some improvement efforts focus heavily on tools and methods. At best they give only lip service to the people and organizational culture elements of improvement, and at worst they ignore them. Other efforts focus heavily on addressing people and culture aspects, but give little attention to the tools that people need to improve once there is a more motivated workforce. Rarely do organizations provide a balanced approach to address both "hard" and "soft" aspects of improvement. This book provides principles, tools, and approaches for integrating three of the most proven, successful improvement disciplines available today: Lean Manufacturing, Six Sigma, and High-Performance Organizations.

What can you achieve with this book?

Leaders will find pragmatic advice on how to best integrate disciplines that focus on cycle time reduction, quality improvement, culture change, cost reduction, intrinsic employee motivation, and revenue enhancement. By successfully integrating these disciplines into a single effort, leaders can compress the transformation time that would be required to implement them separately. The book's tools, principles, "war stories," and checklists provide leaders with practical tips on what to expect, and what to do in each major stage of an improvement effort. Leaders can use the information in this book to start a great transformation effort from scratch or to energize a stalled improvement initiative.

How is this book organized?

There are two distinct parts and an appendix. Part 1 provides fundamental "must know" information for leaders charged with implementing dramatic, sustainable change. It covers the basics of Lean Manufacturing, Six Sigma, and High-Performance Organizations, as well as their combination into one integrated discipline: Lean Six Sigma/HPO (LSS/HPO). Part 2 contains pragmatic, "in the trenches" information, lessons learned, and best practices for leaders of LSS/HPO transformations. Information is organized according to the major stages of an LSS/HPO transformation: Initiation, Direction Setting, Design, Implementation, and Operations and Continuous Improvement. This organization ensures that leaders can access advice in the same sequence in which they will encounter opportunities and challenges during the transformation. The Appendix contains a glossary and a list of other hard copy and online references that will support leaders in their pursuit of improvement excellence.

"Tom Devane has provided a straightforward, practical guide for leaders striving to improve their business results. Moving quickly from theory to pragmatic tips and time-proven tools, Devane offers a leader's road map for performance improvements in today's rapidly changing business environment."

> — Karl Schmidt, vice president, process excellence, Johnson & Johnson

"This is the book that I've been looking for until now! Why? Because it exactly guides us through a practical methodology and concepts that any business enterprise would benefit from. From my experience as a business practitioner and quality trainer, it is vital to integrate and harmonize 'the hard part,' which helps to improve the current processes and products— tackling the vital few causes of the problems—and 'the soft part,' which helps to obtain the buy-in from the key stakeholders and the employees for a change. This book is a wonderful road map for innovation in the combination of productivity, interactive communication, and customer satisfaction."

> — Takashi Masumoto, regional leader and six sigma trainer, General Electric, Japan (as of June 30, 2003)

"This is a breakthrough synthesis of the best of cutting-edge practices for improving organizational performance. Tom Devane has developed a practical handbook for leaders, internal change agents, and consultants, clearly laying out the key principles and methods for achieving improvements that are both dramatic and sustainable. He describes an integrated, comprehensive approach that achieves greater results by building ownership for the change throughout the organization, while implementing process-improvement methods and tools, and building the core competencies required for implementation. The result is a road map for successful change that will work the first time around, start producing results quickly, and continue to work reliably into the future of the organization."

> — Saul Eisen, coordinator, psychology master's program in organization development, Sonoma State University

"Development of a high-potential organization requires dedication, innovation, and a set of proven processes. Tom Devane has given the tools to any company that wants to become a high-quality and -performance organization."

> — Gary Hunt, vice president human resources, administration, and MIS, Operational Management International, Inc. (Baldrige Award Winner in 2000)

THE **COLLABORATIVE WORK SYSTEMS** SERIES

Building collaborative capacity in the world of work

THE **COLLABORATIVE WORK SYSTEMS** SERIES

CENTER FOR THE STUDY OF WORK TEAMS

Integrating Lean Six Sigma and High-Performance Organizations

LEADING THE CHARGE TOWARD DRAMATIC, RAPID, AND SUSTAINABLE IMPROVEMENT

Tom Devane

A Wiley Imprint
www.pfeiffer.com

Published by Pfeiffer
An Imprint of Wiley
989 Market Street, San Francisco, CA 94103-1741
www.pfeiffer.com

For additional copies/bulk purchases of this book in the U.S. please contact 800-274-4434.

Pfeiffer books and products are available through most bookstores. To contact Pfeiffer directly call our Customer Care Department within the U.S. at 800-274-4434, outside the U.S. at 317-572-3985, fax 317-572-4002, or on-line at www.pfeiffer.com.

Pfeiffer also publishes its books in a variety of electronic formats. Some content that appears in print may not be available in electronic books.

ISBN: 0-7879-6973-7

Library of Congress Cataloging-in-Publication Data
Devane, Tom, 1954-
Integrating lean six sigma and high-performance organizations : Leading the charge toward dramatic, rapid, and sustainable improvement / Tom Devane.
    p. cm.
Includes bibliographical references (p.   ) and index.
   ISBN 0-7879-6973-7
1. Organizational effectiveness. 2. Six sigma (Quality control standard) 3. Organizational change. I. Title.
   HD58.9.D48 2004
   658.4′013—dc22

2003018775

Acquiring Editor: Matthew Davis
Director of Development: Kathleen Dolan Davies
Production Editor: Nina Kreiden
Editor: Rebecca Taff

Manufacturing Supervisor: Bill Matherly
Editorial Assistant: Laura Reizman
Illustrations: Richard Sheppard Illustration

Printed in the United States of America

Printing   10   9   8   7   6   5   4   3   2   1

CONTENTS

LIST OF TABLES, FIGURES, AND EXHIBITS

OVER THE PAST DECADE the world has witnessed an exponential growth in improvement initiatives such as Lean Enterprise and Six Sigma. I have been fortunate enough to have been involved in the Motorola deployment as an employee and as a consultant to companies such as AlliedSignal (Honeywell), Sumitomo Heavy Industries, and General Electric in their Six Sigma deployments. While these companies have been well-publicized for their Six Sigma successes, my observation is that their most successful implementations have naturally combined elements of Lean Enterprise (Lean), Six Sigma, and High Performance Organizations (HPO). Combining these three gets you the knowledge, the ownership, and the skills for dramatic, sustainable improvement.

Lean and Six Sigma can, and have, delivered results as stand-alone programs. But the results are often random and unpredictable. This is ironic for programs focused on reducing variation and intended to increase predictability. But by combining Lean, Six Sigma, and HPO practices, a company greatly increases its likelihood of success. Lean Enterprise and Six Sigma provide principles and tools for improvement. HPO provides the impetus for intrinsic motivation and sustainability. While it is possible to have isolated success in Lean and Six Sigma, the results won't be lasting without intrinsic motivation and a sense of ownership of results in the workforce. And those two factors are what HPOs provide.

Unfortunately, in many improvement efforts people focus heavily on improvement tools and virtually ignore the people side of change. These efforts tend to stall, quickly die out, and create resentment in the workforce for future attempts at improvement. I've often been called in for these second-round improvement attempts, and the improvement journey is much more difficult than when starting correctly from scratch.

This book tells leaders how to start correctly from scratch. It presents a straightforward, formalized approach to achieving improvements that are both dramatic and sustainable. In an easy-to-digest format this book encapsulates what excellent leaders have instinctively known for decades: there is tremendous leverage in addressing performance improvement from multiple fronts. Organizations where leaders have done this surpass the "me too" companies simply going through improvement motions and log in with world class results.

Listen to conversations around the water cooler at many organizations today and you'll hear assertions like "This company is experiencing initiative overload" and "I have too much on my plate." This language is symptomatic of companies launching a series of stand-alone programs as they search for the silver bullet that will solve all their problems. But enlightened leaders know better. They understand the effectiveness of simultaneous improvements, and the economics of skill building in critical core competencies for the organization. Instead of a series of one-shot training investments in improvement tools, these leaders favor training fewer resources in multiple disciplines who will drive integrated strategies such as Lean Enterprise, Six Sigma, and HPOs.

Tom Devane has created a book with practical advice on integrating the three most powerful and complementary improvement disciplines on the market today: Lean, Six Sigma, and HPOs. Tom calls on his extensive experience with integrating these disciplines to give leaders principles, tools, and a roadmap to assist them in their transformation to higher performance. In examples from both manufacturing and non-manufacturing settings, Tom provides leaders with insights about high-leverage leader actions, commonly encountered problems, and ways to address those problems.

This book is more than an esoteric treatise on the philosophy of integration. Tom offers up his extensive in-the-trenches experience in an easily comprehensible format for leaders at all levels. The tables, checklists, "war stories," and illustrations succinctly present information leaders need to know. As with Tom's previous book, *The Change Handbook: Group Methods for Shaping the Future,* the reader-oriented layout of each chapter and use of icons make it easy to find critical information. This book will provide today's busy executives and middle managers with an efficient way to extract the significant information they need to develop and design their own strategies.

I believe this book has three audiences. The primary audience is leaders seeking dramatic, sustainable improvements in their organizations. The second audience consists of people familiar with improvement tools, such as Six Sigma Black Belts and Lean experts, who wish to know more about addressing the people side of improvement and implementing sustainable gains. The third audience is internal change agents and organization development specialists who wish to know more about process improvement tools and principles.

This book makes a unique contribution to the improvement literature. Lots of books out there today describe tools for improvement teams. Lots of books talk about high-level theory. This book is a pragmatic guide that tells leaders how to conduct a successful transformation to higher, sustainable performance. This book makes several important contributions to the field:

- It provides practical tips for integrating "hard" and "soft" aspects of performance improvement.

- The templates and lessons learned analyses help leaders develop effective plans *and* execute them.

- It provides a set of tools for leaders that help them focus attention and energy on high leverage activities.

- The book's pragmatic bent and readable style make for a handy reference manual that can be picked up and put down frequently, on an as-needed basis.

This is a "must read" for individuals responsible for driving their organizations to the next performance level. It is a practical treatment of a complex topic by an expert in the field. I see it setting the standard for integrating the three most powerful improvement disciplines in the market today and for integrating the combination of hard and soft aspects of performance improvement.

Mike Carnell
Six Sigma Applications

PREFACE FOR THE COLLABORATIVE WORK SYSTEMS SERIES

IN LAUNCHING THIS SERIES, it is the editors' intention to create an ongoing, dynamic forum for sharing cutting-edge ideas and practices among researchers and those practitioners involved on a day-to-day basis with organizations that depend on collaborative work systems (CWS) for their success.

Proposed publications in the CWS series include books devoted to specific topics, workbooks to guide planning and competency development, fieldbooks that capture lessons learned in organizations experimenting with collaborative work systems, software for facilitating learning, training materials, and assessment instruments. The goal of the series is to produce four new products per year that will build a foundation for a perspective on collaboration as an essential means of achieving high levels of performance in and across organizations. Our vision for the series is to provide a means for leveraging collaborative work practices around the world in for-profit, government, and not-for-profit entities.

Collaborative work systems are those in which conscious efforts have been made to create strategies, policies, and structures as well as to institutionalize values, behaviors, and practices that promote cooperation among different parties in the organization in order to achieve desired business outcomes. While many organizations vocalize support for teamwork and collaboration, collaborative work systems are distinguished by intentional efforts to embed the organization with work processes and cultural mechanisms that enable and reinforce collaboration. New forms of organization continue to emerge with CWS as an essential facet. Team-based organizations and self-managing organizations represent types of collaborative systems. The computer revolution has made possible network, cellular, and spherical forms of organizing, which represent more transorganizational forms of collaboration.

Why the urgency? The challenges organizations face seem to be escalating rapidly. The number of global issues that impact an organization proliferate, including the terrorist threat, continued deforestation of ancient lands by debtor nations, wars, famine, disease, the accelerating splitting of nations' consciousness into the haves and the have-nots around the globe, which fuels hatreds—all aspects of interrelated political, social, economic, environmental challenges that will ultimately reduce quality of life on a worldwide scale if not addressed. These are the systemic, wicked problems that depend on many minds lodged in a common value set committed to improving human welfare in all settings. The business community must work with city, county, and state governments, with nation states, and with transnational organizations, such as the United Nations and the World Bank, to bring enough intellectual and financial capital to bear on the problems to do something about them—demanding collaborative initiatives at all levels.

Individuals working well together—this seems like a relatively simple proposition. Yet barriers abound in organizations that tend to inhibit collaboration at every turn. Social barriers are erected for a variety of reasons, including turf wars and mindsets that lead to hoarding of specialized knowledge rather than sharing. Fear of loss seems to be amplified during economic downturns as operating budgets are trimmed, fueling a multiplicity of negative personal scenarios, including loss of jobs, promotional opportunities, titles, and perks, which in turn can threaten self-esteem and professional identity. Barriers to establishing effective collaborative work systems can also reflect lack of cross-training, cultural norms and reward systems that reinforce individual performance, organizational political realities that reinforce competition for scarce resources among units, and differing technical languages that make communication challenging. However, despite these difficulties, some companies appear to overcome the significant barriers and benefit from the positive consequences of effective collaboration.

People in and around organizations have been experimenting with and learning about designing effective work processes for millennia. Researchers and practitioners have been capturing the lessons learned since the early part of the 20th Century. That process continues as we embark on the 21st Century. There will be much to document as changes in global business practices and new generation technologies enable more effective ways of organizing, operating, competing, innovating, and collaborating. Technical developments during the next quarter century will create unheralded challenges and opportunities in an increasingly interdependent world.

The move from muscle-based work to knowledge-based work has been so profound that some writers have called it the age of the knowledge economy. It demands new levels of collaborative expertise and a shift in focus to intangible forms of capital.

Knowledge grows through the development of organizational routines. Knowledge includes knowing what, but also knowing how and why. Each employee carries a somewhat different library of knowledge and a unique perspective on how to apply it—termed intellectual capital. The network of interaction among knowledge workers creates a rich environment where ideas can grow and blossom in stair-step fashion—termed social capital—and where there is widespread competency around teamwork at all levels of the organization in various forms—termed collaborative capital. This form of capital provides the foundation for leveraging what the other forms contribute, but it demands radically different ways of organizing work and involving employees in its design and practice.

In summary, collaborative work systems provide one of the key competency areas that organizations can focus on for building vitality and excellence, including competitive and collaborative advantage. On a daily basis, people come together to make decisions, solve problems, invent new products and services, build key relationships, and plan futures. The effectiveness of those gatherings and the effectiveness of the systems that emerge from them will depend greatly on the collaborative capacity that has been built in their organizations.

A high level of collaborative capacity will enable more effective work at the local and daily levels and at the global and long-term levels. We can solve our immediate problems more effectively, and we can cooperate more effectively to take on the emerging global issues that threaten us in the 21st Century when we have the skills, values, and processes for effective collaboration. This series of publications is intended as a catalyst in building that collaborative capacity at both local and global levels.

Michael M. Beyerlein, Ph.D.
Susan T. Beyerlein, Ph.D.
Center for the Study of Work Teams
University of North Texas

James Barker, Ph.D.
United States Air Force Academy

Man often becomes what he believes himself to be. If I keep on saying to myself that I cannot do a certain thing, it is possible that I may end by really becoming incapable of doing it. On the contrary, if I have the belief that I can do it, I shall surely acquire the capacity to do it even if I may not have it at the beginning.

Gandhi

THERE IS A CRISIS in organizational improvement programs today. The crisis has nothing to do with the planning of improvement efforts. *Great improvement plans abound.* The crisis has nothing to do with the tools and methods. *There are plenty out there.* The crisis has nothing to do with desires of the improvement method originators or organizational sponsors. *Most want their methods to deliver highly successful change.*

The serious crisis that organizations face today is in the *execution and sustainability* of improvement programs. Experience and research have shown that these two areas are the most troublesome for getting improvements and new ways of thinking into an organization. The ability to execute—both strategy and improvement plans—is a highly sought after skill in executive offices these days. In 2000, a *Fortune* magazine article reported that the primary reason for most CEO firings was "poor execution."

For many organizations the element of sustainability remains equally as elusive as execution. It's not uncommon for improvement efforts to start off with a bang, and end with a whimper only six to nine months later. So what's an approach for getting dramatic gains that stick around?

People have talked about the need to integrate the "hard" aspects of improvement with the "soft" aspects for many years. This book offers best practices for doing just that. By combining three proven disciplines with highly successful track records, an organization can maximize both the long-term and short-term benefits of time invested in a change effort.

None of the disciplines—Lean, Six Sigma or High-Performance Organizations—is entirely "hard" or "soft." While Lean and Six Sigma provide a predominantly "hard" perspective that offers principles, tools, and methods for improving profits, quality, and cycle time, they also seek to influence behavior through links to an organization's management systems. And while the High-Performance Organization discipline has a strong focus on "soft" aspects, such as creating intrinsic motivation, organizing into teams, and increasing organizational capabilities, there is also an obsessive execution focus built into the culture that it creates. When combined in an overall improvement strategy, each magnifies the strengths of the other while compensating for the weaknesses.

Improvements for Lean, Six Sigma, and High-Performance Organizations—when implemented separately—have ranged from 35 percent to 300 percent, and even greater in some unique cases. Individual improvement numbers like that may prompt an astute reader to ask, "Why bother to combine these three disciplines when each, implemented individually, can achieve such great results?" For one thing, not all implementations reach that high-end 300 percent level. Far more modest achievements are common. There are five additional good reasons for combining the three instead of selecting one over the other:

- Increased speed of implementation;
- More improvement projects can occur simultaneously, thus increasing profits faster;

- Less time and energy on the part of senior management than they would expend for Lean, Six Sigma, or High-Performance Organizations implemented individually;

- Swifter and more effective adaptation to external events; and

- Greater sustainability of huge improvements.

How are the above possible? The power lies in the combination of the three complementary disciplines. Each discipline compensates for minor weaknesses of the others to produce a result that is greater than any could produce individually.

Traditionally, Six Sigma and Lean efforts have clashed head on with that ever-present, always formidable opponent, the organization's culture. Resistance manifests itself in such ways as managers blocking improvement projects in their area for fear of looking bad, reluctance to give up high performers to become "Black Belts" who will lead the improvement projects, and lack of diligent follow-through on agreed-on plans for improvement. Implementing High-Performance Organization elements quickly changes certain aspects of an organization's culture to lower the organization's ingrained defenses against Lean and Six Sigma principles and methods.

In the past, many High-Performance Organization implementations have succeeded in raising employee commitment to perform at higher levels. But they sometimes have failed to generate desired financial returns. This is because there were no formal methods or tools for improvement, or inadequate attention was paid to driving for financial results. The improvement disciplines of Lean and Six Sigma provide rich tool sets, methods, and financial screening and project assessments to fill this void.

The combination of Lean, Six Sigma, and High-Performance Organization disciplines can be a powerful way to improve profits. It is not, of course, the only way to reach exceptional levels of performance. Many major successful turnaround efforts have not combined Lean, Six Sigma, and High-Performance Organization practices to achieve success. The combination of these three disciplines does, however, make reinventing the wheel unnecessary in large-scale improvement efforts that require integrated "hard" and "soft" aspects of change. This combination forms a solid foundation since each of three disciplines has a rich history of theory, application, and numerous iterations of learning that resulted in pragmatic, robust improvement approaches.

This book presents a set of best practices for integrating these three powerful improvement disciplines. My research surfaced very little written about the topic of their formal integration. I have relied on personal experiences and discussions with practitioners in other organizations for pragmatic advice about what works and what does not work. This research is based on case studies of implementing each discipline separately, sequentially, and also simultaneously. My hope is that this book is frequently referenced by leaders at all levels who are striving for dramatic, sustainable improvement.

Tom Devane
November 2003

ACKNOWLEDGMENTS

If I have seen further, it is because I have stood on the shoulders of giants.

Isaac Newton

IT'S A BIT MISLEADING. There's one name on the cover of this book. This might cause some people to think that one person is responsible for generating all the ideas in this book and getting them into print. This isn't the case at all.

The rich content in this book is rooted in collaboration with clients, learning conversations with colleagues, and research of key pioneers in the area of organizational performance. Collaboration with clients is one of the most important sources of information for me. Consultants who say they don't learn anything from their clients are either not paying attention, or being less than honest. I am indebted to Gerry Fitzpatrick and J.F. DeBetz of StorageTek. It was with Gerry and J.F. that I first worked to formally integrate Lean, Six Sigma, and High-Performance Organization concepts nearly a decade ago. I also thank

Helena Dolny of the Land Bank of South Africa. Working with Helena helped shape and re-shape many ideas I had about leadership during the remarkable turnaround of the half-government, half-financial institution that she headed after the fall of apartheid. Finally, my collaboration on an extended post-divestiture project with Larry Kinney of AT&T provided me with a deep understanding of leading large groups of people in simple and advanced statistical methods for process improvement. These are three of the more influential clients of the many clients I've worked with who contributed to the knowledge base for this book.

Learning conversations with colleagues were another important source of information for this book. I am fortunate to have two great friends who are also business colleagues and outstanding consultants in the field of High-Performance Organizations. Robert Rehm and Nancy Cebula first got me interested in building High-Performance Organizations many years ago. They have been an invaluable source of ideas and inspiration over the years. We have sat on their deck in Boulder, Colorado, late into the night many times and swapped ideas. I also thank Merrelyn Emery for her extensive research and collaboration with me on two earlier publications. Personal conversations with Merrelyn and long-distance e-mail correspondence with her in Australia vastly added to my knowledge of team performance and participative planning. Thanks to technology, these days cross-continent collaboration and learning are but a few keystrokes away.

The last source of information for this book are the pioneers in research, original thought, and action learning. I am indebted to Fred Emery for his forty years of brilliant research. His research and fieldwork illustrate how to get groups of people involved in meaningful ways that benefit both the organization and the people within the organization. In addition, Merrelyn Emery's research and collaboration with me on several projects proved invaluable as a source of open systems theory and methods for getting large groups of people productive quickly. W. Edwards Deming's teachings appear throughout this book. I suspect they will most likely still be relevant a hundred years from now. Barry Oshry's research and practical advice on the interaction of Top, Middle, and Bottom groups provides important insights into organizational behavior for leaders. Barry's research, his course offerings, and his collaboration with me on another project have given me a deep understanding of group interactions and how to optimize them in a large-scale change effort. Finally, Jim Womack's work on consolidating "lean" principles from Henry Ford to the Toyota Production System form the foundation for Lean Enterprise principles and tools presented in this book. I've learned more from Jim Womack in a couple of his e-mails than I've learned from high-priced Lean consultants in day-long courses. Jim's work is the seminal work in the area of Lean.

The production of this book is the result of many people's hard work, research, and pre-publication activities. I thank Mike Beyerlein for the opportunity to include this book in his series on collaborative work systems. In addition to extending the invitation to participate, Mike was extremely helpful and very supportive throughout the entire writing process. I also thank the Jossey-Bass/Pfeiffer team of Kathleen Dolan Davies, Matt Davis, Nina Kreiden, and Gabriela Bayardo for guiding the book through its development process and ensuring the book launch went smoothly. My heartfelt thanks go out to the book reviewers: Leigh Wilkinson, Lonnie Thomas, Jerry Dake, Mike Carnell, J.F. DeBetz, and Rachel Livsey. Each made significant contributions to the quality of the final manuscript. I also thank my Dad, Jim Devane, for briefly stepping out of retirement and into the role of unofficial book reviewer. He provided some terrific ideas for reader friendliness and useful content based on his long career as a business consultant. The book is a better book because of all the reviewers involved.

There are also historical influences on the book. I am grateful to Peggy Holman for co-writing *The Change Handbook: Group Methods for Shaping the Future* with me. Peggy was the first person who got me interested in publishing my ideas into a full-blown book, instead of just articles. She had the connections, stamina, and incredible drive that helped make that book happen. I am also grateful to my college dean, Emerson Cammack, who instilled in me a lifelong desire for learning, communicating, and writing.

In many ways writing a book is harder on the author's family members than on the author. I thank my wife, Susan Conway Devane, my daughter Krista, and my son Kiernan for being so patient during the writing of this book. And Susan, a special thanks for your words of encouragement and your suggestions throughout the process. Without my family's patience, understanding, and support, it wouldn't have been possible to make this contribution to organizations seeking higher levels of performance.

IS YOUR PLAN for dramatic, sustainable organizational improvements viable?

Find out at www.LeanSixSigma.com.

This site includes an interactive diagnostic tool that can help you map out critical milestones and activities for your improvement plans. In addition, the site contains book excerpts, updates to book topics, case studies, additional references, and other helpful information and tools.

If this is coffee, please bring me some tea. If this is tea, please bring me some coffee.

> Abraham Lincoln, upon sipping a beverage
> brought to him in a sitting room

MOST ORGANIZATIONS TODAY are involved in some sort of improvement effort. The pace of technological change, escalating demands of customers, and fierce competition mandate continual change. Unfortunately, not all change efforts are resounding successes. Many leaders jump from one improvement effort to another, seeking a "silver bullet" for success.

Core Elements of Successful Change

Numerous studies over the past ten years point out that nearly 70 percent of all change efforts fail. This dismal failure rate has been cited for a variety of different improvement efforts such as reengineering, total quality projects, self-managing teams, enterprise resource planning systems (ERP), employee involvement, and outsourcing efforts.

So what are those successful 30 percent doing that puts them so far ahead of the pack? Obviously, a number of interrelated factors contribute to an organization's success. Some highly visible factors—such as an extraordinary leader or proprietary technological innovation—seemingly explain much of an organization's success. But a closer look shows that these are not always present or even necessary for success, and they don't tell the whole story of successful change efforts. Research shows that the subtle interplay of the following key elements are present in all well-executed improvement efforts that yield dramatic and sustainable results:

- *"Know-how"*—a detailed knowledge of what to do for the improvement, that is, a set of methods, tools, and processes that would help rapidly implement the proposed improvements;

- *"Want to"*—intrinsic motivation of a critical mass in the workforce who were willing to make the changes, and were willing to pay the price, to implement the new improvements; and

- *"Pay for"*—the ability of improvement effort benefits to consistently return more than the costs incurred.

In the 70 percent of the improvement efforts that fail, it's rare to find high levels of each of the above elements and a robust interplay among them. In most organizations, change efforts lean toward just one or two, heavily influenced by the leadership style of the sponsor, the success of the last change effort, and the type of change effort deployed. For example, if the last improvement effort in an organization failed because there was too much emphasis on using statistical tools to solve problems, the next change effort will likely shy away from the "know how" element and try to focus more on increasing motivation for people to change.

"Know how," "want to," and "pay for" factors are so important they form the core elements of the Performance Framework tool presented later in the book. This tool helps leaders plan, monitor, and communicate the results of the transformation. But knowing that these core energizing factors are required is not enough; there must also be a discipline to apply them.

Combining Lean Manufacturing, Six Sigma, and HPOs into a Single Discipline

Three improvement disciplines have yielded huge benefits for some organizations that have implemented them. These disciplines are

- Lean Manufacturing, which focuses on cycle time reduction and eliminating waste;

- Six Sigma, which deploys statistical methods to reduce variation and eliminate defects, as well as linking objectives to the formal management system; and

- High-Performance Organization (HPO), which focuses on developing an execution-based culture through organizational restructuring and increasing levels of intrinsic motivation, ownership, and commitment.

Not all organizations that have attempted to implement these disciplines have been successful. The truth is, each discipline has its own set of strengths and weaknesses. Organizations that have been highly successful have actually borrowed a bit from each of the three disciplines. For example:

- Well-known Six Sigma successes like General Electric and AlliedSignal also used Lean Manufacturing techniques and execution-focused teams in many plants.[1]

- The highly successful retailer Home Depot focuses on building an execution-based culture while using Six Sigma and Lean Manufacturing principles.

- Financial institutions like the Land Bank of South Africa have deployed process improvement principles to enhance performance in their highly successful implementation of HPO.

- Government organizations such as the United States District Court System combines HPO principles of teams and an execution focus with process improvement methods to increase throughput and job satisfaction.

The premise brought forward in this book is that formally combining the three disciplines makes it possible to capitalize on the strength of each and makes the weakness of each irrelevant. Below is a brief description of the "pure" elements of each and its strengths and weaknesses in terms of the three core elements of successful, sustainable efforts: "know how," "want to," and "pay for."

Lean Manufacturing   This method can be taught quickly to many and can yield rapid improvements that address the "pay for" element of a successful improvement approach. However, "know how" is limited to addressing a selected set of problems since Lean cannot bring a process under statistical control or identify problems in measurement systems that can wreak havoc if tests are not repeatable and reproducible. In addition, culture change is localized to the areas doing improvements. The "want to" element can quickly fade if management does not consistently make time for, reward, and encourage consistent application of the tools and principles.

Six Sigma   These improvement principles and tools take longer to learn than Lean ones do, but once learned they can solve more complicated problems. Six Sigma's statistical body of "know how" can bring processes under control and determine whether or not the measurement systems require adjustment. But because extensive data collection and analysis are often required for Six Sigma projects, an impatient organization may prematurely stop projects because they don't seem to be addressing the "pay for" element. Even though at most companies proposed projects must pass a minimum return on investment to start, sometimes lengthy completion times cause top management to stop projects. As with Lean, culture change is localized to the project teams doing improvements and teams sometimes experience backsliding once the improvement is implemented. The lack of a universal "want to" attitude has caused many Six Sigma projects to stall. A final shortcoming of Six Sigma is that it dives right into collecting data about and fixing a process, instead of asking if the process should even exist.

High-Performance Organization   These principles and methods focus on quickly changing the organization's structure and culture to foster ownership, accountability, job satisfaction, intrinsic motivation, and commitment to the organization's strategy. By addressing these "want to" elements, organizational members often make improvement suggestions that "pay for" themselves quickly. However, "know how" is limited to applying organizational design principles and there is no formal instruction in principles or tools for improvements.

Combining these three powerful disciplines compensates for the inherent weaknesses of each. The combination provides "know how" of simple and advanced improvement techniques, widespread "want to" for execution and continuous improvement, and rapid and long-term returns that "pay for" the improvement effort. In addition, because High-Performance Organization principles distribute decisions and increase motivation throughout the organization, there is typically less time required of senior management than in a pure Six Sigma or Lean implementation once the project begins.

Important Notes for Leader Practitioners

Time is one of the most important assets that leaders have today. To make best use of leaders' time, this book is focused on the most important things, organized into groups of eight to ten critical items for key topics that leaders need to know about. While obviously many more points could be made, I have invoked the Pareto principle and separated the trivial many from the truly critical few and presented only the latter.

The formal integration of Lean, Six Sigma, and HPO disciplines is a new approach for many organizations. This book cites principles and examples of leadership both for separate and for combined instances of those three disciplines. In addition, exemplary leadership examples outside the realm of LSS/HPO implementations are provided to provide leaders with great ideas for enabling change.

The principles, concepts, methods, tools, and sample templates set forth in this book have relevance across a wide variety of industries. However, if these are to be used in a particular organization, individuals in that organization will most likely want to tailor them to local circumstances. I wholeheartedly support that desire. In my experience, unless an organization is able to put its "fingerprints" on a particular tool or method, the chance of it being implemented well is very low.

What You Will and Won't Get from This Book

This is a book about leading dramatic, sustainable performance improvements. It's about what it takes to mobilize a group of people to achieve significant improvements in cycle time, cost, quality, and revenue enhancement.

The book takes a systemic approach to improvement. It considers the inter-relationships of key aspects of organizational performance such as:

- Return on investment targets;

- Intrinsic motivation for change;

- Knowledge of methods and tools;

- Strategy;

- Business processes;

- Organizational structure;

- Human resource practices;

- Core energizing improvement elements;

- Knowledge and learning; and

- Organizational culture.

This is *not* a book about how to implement the many tools of Lean, Six Sigma, or the technical details of a High-Performance Organization. There are excellent books on those topics available and listed in this book's Reference section. This is a pragmatic book for leaders in their day-to-day LSS/HPO leadership tasks.

Intended Audience

The primary audience for this book is leaders seeking dramatic, sustainable improvements in profits, quality, and cycle time. In this book the term "leaders" refers to those who exercise influence in achieving the new goals, irrespective of organizational level. Of course, top and mid-level managers have special powers vested in them by virtue of their positions in the organization. Where certain techniques and actions are level-specific, it is noted.

Research conducted for the book indicated that interest in this topic has spread beyond the primary audience. Parties who indicated strong interest in focus groups were senior managers, change agents at all levels, internal quality consultants, internal organization development consultants, statisticians, MBA students, academics, and external consultants.

The principles, tools, and concepts in this book apply equally to corporations, government, and not-for-profit organizations.

The most likely "unit of transformation" for LSS/HPO would be a division or several large departments that work together in a relatively self-contained mode. This self-contained aspect is important because many process improvement and cultural changes suggested may be very foreign to an organization. Focusing on a self-contained chunk of a large organization makes it easier to (1) implement new mindsets and techniques quickly and (2) "protect" organizational members from those outside the unit who may actively oppose the unit's new ways of doing business.

This book was written as a reference manual with entry points for leaders at any stage of a transformation. Leaders beginning an LSS/HPO transformation will most likely want to start by looking at some fundamentals and then jump into the Initiation Stage chapters. Leaders who are implementing a standalone Lean, Six Sigma, or HPO effort and find their project stalled can begin by looking at the stage they are in and then analyzing what is missing. By examining what has been done to date and what still needs to be done from an LSS/HPO perspective, leaders can take a slow-moving effort and put it back on track by including the elements that have been missing. To use the book most effectively, leaders will need to understand the two main parts of the book and some general guidelines for navigating between those two parts.

How to Use the Book

This book is divided into two primary parts and an appendix to help leaders select the most relevant material at the time when they need it. Leaders can start any place that makes sense for them and their organizational situation. Here is a brief description of the book parts.

Part 1: Practical Foundations

The first three chapters in Part 1 cover the basics that leaders must absolutely know about Lean Six Sigma, High-Performance Organizations and about their combination into one integrated discipline. Basics for each chapter include items such as representative results a leader can expect, the value proposition, historical notes, key concepts, key players, and the ten important "pay attention to" items for leaders.

Leaders wishing a solid grounding in the basic principles of LSS/HPO would find it beneficial to start in Part 1. If the topics in Part 1 are too familiar, a leader may wish to move immediately to Part 2.

Part 2: Pragmatic Practice

Knowing exactly what to do and when to do it can make the difference between raving success and dismal failure. This second part of the book contains two sections that provide leaders with pragmatic advice for implementing LSS/HPO. The first section contains information about lessons learned from previous implementations, high leverage leadership fundamentals, useful distinctions, and a basic toolkit for leaders. The second section is organized according to the major stages of an LSS/HPO transformation: Initiation, Direction Setting, Design, Implementation, and Operations and Continuous Improvement. This organization ensures that leaders can access advice in the same sequence in which they will encounter opportunities and challenges during the transformation.

For leaders who are pressed for time and need to get going right away, Part 2 is the place to start. In addition to tools to use in each stage, leaders will learn the key outputs, high leverage leader to-dos, large group interventions, and common traps. There is also a leadership checklist at the end of each stage to help leaders figure out what absolutely needs to be done before moving on to the next stage.

The book is organized to enable leaders to find topics of interest quickly. To increase navigation ease, visual icons introduce major topics within a chapter. Some leaders will also find it helpful to navigate topics of interest using the list of all the tables, figures, and exhibits that appears immediately after the table of contents.

Appendix

Within the Appendix, a Glossary provides information about key terms associated with an LSS/HPO transformation. In the Large-Group Interventions section, leaders can find templates for conducting large group meetings that provide transformation products and generate buy-in. Finally, the Reference section provides leaders with a list of books and websites that can be helpful throughout the LSS/HPO transformation.

It is highly likely that LSS/HPO is a field in which information will be exploding over the next few years. Traditional technologies, such as books, won't be able to keep up with all the advances fast enough to satisfy the needs of thirsty innovative practitioners. Therefore, there is a companion website to this book at LeanSixSigmaHPO.com that will contain timely updates to the topics presented in this book. It will include contributions from practitioners in the field, newly discovered principles, transformation tips, and late-breaking best practices for integrating Lean, Six Sigma, and HPOs.

Note

1. Personal interview with Mike Carnell.

PART 1

Practical Foundations

It is more important that you know where you are going than to get there quickly. Do not mistake activity for achievement.

Mabel Newcomber

THE DISCIPLINES OF LEAN, SIX SIGMA, AND HPOs are very rich and have evolved over numerous implementations and iterations. It would be possible to fill several books on each topic and still not cover all the information on each discipline. In this section, leaders will find a summary of each discipline that contains the *essential elements* that a leader must know in order to begin to champion change in these areas. Knowledge of these essential elements will help leaders apply their energy to achieving goal-oriented outcomes, instead of merely performing activities during the transformation. For some excellent books and articles that dig deeper into each topic, please consult the Reference section of this book.

Some readers may be tempted to bypass Part 1 of the book and get to the more "practical" part of the book. However, as social scientist and early leadership researcher Kurt Lewin pointed out, "Nothing is so practical as a good theory."[1] And quality pioneer W. Edwards Deming seconded the notion that it's important to have a foundation in some theory when he repeated in many of his lectures, "No theory, no learning."[2]

Each chapter in Part 1: Practical Foundations is organized according to nine topic areas, shown below. Icons will help leaders navigate the topic area within each of the three chapters in Part 1. The topic segments and associated icons are

      Representative results

      Value proposition

      Typical outcomes

      Brief historical notes

      Key concepts

      Ten important "pay attention to" elements

      Key players

Hallmarks of the discipline

 What it's not

After reading Part 1, leaders will have a solid understanding of the basic building blocks of the improvement disciplines and how they can be combined into a single, more powerful discipline.

Notes

1. Christie, C. (Editor) (2003). *The practice-theory relationship in evaluation.* San Francisco: Jossey-Bass.
2. Deming website, http:/deming.eng.clemson.edu/pub/den/deming_assoc.htm.

1

Overview of Lean Six Sigma

There are risks and costs to a program of action, but they are far less than the long-range risks and costs of comfortable inaction.

John F. Kennedy

L EAN MANUFACTURING AND SIX SIGMA are two powerful process improvement disciplines that provide a set of tools, methods, and principles to improve processes that meet or exceed customer requirements. The ultimate goal of any improvement initiative is to provide products or services of *high quality to customers when customers want them at a price customers will pay that result in a profit for the provider.*

Lean Manufacturing ("Lean" for short) and Six Sigma each support this high-level goal, although each approaches it differently. Six Sigma provides an advanced statistical toolkit and a management system that focus on reducing output variation by controlling inputs and virtually eliminating defects. Lean provides principles and simple tools that focus on eliminating waste, increasing speed, and increasing throughput. Novices in each discipline take great delight in debating which discipline is better or which discipline is a subset of the other. However, skilled process improvement practitioners choose to combine the two in a complementary package that judiciously uses tools and principles appropriate for a particular situation. This approach is used for the remainder of this book.

Lean and Six Sigma have been successfully implemented, both separately and together, across a variety of manufacturing and non-manufacturing industries. Many organizations that reached dramatically higher levels of performance have instinctively combined Lean and Six Sigma, although they haven't always called the combination "LSS." For example, part of General Electric's highly publicized success under the Six Sigma banner also combined cycle time reduction and waste elimination elements of Lean with the advanced statistical tools of Six Sigma.[1] Raytheon's highly successful Six Sigma program complements advanced statistical tools with elements of Lean, agile corporation practices and business process redesign and management.[2]

This chapter presents essentials that leaders must know about Lean Six Sigma (LSS) for the following: representative results, the value proposition, typical outcomes, brief historical notes, key concepts, ten important "pay attention to" elements, key players, hallmarks of the discipline, and specifically what it is not.

Where it is helpful for leaders to consider Lean and Six Sigma disciplines separately, information appears separately.

Representative Results

By providing tools and principles for process improvement, LSS leaders have achieved extraordinary gains. One of the more well-known Six Sigma implementations is the General Electric story. Jack Welch, then CEO of GE, stated in the 1998 annual report that in just three years Six Sigma saved the company over $2 billion. GE's 1997 annual report listed these benefits:

> In Superabrasives—our industrial diamond business—Six Sigma quadrupled its return on investment by improving yields, and giving it a full decade's worth of capacity despite growing volume—without spending a nickel on plant and equipment capacity.

The plastics business, through rigorous Six Sigma process work, added 300 million pounds of new capacity (equivalent to a "free plant"), saved a $400 million investment, and will save another $400 million by 2000.

Additional Six Sigma success stories abound in a variety of industries:[3]

- Six Sigma enabled AlliedSignal to avoid having to build an $85 million plant to fill increasing caperolactan demand, realizing a total savings of $30 to $50 million a year.

- Lockheed Martin used to spend an average of two hundred work hours fitting a part that covers the landing gear. For years employees had brainstorming sessions that resulted in many seemingly logical solutions. However, none worked. The statistical discipline of Six Sigma discovered a one-thousandth of an inch deviation in the part that caused the problem. Now that it has been corrected, the company saves $14,000 a jet.

Lean success stories are equally impressive:

- Porsche implemented a Lean system in 1993. In the final assembly area, the space for inventories was reduced from 40 percent to zero, the amount of parts on hand was reduced from 28 days to essentially zero, and parts were held in the assembly area for about twenty minutes before the completed engine was sent to the final assembly area.[4]

- At Credence Systems, a leading global supplier of automatic test equipment, a work team doubled the output through a bottleneck circuit-card testing work center within six weeks using Lean techniques.

- At Pratt's North Haven, Connecticut, turbine airfoil facility, a Lean program caused overdue parts to fall from $80 million to zero, inventory was cut in half, the manufacturing cost of many parts was cut in half, and labor productivity nearly doubled.[5]

And some companies are now beginning to report results from the combined efforts of Lean and Six Sigma. The Preferred Technical Group, a former division of United Technologies Automotive, announced that the combination of the two helped achieve:

- An operating margin increase from 5.4 percent to 13.8 percent;

- Return on invested capital increase from 10 percent to 33 percent; and

- Reduction of manufacturing lead time from fourteen days to two days.[6]

The above results stories illustrate the potential gains when organizations pay specific attention to Six Sigma, Lean, or combined LSS efforts. In order to better understand how the two complement each other, it is necessary to look at the value proposition of each and the combined value proposition of both.

Value Proposition

Both Lean and Six Sigma propose to add value to an organization, but each does it in a different way. By examining each value proposition separately and considering how each complements the other, we can develop a combined proposition. Although they share the same ultimate goal, each one's primary area of focus excludes certain elements.

Six Sigma's basic value proposition: principles for process improvement, statistical methods, a customer focus, attention to processes, and a management system focusing on high-return improvement projects result in continuous improvement and significant financial gains.

Lean's basic value proposition: principles for improving workflow, decreasing setup time, eliminating waste, and conducting preventive maintenance will speed up business processes and return quick financial gains.

The combination of the two disciplines allows each to compensate for missing elements in the other. As mentioned previously, many organizations have intuitively known this and begun to informally merge tools and principles of the two disciplines in their implementations. Therefore, while it may be difficult to find a "pure" implementation of either, it is nevertheless useful to examine them in their "pure" forms to illustrate why combining them makes sense. A "pure" Six Sigma approach lacks three desirable Lean characteristics:

1. No direct focus on improving the speed of a process;

2. No direct attention to reductions in the amount of inventory investment; and

3. No quick financial gains due to the time required to learn and apply its methods and tools for data collection and analysis.

Shortcomings of a "pure" Lean improvement effort, however, include:

- Processes are not brought under statistical control;

- There is no focus on evaluating variations in measurement systems used for decisions; and

- No process improvement practices link quality and advanced mathematical tools to diagnose process problems that remain once the obvious waste has been removed.

Six Sigma provides complementary support to Lean in all these areas. The combined LSS value proposition then becomes "through a combination of principles and simple and advanced tools that seek to improve processes based on customer requirements, an organization can realize a stream of short-term and longer-term benefits."

Typical Outcomes

The basic outcomes of an LSS effort are

- Increased profitability and quality that will initially come through a set of carefully screened and focused improvement projects;

- Rapid payback on some initial improvement projects;

- Increased process speed resulting from the elimination of waste and preventive maintenance to keep processes running smoothly;

- Changes in workforce mindsets and day-to-day operating practices that support management by data and facts, a customer focus, general workplace orderliness and organization of tools, and attention to processes; and

- Increased profitability and quality that will eventually come from numerous places in the organization when most people in the organization possess basic competencies for LSS improvement projects.

Brief Historical Notes

Many Lean concepts are not new. Some date back to Henry Ford's ideas on cost-effective production techniques in the 1920s. Many others have been familiar to industrial engineers for decades.

The Toyota Production System, developed by Eiji Toyoda, Taiichi Ohno, and Shigeo Shingo in the 1940s through 1960s, is the foundation of today's "Lean Manufacturing."

In a five-year, $5 million MIT funded study from 1985 to 1990, researchers Jim Womack, Dan Jones, and Dan Roos conducted extensive research that provided a clear picture of what Lean companies do to eliminate waste in their processes. Their findings were published in *The Machine That Changed the World*.[7]

In 1996 Womack and Jones followed up with *Lean Thinking*[8] that brought further clarification to Lean principles through additional case studies and analysis.

Six Sigma has a more recent history. Bill Smith, a senior engineer and scientist at Motorola, is the father of Six Sigma. He brought his passion for the concept to then CEO Bob Galvin. Galvin gave him strong encouragement and on January 15, 1987, Galvin kicked off Motorola's "Six Sigma Quality Program" with a speech that was distributed in a letter and videotape. Motorola set a target to achieve Six Sigma within five years.[9] The typical project return of six figures appealed to other large corporations, and soon firms like AlliedSignal, General Electric, Sony, and Texas Instruments adopted the program and had their own success stories to tell.

Key Concepts

While there are many important LSS concepts, there are seven that leaders must know about:

1. The voice of the customer and "CTQ."

2. The Six Sigma metric.

3. Elimination of waste and non-value-added activities.

4. Process.

5. Unintended variation is the enemy.

6. Value streams.

7. The "DMAIC" improvement process.

The Voice of the Customer and "CTQ"

The customer is king in LSS. If it weren't for customers, an organization would not exist. Therefore, people need to link all improvement activities, metrics, and investments to the customer.

Customer requirements and expectations are called "CTQs." This abbreviation stands for Critical to Quality. At the start of a project one of the early activities is that team members define those product or service attributes that are CTQs. These CTQs are continually referred to during the process improvement process to ensure that customers will benefit from the time and resources the organization is spending on an improvement project.

The Six Sigma Metric

There was a time when people thought a 99 percent level of quality was pretty good. That was before the Six Sigma revolution. That old 99 percent target level just doesn't cut it in today's competitive global economy. The "goodness level" of 99 percent equates to [10] 20,000 lost articles of mail per hour; unsafe drinking water almost fifteen minutes per day; 5,000 incorrect surgical operations per week; two short or long landings at most major airports each day; 200,000 wrong drug prescriptions each year; and no electricity for almost seven hours per month.

Most people would agree that the above results of a 99 percent quality level are not desirable, and in some cases are downright scary (I personally fly over 100,000 miles per year, and the airport statistic really caught my eye)! So how does Six Sigma relate to this problematic 99 percent quality level?

Sigma is a letter in the Greek alphabet used to denote the amount of variation, or spread, around an average. For example, if you weigh a bunch of watermelons of many different sizes, you'll end up with a much higher variation—or, as statisticians like to refer to it, "standard deviation"—than if you weigh a bunch of watermelons that are all the same size. In a well-run Six Sigma organization, one goal is to have processes that impact the customer have as little variation as possible. The more variation goes up, the lower the Sigma level. Table 1.1 illustrates this principle.

When we're talking Six Sigma, we're talking about near perfection. Reducing errors directly translates into bottom-line financial results. Raytheon

Table 1.1. Six Sigma Level Associated with Customer Requirements and Defects Per Million Opportunities

Sigma Level	Percentage of Time Customers' Requirements Were Met	Defects Per Million Opportunities
1	68.27	690,000
2	95.45	308,537
3	99.73	66,807
4	99.9937	6,210
5	99.999943	233
6	99.9999998	3.4

figured it spent 25 percent of each sales dollar fixing problems when it oper-ated at four sigma. However, if it raised its quality and efficiency to Six Sigma, it would reduce spending on fixes to 1 percent.[11]

Although it is becoming a source of competitive advantage in many indus-tries, not all organizations are at, or even near, Six Sigma yet. In the year 2000, research from the statistical software firm Minitab found that most firms oper-ate between two and three sigma.[12] A separate study reported that manufac-turing firms frequently attain four sigma quality levels, while service firms operate at quality levels of one or two sigma.[13] (The latter finding should be no surprise to anyone who travels extensively on business.)

Elimination of Waste and Non-Value-Added Activities

On first glance this concept may seem to be such common sense that it is of little value. Who wouldn't want to get rid of waste and non-value-added activ-ities? But the sad truth is that unless employees actively seek to rid the work-place of these, they will remain and slow down processes and make products more expensive. In most shop environments that I've observed, material usu-ally spends about 95 percent of its time waiting to be processed. This number has been confirmed by numerous industrial engineering studies over twenty years. As the saying goes, "there is gold to be mined" by attacking waste and non-value-added activities. The good news is that it does not require a lot of training and long learning curves to get people going on attacking waste. Sim-ply an awareness—coupled with permission from management and a culture that supports continuous improvement—goes a long way.

Process

A process can be defined as a collection of activities and decisions that produce an output for an internal or external customer. Processes often span departmen-tal or group boundaries. In processes that span major functional silo boundaries, there are often great opportunities for improvement, as each silo is typically try-ing to maximize its output to have its metrics look good, while no one is striving to optimize output for the customer. As qualitiy pioneer W. Edwards Deming fre-quently pointed out, "If everyone in an orchestra tried to maximize his output, that would not create music." Some sample processes from different industries appear in Figure 1.1. A new product development process for a high-tech firm

Figure 1.1. Processes in Various Industries

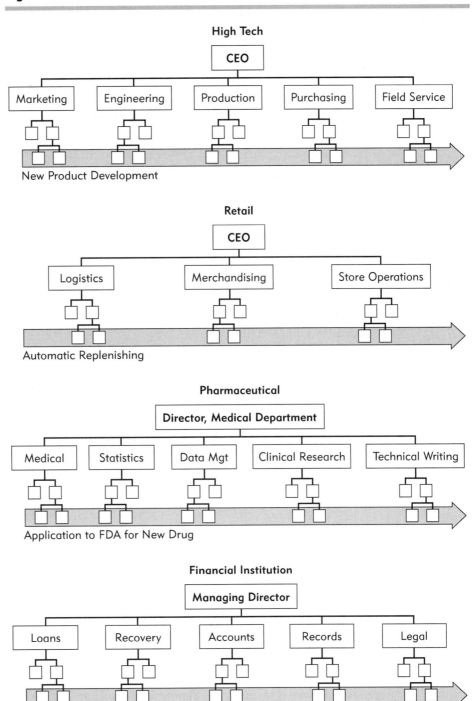

would span the departments of marketing (to articulate what the customer wants), engineering (to design the product), production (to ensure engineering designed a product that could be manufactured at a reasonable cost), purchasing (to ensure parts would be available), and field service (to provide input on what would make it easy to diagnose and repair while on customer sites). An automatic replenishing process in a retail environment would span the departments of logistics (responsible for getting products to a store), merchandising (responsible for determining how much to buy), and store operations (responsible for stocking, displaying, and selling the product).[14] Additional process examples for a financial institution and a pharmaceutical company are provided in Figure 1.1 also.

The concept of process is central to higher levels of operating performance. People work to remove waste from processes. Many people manage processes, instead of functional departments. And people work to reduce unintended variation in key processes.

Unintended Variation Is the Enemy

In some situations in life, variation is desirable. Life would be quite boring with only one ice cream flavor, one television station, and one item on your favorite restaurant's menu. But unintended variation in a manufacturing or service process is the enemy.

It is important to minimize variation in order to get a stable, reliable, repeatable process. Leaders can help by asking focusing questions. For example, when a leader hears an improvement team member say, "The first pass yield for these electronic components is 70 percent, and that's awful" the leader should ask, "And what's the variability of the process that produced those components?" Six Sigma most definitely requires a new way of thinking about quality, and leaders need to take every opportunity to set new, higher standards of performance and ask attention-directing questions that reinforce new ways of thinking and acting.

Value Streams

A value stream is a flow of activities and decisions that produces an end deliverable for a "family" (that is, a general grouping) of products or services.[15] The two principal types of value streams are *new product development* (starting with product concept and ending with product launch) and *delivery* (starting with raw material and ending with shipment to the customer). Value streams tend to cross traditional functional department boundaries, which tends to cause two problems. First, no one person is responsible for looking out for the overall performance of the value stream. For example, a delivery value stream may pass through the purchasing, order entry, production, and shipping departments. No one person is looking out for the end-to-end process and trying to optimize the handoffs between departments. The second, related problem is that each department seeks to maximize its own departmental metrics, instead of the performance of the entire value stream of greater customer interest.

Middle managers and supervisors need to develop high-level value streams for each product or service family. The book *Learning to See*[16] provides an excellent approach to mapping current value streams and improving them. Data collected includes information about lead times between key operations, a designation of value-added or non-value-added time, setup times, number of people it takes to do a task, and other information useful for reducing overall process time and waste.

The "DMAIC" Improvement Process

DMAIC is the Six Sigma problem-solving process teams use. It stands for Define-Measure-Analyze-Improve-Control. (It is pronounced duh-MAY-ick.) By methodically following this simple, but highly effective five-step process, teams can make significant process improvements. DMAIC is useful for:

- Helping teams design solutions that are sustainable once implemented;
- Providing a framework for when tools should be used;
- Providing a sequence of optimal tool usage and linkages among tools; and
- Helping practitioners understand how the tools and improvement phases are related, and how the tools support each other to produce an output that can be acted on.

It is essential that leaders understand the high-level steps of the DMAIC improvement process. In project status meetings leaders should require that teams state which DMAIC phase they are in to provide a context for productive discussion. This provides a common ground for discussion, a context for applying lessons learned from previous similar steps, and a useful context for applying step-specific questions to the discussion of process improvements.

The above are seven concepts that top leaders need to know about LSS. Many more are covered in excellent books such as *Lean Six Sigma,*[17] *Leaning into Six Sigma,*[18] *The Perfect Engine,*[19] and *Managing Six Sigma.*[20]

Ten Important "Pay Attention to" Elements for LSS leaders

Senior managers need to pay attention to where members of the workforce focus their efforts. In an LSS effort these managers must be concerned with the implementation and fostering of LSS concepts, methods, and tools in the organization. To that end, it is helpful for them to focus on

1. The use of data and facts, rather than opinions, to make decisions.
2. Managing variation in processes, instead of just managing reject levels for a product.
3. An awareness of and management of business processes and value streams that cut across functional department boundaries.
4. Opportunities to pull work through operations rather than push it.
5. An emphasis on prevention, not reaction.
6. Processes and culture that foster the continual search for ways to streamline and eliminate waste.
7. Impacts of activities and solutions on customer requirements.
8. Checks and balances to ensure that LSS experts do not become overloaded and leave.
9. Workplace orderliness and cleanliness.
10. Links between LSS improvement efforts and the organization's reward and recognition system.

Key Players

There are six primary types of players in an LSS initiative. Although many of the designations have roots in the Six Sigma discipline, in this context the players have training and develop expertise in both Lean and Six Sigma disciplines. The players and their general responsibilities appear in Table 1.2.

Table 1.2. Lean Six Sigma Key Players and Their Responsibilities

Player	Roles and Responsibilities	Typical Training	Six Sigma Dedication
Black Belt	Works with a team, usually of Green Belts and people with no LSS training, assigned to a specific LSS improvement project. Black Belts help with both the technical aspects (statistical tools) and people issues (team dynamics and change management). Typically a Black Belt will deliver about $1 million to the bottom line annually.	Four weeks of training spread over four months	Full-time[i]
Master Black Belt	Acts as instructor, coach, and mentor to several Black Belts. Frequently Master Black Belts (MBBs) become involved in large-scale organizational change efforts and promotion of LSS within the organization. In many organizations MBBs organize into a learning group in which they challenge, advise, and support each other and Black Belts. They also often formulate business strategies with top management. In addition, they may also lead "super projects" that are high impact and staffed with multiple Black Belts.	Usually on the job	Full-time
Green Belt	Participates in LSS by collecting data, providing process expertise, completing improvement tasks, and communicating changes to colleagues.	Three sessions of three or four days	Part-time, as project needs dictate
Champion (Executive)	Provides business guidance to teams, assists in selecting projects, acts as an organizational "evangelist" for Six Sigma, allocates resources, questions the team, anticipates and prevents problems with the LSS before they occur, removes roadblocks if they do occur.	Five days	Part-time, as active executive sponsorship needs dictate
Executive Sponsor	Actively supports and encourages project teams, participates in LSS meetings, demonstrations, and celebrations.	One or two days	Part-time, as executive support needs dictate
Process Owner	Ensures high quality design and peak performance of business processes. Helps triage problems as those addressable by simple process improvement methods or problems requiring use of complex, lesser-known statistical tools.	One week	Half-time to full-time, depending on process size

[i]Full-time dedication means that the person spends 100 percent of his or her time on Six Sigma activities. They are taken out of their line responsibilities, usually for a period of eighteen months to two years.

Hallmarks of the Discipline

 There are eight hallmarks of the discipline of LSS:

1. *Statistical methods.* An important part of reducing variation in processes.

2. *Attention to workplace and tool organization.* A set of mindsets, practices, and discipline that keeps work areas clean and uncluttered with tools and materials and instead sorts and neatly arranges these items for easy retrieval and use.

3. *Fanatical focus on the external customer.* One key element that distinguishes LSS from earlier "total quality" efforts is the high amount of attention paid to meeting external customer requirements and expectations. Senior managers as well as team members alike constantly ask, "How will what we're doing here affect the external customer?"

4. *Attention to process.* A process is a set of activities and decisions that collectively produce an output for an internal or an external customer. Often these processes span departmental boundaries, and improving them tends to have the highest likelihood of producing significant financial gain. Processes are the heart of "where the action is" with LSS.

5. *Pre-screening and ongoing screening of improvement projects to ensure fit with strategy and financial return.* Another important departure from traditional quality efforts is the initial and ongoing requirement that projects must support strategy and yield a targeted financial return. This is true throughout the project.

6. *People strive for perfection, but noble mistakes are tolerated.* People must feel safe to make a mistake. If they don't, then it is unlikely they will try anything really different that could yield significant gains. Obviously, certain types of mistakes, such as repeated mistakes and lack of follow-through, cannot be tolerated, but other types of mistakes should be considered potential learning opportunities.

7. *An analysis-rich and measurement-rich environment.* LSS environments collect lots of data, and project participants perform numerous data analyses. In addition, in LSS companies, measurement is something that happens *everywhere*.

8. *A classification and sorting process to determine the type of tools to apply.* Some problems are simple, while others are complex. Organizations need to develop internal rules that specify when a problem would benefit from simple tools like process maps and the application of streamlining principles, and when a problem would require more extensive data collection and statistical analyses.

What It's Not

In helping to define what LSS is, it is also helpful to consider what it is not.

It is not just a collection of tools that people can be trained in and shortly thereafter deliver outstanding results. Successful LSS efforts require strong management support, training, and formal ties to the organization's management system.

It is not just a statistics program. It is a results program.

It is not recycled TQM from the 1970s with the letters DMAIC slapped onto training materials and status reports. While many tools and some methods from the quality movement are present in LSS, it has formal links to the compensation system, financial screening of potential projects, and a fanatical emphasis on the needs of the external customer.

It is not a training program, as many TQM programs became. It is a system of tools, principles, and management practices that are applied to improve processes.

In summary, combining the already powerful disciplines of Lean and Six Sigma provide organizations with a set of process improvement principles and tools for significant improvement. The next chapter will cover another powerful discipline that focuses directly on changing organizational culture and structure.

Notes

1. Personal interview with Mike Carnell of Six Sigma Applications on November 15, 2002. Carnell was a consultant to General Electric during their early Six Sigma efforts.
2. Personal conversation with Mike Grimm, Six Sigma Expert at Raytheon in Tucson, Arizona.
3. Jones, D. "Firms aim for six sigma efficiency," *USA Today*, 7/21/98 Money Section.
4. Womack, J., and Jones, T. (1996). *Lean thinking: Banish waste and create wealth in your corporation.* New York: Simon & Schuster.

5. Womack, J., and Jones, T. (1996). *Lean thinking: Banish waste and create wealth in your corporation.* New York: Simon & Schuster.

6. George, M. (2002). *Lean six sigma.* New York: McGraw-Hill.

7. Womack, J., Jones, D., and Roos, D. (1991). *The machine that changed the world.* New York: Harper-Collins.

8. Womack, J., and Jones, T. (1996). *Lean thinking: Banish waste and create wealth in your corporation.* New York: Simon & Schuster.

9. Breyfogle, F. (2001). *Managing six sigma.* New York: John Wiley & Sons.

10. Harry, Mikel. "The nature of six sigma quality." Technical Report, Government Electronics Group, Motorola, Inc., Scottsdale, Arizona.

11. Jones, D. "Firms aim for six sigma efficiency," *USA Today,* 7/21/98, Money Section.

12. Minitab, Inc., Internal study in 2000, 3081 Enterprise Drive, State College, PA 16801, http://www.minitab.com.

13. Blakeslee, J. "Implementing the six sigma solution: How to achieve quantum leaps in quality and competitiveness." *Quality Progress, 32*(7): 77–85. 1999.

14. The automatic replenishment process is an improvement process currently underway at Home Depot. Information obtained from Tammy Bess in a personal interview.

15. Experience has shown it is more useful to map and manage value streams at the "family" level instead of at the more detailed individual product or service level.

16. Rother, M., and Shook, M. (1999). *Learning to see.* Brookline, MA: The Lean Enterprise Institute.

17. George, M. (2002). *Lean six sigma.* New York: McGraw-Hill.

18. Wheat, B., Mills, C., and Carnell, M. (2001). *Leaning into six sigma: The path to integration of lean enterprise and six sigma.* Boulder City, NV: Publishing Partners.

19. Sharma, A., and Moody, P. (2001). *The perfect engine.* New York: The Free Press.

20. Breyfogle, F. (2001). *Managing six sigma.* New York: John Wiley & Sons.

CHAPTER 2

Overview of High-Performance Organizations

Ability without opportunity is nothing.

Napoleon

THE DISCIPLINE OF HIGH-PERFORMANCE ORGANIZATIONS (HPOs) focuses directly on changing the organizational culture, changing the organizational structure, and creating conditions for employees to assume more ownership and accountability. The structure—composed primarily of High-Performance Teams—within an HPO helps increase the opportunities of all to participate in achieving objectives that support the strategy, take part in continuous improvement activities, and develop their own personal capabilities. An important part of the High-Performance Team (HPT) structure is that teams feel a great deal of solidarity and peer pressure to perform well and improve. Benjamin Franklin's observation, "If we don't all hang together, we shall surely hang separately," characterizes the closeness of team members and their willingness to coach and help each other. HPOs have been widely implemented across a variety of industries in both manufacturing and non-manufacturing settings.

There is actually no universally accepted definition of an HPO. While numerous references are made to HPOs in business literature and there is general agreement about some shared principles, no one definition exists. Definitions vary by implementation at each HPO site. For purposes here, I offer the following key points based on my experiences with highly successful HPOs.

An HPO is a structure composed principally of high-performance teams (HPTs) whose members work interdependently to address specific performance challenges. HPTs collectively set their own goals based on upper management input and subsequent negotiation with upper management and peer teams.

HPTs are responsible for executing daily technical and managerial duties usually related to making products and delivering services. They are "standing teams," that is, the teams have the same members over time. HPTs are held collectively accountable for performance outcomes.

In addition to HPTs, which function as standing teams that make products and deliver services, HPOs also contain temporary process improvement teams. These improvement teams, whose membership is drawn from HPTs—usually on a part-time basis—form to address an improvement issue and then disband when they've completed the work.

Throughout an HPO, decisions, information, and rewards are pushed to the lowest possible level. This keeps planning, error detection, and correction close to the source and to customer needs.

Not all individuals in an HPO are continuously on an HPT. HPTs are only required when two or more people must work interdependently to achieve a desired outcome. While in today's complex world most work does require collective efforts, this is not always the case, especially at higher management levels. For example, sometimes it makes sense for senior managers to act as a team because their end objective requires a high level of interdependence, such as a successful LSS/HPO transformation. In other cases they need to operate as individuals who provide guidance and learning opportunities for those in the organization who share their functional discipline.

An HPO must be well-supported by enabling functions. In highly successful HPOs, human resources establishes policies to reward team behavior, provides team bonuses based on achieving goals, shares gains the organization realizes, and provides for varying levels of individual compensation by paying for skills or knowledge held. Information technology groups provide access to key information for teams that allows a flatter hierarchical structure.

Similar concepts appear today under various names such as "High-Performance Work Systems," "High-Performance Work Organizations," "High-Performance Systems," and "High Involvement Workforces."

This chapter presents essentials that leaders must know about HPOs for representative results, the value proposition, typical outcomes, brief historical notes, key concepts, ten important "pay attention to" elements, key players, hallmarks of the discipline, and specifically what it is not.

Representative Results

 By creating a culture that highly values execution and accountability, HPO leaders have achieved dramatic results in very short periods of time. Representative results include:

- Westinghouse-Airdrie decreased cycle time from seventeen weeks to one week.[1]

- In Brazil, Semco increased productivity by 264 percent.[2]

- AT&T Credit Corporation used high performance cross-functional teams to improve efficiency and customer service. The teams doubled the number of credit applications handled per day and cut loan approval time by 50 percent.[3]

- Eli Lilly used high performance teams to bring a new product to market. Its rollout was the fastest in the company's history for a medical product.[4]

- Cycle Hardware P&N Tools in Australia increased equipment utilization by 30 percent.[5]

- The Northern Telecom plant in Harrisburg, Pennsylvania, doubled productivity.[6]

- SEI Investments revenues went from $300 million in 1997 to $658 million in 2001. The combination of the company's unique innovation focus, culture, and organizational structure consisting of 140 self-managed teams accounted for a good deal of the growth, especially during a time when other investment firms were losing substantial amounts of money.[7]

- Kodak's high performance teams improved productivity so much at one plant that the work of three shifts could be completed in one.[8]

- The Land Bank of South Africa (a quasi-governmental and financial institution) increased approved loans by 90 percent within ten months. Within eighteen months after the change effort, approved loans increased 300 percent—with the same number of employees they had at the start of the HPO transformation. In addition, all the branch banks operated at a profit for the first time in three decades.

Value Proposition

The value proposition of a High-Performance Organization (HPO) is that a structure composed principally of High-Performance Teams (HPTs) practicing *high levels of collaboration* creates a widespread culture of motivated individuals that is highly focused on metrics, extremely execution-driven, and committed to continual improvement and rapid adaptation.

Within HPTs local team structuring, goal setting, and metrics monitoring processes instill high levels of accountability, and ownership and commitment. These translate directly into profitability and job satisfaction.

Typical Outcomes

The basic outcomes for an HPO effort are

- Distributed responsibility and accountability throughout the organization;

- An organizational structure composed primarily of HPTs in which technical and business decisions and needed information are pushed down as far as possible into the organizational structure;

- Increased levels of intrinsic motivation and commitment to the organization's strategy resulting from increased power over local activities, local goal-setting and feedback, and the sense of achievement of meeting clearly articulated performance goals;

- An extreme focus on execution driven by collective goal-setting, measurement, and variable compensation based on meeting goals;

- Fewer hierarchical levels in the organization than existed before the HPO conversion (although headcount is not necessarily reduced);

- A workforce that understands the strategy and the business operations resulting from local team goal-setting;

- An organization with the structure and the motivation to quickly adapt to changing external conditions; and

- Changes in the workforce's mindset and day-to-day operating practices that support high levels of collaboration; individuals acquiring additional technical, business improvement, and business management skills that will ultimately yield high performance; more peer-to-peer interactions (instead of one-up, one-down), especially in the areas of peer technical reviews, performance feedback, and coaching; and numerous improvements in the organization from many places within two to six months resulting from teams having the power to improve their work based on the strategy.

Brief Historical Notes

The most significant HPO roots go back to the 1960s and the concept of "sociotechnical systems"—a set of principles and methods that restructured work so the social (people) and the technical (job tasks) aspects of work were optimized and worked in combination. HPOs are also influenced by the Hawthorne Studies at Western Electric in the 1920s that demonstrated how work teams provide mutual support and effective resistance to management actions to increase productivity. In this study workers were more influenced by rewards and punishments bestowed by their own work team than by management-applied extrinsic motivation techniques. HPOs incorporate this finding in the strong development of team unity and collective accountability.

The most contemporary influences on HPOs as presented in this book come from research pairs Fred and Merrelyn Emery and Jon Katzenbach and Douglas Smith.

The Emerys provided breakthroughs in (1) the concept of an organization as an adaptive work system that can quickly respond to, and in some cases even shape, the external environment if it periodically scans the environment and is organized for quick response, (2) the principle that for exceptional performance, the coordination and control of and work should be located as close to the team doing the work as possible,[9] and (3) designs for pragmatic participative planning sessions and restructuring workshops that transition traditional organizational structures into HPT structures.[10]

McKinsey & Co. researchers Katzenbach and Smith found that "teams out-perform individuals acting alone or in larger organization grouping, especially when performance requires multiple skills, judgments, and experiences."[11]

They also made an important distinction between work groups with a single leader and truly high performance teams. In *work groups* with a single leader, performance depends heavily on the leader and how he or she coordinates the work of the individual players. In a *truly high performing team*, leadership shifts among group members based on the performance challenge at hand, and there is mutual as well as individual accountability among team members.[12] The latter type is desired throughout most of an HPO,[13] although the ability to shift back and forth based on the performance challenge at hand is an important team competency.

Katzenbach and Smith also found that teams can work very well within a hierarchical structure.[14] In fact, for large organizations, hierarchies are essential. The critical point for LSS/HPO is that, because there are fewer bureaucratic practices and because considerable "manager" work (such as planning, scheduling, and coordinating work) has been pushed down to teams, far fewer levels of the hierarchy are needed.[15]

The above research, in addition to field work and action research that I have done, constitute the basis for HPO practices presented in this book.

Key Concepts

While there are many important concepts within the HPO discipline, here are the seven that leaders absolutely must know about:

1. The Six Criteria for productive work;

2. Collective accountability;

3. Balancing empowerment and control;

4. Structural differences between traditional and HPO organizations;

5. The transition process to HPTs;

6. Multi-skilling; and

7. Rapid team reconfiguration as conditions change.

The remainder of this section describes each of these in detail.

The Six Criteria for Productive Work

A central theme of HPOs is the six criteria for productive work. These criteria were developed over thirty-five years of research in a variety of work situations.[16] Research shows that employees who score high on the following criteria are more productive:[17]

1. Autonomy in local decision making;

2. Continual learning, for which there must be (a) the ability to set goals, and (b) accurate and timely feedback;

3. Variety in the content, rhythm, and pace of work;

4. Mutual support and respect;

5. Meaningfulness, which consists of (a) doing something with social value and (b) seeing the whole product or service; and

6. A desirable future.

You can perform a quick validation check on these now. Simply think about a time when you believed you personally had the "right amount" for each. How productive were you at work? And how productive were you when you had low scores? While it may seem obvious that these factors contribute to high performance, often today's multi-layered hierarchies, functional silo structures, and directive management styles tend to lower individuals' scores on these criteria and subsequently adversely affect productivity. HPO structures support high scores for individuals on each of the criteria. These criteria are used in at least four ways in an HPO effort:

- To explain the benefits of HPOs to the top management team;

- To record initial individual benchmarks for later progress evaluation;

- As a checklist within the HPT transition workshop to ensure the newly designed organization improves member criteria scores; and

- As a periodic diagnostic after the initial redesign.

Collective Accountability

A difficult paradigm shift for many new HPO leaders is the concept of *collective* (versus *individual*) accountability. Since teams, not individuals, are the basic performance unit in HPOs, it stands to reason that teams plan goals collectively and are collectively responsible for meeting these goals.

Holding groups (teams, groups of teams, or a division) collectively accountable instead of holding employees individually accountable can help transform
groups into cohesive, high-performing units. The introduction of financial
incentives can amplify this message. Corning did just that in the 1980s:

> Corning developed a performance bonus that paid handsomely if the
> entire company met its goals for stock performance and return on equity.
> And those potential bonuses far outweighed any rewards team members
> could receive based on their particular unit's performance. The plan
> instantly changed behavior; in one instance, the head of one operating
> unit voluntarily transferred two of his best managers to the company's
> most troubled unit. He did it with the full realization that no matter how
> much better his own unit did, there was no way the executive bonus plan
> would pay out unless the troubled unit's performance improved dra-
> matically. The underlying concept soon became clear to everyone: It was
> much more important for the entire organization to meet its goals than
> for one unit to look good in relation to the others.[18]

Many have heard the old adage, "When everyone's responsible, no one's
responsible." This is clearly *not* the case with well-run HPTs. Team members
serve as coaches, internal motivators, and disciplinarians, if need be, to achieve
the team's mutually set goals. From a motivation standpoint, teams have external motivation through the reward system that provides bonuses for teams
meeting goals, as well as internal motivation from a sense of achievement for
meeting the goals they themselves set and the ability to improve local work
flows and conditions. This may seem a minor point, but it is a huge leverage
principle when applied in the workplace.

Collective accountability does not eliminate individual responsibility in an
HPO. Team members still depend on their peers to perform tasks that fall
within agreed-on responsibility areas. Team members hold each other mutually *and* individually accountable. The team is collectively accountable to those
outside the team. What collective accountability looks like in practice is that the
team shares credit when things go well, receives disciplinary action together,
and collectively approaches management with important team requests.[19]

Balancing Empowerment and Control

The redistribution of decision making to lower levels of the organization is an
initial cause of concern for many senior and middle managers. It needn't be.

By practicing "intelligent empowerment"—an HPO best practice in which teams receive new decision-making authority accompanied by relevant information, skills training, and rewards—top leaders can initiate a balance of empowered employees and systemic controls.

In HPOs, both technical *and* management responsibilities are redistributed to lower levels of the organization. Simple managerial responsibilities such as goal setting, planning, scheduling, and controlling work quality are often redistributed early. More complex management decisions such as budgeting, hiring, and disciplining are pushed down later, and only when accompanied by training. In many technology-intensive organizations, pushing down technical responsibilities requires accompanying training and apprenticeship programs.

HPOs contain strong elements of control to ensure intelligent empowerment succeeds. Checks and balances appear in the form of:

- Initial guidelines and constraints that top management establishes for HPT redesigns;

- Negotiation of goals with the team's manager(s) to ensure alignment with strategy;

- Self-monitoring, internal team peer reviews and necessary corrective actions;

- Inter-team peer reviews; and

- Periodic manager reviews of team performance metrics.

In some cases of highly specialized work such as medicine, engineering, or research, higher organizational levels often review a team's work because the team or other peer teams do not have the knowledge required to ensure technical accuracy. When this higher level review occurs in a well-run HPO, the higher level teaches as well as reviews at every opportunity.

Structural Differences Between Traditional and HPO Organizations

Some key differences between traditional and HPO organizations are summarized in Table 2.1. In addition, leaders can expect to see a different organizational structure than the traditional lines and boxes depicted on an organization chart. Figure 2.1 shows the traditional representation as well as three sample HPO configurations. The first HPO structure (2a) shows a top leader with a manager (depicted by a box) and a team (depicted by a circle) reporting in to the top leader. The lowest level of the structure consists of teams. The second structure (2b) shows a network arrangement of teams with a central team providing coordination for all the others. The final sample structure (2c) shows a team at the top, two management teams (the medium-sized ellipses), and two HPTs underneath those two management teams. The long ellipse at the bottom of the structure represents a team that provides services to all the other teams, such as an information systems or legal team. The absence of lines indicates that each team negotiates its goals with other teams both vertically and laterally.

Table 2.1. Key Differences Between Traditional and HPO Organizations

	Traditional	HPO
Basic unit of performance	Individuals with a supervisor	High-Performance Team that negotiates goals with their manager and pulls down selected managerial responsibilities such as work goal setting, planning, scheduling, and budgeting.
Layers of management	Many layers of management; organizing rule of thumb is that one person cannot have more than eight to twelve people as direct reports.	Fewer layers of management than traditional structures; managers may still only have eight to twelve "direct reports" but those reporting units are teams. With, for example, an average team size of twelve people, there could be 144 people with one manager. However, this does not mean 144 people reporting to the manager; there are twelve teams reporting as units that have taken on many managerial tasks and controls.
Responsibility for coordination and control of work	One level above the actual work	At the level where the work is performed.
Necessary redundancy to absorb business fluctuations.	Redundancy of parts (one skill to one person, more people than needed with the same skill)	Redundancy of function (multiple skills to one person; a person has more skills than he'll use).

Table 2.1. Key Differences Between Traditional and HPO Organizations, Cont'd

	Traditional	HPO
Goal setting	Done at one level above the actual work.	Done at the actual work level.
Work quality	Responsibility of supervisor or quality department.	Explicitly built into HPT goals. Peer and other group or individual reviews occur as required.
Work product development and accountability	An individual is responsible for one or more tasks. Specific task assignments to individuals are decided by the individual's supervisor. The individual is held accountable for the set of tasks assigned to him.	Groups of people are responsible for groups of tasks. Specific task assignments to individuals are decided by the team. The team is held collectively accountable for the group of tasks assigned to the team.
Specialist work, such as R&D, medical care	People with specialized skills treated as replaceable parts, often uncoordinated.	Where steep learning curve and legal requirements prevent multi-skilling, work coordination is the group's responsibility and the technical control of the content lies outside the group.
Requirements for productive work	Not consciously designed into day-to-day interactions (often are counter to the requirements).	Information provided to all and designed into the work structure.
Knowledge of HPO design principles	Known by a select few, usually human resources and senior manager who have the authority to reorganize.	Known by all, and all have authority to redesign as conditions change.
Rewards and compensation	Individuals receive bonuses and other rewards based on individual performance. Individual compensation based on job title, compensation band. Sharing of organization's gains sometimes exists.	Teams receive bonuses and other rewards based on teams meeting goals that were aligned with the organization's strategy. Individual compensation based on skills held. Sharing of organization's gains frequently exists.

Source: Reprinted with permission of the publisher. From *The Change Handbook: Group Methods for Shaping the Future,* copyright © 1999, by M. Emery and T. Devane, Berrett-Koehler Publishers, Inc., San Francisco, CA. All rights reserved. www.bkconnection.com

Figure 2.1. Traditional vs. HPO Structures

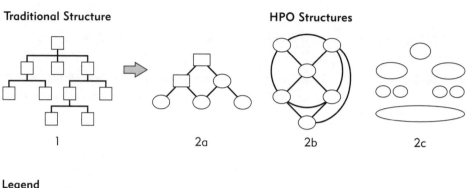

Traditional Structure

1

HPO Structures

2a   2b   2c

Legend

☐ = Individual

◯ = Team

Another important difference is that many—although not all—HPTs are composed of members of different disciplines. Often these team compositions correlate to cross-functional processes, as presented in the previous chapter. For example, a high-tech company might have a new product development HPT containing people with skills in marketing, engineering, and manufacturing. While they do not learn one another's skills completely, team members work jointly on work products and gain a better understanding of how the disciplines fit together. In another example of cross-disciplinary teams, for a deepwater drilling operation Shell Oil had teams containing people from exploration, drilling, development, surveillance, production, and abandonment. The result was a much better work product than if the people had remained in functional departments and tried to work across departmental lines.[20]

The Transition Process to HPTs

The transition process from the organization's current organizational structure to HPTs is accomplished through a series of two-day workshops in which participants consider the organization's strategy and performance challenges and then design HPTs to address them. Within each session, teams address important considerations such as team purpose, boundaries, goals, required resources, and needed training . The typical sequence of an HPO redesign is as follows:

1. Top leadership provides guidelines and strategic inputs for all redesign efforts.

2. The bottom level of the organization redesigns into HPTs. They negotiate their HPT goals with their manager to ensure strategic fit with the organization's goals.

3. The middle level of the organization redesigns into some mid-level HPTs and some single manager positions. Each negotiates goals with their manager(s) to ensure strategic fit.

4. Top leadership redesigns into an HPT, single executive positions, or a combination of the two.

To many this sequence may seem counterintuitive. Often people assume the top level should redesign first, followed by the middle level, and then the bottom level. The problem with this sequence is that there is little substantive change as each level merely "tweaks" the level design a bit and passes the baton down to the next level to do likewise. With a bottom-up approach, people at lower levels pull down some time-consuming responsibilities traditionally held by middle managers. Middle managers then have time to assume some responsibilities held by top leaders. This frees up top leaders for more strategic work and customer interactions, creating a much more powerful work system. Harvard author and researcher Gary Hamel found that typically top leaders spend a mere 3 percent of their time on high-leverage strategic activities![21] After an organizational restructuring into HPTs that starts at the bottom with top-established boundaries, top leaders have substantially more time for strategic activities, and the entire organization benefits.

Multi-Skilling

Within HPTs it is beneficial to have people learn as many skills as possible. This provides maximum flexibility, as people are able to swap tasks when workload demands are imbalanced or a team member is ill and doesn't show up. I broadly classify skills into four categories: technical (the tasks to get products and services out the door); managerial (tasks such as scheduling, budgeting, and coordinating activities among groups); interpersonal (negotiation and conflict management); and analytical (solving problems and evaluating alternative courses of action). While it is not always possible to multi-skill highly specialized technical skills (a neurosurgeon and scrub nurse would never be able to swap roles during surgery), it is possible—and highly desirable—for team members to learn about each other's specialties so they can interface better.

Rapid Team Reconfiguration as Conditions Change

One unique characteristic in an HPO design is that a single HPT or a group of HPTs can reconfigure themselves into different HPT structures as external or internal conditions dictate. For example, if a new market niche opens up, the current sales, marketing, and production teams may reconfigure themselves to take advantage of the new opportunity. They may swap members across teams or design an entirely new set of teams. This behavior is acceptable, and in fact encouraged. During the initial set of workshops in which people redesign themselves into HPTs, everyone in the organization learns the principles of HPT redesign and teams are given the authority to redesign so they can quickly adapt to change. This provides a significant competitive advantage for a company.

Freedom to redesign, of course, it not without boundaries. There are two important guidelines. The redesigning units are asked to check with lateral teams to whom they currently owe deliverables and ensure they have what they need after the redesign and with their management to ensure the proposed new structure is consistent with the organization's strategy.

In addition to the seven concepts just described, leaders must pay close attention to a number of other items.

Ten Important "Pay Attention to" Elements for HPO Leaders

With the HPO discipline we are very concerned about how people are organized, how they interact, and their continued development. The "people elements" of the change equation that need to be addressed to generate motivation to change and to influence subsequent operation in the new environment are

1. *Formal reporting relationships.* People need to know team boundaries and what is expected of them by whom.

2. *The social element of work.* HPO leaders need to acknowledge and allow time for people to share work and non-work-related stories informally, outside the main workflow. This contributes to a strong team orientation.

3. *Connection to existing values and organizational norms.* In an HPO values and organizational norms "manage" or influence people, at least as

much as managers and supervisors do in traditional environments. Leaders ensure people know the values and norms and manage to them.

4. *Connection to existing patterns of interaction.* People have a tendency to cling to old patterns, especially in their networks of interactions and with selected people. Leaders need to identify their own destructive patterns, such as meeting for hours and not reaching a decision, and discontinue them.

5. *Actions and new norms that negate undesirable aspects of the current culture.* Elements of the old culture will need to be shed to reach dramatically higher performance levels. HPO leaders need to introduce what the old organization might deem "countercultural" actions such as requiring data for major marketing decisions and applying financial screens to improvement projects before they are allowed to proceed. HPO leaders strive to actively manage culture and prevent backsliding to old practices.

6. *The nature of supervision.* The practice of supervision changes considerably as teams take on responsibilities typically held by supervisors and managers. For example, more intra-team and peer team reviews to ensure quality occur.

7. *Feelings of competency and achievement.* When people feel competent and that they have achieved something, their energy level and motivation levels tend to increase. Leaders must structure conditions in which people can demonstrate competence and achieve in the new environment.

8. *Local goal-setting and decision-making authority over local work-related issues.* Motivation levels also rise as people feel they have some control over their immediate destiny. They initially gain this feeling in the workshops in which they redesign the organization. Leaders must continue to grant authority to front-line workers after the first redesign so that worker commitment levels continue to rise.

9. *Continual development of employee skills.* HPOs are built on the foundation of the organization developing internal capabilities, including new capabilities for technical performance, process improvement, interpersonal skills, managerial skills, and problem solving.

10. *Conditions and structures exist for productive work criteria.* Leaders need to pay attention to ensuring that the six criteria for productive work described earlier in this chapter are always kept in mind by individuals.

Throughout the course of a transformation effort leaders need to address these ten elements to enable acceptance of the proposed changes by employees.

Key Players

The primary players in an HPO transformation and beyond are shown in Table 2.2.

Table 2.2. HPO Key Players and Their Responsibilities

Player	Roles and Responsibilities	Training	HPO Dedication
Senior managers	Ensure that a clear vision of the future exists, communicate the vision, ensure opportunities for meaningful participation exist, create time and space to accomplish new tasks and reflection, remove barriers, model new behaviors, reward new behaviors and mindsets	Group sessions of two hours each month for the first six months; as needed after that[i]	Full-time
Middle managers	Integrate the work of their teams with other teams, remove barriers for lower levels, negotiate lower level goals to ensure fit with strategy, ensure lower levels are meeting metrics	Group sessions of two hours each month for the first six months, as needed after that[ii]	Full-time
Front-line workers	Set goals, perform work, continuously improve	One two-hour briefing session initially; then a two-day workshop; then often team skills training of three days from three to six months after the initial redesign	Full-time
Workshop manager	Ensure that the principles of HPOs are applied	Five days, often followed by an apprenticeship program in which the new workshop manager is accompanied and coached by an experienced workshop manager for two additional workshops	Full-time during the two-day workshops

[i]It is recommended that these sessions be conducted by the senior managers themselves, but external facilitators may be called in for especially challenging situations or topics.

[ii]It is recommended that these sessions be conducted by the middle managers themselves, but external facilitators may be called in for especially challenging situations or topics.

As you can see, the HPO discipline reaches a far broader and deeper audience initially than does Lean Six Sigma. There is a much shorter learning curve for being able to apply HPO principles initially (although it may take some people several months to become entirely comfortable with the new ways of thinking and interacting).

Hallmarks of the Discipline

There are nine hallmarks of the discipline of HPOs:

1. An execution-oriented workforce.
2. Technical decisions, managerial decisions, and information are pushed to the lowest possible level.
3. Teams, not individuals, are the fundamental unit of performance.
4. The culture relishes productive conflict and status quo challenges.
5. Teams set their own goals and are held collectively accountable.
6. There are few levels in the organizational hierarchy.
7. Top-down direction and bottom-up implementation prevail.
8. People and teams are multi-skilled whenever possible for flexibility and speed.
9. It is a measurement-rich and feedback-rich environment.

What It's Not

In defining what an HPO is, it is also helpful to consider what it is not.

An HPO is not merely an organization that has a *few* high performing teams in it. In an HPO nearly *all* the organization is composed of high performing teams. While some individuals will continue to be the basic performance unit for some tasks at middle management and top management levels, the organization is primarily composed of teams. In quality improvement people make a distinction between "big Q" and "little q." Big Q is when quality is present everywhere in the organization. Little q is just a process improvement effort here and there.

The same important distinction exists for teams. HPO is "big T, not little t." In an HPO workers are on at least one standing team, and some people may devote part of their time to formal, cross-team improvement efforts. By having everyone on a team, getting together in a team to solve a problem is not some sort of unnatural act. And more than just the people who were on the team have the benefit of knowing how to collaborate and jointly solve problems. Unfortunately, many Six Sigma consultants these days focus on how to improve performance of a single improvement team at a time. This is not as effective as having an entire organization of teams, with individuals who can move in and out of teams smoothly because they live in a culture that actively supports teams and reconfigures itself around the team concept.

An HPO is not an organization that is structured according to functional departments that frequently employ the use of temporary teams to address process improvement issues and then disband and return to the functional department organization. Teams are the basic organizing unit in an HPO, and they are standing teams, not just temporary teams.

An HPO is not a recycled plan for self-directed work teams resurrected from the 1980s. While there is a semiautonomous element in the design of high performance work teams, in an HPO there are also controls built in to ensure alignment with strategy and culture. Specifically, top management provides guidelines for the teams, team-set goals are negotiated with management and peer teams, and team operating principles are consistent with the organizational structure. In addition, there are changes to the organization's compensation and reward system that were rarely made in the self-directed teams of yesteryear.

An HPO is not a renewed 1970s attempt at "empowerment." HPOs go far beyond empowerment by systematically distributing decisions, information, business skills, and controls throughout the workforce. Specifically, in an HPO there are five controls, as discussed earlier in this chapter, to ensure teams are supporting the organization's strategy.

This chapter has provided some insights into HPOs and the HPTs that comprise them. HPOs exert a considerable influence on organizational culture and individual motivation. Through participation in restructuring workshops and setting their own goals in a team environment, individuals gain a higher level of enthusiasm for supporting the organization's strategy. In the next chapter we will see how combining HPOs with high leverage process improvement methods can bring the organization to even higher levels of performance.

Notes

1. Fisher, K. (1999). *Leading self-directed teams.* New York: McGraw-Hill.

2. Semler, R. (1995). *Maverick.* New York: Warner Books.

3. Fisher, K. (1999). *Leading self-directed teams.* New York: McGraw-Hill.

4. Boyett, J., and Boyett, J. (1998). *The guru guide: The best ideas of the top management thinkers.* New York: John Wiley & Sons, Inc.

5. Emery, M., and Devane, T. (1999). Participative design workshop. In Holman, P., and Devane, T. *The change handbook: Group methods for shaping the future.* San Francisco: Berrett-Koehler.

6. Fisher, K. (1999). *Leading self-directed teams.* New York: McGraw-Hill.

7. Kirsner, S. (1998, April). Total teamwork: SEI investments. *Fast company, 18,* p. 130.

8. Boyett, J., and Boyett, J. (1998). *The guru guide: The best ideas of the top management thinkers.* New York: John Wiley & Sons, Inc.

9. Emery, F. (1995, January/February). Participative design: Effective, flexible and successful, now! *Journal for Quality and Participation,* pp. 6–9.

10. Holman, P., and Devane, T. (1999). *The change handbook: Group methods for shaping the future.* San Francisco: Berrett-Koehler.

11. Katzenbach, J., and Smith, D. (1993). *The wisdom of teams.* Boston, MA: Harvard Business School Press.

12. Katzenbach, J., and Smith, D. (1993). *The wisdom of teams.* Boston, MA: Harvard Business School Press.

13. Katzenbach and Smith argue that if the required performance challenge can be best met through the sum of individual contributions, then the single-leader discipline makes the most sense. However, most business tasks today have a level of complexity that requires collective work of multiple skills, which would require a truly high performing team, in their terminology.

14. Katzenbach, J., and Smith, D. (1993). *The wisdom of teams.* Boston, MA: Harvard Business School Press.

15. Here are some examples that may serve as general guidelines. I have seen organizations of 250 people and below operate effectively with two levels (the top person or top team, and the level of HPTs below). Facilities of up to 2,000 people have been effectively operated with three levels (the top person or team, a middle level that integrates work across HPTs, and the HPT level).

16. Holman P., and Devane, T. (1999). *The change handbook: Group methods for shaping the future.* San Francisco: Berrett-Koehler.

17. It is important to note that the emphasis is on creating productive employees, not happy employees. Although numerous efforts have been undertaken to increase happiness and job satisfaction in the workplace, research from the Center for Effective Organizations in Los Angeles shows there is no significant statistical correlation between employee job satisfaction and improved performance.

18. "The mythic leader and beyond." Mercer Delta white paper at www.mercerdelta.com.

19. As teams and the concept of collective accountability become more widely accepted in the organization, teams may choose to send a delegate to upper management to make a request. It is extremely important at the start of an HPO, however, that teams embrace the notion that teams are an organizational unit that in many cases will behave as individuals behaved in the old structure. Although to many this may seem wasteful (why have eight people in a meeting when you could just have one?), the solidarity and "oneness" of the newly formed groups will be critical to their future performance.

20. Personal conversation with Ann Burress, Shell Oil.

21. Hamel, G., and Prahalad, C. (1994). *Competing for the future.* Boston, MA: Harvard Business School Press. The study results showed that executives spend "3 percent of their energy building a corporate perspective for the future." In some cases, the study showed that executives spent less than 1 percent of their time on such activities.

Lean Six Sigma and High-Performance Organizations Combined

Some are born great, some achieve greatness, and some have greatness thrust upon 'em.

Shakespeare, *Twelfth Night*

THE COMBINED DISCIPLINES of Lean Six Sigma and High-Performance Organizations have not yet been widely implemented. This is why many independently implemented Lean Manufacturing, Six Sigma, and HPO efforts have faltered. Early successful adopters of aggressive process improvement programs, such as Motorola, StorageTek, and AlliedSignal on many sites naturally combined these LSS/HPO elements of simple process improvement principles, advanced process improvement using statistical methods, and the use of teams to generate high levels of energy and commitment.[1] Experience has shown that LSS/HPO is best implemented at the level of a plant, a site, or other relatively self-contained organizational unit. This strategy, as contrasted to a "big bang" approach that attempts to mandate standard approaches simultaneously across multiple global locations, provides for an easier to manage transition and the resulting operation and local motivation to continuously improve.

This chapter presents essentials that leaders must know about HPOs for the following topics: representative results, the value proposition, typical outcomes, brief historical notes, key concepts, ten important "pay attention to" elements, key players, hallmarks of the discipline, and specifically what it is not.

Representative Results

Representative successes of LSS/HPO implementations include:

- In 1988 StorageTek's HDA production line organized into HPTs and used advanced statistical tools to dramatically improve quality and costs. Within two and one-half years, the product went from a mean time-to-failure of 200 months to mean time-to-failure that exceeded 2,000 months—a 1000 percent increase in product quality. Workmanship errors decreased by 90 percent. Scrap cost was reduced by 85 percent. Rework costs were reduced by 73 percent. Process yield improved by 80 percent. Manufacturing cost was reduced by 60 percent.[2]

- The General Electric plant that manufactures jet engines in Durham, North Carolina, reduced the number of defects per engine delivered to Boeing by 75 percent and is close to producing twice the output for one major engine with the same number of people within a four-year timeframe.[3]

- In 1995, in a second LSS/HPO effort in a different StorageTek division than the HDA production line mentioned above, within three months StorageTek increased group productivity of four combined departments of knowledge workers by 60 percent and yielded $400,000 in cost savings.

Value Proposition

Combining existing powerful disciplines with complementary strengths is a key to success. Table 3.1 provides an overview of Lean, Six Sigma, and HPO disciplines so leaders can understand how the roots of each discipline contribute to the more comprehensive LSS/HPO approach. Additional information on these topics can be found in books and websites listed in the Reference section of the Appendix.

Table 3.1. Top Leader Overview of Lean, Six Sigma, and HPOs

	Value Proposition	Critical Assumptions	Hallmarks of Discipline	Key Tools and Methods	Observed Side Effects	Off-Missing Elements
Six Sigma	Principles for process improvement, statistical methods, a customer focus, attention to processes, and a management system focusing on high return improvement projects result in continuous improvement and significant financial gains	Measurement results in process understanding and will guide the way to process improvement A process is in fairly good shape at the start of a detailed data collection and statistical analysis effort Substantial financial incentives for senior managers will cause Six Sigma to be practiced throughout the organization	Statistical methods Fanatical focus on the external customer Attention to process Pre-screening of improvement projects to ensure fit with strategy and a minimum financial return before chartering team People strive for perfection, but noble mistakes are tolerated Top-down implementation lasting eight months to three years Analysis-rich and measurement-rich environment Executive bonuses tied to Six Sigma improvements	Control charts to analyze process variation Charts to determine where errors might occur in a process Regression techniques to determine input effects on outputs Techniques to determine the effect of multiple inputs on output	Target areas for improvement often resist out of fear Senior managers sometimes game the system to get large financial bonuses Six Sigma avoided because of its "bigness"	No direct focus on time or inventory reductions Doesn't focus on quick, large wins High level of motivation exists in internal people trained in Six Sigma, but often not in the general workforce
Lean	Principles for improving workflow, setup time, elimination of waste, and preventive maintenance will speed up business processes and return quick financial gains	Dramatic improvements in cost, time, and quality metrics are possible by focusing on process cycle time and compressing it Effective maintenance can virtually eliminate unscheduled downtime	Identify, prioritize, and address time traps within key processes Eliminate waste Improve quality and simultaneously reduce cost Minimize "things in process," such as work in process inventory Provide make-to-order products to customers efficiently Make visual control and lean production possible by having uncluttered work areas in which work materials are separated from unneeded materials and then neatly arranged and identified	Pull systems Work cells Setup reduction Preventive maintenance Value stream mapping across organizational boundaries	People become frustrated as improvements hit a plateau that requires statistical methods Lack of formal tie-in to management system makes participation strictly voluntary	Cannot bring process under statistical control Motivation for improvement limited to people using the Lean principles

Table 3.1. Top Leader Overview of Lean, Six Sigma, and HPOs, Cont'd

	Value Proposition	Critical Assumptions	Hallmarks of Discipline	Key Tools and Methods	Observed Side Effects	Oft-Missing Elements
HPOs	A structure composed mainly of high performance teams and a set of operating principles creates a widespread culture of motivated individuals that is highly focused on metrics, extremely execution-driven, and committed to continual improvement and rapid adaptation	Flexible team structures enable rapid adaptation to external challenges Pushing technical and business/managerial decisions down to the lowest level, accompanied by needed information and employee development efforts, create intrinsic motivation for employees to perform at high levels and to actively seek opportunities for continuous improvement	Execution-oriented workforce Technical decisions, managerial decisions, and information pushed to the lowest possible level Teams, not individuals, are the fundamental unit of performance The culture relishes productive conflict and status quo challenges Teams set their own goals and are held collectively accountable Few levels in the organizational hierarchy Top-down and bottom-up implementation lasting one to six months Multi-skilling for flexibility and speed Measurement-rich and feedback-rich environment	Workshops for collective planning, process understanding, and organization redesign Matrices that map responsibilities to individuals and groups Peer technical reviews and evaluations where possible Straight talk Processes for managing culture	Managers become detached from the work of their teams and let teams do whatever they want, compromising organizational strategy or else managers fail to discard old paradigms and micromanage teams Teams become consensus-crazy and decision processes slow	No tools for consistently reducing variation No principles for process improvement provided by HPO discipline; improvements are mainly of the "low hanging fruit" variety, and results of local, isolated innovations initiated within high-performance teams

The LSS/HPO value proposition is that an organization can achieve dramatic, sustainable results by integrating:

- Lean's simple improvement principles and tools that focus on waste elimination and process speed;

- Six Sigma's statistical analyses and other advanced methods that focus on reducing variation, plus a financial screening rigor for projects; and

- High-Performance Organization's cultural focus and creation of accountability, energy, and ownership through a new structure and set of principles.

This combination also provides a balance of short-term and long-term gains within an overall improvement portfolio. Applying simple streamlining principles and organizing teams with authority to improve local work flows can produce quick gains within three weeks to two months. Advanced statistical methods that require lengthier data collection and analysis times round out the improvement portfolio by providing gains in a six-month to eighteen-month timeframe.

Typical Outcomes

The previous chapters described the basic LSS and HPO outcomes. Organizations that implement LSS/HPO will achieve those benefits plus three additional outcomes resulting from the combination:

1. Easier change management than with LSS alone because HPO specifically addresses culture change;

2. More sustainable outcomes than typically accompany LSS alone because HPTs own their goals and have a mindset of execution and continuous improvement; and

3. More rapid, dramatic gains than with HPO alone since LSS tools provide the HPO teams the LSS tools needed to be successful.

The analogy of a car and gasoline is useful. LSS is the car and HPO is the gas. Put them together and you can go fast to a selected destination. But the car alone without gas—or the LSS alone without HPO—is just an idle combination of simple and complex moving parts. The gasoline alone—like HPO without LSS—can be set afire and produce a lot of heat, but won't get you to your destination. The two need to work together for the best results.

Brief Historical Notes

In a recent conference, the title of a Lockheed Martin presentation was "It's not Lean or Six Sigma, it's not Lean then Six Sigma, it's Lean and Six Sigma."[4] The *informal* combination of the elements of waste elimination, statistical tools, teams, and culture change has been going on in selected high performing organizations for years. However, for most organizations, the notion of *formally* planning and integrating Lean Six Sigma and High-Performance Organizations is relatively new.

Several companies, however, have formally combined quality improvement and *team-based* organizations (not just organizations that convened and disbanded ad hoc teams). Years ago, Procter & Gamble developed innovative, highly effective work system designs for new plants. Some key people transported successful best practices of combining quality and high-performance teams to different companies such as Weyerhaeuser and Champion International.[5] And finally, although Motorola and AlliedSignal have more noticeably been in the press for Six Sigma, historically they have also implemented Lean and high-performance teams in many successful plants.[6] Historically, the initial focus in the above companies was on planting improvement seeds and watching the evolution unfold over the course of years. This was a slow process. The emphasis with today's LSS/HPO approach is on speed. Innovations have been made since the early days of connecting the two piecemeal, and the LSS/HPO approach incorporates those innovations.

Key Concepts

LSS/HPO is far more than just putting activities and tools from each into one work plan. Organizations using LSS/HPO combine the two disciplines into one formalized, well-planned effort to achieve the benefits from both. Consequently, leaders must consider the following four concepts along with those that appeared in the previous two chapters:

1. The importance of blending the two disciplines;
2. The need to provide both extrinsic and intrinsic rewards;
3. Ownership of process improvement and results; and
4. Critical sequencing considerations.

The Importance of Blending the Two Disciplines

It's slower and far less effective to implement only one of the disciplines initially and then the second. Combining LSS and HPO tools and methods is critical. A garden analogy is helpful (see Figure 3.1). In this analogy flowers are the ultimate financial and human motivation rewards, seeds are the principles and LSS methods of process improvement, and the fertile soil is the execution-oriented culture provided by HPO.

Figure 3.1. Flower Garden Analogy

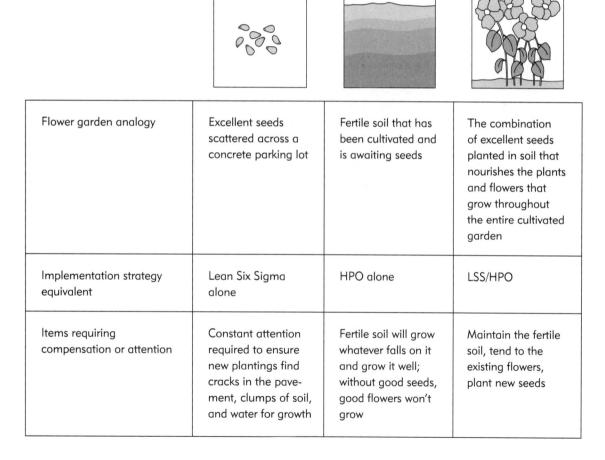

Flower garden analogy	Excellent seeds scattered across a concrete parking lot	Fertile soil that has been cultivated and is awaiting seeds	The combination of excellent seeds planted in soil that nourishes the plants and flowers that grow throughout the entire cultivated garden
Implementation strategy equivalent	Lean Six Sigma alone	HPO alone	LSS/HPO
Items requiring compensation or attention	Constant attention required to ensure new plantings find cracks in the pavement, clumps of soil, and water for growth	Fertile soil will grow whatever falls on it and grow it well; without good seeds, good flowers won't grow	Maintain the fertile soil, tend to the existing flowers, plant new seeds

In the case of LSS and HPO implemented separately, expert practitioners may argue that when they implement each of these disciplines they don't encounter the problems mentioned here. And they're right. Experts instinctively compensate. But inexperienced implementers do tend to encounter these problems because of the nature of the methods and how they are typically taught to implement them.

The Need to Provide Both Extrinsic and Intrinsic Rewards

There's no doubt that extrinsic motivators, such as money and stock options, play a role in motivating people. If you have any doubt about that, stop paying people and see what happens to their motivation. Extrinsic motivation is great for some objectives, such as motivating people to implement a given strategic direction and monitoring its implementation. But it often falls short in areas such as increasing people's initiative to seek out potential errors or opportunities and organizing a group of people to address them.[7] Intrinsic motivators, such as allowing workers a say in how work is done and letting them set their own goals, do a better job of addressing this type of behavior, which is absolutely critical in an LSS/HPO. When combined, extrinsic and intrinsic motivation have a significant impact on workforce output and satisfaction.

In 1990 the Brookings Institution's conference on pay and productivity uncovered an important relationship that wasn't even part of the study. When all the results were in, conference chairman Alan S. Blinder concluded from the data that "Changing the way workers are treated may boost productivity more than changing the way they are paid. Worker participation apparently helps make alternative compensation plans like profit sharing, gain sharing, and employee stock ownership plans work better and also has beneficial effects of its own. This theme, which was totally unexpected when I organized the conference, ran strongly through all the papers."[8]

Ownership of Process Improvement and Results

As with most expert-driven projects, at the start of a typical Six Sigma project (without the HPO element or a longstanding successful history of teams in the organization), the ownership for success lies primarily with the expert—the Black Belt. One hopes that, as the project progresses, ownership passes from the Black Belt to the people responsible for implementing and subsequently operating the solution. The challenge in this process is that this ownership transition process is a change management issue, for which Black Belts are often ill-equipped and under-trained. As Val Larson of Becton, Dickinson, and Company and Mike Carnell point out, the role of a Black Belt is typically described as a "change agent." In fact, the two terms are frequently used interchangeably in Black Belt training. Ironically, though, while Black Belt training lasts four to six months, there is often just several hours dedicated to the process of effecting change.[9] Quite predictably, passing the baton of responsibility from the Black Belt to the operations group can take a long time, and in some cases it fails to happen at all.

Ownership of improvements evolves quite differently in a team-based environment. Teams want to improve because it is part of the culture and they are rewarded for it, both intrinsically (through job satisfaction and sufficiently challenging work) and extrinsically (through compensation, rewards, and other recognition). Black Belts are not viewed as threats, or superior members in the organizational caste system, but rather as peers who hold a different skill set. The theme of peer-to-peer relationships in joint pursuit of organizational goals is pervasive in an LSS/HPO. This theme fosters a joint ownership of process and results by the Black Belt and improvement team from the first day of the project. In one LSS/HPO organization, I saw a team challenge and assertively question the Black Belt's process and recommendations the first week of the project. The team wanted to make sure they were making best use of their time and would achieve the best possible results. I have rarely seen such questioning of a Black Belt early in a pure Six Sigma implementation, where Black Belts hold a position of unquestionable, esteemed regard.

In an LSS/HPO, ownership throughout the improvement process resides with the operating group as well as with the Black Belt. However, to achieve that early ownership of the operating group it is important to consider sequencing of LSS/HPO transformation activities.

Critical Sequencing Considerations

There are three general guidelines for sequencing activities in an LSS/HPO transformation. Astute leaders will consider Voltaire's trenchant observation that "All generalizations are wrong, even this one" when applying these general guidelines. For the most part, leaders will find these guidelines to be applicable to a majority of cases where such judgment is required. The rationale for each guideline is presented below, along with an example of when the guideline might not apply.

Guideline 1

Use LSS principles and tools in principally HPO activities and HPO principles and tools in principally LSS activities. For example, high participation planning events have roots in the HPO discipline, but in an LSS/HPO transformation it's helpful to also have the group discuss continuous improvement and waste elimination in these events. Conversely, it's good to consider the HPO principles of ownership and intrinsic motivation when conducting LSS process improvement sessions. Exceptions to this guideline would be when the purpose, time available, and combination of tools and principles simply do not lend themselves to a combination. An example would be using a group method called "Dialogue" (see Appendix) rooted in HPO to exclusively discuss issues of employee motivation.

Guideline 2

Do ownership-generating activities before improvement activities. A perfect 50/50 balance between LSS and HPO will not always be possible, since many activities have strong roots in one or the other of the two disciplines. In these cases it's best to sequence the primarily HPO activities before the primarily LSS activities, while still trying to include elements of each discipline in each activity. By sequencing the HPO activities in a staggered fashion slightly before the LSS activities, leaders can begin to create buy-in and ownership of the upcoming process improvement related activities.

Figure 3.2 shows the key LSS/HPO transformation stages and sequencing of combined major LSS/HPO activities (A's), predominantly HPO activities (B's, D), and predominantly LSS activities (C's). Details of these major activity blocks appear in Chapter 11, titled "Activity Map and Leader To Do List." An example of preceding improvement activities with ownership-generating activities would be the sequencing of B and C in the Design stage. In B people redesign the structure into HPTs and increase conditions for job productivity and satisfaction. In C people launch process improvement projects. By having B slightly precede C, the workforce is more likely to accept and own the process improvements. An exception to this sequencing guideline would arise in a crisis situation, such as FDA threatening to close a pharmaceutical plant for compliance infractions. In such cases there would be no time to build ownership through massive team goal-setting exercises, and people would need to quickly move to improve the process and avoid a shutdown using LSS methods.

Figure 3.2. Activity Map for LSS/HPO Transformation

LSS/HPO Combination	Stage 1: Initiation	Stage 2: Direction Setting	Stage 3: Design	Stage 4: Implementation	Stage 5: Operations and Continuous Improvement
LSS/HPO together	A	A	A	A	A
Predominantly HPO activities		B	B	B D	
Predominantly Lean Six Sigma activities		C	C	C	
Duration	1–2 months	1–3 months	1–4 months	4–9 months	ongoing
Cumulative time	1–2 months	2–5 months	3–9 months	7–18 months	8–19+ months

Guideline 3

When considering process improvement, first question whether the process should be done at all, then do Lean methods before statistical Six Sigma methods. Before trying to improve a process, leaders should determine whether or not customers or the market want such a process, at least in its current form. If the answer is yes, leaders should consider applying Lean first. (Since the bodies of research and knowledge of Lean and Six Sigma remain separate and most likely will for some time, it make sense to split them out here.) Most Lean techniques require a shorter learning curve and shorter data collection time than Six Sigma tools. Therefore, for purposes of quick results, it makes sense to first apply Lean methods such as process and value stream mapping and identification of non-value-added activities. However, we don't want to universally apply this rule if other conditions suggest another, more beneficial course of action. An exception would be a machine process that involves very little human intervention, such as a highly automated precision lathe or a bioreactor for cell growth. With minimal human interaction, there is little chance that people will introduce variability in the process. Therefore, process maps and attempts to identify non-value-added activities may yield little benefit and it would be better to start by establishing control charts to identify the impact of the key process inputs on process variability.

Ten Important "Pay Attention to" Elements

With the combination of LSS and HPO disciplines, leaders need to be concerned with simultaneously introducing improvement methods and establishing a culture of performance and continuous improvement. To do this requires big picture, systemic thinking about how the various parts of the performance puzzle fit together.

The first four elements that help maintain a systemic focus are rooted in a discipline called "systems thinking." Systems thinking was popularized in the early to mid-90s by Peter Senge of MIT. It can help leaders think creatively about, and effectively address, the big picture for complex issues because it focuses on the interconnectedness of factors in a "system." The intent of presenting systems thinking concepts here is not to make you an expert. I highly recommend that some people in your organization be trained in detailed tools and principles of systems thinking to assist in the transformation effort. The intent of presenting elements one through four below is to make you aware of, and conversant with, some of the key systems thinking concepts and tools that are relevant for an LSS/HPO transformation. For further information about systems thinking, you may want to read *The Fifth Discipline Fieldbook: Strategies and Tools for Building a Learning Organization.*[10] Elements five through ten below provide additional leverage for leaders in working toward a highly effective, seamless integration of LSS and HPO.

1. *Think in terms of the "structure of systems."* In systems thinking parlance, a system is a "perceived whole whose elements 'hang together' because they continually affect each other over time and operate toward a common purpose" and a structure is "the pattern of interrelationships among key components of a system."[11] Examples of systems are organizations, business processes, teams, communities, and biological organisms. Senge observed that "systems of which we are unaware hold us prisoner."[12] LSS/HPO leaders need to pay attention to systems and the structures that determine how they operate and the outcomes they produce. Structures, or the rules that hold the components of a system together, are often invisible and are sometimes constructed unconsciously.

   It is helpful for leaders to think about, and in some cases draw pictures of how various components of a system interact so that leaders can take appropriate action. Three basic building blocks for systems thinking that leaders need to consider are

- *Reinforcing loops,* which amplify the effects of an action. Sometimes referred to as virtuous cycles, or vicious cycles, they can be positive or negative for an organization. Leaders must identify critical variables to fuel virtuous cycles (such as increased intrinsic motivation that leads to more improvement suggestions that leads to more intrinsic motivation, and so on) and put the brakes on vicious cycles (people feeling negative about the proposed changes so they sabotage them, resulting in the changes being ineffective, and so on).

- *Balancing loops,* which seek to move the current state to a targeted state, much as the thermostat in a room regulates room temperature to the desired setting. Positive uses of this building block include setting stretch goals and imposing a limiting factor or "brake" on an undesirable reinforcing loop (such as introducing participation to obtain buy-in for the next improvement stage).

- *Delays,* which make the link between cause and effect longer than one might expect. Unless leaders consider and allow for delays, they will often redouble their efforts, thinking that nothing has happened, or, as we used to say in the old TQM days, frequently yanking up the newly planted flowers to see if they had taken root. Each of these actions has adverse long-term effects.

The basic building blocks can be combined to explain workplace phenomena and design ways for improved performance. There are some standard, recurring situations and structures that systems thinkers have dubbed "system archetypes." More detailed explanations of the specific systems archetypes mentioned below can be found in *The Fifth Discipline Fieldbook*[13] or www.LeanSixSigmaHPO.com. One useful system archetype for LSS/HPOs is the Limits to Growth archetype, which contains each of the three building blocks. In an LSS/HPO transformation, workers may have a strong desire to improve operations because they have had a voice in the initial direction setting for their area. This could be a strong reinforcing loop in which intrinsic motivation and improvement each serve as a cycle of cause and effect for each other. However, a balancing loop often enters the picture because not enough people know tools and methods to improve. There is a delay in getting people trained in both simple and advanced improvement techniques, which leads to a decline in intrinsic motivation. A key strategy to address this Limits to Growth archetype is to zero in on the limiting factor—in this case, dissemination of knowledge through apprenticeships, training, or e-learning—and take action to remove that limit.

2. *Consider undesirable, unintended consequences of positive leadership actions.* The best-intentioned actions may have serious side-effects, and leaders need to consider what those might be. Leaders may try to help teams by making key decisions that the teams need to gain experience in making. (This is known as the Shifting the Burden archetype since the capability to solve problems is shifted from where it belongs to another place). Another example is when some leaders genuinely try to accelerate change by modifying the compensation system before the new skills and organizational structure are in place. (This is known as the Fixes That Fail archetype, as the attempted fix ends up failing to achieve long-term benefits because the new pay system is inappropriately based on old skills and an old structure that both change dramatically in the LSS/HPO transformation.)

3. *Be alert to overburdening key resources and processes.* Problems will invariably ensue when everyone asks for the best talent on their improvement efforts. Burn-out results. It can also result for teams and business processes. For further details of this situation and tips for remedying it, refer to the Tragedy of the Commons archetype in one of the above-mentioned resources.

4. *Encourage and hold fast to aggressive, achievable goals.* Goal setting is a foundation for improvement and for increasing worker intrinsic and extrinsic motivation. Leaders should not permit people to set goals that do not stretch their capabilities, just so the people can say they met their goals. (This specific practice would be classified as the Drifting Goals archetype.)

5. *Periodically meet to understand, not to decide.* For complex topics where people hold widely differing views, it can be helpful to hold a "Dialogue" session (see the Appendix for a detailed description of the Dialogue method).

In such a session people strive to surface each other's assumptions and understand the key variables impacting the situation at hand. No decisions are made in a Dialogue session, as this tends to decrease openness and willingness to listen non-judgmentally to others' ideas. Dialogue sessions are then followed up by decision-making sessions once everyone has had an opportunity to better understand the situation and others' views.

Unfortunately, the "not-meeting-for-a-decision" element of Dialogue often scares people off and they avoid Dialogue, thinking it a huge waste of time. I once conducted a Dialogue session for an eighty-person department in a pharmaceutical company. After the session the director came up to me and said she was very pleased with the ultimate outcome, but if she had known the proposed process in advance she would not have permitted it to happen because it seemed unstructured and did not drive to any decisions. This organization now holds regular Dialogue sessions for controversial and complex topics.

6. *Make great personnel selections.* For an LSS/HPO it is essential to have great people in leadership positions. "Great" in this context does not mean charismatic, but rather focuses on the appropriate blend of a results-orientation and people skills. Carole Jacobson, an organization development manager at Weyerhaeuser, has two questions she asks potential managers of high-performance teams: "Do you like people" and "Are you willing to do this type of work the rest of your life?"[14]

    Researcher Jim Collins believes people selection to be of the utmost importance. Collins studied details of what eleven companies did from 1965 to 1995 that brought them from good to great companies. In the third chapter of his book *Good to Great,* Collins writes, "To be clear, the main point of this chapter is not just about assembling the right team—that's nothing new. The main point is to first get the right people on the bus (and the wrong people off the bus) before you figure out where to drive it. The second key point is the degree of sheer rigor needed in people decisions in order to take a company from good to great."[15]

7. *Structured assumption checking.* The assumptions that were once valid may no longer be valid. Since assumptions influence behavior, rules, and goals, it makes sense to periodically, in a structured fashion, discuss articulated and unarticulated old assumptions and see if they are still valid.

8. Plan-Do-Study-Act (PDSA) continually. Quality pioneer W. Edwards Deming developed the concept of PDSA to assist in continual improvement. This cycle has applications in both "hard" improvement skills (such as the application of statistical methods) and "soft" skills (such as coaching and self-reflection).

9. *Seek to increase variety and eligibility.* For most people, variety is a great motivator. Giving people more variety in their work provides the added benefit of developing a multi-skilled workforce that can tackle more difficult problems and cover for each other in the event of the temporary loss of a member.

    Increased variety goes hand and hand with increased eligibility. In an LSS/HPO, leaders must help people at all levels increase what they are "eligible" to do. This means providing appropriate training and information that accompany new responsibility levels so that the entire organization benefits. When people are provided an opportunity, it is often amazing at how they can excel. In 1760, at the age of 25, John Adams lamented, "I shall never shine 'til some animating occasion calls forth all my powers."[16] With the American conflict with England providing sufficient stimulus and opportunity, Adams went on to become a great leader in America's independence, co-authored the Declaration of Independence, served in diplomatic roles in France and Holland, and was vice president and president of the United States. Similar amazing performance is possible when people in organizations have opportunities that they have not had before.

10. *Establish conditions for and reinforce flawless execution at every opportunity.* Organizations that execute well will consistently outperform those in their industry that do not. When many people hear the recommendation to "actively manage the organization's culture," they think it means to make the organization a more fun place to work. This is not the objective of managing culture. The objective is to achieve an execution-oriented culture that fosters ethical behavior. Fun is often a by-product of this, but it is not the primary cultural objective. Top leaders must continually seek opportunities for flawless execution to occur and provide rewards and recognition when it does. In an LSS/HPO, rewards and recognition are most often done at the team level, but can also be done at the individual level.

We are now ready to explore the people involved in the transformation and their interrelationships.

Key Players

Figure 3.3 shows the key groups that organizational members form for the LSS/HPO transformation. The many LSS/HPO structures are represented by ellipses, concentric circles, and overlapping circles and ellipses rather than as lines and boxes connected in a traditional structure.

Figure 3.3. Key Groups During the LSS/HPO Transformation

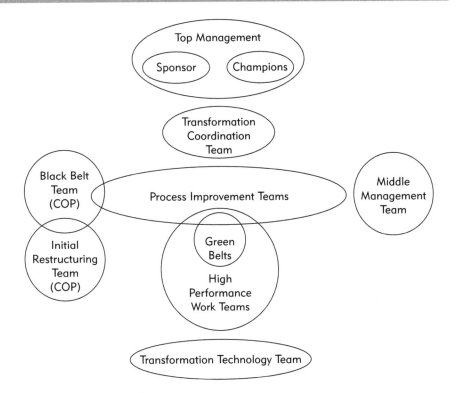

In the figure ellipses contained within ellipses represent subgroups of a larger group; overlapping ellipses indicate that certain individuals are members of both overlapping groups. Ellipses that are not connected does not mean that they have no relationship to other groups. Rather, it indicates that the exchanges of materials or information are negotiated between the ellipse groups and are subject to change as customer needs change.

Figure 3.3 makes a distinction between two types of groupings, a *team grouping,* a collection of individuals who share common goals and whose collective skills are need to achieve those goals, and *communities of practice* (COP), individuals who share a common interest and periodically gather to exchange best practices and learn more about topics of interest. Table 3.2 describes the critical interrelationships of each of the groups.

Table 3.2. Key Group Interrelationships in LSS/HPOs

Group	Interactions with other groups and notes
Top Management	Provide strategy and restructuring guidelines to Initial Restructuring Team
	Review process improvement recommendations from Middle Management group
	Provide initial list of improvement projects (that meet financial screening criteria) and strategic inputs to Transformation Coordination Team for development of the Integrated Work Plan
	Review improvement project status prepared by Process Improvement Teams and Transformation Coordination Team
	Model new behaviors and reward desired new behaviors for all groups
Champions	Assist Process Improvement Team in creating business case for the project
	Ensure appropriate resources are allocated and scope is correctly defined for the Process Improvement Teams
	Ensure Process Improvement Team is chartered and meets tollgate requirements before moving from one stage of DMAIC process to the next
	Remove roadblocks for process improvement projects getting completed and meeting their objectives
	Ensure alignment of operational project goals and strategic organization objectives
	Major participants in first wave of project selections in discussions with Top Management peers; very responsible for the quality or project selection in subsequent waves
	Meet periodically as a Champion team to prioritize resource allocation and share lessons learned about being Champions
	Ensure lessons learned are captured and celebrations of success occur
Sponsors	Provide encouragement to Process Improvement Teams
	Attend process improvement functions and demonstrate top management commitment to LSS/HPO
	Sponsors would meet periodically as a team to prioritize resource allocation and share lessons learned about being Sponsors

Table 3.2. Key Group Interrelationships in LSS/HPOs, Cont'd

Group	Interactions with other groups and notes
Transformation Coordination Team	Ensure that an Integrated Work Plan is developed that addresses all activities related to process improvement, restructuring, change management, reward and compensation modifications, and other LSS/HPO activities
	Act as the "project management" arm of the top management to ensure LSS/HPO activities are being accomplished when they need to be. While it is true that top managers need to visibly lead the transformation effort, they should not have to attend to detailed planning, project management, and logistics activities. In some organizations this responsibility may rest with one individual and a dedicated administrative resource (keeping track of all that's happening during the conversion is a significant task). In the new spirit of High-Performance Teams, where the fundamental performance unit is teams, not individuals, organizations may wish to have a team of multi-skilled individuals perform these project management tasks, for which they would collectively be held accountable.
	Ensure appropriate training occurs and that knowledge is transferred from any external sources to internal sources
	Provide a central clearinghouse for measurement of progress
Black Belt Team (community of practice)	For the most part Black Belts operate independently of other Black Belts, spending most of their time with process improvement teams and part of their time reporting to their Champion. In an LSS/HPO it is recommended that Black Belts form a "community of practice," that is, a group that periodically convenes with the purpose of keeping their skills sharp in their selected discipline
	Periodically meet to discuss what's working and what's not in process improvement projects
	Periodically meet to swap the use of key tools and provide examples of how they were used in the organization
	In an LSS/HPO there should be an overlap of members of the Black Belt Team and the Initial Restructuring Team so as to cross-pollinate Six Sigma and HPO principles in the context of the actual work occurring in the organization
	If there is no experience internally in process improvement principles and statistical methods, this Black Belt Team will need to obtain start-up training from an outside source such as public workshops or consultants familiar with these topics
Initial Restructuring Team (community of practice)	Facilitate the initial conversion from a traditional structure to one of high-performing teams
	Teach all HPT members the principles and tools to restructure to HPTs so that teams can reorganize themselves in the future as external conditions require
	Provide temporary guidance to new HPTs as they learn to function in the new structure
	Disband after the initial round of restructuring to HPTs since all HPT members will have learned how to design and operate an HPT

Table 3.2. Key Group Interrelationships in LSS/HPOs, Cont'd

Group	Interactions with other groups and notes
	If there is no experience internally in converting to HPTs, this Initial Restructuring Team will need to obtain start-up training from an outside source such as public workshops or consultants familiar with HPT redesign
Green Belts	Learn simple process improvement principles and techniques
	Apply simple process improvement principles and techniques to their work situation with the assistance of a Black Belt
High-Performance Work Teams	Based on strategic inputs from the Top Management Team and the Initial Restructuring Team, people organize themselves into HPTs under the facilitation of Initial Restructuring Team members
	As the new official structural units of the organization, HPTs set goals and metrics and negotiate them with the middle managers (either an individual or a team) to whom they report
	HPTs are held collectively accountable for meeting their goals, first among themselves, and then to their middle manager(s)
Middle Management Team	In an LSS/HPO middle managers interact laterally with other middle managers as well as the traditional vertical way (with one's boss and with one's direct reports), which provides for the integration of work done by the lower level HPTs and also provides a way for middle managers to share best practices in the new skills of leading and managing an LSS/HPO
	Middle managers become a team that performs tasks that include, in ascending order of complexity: informal information sharing, problem solving, collective planning, and forming a coalition to lead a work group or divisional leadership with minimal supervision from Top leaders.[i]
Transformation Technology Team	Consisting of dedicated or nearly dedicated resources, this team provides quick hit and long-term information technology solutions for organizational members involved in the transformation to LSS/HPO. One reason the group exists is to avoid the traditionally long queue times associated with information technology projects. Although new system development requests could be handled with the existing information technology organizational structure, many organizations have found it useful to form a separate team as recommended here
	Quickly build applications like intranets for transformation (containing communications and project status information) and programs to support analysis and dissemination of lessons learned

[i]This order of increasing complexity of middle management integration was first articulated by Barry Oshry in the book *In the Middle*.

Hallmarks of the Combined Disciplines

The hallmarks of the individual Lean Six Sigma and HPO disciplines appear in the previous two chapters. An LSS/HPO contains all those hallmarks and, in addition, some unique aspects obtained by combining the two programs:

1. *Speedy acceptance of new improvement concepts.* Because of team achievement, greater control over their work, increased job satisfaction, and collective rewards, teams have a high motivation to meet goals and set new stretch goals. For this reason teams are anxious to learn more about process improvement principles and tools and tend to "pull" these practices rather than the practices being "pushed" from organization unit to organization unit by brute force.

2. *Less top management time required as the implementation progresses.* An LSS/HPO fosters high levels of motivation and a structure that provides for controls through metrics monitoring. Consequently, in an LSS/HPO implementation top management is able to devote less time to shepherding the implementation than with standalone Lean or Six Sigma efforts.

3. *Rapid widespread improvement.* Since HPOs by themselves provide only simple process improvements that don't capitalize on advanced statistical methods, with an LSS/HPO people enthusiastically receive principles and tools to channel the energy they have for execution resulting from their motivation.

4. *Consistent messages employees can act on.* Management failing to create a supportive culture before distributing tool books such as the Memory Jogger™[17] with the expectation that employees will use them in their improvement project dooms the effort to failure. I once talked with a manager in a brewery about process improvement there. He boasted, "I know thirty-five process improvement tools." When I asked how many he'd used in the past six months, he replied, "None. Actually, management never seemed to care too much about us using the tools once we were trained." This situation is all too common. Implementing LSS/HPO dramatically increases the likelihood of sustaining new mindsets and processes for improvement.

5. *Sustainability of results.* In many LSS implementations after a Black Belt moves on to another project there is often a danger of backsliding—to

old methods and to old performance. This risk is mitigated in an LSS/HPO because people have set new goals for the improved process and are intrinsically and extrinsically motivated to achieve them.

By combining LSS and HPO disciplines, an organization can achieve the benefits of each, plus additional benefits from the combination. The logic of putting LSS and HPO together is inescapable. The combination provides definite synergy by putting together proven improvement methods (LSS) and a rapid way to restructure the organization, foster ownership, and reshape the culture (HPO). However, based on my experience, during early project stages there are sometimes questions about the necessity of the significant operating change associated with deploying HPO. Do we have to do the HPO part of LSS/HPO to get the dramatic, sustainable results? This question and related concerns are addressed in Exhibit 3.1.

Exhibit 3.1. Combining HPO and LSS for Dramatic, Sustainable Results

There's no doubt about it. Implementing HPO definitely requires a different set of leadership mindsets and practices than a traditional functional, multi-layered hierarchical organization. The big question in top leaders' minds is, "Is it worth the effort?" Here is a summary of a conversation I recently had with a CEO considering LSS/HPO. It's about the sixtieth time I've had a similar conversation, so I thought it might be helpful for leaders if I included it here.

CEO: I'm sold on combining Lean and Six Sigma. I like the fact that Lean will help me get quick returns. I like the fact that Six Sigma will help solve the organization's really complex problems. What I'm hesitant about is this HPO part.

Tom: Okay. Say more.

CEO: It looks like a pretty radical departure from the way we do things around here now. I mean, fewer layers in the hierarchy, people held collectively responsible for work, and decisions pushed down in the organization. . .

Tom: It is a radical departure. It's intended to quickly change the culture and get it in line with the new "hard" aspects of the transformation.

CEO: I do understand that Lean Six Sigma is the "hard" aspect and that we need a "soft" aspect to address culture and the people parts of the transformation. Otherwise the changes won't stick. Improvements may backslide and all that. But I'm wondering, is there another way we could get the same result without reorganizing the organization into teams? Aren't there some companies out there performing exceptionally well with Lean Six Sigma, but that aren't organized into teams?

Tom: Yes, there is another way. And yes, there are some companies doing great with Lean Six Sigma without the HPO aspect.

Exhibit 3.1. Combining HPO and LSS for Dramatic, Sustainable Results, Cont'd

CEO: But so far we've only talked about doing HPO with Lean Six Sigma. Who are these other companies, and why can't we take the approach they took?

Tom: The issue is speed. Organizing people into teams is the fastest way to address the "soft" aspects of change. The reason some other companies have been able to be successful at Lean Six Sigma without organizing into teams is because of their existing strong culture that already tends to support initiatives like Six Sigma and Lean.

CEO: "Strong culture?"

Tom: Yes. There's a great book called *Built to Last* by Collins and Porras that emphasizes the importance of culture in the long-range success of a company. Collins and Porras' research showed that companies that pay attention to actively managing culture tend to have a "strong culture" and they consistently outperform industry peers who do not pay as much attention to managing culture. In a strong culture, people know the rules, values, and behaviors expected. This manifests itself in seemingly minor things like people showing up to meetings on time, if that happens to be a cultural norm. In weak cultures people tend to do pretty much whatever they want, because there are no accepted rules or behaviors.

CEO: By your definition, we really don't have a very "strong" culture here. So how does a company go about getting a strong culture?

Tom: Strong cultures get built over time through leaders modeling and reinforcing certain behaviors. Stories, myths, and legends about an organization also help spread and reinforce the culture. What people get rewarded for, and what they get punished for, also shape the culture. Behaviors that work get rewarded, become part of the folklore, and tend to be perpetuated.

CEO: So a strong culture would get us what we need from a "soft" aspect of change?

Tom: Actually, I believe a strong culture only gets you part of the way there. The strong culture must also be appropriate for what you're trying to accomplish internally and what that external condition requires. For example, for a culture that works well with Lean Six Sigma, it would need to be a culture that was strong *and* that reinforced values like cross-functional and cross-level collaboration, innovation, intelligent risk taking, not punishing people for mistakes, continuous improvement, people seizing the initiative to fix things without being told, and top and middle managers who believed it was their job to enable the people below them to do the best work possible.

CEO: Sounds like a lot of subtle, behind the scenes work. How long does it take to build a strong culture that has those characteristics and values you just described?

Tom: If you're just focusing on changing culture, it could take five to twenty years to get something like the culture I just described. Just consider trying to instill all those values in a hierarchy with multiple layers, where people had for years been afraid to make a mistake because mistakes cost other people their jobs.

Exhibit 3.1. Combining HPO and LSS for Dramatic, Sustainable Results, Cont'd

CEO: Yes, I see how that could be difficult to instill new values as you'd described there.

Tom: On the other hand, if you flatten the organization, restructure people into teams, and push down goal setting and decision making, you can begin to get the desired "soft" aspects addressed in as short a timeframe as one to four months. This is why HPOs are a favored "soft" strategy in trying to support and sustain Lean Six Sigma.

CEO: But you said there are companies who do Lean Six Sigma without organizing people into teams. Let's return to that topic for a moment. Who might some of those be so I have an idea what it might take for us to select the "changing culture" approach?

Tom: Two come immediately to mind. One is Operational Management International, Inc. (OMI). They won the Baldrige Award in 2000. It's a very strong culture that supports all those things I mentioned, which works well for supporting their process improvement efforts. It started building those attributes long before they won the Baldrige Award and then accelerated the shaping of that culture in response to the challenge of trying to win the Baldrige Award. And I suspect they'll have those attributes and values forever because they focus on reinforcing them every day.

CEO: You mentioned two. Who else?

Tom: The other company is Johnson & Johnson. They have a very strong culture built over many years, shaped during reactions to key events, such as the Tylenol poisoning crisis. During that time they recalled all the Tylenol in the field so they could assure consumers and hospitals that the Tylenol supply was safe. I've visited many different J&J sites in different countries, and although it's a highly decentralized company, their core values are present every place I've been. And those core values all support the Lean Six Sigma we've talked about here.

CEO: So they're doing Lean Six Sigma?

Tom: They are doing the essence of waste elimination, process streamlining, and advanced statistical methods. Internally they call the initiative "Process Excellence," and it's yielded quite dramatic results for them.

CEO: And they do this without teams?

Tom: As I'd mentioned, J&J is a very decentralized company. Many parts of J&J are not organized into full-time teams, but some are. It depends on the preference of the organizational unit and the performance challenges they need to address. The Process Excellence methods work well in both because J&J's core values support it.[i]

CEO: Okay, I'm convinced we don't have as strong a culture that supports Lean Six Sigma as a Baldrige Award Winner like OMI. And we definitely haven't been shaping our culture as long as Johnson & Johnson. So it seems we're back to the concept of HPO. Why is it that HPO can bring about the desired "soft" aspect that supports Lean Six Sigma in one to four months, instead of the lengthy five to twenty years required for the culture-shaping process you described?

Exhibit 3.1. Combining HPO and LSS for Dramatic, Sustainable Results, Cont'd

Tom: De-layering the organization and having most of the organization restructure themselves into High-Performance Teams are critical parts of the overall HPO strategy, and also why it works so quickly. This process rapidly involves everyone and starts to build local ownership within the teams immediately through local goal setting and collective accountability.

CEO: Yes, yes. It does seem like we're back to talking about very dramatic departures from current management practices. I'm still concerned about that. Isn't there something like an "HPO-Lite" process that we could use that wouldn't be so disruptive?

Tom: I understand that you're concerned about how disruptive this will be to current management practices. However, it's the disruptive nature of this process that makes it so powerful and effective.

CEO: How so?

Tom: Many change efforts are ineffective or extremely difficult because people backslide into their old ways of doing things. There is an especially strong tendency to do so in a crisis. And once people slip back, it is hard to regain the lost ground. With the HPO approach described, it is difficult to revert to old ways of doing things because nearly all the undesirable structural and cultural footholds of the past are removed. A manager's direct reports can't blame her if the direct report's goals aren't met, because the team set the goals. Unhealthy competition to claw one's way to the top of the corporate ladder dissipates as the new structure flattens and people are rewarded for skills held, meeting goals, and the organization's overall success. People can't complain they never get a say in how things are done because everyone was involved in redesigning the work group. In addition, teams have the ability to reorganize as external or internal conditions dictate. Slackers who are on teams can't continue to hide and slack off. They are watched by and dealt with by all the team members, instead of just by their immediate supervisor as in the old environment. And people rise to the occasion to improve their processes because their intrinsic sense of accomplishment and their group bonus are based on meeting those goals that they themselves set. These are just a few of the things that are different that represent new paths that must be gone down, and old paths that have been closed off after the HPO redesign activities.

CEO: I see. And it sounds like that's going to do more for us than just a good solid toolkit.

Tom: The tools will work fine, for what they do. Control charts will still track a key variable over time and allow us to look at its average and variability. Pareto charts will still help us separate the vital few from the trivial many. But transformations don't fail because the tools don't work. We know the tools work—they're mathematical. Transformations fail because of the people part of the change equation. And it's the people part that we're trying to address, as quickly as possible, so that the use of the tools can be enthusiastically supported now, and forever. The HPO strategy addresses the people side of change very quickly and effectively.

Exhibit 3.1. Combining HPO and LSS for Dramatic, Sustainable Results, Cont'd

CEO: Okay. I'm beginning to see that, although the HPO method of change is quite different from what we're used to, it can be quite beneficial in accelerating the culture change needed to support LSS/HPO sustainability. And it seems to be a more viable alternative than trying to keep our existing structure and operating practices and embarking on a major culture change effort. I guess the only thing still gnawing at me is this whole business of pushing decisions down to these newly formed teams. Are there any sort of controls that can be put in place to make sure they're not just running wild and doing their own thing?

Tom: Absolutely. In fact, there can actually be more controls in an LSS/HPO, because as decisions are moved to lower levels, controls are also designed in to ensure fit with strategy and to report progress and trends. The website www.leansixsigmaHPO.com provides details.

CEO: Okay. I'll take a look at it before we get together again next week and decide next steps. See you then.

Tom: See you then.

[i]Personal conversation with Karl Schmidt, vice president of process excellence for Johnson & Johnson.

What It's Not

An LSS/HPO is not a strong implementation of one discipline (either LSS or HPO) with a diluted implementation of the other, just to give the appearance that the change effort addresses both "hard" and "soft" aspects. To achieve truly radical benefits, maintain profit sustainability, and create a cultural mindset of continuous improvement it is necessary to strongly pursue both disciplines simultaneously.

It is not two sets of tools and principles tossed into one implementation bag for later independent removal and application as needed. An LSS/HPO effort must be a blended one to succeed. LSS process improvement events also need to contain reminders of the new culture. HPO restructuring events must establish goals in the context of continuous improvement and identification of where statistical tools may help. While events may have originated in the LSS or HPO discipline, the majority of time in an integrated LSS/HPO transformation they need to contain the other element.

Now let's move on to the Pragmatic Practice part of this book, where you'll learn how to implement the tools.

Notes

1. Personal conversations with Rob Tripp, Mike Carnell, John Lupienski, and J.F. DeBetz.

2. Personal conversation with Robert Rehm and Gary Frank, who were both StorageTek employees during the dramatic turnaround.

3. Fishman, C. (1999, October). Engines of democracy. *Fast Company, 28,* p. 174.

4. George, M. (2002). *Lean six sigma.* New York: McGraw-Hill

5. Personal interview with Carole Jacobson of Weyerhaeuser on March 26, 1999.

6. Personal interview with John Lupienski of Motorola and personal interview with Rob Tripp, who worked at AlliedSignal in the Maryville, Tennessee, facility.

7. Argyris, C. (1998, May/June) "The emperor's new clothes." *Harvard Business Review.*

8. Blinder, A. (1990). *Paying for productivity: A look at the evidence.* Washington, DC: Brookings Institution.

9. Larson, V., and Carnell, M., "Surviving the valley of despair and pity city." www.isixsigma.com.

10. Senge, P. (1990). *The fifth discipline: The art and practice of the learning organization.* New York: Doubleday.

11. ibid

12. ibid

13. Senge, P. et al. (1994). *The fifth discipline fieldbook: Strategies and tools for building a learning organization.* New York: Doubleday.

14. Personal conversation with Carole Jacobson on May 12, 2000.

15. Collins, J. (2001). *Good to great.* New York: HarperCollins.

16. McCullough, D. (2001). *John Adams.* New York: Touchstone.

17. Brassard, M., Ritter, D., Rilter, D., and Oddo, F. (Eds.). (1994). *Memory jogger II.* Methuen, MA: Goal/QPC.

PART 2

Pragmatic Practice

Success is determined not only by knowing what to do ultimately, but by knowing what to do next.

Winston Churchill

L EADERS OF SUCCESSFUL LSS/HPO transformations have a firm grasp of what needs to be done and on when it needs to be done. The *first section* in this second part of the book—The Fundamentals—provides information about the *role of leaders* in a successful LSS/HPO implementation. The *second section*—The Leader's Stage-by-Stage Guide—provides advice on *implementation* as leaders move from stage to stage.

Section 1: The Fundamentals

The chapters in Section 1 provide leaders with insights based on lessons other leaders have learned and high leverage leadership principles (Chapter 4).

Section 1 also addresses fundamentals for leaders (Chapter 5). Throughout the transformation, leaders will need to make subtle, but highly important, distinctions between situations they encounter (Chapter 6). Knowing these distinctions—such as compliance-based change versus intrinsically motivated change, the different levels of problem complexity, and different types of leadership challenges—will enable leaders to apply their energy to the highest leverage course of action for a given situation. Section 1 finishes up with a chapter that provides a powerful set of core tools for leaders to use in each stage of the transformation (Chapter 7).

Section 2: The Leader's Stage-by-Stage Guide

Section 2 is organized according to the five major stages of an LSS/HPO transformation: Initiation, Direction Setting, Design, Implementation, and Operations and Continuous Improvement. Each of the five stages is covered in a set of three repeating chapters:

- Activity Map and To Do List;
- Tools Application; and
- Pragmatic Tips.

A brief overview of each type of chapter appears below.

Activity Map and Leader To Do List

These chapters contain a high-level map of the various types of improvement and culture-changing activities that occur in a stage. In addition, a Leader To Do List organizes leader actions by high leverage category. Not all high leverage categories are invoked in each stage, of course, but only the ones that will provide leaders the highest leverage. The categories and associated icons for the Activity Map and To Do List are shown below.

 Activity Map   A pictorial representation of the timing of certain activity blocks and associated narrative descriptions.

 Leader To Do List   A list of high leverage actions that leaders can take to move the transformation along. The high leverage actions are organized into the following categories:

- Key shaping actions—high leverage actions leaders can take to create conditions for the workforce to succeed in the LSS/HPO transformation.

- Participative planning—opportunities for groups of people to take part in setting direction for selected topics during the transformation. Such participation tends to generate high quality work products and also increase ownership and commitment to the change.

- Process awareness—dissemination of information about what a process is, what it takes to improve one, and what it takes to manage one.

- High participation restructuring—opportunities for groups of people to take part in reconfiguring the organizational structure to produce a higher performing organization.

- Leadership development—specific areas for leaders to expand their knowledge and sharpen their skills.

- Support—general assistance provided to the transformation, usually from the perspective of areas such as communications, human resources, and information technology.

The "Activity Map and Leader To Do List" chapters all provide a high-level overview of what's happening in the transformation and point out the high-level areas leaders need to focus their attention and energy on.

Tools Application

Tool Application chapters also appear for each of the stages. These describe the core tools that a leader will use in all transformation stages. While other tools are presented throughout this book, leaders will consistently use the three tools (Performance Framework, Top/Middle/Bottom Space Analysis, and Integrated Work Plan Shaping and Quality Assurance Guide) in each stage. These tools and their associated icons are shown below:

 Performance Framework   A tool that focuses leaders' attention on high leverage, interrelated performance factors such as business processes, human resources practices, and organizational structure. It is a visual tool that helps leaders develop congruent change plans among the performance factors, monitor progress, debate alternative courses of action, and conduct lessons learned analyses to continuously improve from stage to stage throughout the transformation.

Top/Middle/Bottom Space Analysis   A tool that helps leaders understand human interactions among organizational levels and groups. The tool enables leaders to develop powerful change actions and communications by providing insights into how targeted change audiences will interpret communications about upcoming changes and react to proposed improvements. In addition, the tool provides insights into a leader's own condition and options for high leverage actions.

 Integrated Work Plan Shaping and Quality Assurance Guide for Leaders   This tool provides leaders with the opportunity to shape the Integrated Work Plan and ensure it is executed well.

These three tools appear in each chapter entitled "Tools Application" for each of the five stages of the transformation process.

Pragmatic Tips

The final chapters for each stage—Pragmatic Tips—contain vital information that will help leaders navigate the opportunities and challenges. The tools and their associated icons are shown below:

 Key Outputs and Deliverables   What leaders can expect from a particular stage.

 Important Questions to Ask   Questions leaders ask of themselves and of others to direct attention, foster self-reflection, and shape attitudes for the new performance environment.

 Large-Group Interventions and Key Meetings   Gatherings in which members of the workforce develop key work products for the transformation. These gatherings, most of which are guided by a semi-structured agenda, promote widespread understanding of proposed changes, increase energy and commitment toward those changes, and help develop leadership capabilities of all involved.

 Interesting Options   Unique actions that some organizations have taken that are consistent with the basic LSS/HPO principles, but are not part of the core activities presented earlier.

 Common Traps   Advance warning to leaders about problem areas that other leaders have faced during a particular stage. This advance warning enables leaders to plan for likely project problems, instead of just reacting to them.

Counterintuitive Elements LSS/HPO leadership thought patterns and practices that differ, often in a seemingly illogical way, from those of traditional leadership.

 Leadership Checklist Used before proceeding to the next phase, the checklist presents key items that should be completed prior to moving from one stage to the next.

These topics appear in the "Pragmatic Tips" chapters, one for each stage.

 Leaders need to consider many things before embarking on an LSS/HPO transformation. Part 2 of this book provides them with a solid understanding of the new leadership principles required; presents some lessons learned from those who have preceded them; gives them a core toolkit, a stage-by-stage roadmap, and instructions for achieving success.

CHAPTER 4

Lessons Learned from Integrating Lean Six Sigma and HPO

Only a fool learns from his own mistakes.

Bismarck

PLENTY OF PEOPLE HAVE TRIED TO IMPLEMENT Lean improvement principles, Six Sigma tools and methods, and teams. By exploring others' successes and failures, today's leaders can develop plans that steer clear of commonly encountered problems and focus on high leverage opportunities. When today's leaders couple this valuable learning from others with a different way of thinking about commonplace organizational phenomena, they are well on their way to becoming effective transformation leaders who achieve results that are both dramatic and sustainable.

This chapter provides valuable insights gained from healthy as well as unhealthy LSS/HPO transformations. Both types of story illuminate the upcoming path for future leaders. The lessons learned are drawn from a variety of industries and different sized organizations in both public and private sectors.

After the groundwork has been laid for what to do and what not to do, the chapter introduces new ways of thinking about everyday organizational issues that will provide insights and high leverage choices leaders had not previously thought were possible.

In contrast to the lists of ten important lessons learned presented in other chapters, here we have twenty-eight. There are just too many lessons, and they are too important, to condense to a "top ten" listing. Lessons are organized according to relative timeframe: transformation, operations, and lessons applicable to both transformation and operation.

Transformation Lessons Learned

The transformation phase spans from the initiation through the implementation of the first wave of process improvements. During transformation, organizational members are in transition and are often confused about whether to behave according to the old rules or adopt the new operating rules leaders are espousing. Leaders must help guide workforce members through this challenging transition state and have people focus on both the change process and their daily jobs. The eleven key lessons that apply to the LSS/HPO transition phase are

1. *An understanding of business processes—their characteristics, management, variation, and improvement—is an important foundation for LSS/HPO high performance.* At the start of the transformation there is often widespread misunderstanding at all levels about what a business process is and why it is important to improve and manage one. Leaders must ensure that process training occurs swiftly and is reinforced by the words and actions of senior management.

2. *Develop and frequently communicate the "burning platform" for change.* Leaders must clearly articulate the logical and emotional reasons for change—sometimes called a burning platform—to the workforce at least five times in a variety of different communication modes, such as town hall meetings, newsletters, one-on-one conversations, and the organization's intranet.

3. *Develop organizational restructuring guidelines and boundaries early in the transformation.* Providing information early about what can or cannot be

redesigned is a big advantage. It allows time for feedback and timely modifications if required prior to lower levels beginning their redesign efforts.

4. *Develop* one *integrated work plan for all key elements of the change effort.* Because different groups are initially involved, there are often separate work plans for each effort. This results in delays, redundant work, overloading of key individuals, and coordination problems. One work plan should incorporate all the different improvement, restructuring, and change management efforts.

5. *Assign responsibility for the tactical elements of the transformation.* While it's true that top leaders need to be visible and actively supporting the transformation, they cannot be responsible for day-to-day transformation activities, scheduling of resources, transformation logistics, and coordination of key people's schedules. One person—or a team of people (if the organization is ready to embrace the emerging concepts of teams and collective responsibility)—can assume these responsibilities and be held accountable for their timely execution. If only one person is charged with overall project management, he or she should be assigned a dedicated administrative assistant. This role is described in detail under the Transformation Coordination Team heading on page 59.

6. *Develop and publicize a diagram and descriptions of the interrelationships of key groups in the transformation.* During the transformation it will seem like there are a lot of groups running around the organization that never existed before. There are, so it is important for the workforce to know what groups are involved in transformation activities, what the functions of the groups are, and how the groups are interrelated. Figure 3.3 in Chapter 3 shows a sample diagram of the various groups that may be involved in an LSS/HPO transformation. Table 3.2 describes how the groups in Figure 3.3 are interrelated. For details of each group's function, see the relevant LSS or HPO overview chapters earlier in this book. In Figure 3.3, overlapping ellipses indicate shared membership between groups and small ellipses completely contained within larger ellipses indicate that all members of the smaller group are drawn from the larger group.

7. *Design for quick successes.* Quick successes provide funding for future efforts, prove that concepts can work in the organization, and generate energy based on employees' success at deploying new tools and methods.

8. *Give people at middle and lower levels more responsibility.* These people can take on more responsibility than upper level leaders might initially think, so relocate decisions and responsibilities accordingly.

9. *Do not exclusively focus on large group events as a vehicle for change.* Large group gatherings such as town hall meetings, participative planning sessions, and redesign workshops are highly visible events and can create a lot of energy. Unfortunately, they are often viewed as the *only* time that change is considered, and people conclude the session saying, "Well, that was a great event, now it's time to get back to our real work." The real job of change goes on during the events and between them also, and everyone needs to understand this point. When Motorola was implementing Six Sigma, CEO Bob Galvin personally reviewed Six Sigma results monthly. He also stated that Motorola meetings should begin by discussing quality.[1]

10. *If leaders can successfully manage the common transition questions, leaders can accelerate the workforce's desire to participate in the new environment.* At the start of an LSS/HPO transformation, the general rule of thumb for change supporters holds true, that is, 20 percent will actively support the change; 20 percent will actively be against it and oppose it overtly or covertly; and 60 percent will be on the fence. Top leaders and change agents can accelerate moving that 60 percent to the side of the proposed transformation. For front-line workers and some middle managers, I have found the following common questions in most large-scale changes, especially those that relocate decisions and responsibility lower in the organization. While some people progress from question 1 to question 7 faster than others, the general sequence appears in Table 4.1.

11. *Executive efforts can decrease as the transformation progresses if HPO elements are successfully anchored.* As mid-level and lower level teams assume greater ownership through local team goal setting and increased understanding of the organization's strategy and increased participation that fosters intrinsic motivation, they do not require as frequent check-ins.

Table 4.1. Seven Questions Employees Ask

Internal question in employee's head	Usual internal default response	However, when it's addressed by . . .	. . . then the employee can . . .
1. Is this another flavor of the month improvement program?	Yup	Showing how this change is different and proving it through quick, even if small, experiences for employees	Move on to question 2
2. Will this go away if I wait long enough?	Absolutely, we don't do well with big changes around here	Leaders publicly showing support for (not just talking about) the new ways, removing people who don't get with the program and rewarding those who do	Move on to question 3
3. Since it appears this isn't going away immediately, what's it about again?	Now I'll listen a little	Providing quick opportunities for employees to see they can have an effect, and that there are benefits for employees in having greater control of their local work and potentially greater pay	Move on to question 4
4. Is management really going to let us do this?	I doubt they'll really give up that much control	Several presentations and two-way dialogue sessions about how leaders and teams will operate in the new environment	Move on to question 5
5. What's the catch?	There must be a catch	Additional dialogue sessions and conversations about operating rules in the new environment	Move on to question 6
6. What does this mean for me?	I can't tell if I'll be screwed under this new plan, or if I'll be okay	Additional presentations and opportunities for small peer group discussions and resulting quick hit improvements to the employee's local work environment	Move on to question 7
7. How can I work this change for my benefit?	I think I could give this a try, if I can make it work for me	The details of the redesign workshop and how the outcome is highly reliant on what the individual employee does in the workshop	Become engaged in the program, even if only on a trial basis until more positive reinforcement occurs

Operations Lessons Learned

The operations phase begins after the implementation officially concludes. In the operation phase organizational members begin to settle down from the transition and some behave according to the old rules. In this phase leaders need to help sustain the impressive gains from the first round of improvements. The eight key lessons learned that apply to the LSS/HPO operations phase are

1. *Executives need to agree on their individual and collective areas of responsibility for business processes.* Without top level agreement, confusion reigns among middle managers and workforce members as they are unclear about priorities, improvement responsibilities, and their team and personal boundaries.

2. *Leaders at all levels must focus on evaluating employees in terms of both results and new behaviors desired.* Managers who violate new values—even though they achieve their business goals—should be coached to live the new values. If several rounds of coaching do not initiate the proper level of enthusiasm for the new values, the manager must be removed. It is best to communicate any such decisions to the rest of the organization so employees know top leaders are serious about the new values and their associated behaviors.

3. *Conduct process improvement status reviews and analyze process improvement efforts with a finance person on the team.* This provides a higher level of certainty that improvement goals are likely to be met. Once the project is completed, the finance person can provide an independent certification that goals have been met.

4. *The shift to the LSS/HPO leadership paradigm must be actively managed.* For many, the shift to an LSS/HPO is significant and initially uncomfortable, so the transition must be managed with education, feedback loops, coaching, and personal and group reflection sessions. In addition, it is helpful to have peer sessions in which people discuss common problems and best practices in the new LSS/HPO leadership paradigm.

5. *Don't exclusively focus on monetary rewards, but don't forget them.* In an LSS/HPO much is geared to creating intrinsic motivation. However, as one employee in a dot-com asked his boss after a 75-hour workweek, "What, is this just about the love?" Obviously money needs to be

included as part of an overall reward structure, but money shouldn't be given for everything. Companies that have successfully instilled quality as a way of life, such as Motorola, Matsushita, Shell Oil, and Hewlett-Packard, have historically given annual quality awards from the president or other high ranking official, but have had no money, just huge recognition, tied to the award.

6. *Team goals must be negotiated with manager(s) before they become the "official" goals of the team.* This ensures alignment of goals to the strategy from the top of the organization to the bottom. Without this step there is no opportunity to ensure the team's interpretation of the strategy is correct and that the team has considered all that has to be considered.

7. *"Boundaryless" is a good concept for cross-group information sharing, but leaders must establish and defend team boundaries.* General Electric popularized the concept of a "boundaryless" organization, which is fine when applied to sharing information across organizational boundaries. However, HPTs need very clear boundaries surrounding task responsibilities or there may be overlap, redundant work, and confusion about which team is responsible for which components of a process.

8. *Ensure the HR systems support the new business paradigm.* All too often people toss up their hands in defeat and cry, "Okay, okay, I finally understand we can't change the human resources systems!" But HR systems must be changed to support the new work environment. Formal employee evaluations must include team as well as individual performance. The compensation system must recognize and reward groups and individuals for meeting goals and radical process improvements. Career paths must be plotted more carefully to ensure that people are satisfied, even though levels in the organization chart have been reduced. And people need to be visibly hired and fired on the basis of culture as well as goal attainment. Such bold but necessary acts are not possible unless the official HR policies are changed.

Lessons That Apply to Both Transformation and Operations

Some lessons apply to both the transformation part of the project and the ongoing operation after the first wave of LSS/HPO projects has been successfully completed. The nine key lessons learned that apply to the LSS/HPO operations phase are

1. *There is a natural tendency to focus on the "gee whiz" nature of the new problem-solving tools that the Six Sigma discipline provides.* From the start leaders need to focus people's efforts on the application of the tools and how they help support company strategy and contribute financially—not on the nifty tables and charts the tools produce.

2. *Dispel the notion that all decisions require group participation.* This common misperception needs to be addressed early in the transformation. Although the HPO element of an LSS/HPO does help construct a more participative environment, all decisions do *not* require group participation, and in fact should not have group participation. The "everybody-in-the-pool!" philosophy needs to be replaced with intelligent event invitations that consider the objectives of the event and the perspectives required for a high quality decision.

3. *Executives must visibly support the new environment continually or it will fail to yield the desired results.* Visible support includes conducting town hall meetings about the changes, celebrating victories in the new environment, and publicly rewarding and punishing people as appropriate to reinforce the desired results orientation and behaviors.

4. *Only hire external consultants who will build internal capability.* Unless an organization can pull off a massive raid of Black Belts and HPO design experts from an existing LSS/HPO, it is likely it will require external assistance. It is important that any consultants hired be training internal personnel from the first day they are on site to the day that they leave. In addition, strive to have internal Black Belts lead projects instead of external consultants so that internal capability is built up and consultant dependence is decreased. Otherwise, an organization has only funded an expensive temporary fix and built no internal capacity.

5. *Develop and publicize the method for disseminating strategy to the organization.* Getting the strategy out to the entire organization is essential. Everyone must know what the strategy is so they can support it through local goal setting and execution as well as through process improvement efforts. Figure 4.1 depicts the cascade of strategy through an organization and the importance of goal setting and measurement at critical points. Strategic information flows downward so that local goal setting

can support that strategy. Performance and inputs for strategy flow upward. Leaders have to ensure easy upward and downward flow. It is important to point out to the workforce that a person can simultaneously be on a standing HPT within the organizational structure and also on an ad hoc process improvement team formed to address a specific process issue. It is also important to note that in the *initial* redesign to HPTs, the HPT goal-setting process precedes the Manager goal-setting process. HPTs set their initial goals based on the organization's strategies, objectives, and goals. Subsequent HPT redesigns need to be aligned with the manager and organization goals.

Figure 4.1. Sample Strategy Dissemination Through Goal Setting

6. *Create and support a learning-rich environment to accelerate the transformation and yield better business results.* Research and personal experience show that organizations that actively support learning and inquiry can change significantly faster and more effectively than those organizations that do not.

7. *What top leaders say really matters.* During the transformation, the workforce evaluates how serious the organization is about the proposed changes by listening and watching top leaders. After the transition is over, top leaders must continue reinforcing what is important. One of the reasons Six Sigma has gained such dramatic results at Raytheon is that whenever CEO Dan Burnham gives a speech within the first ten minutes he mentions Six Sigma. This sends a powerful message to the workforce about what is important.[2]

8. *Information dissemination and two-way dialogue at all levels of the organization are essential to a successful implementation.* All too often the only communication attempts are one-way. While slightly better than no communication, these fail to engage people and do not respond to unique questions they may have.

9. *Actively manage the organization's culture.* Culture needs to be managed just as much, if not more, than day-to-day technical tasks. The transformation to an LSS/HPO requires substantial changes to an organization's culture. As John Lupienski, the head of quality for one of Motorola's most successful quality plants in 2001 and 2002, once said, "When strategy and culture clash, culture always wins." Paying adequate attention to culture pays big dividends in any large-scale change effort.

This chapter provided insights that can be quickly and easily referenced during the LSS/HPO implementation and the subsequent operation phase. The lessons learned help focus leaders' attention on key knowledge elements, actions to take to accelerate the change process, and the important support factors to address when managing results and culture.

Notes

1. Interview with Mike Carnell on December 18, 2002.
2. Interview with Mike Grimm, Six Sigma Expert at Raytheon, on April 9, 2003.

5

Leadership Fundamentals

There is a loftier ambition than merely to stand high in the world.
It is to stoop down and lift mankind a little higher.

Henry Van Dyke

L SS/HPO LEADERS MAKE A DIFFERENCE. They make a difference in the overall performance of the organization. They make a difference in their followers' lives. They make a difference in their own lives as they develop their full potential as leaders and human beings. They constantly challenge the status quo and seek ways to make a positive difference.

The good news is that leadership opportunities in an LSS/HPO abound. Leaders help develop and support teams. Within teams leadership often rotates depending on who has the most expertise for the issue at hand. Even a person with no direct reports can convene and lead a cross-functional improvement team. Clearly more opportunities to lead exist than in a traditional organization.

The "other" news is that many leadership practices that worked in the past may not be applicable in an LSS/HPO. This is a critical point that many fail to grasp. Leadership is neither a tight command-and-control style that directs others nor a loose "let-the-teams-do-whatever-they-want-because-they're-a-high-performing-team-and-know-what-they're-doing" approach. It requires different mindsets and interaction patterns from those historically practiced in most organizations.

Leadership researcher Joseph Rost describes leadership as "an influence relationship between leaders and followers who intend real changes that reflect their mutual purposes."[1] This definition provides an excellent introduction to LSS/HPO leadership. It addresses the key issue of having a clear performance challenge requiring significant change. It takes into account that leaders must find or establish common ground with followers if anything worthwhile is to happen. And it highlights the fact that influence relationships between leaders and followers require as much consideration as technical requirements. LSS/HPO leadership clearly has a unique combination of themes, principles, and style elements. This chapter presents each of those, as well as a summary checklist for leading successfully in the new environment.

This chapter is not intended to substitute for other leadership books. Rather, it presents the combination of certain elements leaders can use to help LSS/HPOs reach peak performance. Other books I highly recommend are *The Leadership Challenge*,[2] *Results-Based Leadership*,[3] *Credibility*,[4] *The Leadership Engine*,[5] and *Leadership Without Easy Answers*.[6] Additional information can be found in the Reference section of the Appendix. These complement the themes, principles, and style presented below for LSS/HPO leadership.

Themes

Four distinctive, pervasive themes are woven into an LSS/HPO leader's day-to-day thoughts, actions, choices, biases, and conversations. These recurring themes are

1. *Leadership is an activity, not a position.* Leadership can—and in fact, *must*—be exercised at all levels in the organization in an LSS/HPO. Teams should rotate leadership roles where possible.

2. *Conditions must be created for high performance and continuous improvement.* In the new environment leaders need to get out of the "doing" mode and into the mode of "creating conditions" for desired situations. There are

many ways to accomplish this. One is by ensuring that the right resources (people, tools, equipment, and processes) are in the right place at the right time. Another is by sharing information. Yet another is by allowing people time for learning and continuous improvement activities. These are a few of the many ways covered in greater detail later in this book.

3. *Leaders must take advantage of the power of groups.* Far too many change efforts focus solely on *individual* change strategies and ignore *groups.* While it's true that each individual must deal with proposed changes, a person's peer group has a tremendous impact on that person's attitudes and actions regarding change. Leaders should focus on influencing groups. This requires less time and frees leaders up for other tasks. Ways to accomplish this include conducting group events, briefing small groups, and influencing key opinion leaders associated with targeted groups for change.

4. *Leaders have to create and sustain energy.* In addition to the technical performance of the organization, leaders are responsible for the organization's energy. In well-run organizations energy is palpable—you can feel it as you walk through the hallways. Good leaders create energy by hosting participative planning events, celebrating successes, and even celebrating "noble failures," as Motorola called mistakes to encourage innovation. They create healthy internal competition for the CEO's annual quality award. Leaders also create and sustain energy by establishing and living by important organizational values, even in times of crisis. Johnson & Johnson's CEO James Burke's decision to pull Tylenol off store shelves in 1982 because of a cyanide poisoning scare resulted in a $100 earning loss.[7] To this day people inside and outside the company talk about the courageous commitment to customers. But this values story began three years before when Burke, fearful that that credo had become an interesting but currently irrelevant artifact, pulled twenty top executives and had them take a critical look at the thirty-six-year old credo, which contained statements like "We hold these truths to be self-evident of the Johnson & Johnson Co." among them a higher duty to "mothers and all others who use our products." Burke said, "Here's the credo. If we're not going to live by it, let's tear it off the wall. We ought to either commit to it, or get rid of it."[8] What followed was a series of worldwide discussions and emotional recommitment the credo, making intense debate in 1982 unnecessary because it had already been conducted.

These are but a few ways for leaders to crank up and manage organizational energy.

The Leader's Inner Voice

Six messages constantly play in a leader's head. These six messages, shown in Figure 5.1, impact short-term and long-term decisions that are made.

Figure 5.1. Six Messages of the Leader's Inner Voice

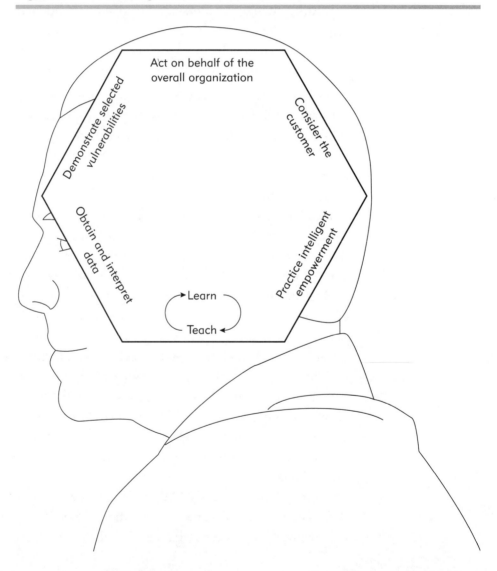

Message 1: Act on Behalf of the Overall Organization   No matter what organizational level a leader resides at, the survival and development of the larger organizational system are of paramount importance. Although other distractions, personal interests, and priorities may attempt to pull the leader in different directions, leaders should assess each decision in the context of impact on the overall organization.

For a great example of a tough call a leader had to make along these lines, please see page 346 for a detailed description of how a manager in the U.S. District Court System revoked a High-Performance Team's self-managing status for two months until they upgraded their time management and general business skills. This action seemingly is counter to HPO philosophy since it was non-participatory and limited the team's influence on local work. However, it was necessary to meet the organization's short-term and long-term goals. Leaders require the necessary fortitude to make the tough calls when needed. To coin a new LSS/HPO phrase based on traditional wisdom, leadership courage is not the absence of fear or discomfort, but the ability to act in their presence for the organization's goals.

Message 2: Consider the Customer   Great LSS/HPO leaders always consider external customer impact. Internal customers are also important, but the first thought that comes to a leader's mind when faced with a problem, decision, or improvement opportunity is, "What will be the impact on the external customer?"

Message 3: Practice "Intelligent Empowerment"   Previous failed attempts at redistributing responsibility in organizations have given the term "empowerment" a bad name. Leaders for LSS/HPOs need to focus on the concept of "intelligent empowerment." Exhibit 5.1 is a checklist for intelligent empowerment, organized by set-up and execution requirements.

Exhibit 5.1. Checklist for Intelligent Empowerment

Setup

☐ A genuine desire on the part of a leader to distribute work to her direct reports

☐ Clear goals exist that are aligned with the strategy

☐ Where possible, distribute decisions to groups of people who will have collective responsibility for their implementation instead of to individuals; this provides an instant support and coaching group for the work to be done

Exhibit 5.1. Checklist for Intelligent Empowerment, Cont'd

☐ Clear boundaries specifically state what the group can and cannot do

☐ Clear definition of roles and responsibilities

☐ Principles and values help employees make choices; with intelligent empowerment, people's behavior is not determined solely by a management direction. Principles, such as, "The external customer needs to be considered in every key decision" and "When changing conditions dictate, a team or unit of teams has the authority and responsibility to reorganize" end up managing people's behaviors more than managers.

☐ A clear escalation path for problems that cannot be solved at a lower level and criteria for activating that escalation path

Execution

☐ Information required to make decisions is available

☐ Use of data rather than organizational position to drive decisions

☐ The team or individual possesses the needed skills for making the decision and taking subsequent action (If not, training is provided)

☐ Built-in controls that manifest themselves through metrics when things start to go wrong

☐ A two-way feedback session between the "empowerer" and the "empowered" conducted every two to four weeks in which they candidly discuss how the empowerment is going

☐ Feedback mechanisms established and executed so the empowered team or individual can continually assess performance and improve

☐ Rewards and recognition for performance

Message 4: Learn-Teach-Learn-Teach   Effective LSS/HPO leaders understand that, to create an environment in which people value learning and continuous improvement, a leader must model that behavior. Workers who see their leaders continually learning and encouraging others to do so tend to adopt those habits, and the entire organization benefits. Repetition can be an important part of leaders teaching and focusing attention.

Raytheon CEO Dan Burnham never gets further than ten minutes into a meeting without mentioning Six Sigma at least once.[9]

Message 5: Obtain and Interpret Data   Rather than allowing others to make decisions on "gut feel," leaders need to direct people's efforts toward collecting and interpreting data. For many, this is a huge mindset shift. Once data is collected, they need to take the appropriate action using the DMAIC improvement process.

Message 6: Demonstrate Selected Vulnerabilities While this may initially appear counterproductive for a leader to do, it can actually enhance a leader's credibility and increase influence. When the managing director of the Land Bank announced in a town hall meeting that she didn't have all the answers on what the transformed organization would look like, the collective group was stunned. Never before had a leader admitted he or she didn't know something about the future. Such acts demonstrate that the leader is human and create a stronger bond with the workforce. It also signals that it's okay for others to have imperfections and make mistakes. This becomes very important for team members to articulate so they can compensate for each other's weaknesses.

Of course, a leader should not admit weaknesses that would clearly damage credibility. For example, it would be inadvisable for the head of research and development at a biologics firm to publicly state that he really never understood organic chemistry. In admitting weaknesses and vulnerabilities it's best to selectively choose items that would not seriously erode credibility or to choose a weakness that could be perceived as a positive, such as, "I set extremely high standards for others because I set them for myself."

By heeding the six inner voice messages, a leader can guide the organization through difficult times during and after the transformation. But the inner voice alone is not adequate to steer the workforce clear of implementation rocks; leadership principles are also necessary for the voyage.

Principles

In addition to the inner voice that provides perspective, LSS/HPO leaders frequently reference a set of fundamental principles to guide their reasoning and conduct. These principles apply to transformation and operations phases. The top ten high leverage principles are described below.

Principle 1: Ensure That a Vision and Strategic Focal Points Exist and Are Adequately Communicated People need to be aware of the expected end-state and what it will be like for them to operate in this end-state. This "vision"—or whatever term plays best in the organization's culture[10]—provides a common direction for people. In addition, people need to know the key target areas for improvement, called *strategic focal points*. The combined vision and strategic focal points provide employees with information and principles for making choices at key transformation points, such as improvement, project selection, and the first HPTs redesigns. For an excellent example of a leader being clear about what needed to be done, and how the organization needed to proceed, see Exhibit 5.2.

Exhibit 5.2. ASDA Turnaround Kickoff Speech

In 1991 the grocery chain ASDA was nearly bankrupt. In the six-year course of the newly appointed CEO's tenure, the chain reshaped the industry. In 1999 Wal-Mart bought ASDA for eight times its 1991 value. The purpose of this speech was to kick off the ASDA turnaround in 1991, not to initiate an LSS/HPO effort. Nevertheless, I believe this kickoff speech for the turnaround, given by Archie Norman, is a remarkable example of leading the kickoff of a major change effort and worthy of study as a leadership example. Leaders I have worked with have borrowed from this speech to craft their own kickoff speeches.

> Today is Day Zero in our recovery program. This business is in poor shape and must change sharply in order to survive. Incremental change is not enough. There are no sacred cows and nothing that can't be examined. Our number one objective is to secure value for our shareholders and secure the trading future of the business. I am not coming in with any magical solution. I intend to spend the next few weeks listening and forming ideas for our precise direction. I am not interested in what has happened in the past. I am only interested in the future, and there is room in the boat for anyone who could pull on an oar.

Norman continued by listing a number of specifics.

- We need cash. We must look at every possible source in the business for realizing cash.
- ASDA stores must be built around the original core values of the ASDA brand, and this includes being price competitive.
- We are going to have two experimental store formats up and running within six months. We need a culture built around common ideas and goals that include listening, learning, and speed of response, from the stores upwards.
- There will be management reorganization. My objective is to establish a very clear focus on the stores, shorten lines of communication, and build one team.
- I want everyone to be close to the stores. We must love the stores to death; that is our business.

After clearly articulating what he wanted to change, he concluded:

> Finally, a few words of warning about me and my management style. First, I am forthright and I like to argue. Secondly, I want to discuss issues as colleagues. I am looking for your advice and your disagreement. I want an organization that is transparent. That means sharing knowledge, plans, and intentions. Lastly, if we can together restore a future for our business, that will be a great achievement. In doing so, I hope we can have some great fun as well. We must not lose sight of the need to make ASDA a great place for everyone to work.[i]

[i]Beer, M., and Weber, J. (1997). ASDA (A1) case. Boston, MA: Harvard Business School.

Principle 2: Design Events for Meaningful Participation   It's common sense that people own and commit to something they have participated in creating. But it's also obvious that all organizational members can't participate in every decision affecting them. Leaders need to strike the correct balance between "top only" and "everybody-in-the-pool" types of participation. The question is: *"Who really needs to be there for the best organizational outcome?"* In one example of poorly matched desired outcomes and participation, a procurement team redesigned their process and top leaders solicited comments from the entire organization during a process fair. An avalanche of comments and suggestions followed from people who knew nothing about the process. When the team was forced to implement others' suggestions it demotivated them, diminishing local control over their work. A better approach would have been to let the team implement their own changes first and develop a feedback mechanism to continually improve.

Level of participation will vary by purpose. For example, in *direction setting events* it's usually sufficient to invite participants so that all parts of the organization jigsaw puzzle are present in the session. One hundred percent participation is not required since the key parts attend. However, in *restructuring events* where people design HPTs, 100 percent participation is desirable. This is because, in addition to the targeted outcome of well-functioning HPTs, another targeted outcome is a high level of ownership gained through participation.

Principle 3: Create a Learning Environment   Organizations where leaders have created and maintained a learning environment have a significant advantage over those that do not have one in a large-scale change effort.[11] Realistically, there will always be pressure to complete technical day-to-day tasks. However, organizations that allocate time for learning tend to outperform those that do not. In a large transformation effort at Shell Oil, workers who engaged in continual learning practices succeeded in the new organization more than their less learning-oriented colleagues. Leaders at Shell sought to foster conditions for learning and error correction in several ways, including:

- Providing money for schooling, even though it may not have been directly related to the job (one employee enrolled in an advanced chemistry course to keep his mind sharp, even though it had nothing to do with his job).
- Establishing an online global information sharing network organized by key discipline areas. People post questions and have them answered either by a Shell expert in the field or by a research monitor responsible

for the topic within twenty-four hours. Other members of the network are all notified of new postings.

- Allowing employees time to engage in problem-solving sessions.
- Rewarding, both formally and informally, those who demonstrate continual learning behaviors.
- Encouraging intelligent risk taking based on data.
- Not punishing those who made mistakes if they could be learned from and were recoverable.

Shell's CEO promotes knowledge sharing as a critical component of the business. Quarterly the CEO publishes a newsletter containing results. People are not rewarded directly for their contributions to the network, but they are listed in the CEO's newsletter. The CEO's message is, "Knowledge sharing is part of the culture. This is the way we need to business at Shell. This is our culture."[12]

Within any learning environment it is critical to design three types of feedback loops: those with customers and suppliers, those with teams and individuals, and those that occur at the end of project milestones (often called "lessons learned analyses").

Principle 4: Create Opportunities for Choice   Human beings, for the most part, prefer choice over being told what to do. Leaders can raise motivation levels and increase commitment to the strategy by crafting situations that provide employees choices when possible.

Hewlett-Packard excels at this practice. In discussions with H-P employees at numerous sites I found choice to be commonplace for design engineers regarding component design and for project managers regarding staffing and other project decisions. Even employees whose positions are being eliminated usually have some choice on their next move within H-P.[13]

"Opportunities for choice" does not translate into "unlimited, unbounded choices." Good LSS/HPO leaders establish boundaries around choices. For example, while H-P design engineers have innovation choices in electronic component design, they still must conform to standards regarding design templates, approved suppliers, and standard components.

Principle 5: Go Slow to Go Fast   Often at the start of a large-scale change effort effective leaders take time to obtain widespread understanding, group participation, buy-in, and commitment to common goals. To an uniformed observer, this seems like wasted time because few "hard results" are produced. However, by taking time like this up-front, leaders can compress the *overall* timeframe since people tend to act more quickly in subsequent project phases. This strategy also yields results that are more sustainable than do approaches that ignore the above steps.

For some people it's difficult to not just provide the "the right answer" to a group and charge ahead. For example, an external consultant learning Six Sigma tools facilitated a major improvement project at a California-based pharmaceutical company. He was especially interested in Fishbone Diagrams, which graphically show causes of problems. Because of his interest and to "save time" he developed a Fishbone Diagram outside the team meeting. This diagram sketched out causes for lengthy lead times required to prepare critical documentation called a batch record. Although he did a thorough job of research and presented his findings to the group, the group did not co-develop the Fishbone Diagram and consequently did not feel ownership. When the consultant left the project it was apparent the group never developed any expertise in improvement tools and also relied on outside expertise to run their meetings. Process performance deteriorated and no one convened a meeting to address it. The moral of the story: sometimes at the start of a project it's necessary for a team to *apparently* go slowly and experience some "thinking together" time, so they can go fast later in the project.

Principle 6: Be Constantly Vigilant for Opportunities for Symbolic Acts

Employees look to leaders' actions, even more so than to their words, to judge commitment to new ways of doing things. Therefore, it is important for leaders to demonstrate commitment in ways such as publicly recognizing and rewarding the desired new behaviors and personally exhibiting a new behavior, such as collecting and analyzing data before making a major decision. Most often opportunities for symbolic acts cannot be neatly scheduled into the integrated work plan, so leaders need to be on the lookout for opportunities and seize them. Not all symbolic acts need to accentuate the positive. Some fall into the realm of what one of my clients termed "public hangings to articulate and reinforce new values."

For example, in 1993 I facilitated a meeting in Austin, Texas, at SEMATECH. One of the IBM representatives told a story in the afternoon that illustrated the then new CEO Lou Gerstner's resolve to change the performance and the culture of the company. Earlier Gerstner said he wanted to change the conduct of divisional meetings. Instead of the historical 120-transparency presentations, Gerstner wanted a conversation with division managers about performance. He was quite adamant in his request for conversations in which there would be give and take between him and division heads, *not* a presentation.

Two Atlanta gentlemen showed up at New York headquarters to present their division's results. As the first gentleman opened his briefcase, Gerstner looked across the table, pointed inside the briefcase, and asked, "What are those?" The second man answered, "Those are our transparencies showing our division's results." To which Gerstner promptly responded, "You're fired. Both of you." This event allegedly transpired in late morning. News traveled very fast. I heard about it at 2:00 p.m. from the IBM representative on the SEMAT-ECH team. Although I haven't checked, I believe it would be reasonable to assume there were few transparency-based presentations of operating results after that story spread through IBM.

Principle 7: Assist Employees in Integration and Sense Making   Many things are going on during an LSS/HPO transformation. At times employees may be confused about how various components of the change effort fit together. Leaders need to periodically move through the following three steps to help:

- Identify confusing or seemingly contradicting aspects of the transformation by soliciting employee feedback and by trying to anticipate potential areas for clarification;

- Prepare remarks that explain how various elements fit and help employees make sense of why these things are needed from organizational and personal employee perspectives; and

- Communicate clarifications and explanations through several communication channels, such as town hall meetings, the organization's intranet, and newsletters.

Principle 8: Maintain a Systemic Focus   Since many activities are often concurrently underway, it is important for leaders to pay attention to congruency of key performance levers such as process redesign and organizational restructuring. For example, it doesn't help to announce that the organization is going to extensively use teams, but keep old HR practices that reward individuals. Leaders may find the Performance Framework Tool (pages 125–133) helpful in planning tactical rollouts of changes and also for assessing whether or not the impact had the desired results.

Principle 9: Seek Intrinsic and Extrinsic Motivation   For people to change their current ways of thinking and acting, they need to *want* to change. This motivation comes in two varieties. One variety is intrinsic motivation, which is an inner drive on the part of an individual to do a task. A leader cannot intrinsically motivate an employee; he or she can only create conditions under which an employee can become intrinsically motivated. The other variety of motivation, extrinsic motivation, such as a bonus, is usually initiated and administered by top leaders and HR departments. Good LSS/HPO leaders ensure conditions exist for both types of motivation. Table 5.1 includes ideas for intrinsic and extrinsic motivation for both the short-term and the long-term. Typically these rewards would be given to the team as a whole. For example, each team member would receive the reward "dinner for two." While in some cases individual awards may be appropriate, providing rewards at the team level tends to increase the team cohesiveness and solidarity.

Table 5.1. Short-Term and Long-Term Extrinsic and Intrinsic Motivators

	Extrinsic	Intrinsic
Short-term	Dinner for two	Feedback on performance
	Theater tickets	Participation in short-term projects of interest to the employee
	On-site massage	
	Spot bonuses	Opportunities for learning (something of interest to the employee)
	Dental work performed in the parking lot	Participation in group events that set direction, develop ideas, structure organizational units, and so forth[i]
	Celebration of project milestones	
		The ability to impact local work conditions affecting the employee
		The ability to change the local organizational structure to improve operating results and for continuous improvement

Table 5.1. Short-Term and Long-Term Extrinsic and Intrinsic Motivators, Cont'd

	Extrinsic	Intrinsic
Long-term	Stock options	Systemic mechanisms for local goal setting and feedback
	Salary increases	
	Annual bonuses	Creation of a culture that supports continual learning
	Stock options for spouse[ii]	
	Profit sharing	A desired level of work variety
		A desired level of autonomy
		Mutual support and respect from co-workers
		Seeing the "whole" of one's work and how it fits into the big picture
		A desirable future, at or outside of company
		A sense of achievement for meeting an operational goal
		A sense of achievement for learning and applying a new tool

Extrinsic motivators adapted from Conference Proceedings for Organizational Design Workshop, Center for Effective Organizations, Los Angeles, CA, 2002.

[i]Intrinsic motivators developed from personal research and research of Fred Emery and Einar Thorsrud.

[ii]Given by one high-tech firm in Silicon Valley in recognition that spouses' mates had spent so many weekends and late nights in the office.

Principle 10: Reshuffle Priorities as Conditions Change   This helps leaders get the outcome desired and send a message about what's important. Leaders need to watch for changed conditions that may require re-prioritization. Karl Schmidt, Vice President of Process Excellence for Johnson & Johnson, advises leaders at all levels of the organization to pay attention to what's really important for the business and make adjustments when required. Sometimes, Schmidt maintains, this means putting an individual's operations job on hold while she completes an improvement project. In addition to getting the necessary improvement project completed on time, this sends a strong message to the organization that process improvement is important.[14]

These ten high leverage principles set the stage for the last element of leadership explored in this chapter, leadership style.

Leadership Style

LSS/HPO leaders have a distinctive way of expressing and conducting themselves. This "style" element of leadership manifests itself in one-on-one conversations, small group discussions, and town hall meetings. Although each leader imparts personal touches to the general LSS/HPO style, consistent style elements persist from leader to leader. The first style element presented in this section is how a leader naturally gravitates toward developing internal organizational capabilities. Successful leaders also focus on both results and behaviors in day-to-day performance, cultivate a style of speaking rich in storytelling, metaphors, and analogies. Finally, LSS/HPO leaders jettison the traditional "command-and-control" style and replace it with "analyze-and-energize."

Continually Seek to Develop Internal Capabilities

Good LSS/HPO leaders are forever on the lookout for opportunities to develop internal capabilities within the organization. This is true for hard technical skills as well as "softer" skills of leadership, interpersonal, and team skills.

One integral part of developing internal capabilities is providing opportunities—with appropriate training—for individuals in areas outside their normal expertise. During Amazon.com's Six Sigma implementation, Leigh Wilkinson was director of operations learning. Wilkinson stated, "There was a great side effect of Black Belt training at Amazon. With Black Belts we got people who could solve problems and get great financial gains. An unexpected side effect was we were also developing exceptional leaders through Black Belt training and subsequent follow-up projects." He continued, "This is an example of how Six Sigma helps a business create internal growth opportunities and the ability to grow their own leadership, something successful companies like Procter & Gamble and General Electric have done for years."[15]

Another integral part of developing internal capabilities is creating an environment where it is safe to make mistakes. Failing to learn from mistakes is unacceptable, but sometimes people make honest mistakes. Leaders who pounce on individuals or teams over an honest mistake shut down future possibilities of improvement and the disclosure of potential problems. In such cases leaders need to work with employees to determine what went wrong and how to prevent errors in the future.

Focus on Results *and* on Behaviors

Ultimately organizations need results to survive and thrive. Leaders need to focus on getting results from their organizational units. But leaders also need to pay attention to how they and peer leaders get results. Good LSS/HPO leaders continually express their requirements for results *and* for accepted cultural behaviors that get those results. For more details on the mechanics of evaluating and managing results and behaviors see Welch's GE matrix on page 233.

Use Stories, Metaphors, and Analogies to Make Key Points

Highly successful leaders use language to help make complex concepts simple and shape people's reality. Stories can be told to help people envision what might happen in the future as a result of the LSS/HPO proposed changes. Metaphors and analogies are useful in explaining complex points and motivating people to action. Leaders can improve these skills by reading a few good books[16] and by practicing.

Move from a Command-and-Control to an Analyze-and-Energize Style

In today's complex, fast-changing world the command-and-control style makes less and less sense. It fosters slow cross-functional decision making because of time spent going up and down the organizational ladder for permission. It tends to demotivate, rather than motivate the workforce. And it tends to protect incompetent managers who have risen in the hierarchy at a time when talent is desperately needed at all levels. While many organizations are trying to get away from command-and-control—and most won't admit to still practicing it, the truth is that many, many places still operate under some form of "the-boss-tells-the-worker-what-to-do-and-how-to-do-it-and-the-worker-does-it" operating rule set. This style clearly does not support—and in fact seriously detracts from—LSS/HPO practices.

Yet even with all the known drawbacks of the command-and-control style, genuine problems exist in abandoning it. To start with, its prevalence presents a problem for any "enlightened" leader who tries to implement another style in an organizational unit surrounded by other command-and-control units. Other roadblocks to displacing the command-and-control style are its perceived value in crisis situations, time constraints that imply no group discussion time, many MBA programs still teaching it, and the lack of a clear alternative and how to apply it. Exhibits 5.3 and 5.4 provide some insights and a tool for moving toward analyze-and-energize leadership.

By examining five key factors leaders can quickly see the case for analyze-and-energize over command-and-control (see Figure 5.2).

Figure 5.2. Leader-Influenced Performance Factors

Motivation

Required Cross-Boundary Teaming

Knowledge of Strategy

Information

Speed

Performance Element	Requirements for High Performance	A Command-and-Control Style . . .	While an Analyze-and-Energize Style . . .
Motivation	People at all levels take initiative to improve performance for their areas and the entire organization	Tends to demotivate workers through close supervision, goal setting at high levels, and frequent instructions on how to perform the work from above	Considers whether or not decisions should be passed down and then seeks to create conditions to energize workers
Knowledge of strategy	People at all levels know the strategy so their goals and day-to-day activities support it	Often only distributes strategy on a "need to know" basis	Passes down the "big picture" as well as detailed elements of the strategy; strategy is further clarified as HPTs develop and negotiate local goals aligned with strategy
Speed	People of different disciplines must act and decide quickly	Decisions must go up the chain of command, tending to slow down decisions	Information and skills exist at lower levels so good decisions can be made
Information	People have the information needed to make high-quality decisions	Information is often hoarded at top and middle levels because information is power	Information is distributed to lower levels where decisions are made
Required cross-boundary teaming	To satisfy customer requirements often members of multiple organizational units must work together, often at low levels	Permission to act must go up one leg of the organizational ladder and down the other and back before agreement is reached	Teams are empowered within boundaries and often negotiate inter-team goals

Analyze-and-energize leadership supports the LSS/HPO performance factors of motivation, information, knowledge of strategy, speed, and required teaming across organizational boundaries. The first step is to analyze what high leverage approach is appropriate. The next step is to energize others to act.

Exhibits 5.3 and 5.4 provide a guide for leaders as they begin to adopt the analyze-and-energize leadership style. These tools capture key LSS/HPO leadership themes, inner voices, and principles, as well as important Lean, Six Sigma, and HPO questions. Exhibit 5.3 contains specific areas to analyze and sample questions to help leaders experiment with the new behaviors. Exhibit 5.4 contains strategies for energizing teams and individuals.

Exhibit 5.3. Leader's Guide for Analyze-and-Energize Leadership (Analyze)

The Analyze Component	
Area to Explore	**Sample questions for leaders to ask**
Type of leadership situation	☐ What does the situation call for and what are my options for responding? An opportunity to jointly address supporting the organization's strategy and developing people? Give an individual or team an entire packet of work they can be responsible for and learn from? Quick action on my part without consulting others? If so, how will I inform others later?
Option Generation	☐ Should the team generate the options for this issue or should I? ☐ What should be the criteria for evaluating the generated options?
Boundaries	☐ What are the boundaries for what the team can and cannot do in this situation? ☐ Should I, as the team's manager, mutually explore boundaries with the team for this project, or should I provide boundaries with an explanation? ☐ If another group has requested work from mine, are their initial boundaries firm, or can we flex them?
Opportunities for Teaching	☐ What key strategy points or other information should I provide that the team may not have? ☐ If I know the team will fail based on the course of action they selected, should I inform them and stop the current course, or do they need to learn this lesson through experience?

Exhibit 5.3. Leader's Guide for Analyze-and-Energize Leadership (Analyze), Cont'd

The Analyze Component

Area to Explore	Sample questions for leaders to ask
Opportunities for Learning	☐ Can a situation be set up in which the team will learn from this situation? What special set-up might be required? ☐ Is there an opportunity for me to learn something from this situation? What special set-up might be required?
Meaning	☐ Given that people are fundamentally "meaning making machines" are there any crucial meanings related to this issue requiring further exploration? ☐ What can I do to help people make sense of the changes—some of which may seem unrelated and even contradictory—in this LSS/HPO transformation and subsequent operation? ☐ Do all parties involved share the same understanding of the problems, root causes, key issues, and implications? If not, should I convene a session to help in collective "meaning making" such as a dialogue session?
Assumptions	☐ Are the assumptions that were valid historically still valid for this issue, or should we revise our assumptions? ☐ Are all parties involved aware of the others' assumptions? If not, how can we make that happen?
Workspace	☐ Is the workspace kept in an orderly fashion and is it easy to find tools and other resources quickly? ☐ Is the workspace clean and safe?
Data and Decisions	☐ Do we have the data we need to make the decision? If not, how do we find it? ☐ Have I personally created an environment that supports the use of data for decisions?
Reactions to Problems	☐ What happened, what is the systemic reason this problem occurred, and how can we best address it? (This questioning approach is favored over assigning blame.) ☐ How can I make it easy for people to come to me when they have a mistake instead of hiding it? ☐ Is the perceived problem within the normal realm of variation of the process of origin? (If so, then we need to be careful not to interfere by tampering with a process that is in control.) ☐ Has a person or team repeatedly made the same mistake that would require that I move them?

Exhibit 5.4. Leader's Guide for Analyze-and-Energize Leadership (Energize)

The Energize Component
Ways for Leaders to Energize Teams and Individuals

High-Leverage Team Energizers

☐ Ensure roles and responsibilities have been clearly defined for all involved

☐ Give people encouragement that they can undertake important work without manager help

☐ For any new task, give people the appropriate related information, responsibility, and authority to act

☐ Ensure boundaries among teams and within teams are clear

☐ Let teams set their own goals and monitor progress

☐ Ensure that successes are celebrated, even small ones

☐ Recognize and reward teams and individuals for accomplishments

☐ Encourage teams to set stretch goals, but not goals that cannot be achieved

☐ Celebrate the use of data to make informed decisions

☐ As a manager, be open to be influenced by input from those below

High-Leverage Individual Energizers[i]

☐ Structure work so coordination and control of the work occurs at the level where the work occurs

☐ Provide individuals with the level of work variety they seek

☐ Provide people with autonomy levels with which they are comfortable

☐ Establish conditions and structures that foster timely receiving and giving of feedback

☐ Ensure conditions exist to encourage and reward learning and continuous improvement

☐ Create conditions and structures that foster mutual support and respect among co-workers

☐ Allow people to see the whole product—not just their component—of their work and how it is used

☐ Where possible, allow people to see how what they produce at work is socially useful

☐ Support people in creating a desirable future for themselves (either in or outside the organization)

[i]Based on over forty years of research by Fred Emery, Einar Thorsrud, and Merrelyn Emery. Research results appear in M. Emery and T. Devane (1999), Participative design workshop. In P. Holman and T. Devane (Eds.), *The change handbook: Group methods for shaping the future.* San Francisco: Berrett-Koehler.

Often the practice of leaders asking questions represents a significant departure from the previous practice of providing direction. Employees may find this a bit disorienting as the old pattern is disrupted, but eventually quite empowering. For example, Operational Management International, Inc. (OMI), a 2000 Baldrige Award winner, is involved in water and waste treatment. When they acquire an operation from a municipality or a competitor, employee satisfaction is typically much higher after just one year of OMI's ownership of the operation. There are many reasons for this: for example, all new employees receive stock in the company, extensive training, and new employee and spouse orientation workshops. But one very important activity that occurs early in the transition is OMI's asking questions of the new employees (who will be called "associates" when working for OMI). OMI asks about personal history, job experiences, and associates' specific ideas to improve the performance of the project. OMI also allows individuals to ask any specific questions that they may have regarding OMI and their jobs. These questions set the tone for a new employer relationship, start the empowerment process, and also begin to shape the new cultural norm of continuous improvement. A useful set of starter questions to diagnose, focus attention, and create intrinsic motivation appears in Exhibit 5.3.

It is important to note that the perceived positives of a command-and-control style, namely speed and usefulness in a crisis situation, are not discarded. Rather, in the flexible analyze-and-energize style leaders can invoke options based on situation specifics diagnosed in the "analyze" segment. Managers can still make quick decisions without consulting others, passing on strategic information, or developing others if the situation calls for immediate action. A primary difference is that in command-and-control the default mode is to give instructions and minimal information. In analyze-and-energize the default mode is to diagnose the situation and lean first toward joint opportunities for meeting strategic objectives and developing people.

In summary, LSS/HPO leadership will most likely look quite different from existing leadership thoughts and practices in an organization. While some elements may already be practiced, it is atypical for the combination of the themes, inner voice, principles, and style presented here to be consistently practiced in non-LSS/HPO organizations. Leaders can greatly increase personal and organizational performance levels by learning and applying these. Leaders can continually improve by obtaining feedback—from all directions—on new skill application and then developing personal action plans to incorporate feedback.[17]

Notes

1. Rost, J. (1993). *Leadership for the twenty-first century.* Westport, CT: Praeger.

2. Kouzes, J., and Posner, B. (2003). *The leadership challenge: How to get extraordinary things done in organizations* (3rd ed.). San Francisco: Jossey-Bass.

3. Ulrich, D., Zenger, J., and Smallwood, N. (1999). *Results-based leadership.* Boston, MA: Harvard Business School Press.

4. Kouzes, J., and Posner, B. (1993). *Credibility.* San Francisco: Jossey-Bass.

5. Tichy, N. (1997). *The leadership engine.* New York: HarperBusiness.

6. Heifetz, R. (1994). *Leadership without easy answers.* Boston, MA: Belknap Press.

7. Collins, J. (2003, July). "The ten greatest CEOs of all times." *Fortune, 148*(2), p. 62.

8. Badaracco, J., and Ellsworth, R. (1993). *Leadership and the quest for integrity.* Boston, MA: Harvard Business School Press.

9. Personal conversation with Mike Grimm, Six Sigma Expert at Raytheon in Tucson, Arizona.

10. In many organizations the term "vision" has been overused and it has under-delivered. If the workforce rolls its collective eyes at the mention of the word vision, top leaders may wish to consider using another term such as end-state, new direction, or future state.

11. Mohrman, S. (2003). *Implementation processes.* Advanced Topics in Organization Design Conference. Center for Effective Organizations, Marshall School of Business, University of Southern California.

12. Personal interview with Ann Burress, Shell Oil Company.

13. Personal communication with Stu Winby, former director of Business Transformation Services at Hewlett-Packard during the Hewlett-Packard and Compaq merger.

14. Personal interview with Karl Schmidt on May 24, 2003.

15. Personal interview with Leigh Wilkinson on December 3, 2002.

16. Some good resources are Simmons, A. (2002). *The story factor: Inspiration, influence, and persuasion through the art of storytelling.* Cambridge, MA: Perseus Publishing; McKee, R. (1997). *Story, substance, structure, style and the principles of screenwriting.* New York: HarperCollins; and Maguire, J. (1998). The power of personal storytelling. In J.P. Tarcher and M. Gass (Eds.). (1995). *The book of metaphors.* Dubuque, IA: Kendall/Hunt. The website www.storytheater.net also provides some useful material and references.

17. For automated assessments, see LSSHPOAssessments.com.

CHAPTER 6

Useful Distinctions

Our todays and yesterdays are the blocks with which we build.
Henry Wadsworth Longfellow

WILLIAM, A WINE CONNOISSEUR of thirty years, met Mark, the restaurant manager of a trendy Chicago restaurant, on an airplane. The twenty-two-year-old restaurant manager boasted he knew quite a bit about wine, having consumed quite a bit in college. He accepted a challenge from William to a series of "blind tastings" in which each would try to match wines poured with their corresponding bottles. In the first round the challenge was to distinguish the Cabernet Sauvignon from the Pinot Noir. The connoisseur was correct; Mark was wrong. The second round challenge was to distinguish the California Cabernet from the French Cabernet. William again prevailed. The final challenge—which Mark also lost—was to match each Cabernet poured to its French Bordeaux or Rhone region of origin.

Forty miles away in an automotive stamping plant Jim, a new hire, struggled to get his punch press working. He fiddled with the bolts. He removed the side plate, cleaned the insides, and fastened the plate again. He even pounded parts of the press with a hammer. After forty-five minutes of working on the press, it still didn't work. Samuel, a forty-year tool and die veteran, stopped and asked what was wrong. After hearing a brief description, Samuel placed his hand on two press areas and felt the vibration in each. He pulled out a hammer, whacked the upper left side of the press once, and it began to work again.

What's the common element in the two stories above and LSS/HPO leadership? It's that an expert makes distinctions that an amateur does not. Based on Mark's college sampling days, all the wines looked red and tasted like they had alcohol in them. But the wine connoisseur made different distinctions Mark wasn't even aware of. Likewise, expert LSS/HPO leaders make distinctions that less experienced leaders do not. These distinctions enable leaders to correctly frame the problem, quickly focus on areas of highest leverage, and apply efforts there. This chapter presents seemingly subtle, but important distinctions for LSS/HPO leaders in four areas: levels of improvement complexity, organizational change, leader challenges, and types of work.

Levels of Improvement Complexity

All challenges are not created equal. Through effective classification leaders can spend the minimum amount of effort and obtain maximum results. There are two dimensions, or "realms," of these challenges:

- *Data-based,* which require data or information to improve, and
- *Interest-based,* which involve varying degrees of emotional attachment to an outcome.

Data-Based Challenges

Data-based challenges range from issues requiring very little data manipulation (Level 1) to a great degree of data manipulation (Level 5) (see Figure 6.1.). Moving up the pyramid from Level 1 to Level 5 requires specialized knowledge, increased learning curves, and a longer times to address the challenge.

Figure 6.1. Data-Based Problems and Opportunities

For each level in the data-based realm, Table 6.1 presents action descriptions.

Table 6.1. Descriptions of Data-Based Realms

Level	Data Type	Description
5	Statistical analysis	Identify variables that are critical to quality for a product or service and use analytical tools to reduce variability. Sample tools include control charts to visually depict process variation and Failure Mode and Effects Analysis to identify potential failures of process components and their impacts on other process components and what should be done to address high priority and high likelihood problems.
4	Basic quality tools	Apply basic quality management tools to the challenge. Examples would include Pareto analyses to classify data and analyze data and Fishbone analyses to determine simple root causes of problems.
3	Streamlining principles	Employ simple principles such as "Identify and remove non-value-added activities," "Map the process and remove duplication," and "It's better to pull work through a work center than to push it."
2	Simple collective thought	Convene a group of people and request their thoughts on how the current situation might be improved. After the session management needs to agree to implement the ideas or provide reasons why they won't.
1	Eligibility/permission	Senior management announces a new work environment of "openness and continuous improvement," in which employees can make improvement suggestions.

In keeping with the LSS/HPO spirit of simplicity, leaders should try to solve as many problems as possible at lower levels, as often quite significant gains are possible at even the lowest level. For example, in 1991 Honeywell's Technical Instruments Division underwent a large-scale improvement effort. I facilitated an early progress review with front-line workers and senior management. At this time workers were trained only in process mapping. A machining area worker who had worked there twenty-two years presented a recommendation that reduced cycle time from twenty-four days to three hours. Senior management was very impressed, but at the end of his presentation one VP couldn't help asking, "If you've been here for twenty-two years, why haven't we heard this dramatic recommendation earlier?" The response was, "Nobody asked me."

Similar scenarios happen frequently in many industry and government organizations. People hold back, either because they are told to or because the culture implicitly supports "not rocking the boat." An important early step for LSS/HPO leaders is to modify the culture to increase people's eligibility to make improvement suggestions (Level 1 in Figure 6.1).

Interest-Based Challenges

Obviously not all challenges can be addressed by considering data alone. Emotions, politics, feelings, values—all those things that make us human—also impact improvement decisions. Potential friction points occur when people's varying interests cause them to want different things from the same situation.

There are four levels in the interest-based realm, based on the interpersonal and team training skill course called PeopleSmart Skills for LSS/HPOs.[1] As with the pyramid for the data-based realm, the simplest level to address in the interest-based pyramid[2] is Level 1. It becomes increasingly complex as leaders move from the first to the fourth level. See Figure 6.2.

For each level in the interest-based realm Table 6.2 presents detailed descriptions, examples, and leadership implications.

Many challenges do not clearly fall within either the data-based *or* interest-based realm. Often challenges present themselves in combination. These combinations can be presented in a matrix that maps the data-based to the interest-based realm. Table 6.3 illustrates this concept with selected concrete examples in selected cells. The simplest combination for a leader to address lies in the upper left-hand corner, with complexity increasing when moving to the lower right.

Figure 6.2. Interest-Based Problems and Opportunities

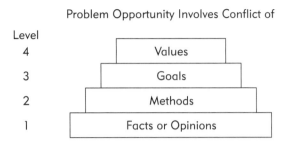

Table 6.2. Descriptions of Interest-Based Realms

Level	Interest Type	Description
4	Values	A clash of deeply held beliefs and life assumptions
3	Goals	A clash between differing target outcomes; such clashes frequently arise when people from two different departments get together and attempt to plan joint improvements that must simultaneously satisfy their respective groups
2	Methods	A clash between different ways of accomplishing the same or similar outcomes
1	Facts or Opinions	Disagreements over whose facts are correct or whose opinions are the most valid in the absence of data

Organizational Change

Just as there are levels of improvement complexity people don't often think about, there are also distinctions in types of change roll-out strategies. Knowing the characteristics of each and how leaders can best support each contributes to LSS/HPO success. Figure 6.3 provides a visual comparison of the two approaches.

Table 6.3. Examples of Combination Challenges

Data-Based Realm	Interest-Based Realm			
	1. Facts or Opinions	2. Methods	3. Goals	4. Values
1. Eligibility/permission				
2. Simple collective thought		The quality management group and production departments in a drug company gather to determine how best to meet the new FDA regulations. Production currently wants it one way, Quality wants it another.		
3. Streamlining principles				
4. Basic quality tools	Linda debates with Ron about the root cause of the fabrication area's high scrap rates. By collecting data and conducting a Pareto analysis they resolve the conflict and determine the true root cause, which was not what either initially thought.			
5. Statistical methods			A Six Sigma statistical study reveals a plant needs to be closed, but the plant manager wants to keep his family in town and there are no other jobs for him in that town.	One set of statistics reveals that capital punishment is a deterrent to crime. Although against his personal values, Steve is assigned to a team to design new ways of administering capital punishment in the prison where he works.

Figure 6.3. Compliance-Based Change vs. Intrinsically Motivated Change

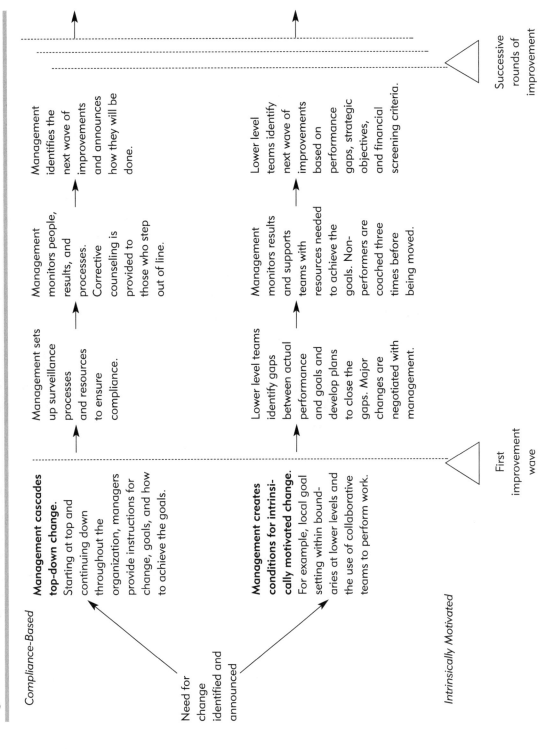

The first is *compliance-based* change, a traditional approach that has been around for centuries. Under this approach top leadership tells people precisely what needs to be done and how to do it. A major downside of this approach is that it requires heavy management attention as long as management wants the desired change. For example, several years ago a Fortune 50 company implemented Six Sigma using a compliance-based approach. Improvement gains were rapid initially as the CEO, a very charismatic individual, spent long hours extolling the virtues of Six Sigma. Six months into the program other strategic issues arose and the CEO worked less with Six Sigma, figuring it had sufficient momentum. The result: Six Sigma faltered. People assumed that since the CEO's public enthusiasm waned that Six Sigma was not important any more. It took the CEO three months to get the effort energized again.

The second approach is *intrinsically motivated* change, in which top leadership provides high-level goals, principles for change, and how to measure if it is going well and then lets people develop their own local goals and tailored approach that they then own. Under this approach:

- Resistance is greatly minimized;
- Top leadership involvement is not as continually necessary; and
- The overall timeframe for implementing impressive changes is shorter (although initially the participation phase may take longer, the execution phase for the change is rapid).

Although compliance-based change is not the preferred approach, good LSS/HPO leaders are flexible and act in the overall organization's interest. There are cases in which the compliance-based approach may be applied, for example, if an outside regulatory agency like FDA or FAA is about to close a facility unless certain violations are immediately addressed. In these cases there may be no time to create conditions for people to own the changes required and develop their own approach to fixing them. However, in most LSS/HPO efforts, intrinsically motivated change is preferred.

Leader Challenges

The way that a leader views a challenge can have a tremendous impact on the leader's leverage. That key distinction of interest is between *technical* challenges and *adaptive* challenges.[3] Ron Heifitz of the Kennedy School of Government at Harvard first highlighted this difference, which is critically important to LSS/HPO leaders.

When dealing with a technical challenge, it is possible to provide a solution that does not require people to change any attitudes or deeply held beliefs. For example, you can prescribe the drug Augmentin to clear up a patient's ear infection. He doesn't have to change how he lives. The ear infection could be thought of as a simple technical challenge that the prescribed drug addresses. However, let's consider another medical problem where a surgeon performs open-heart surgery on a patient to clear artery blockages. The story is entirely different if the problem is to stay "fixed." The patient will need to make major life changes in areas like smoking, eating, stress reduction, and exercise. A heart problem is clearly an adaptive challenge, as it requires a change to deeply held attitudes, beliefs, and habits.

LSS/HPO environments contain challenges aplenty. Leaders can make best use of their scarce time and maximize their value to the organization by striving to address adaptive challenges over technical. Adaptive challenges typically have five characteristics:

1. They require a moderate to significant change in behavior and mindset;

2. They are a complex web of interrelated factors;

3. They involve a clash of interests (either within oneself or among others);

4. They may involve a clash of values; and

5. They require systemic thinking and solutions.

Leading people through adaptive challenges can be difficult, as people often go through painful periods of adjustment. In moving to an LSS/HPO environment, large segments of the workforce will likely

- Have to abandon or place less emphasis on previously built relationships;

- Create new working relationships, sometimes with former adversaries;

- Change the way they lead, as decision making is often more participative and more data-driven; and

- Encounter feelings of incompetence as people experiment with new LSS/HPO tools and learn what it means to work as a team that is held collectively accountable.

The problem is that technical challenges have a strong gravitational pull for leaders at all levels. After all, solving technical challenges is most likely how leaders were promoted.

It's not that top and middle leaders need to completely stop spending time on technical challenges. They can still provide support and, one hopes, continually attempt to develop organizational capability in their areas of expertise. Top and middle leaders must be alert to the fact that there are two types of challenges and that adaptive challenge is often where the most organizational leverage is.

Types of Work

Just as classifying *challenges* can enable leaders to make best use of their time and enhance organizational performance, so can classifying *types of work*. Years ago Doug Englebart, a Silicon Valley pioneer in workplace collaboration credited with developing the mouse and word processing, developed insightful work classifications that have important implications for LSS/HPO leadership. I have adapted Englebart's thoughts on types of work into a diagram and accompanying framework for LSS/HPO leaders, shown in Figure 6.4.

Leaders increase their leverage as they spend more time at the right-most parts of the diagram. The chain of high leverage begins with Type C work, which influences Type B work, which influences Type A work. Two decades ago the U.S. automobile and electronics industries learned the costly lesson of "process" impact on "products and services" from Japan. While U.S. automakers established acceptable quality levels to assess compliance to *product* specifications, Japanese automakers focused on improving *processes* for making cars and grabbed a huge share of the international market.

Type C work's influence on Type B work is subtle, but powerful. The following five areas, taken from the "examples" box for Type C work in Figure 6.4, illustrate important leader Type C work.

Collective and Personal Assumptions

Leaders shape personal and collective assumptions within the organization. These have a tremendous impact on how processes are executed to produce a certain level of quality in products and services. To illustrate the power of collectively held assumptions, consider two quotes that represent different ways of thinking about employees.[4] The first quote comes from Frederick Taylor:

> "Hardly a competent workman can be found who does not devote a considerable amount of time to studying just how *slowly* he can work and still convince his employer that he is going at a good pace. Under our system—

Figure 6.4. Types of Work

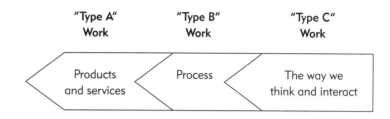

Brief Description	The "what"	The "how"	"Shaping thoughts and interrelationships"
Examples	Car Bank loan TV set Circuit card Consulting advice Credit card billing Movie	New product development process Production process Loan initiation process Computerized processing of credit card charges	Collective and personal assumptions Questions leaders ask Rules leaders make Technology that assists collaboration Language leaders use that shapes peoples' thoughts and actions

Increasing leader leverage

Based on work by Doug Englebart.

that is, the system of scientific management—a worker is told just *what* he is to do and *how* he is to do it. Any improvement he makes upon the orders given to him is fatal to his success."

The second quote comes from Konosuke Matsushita of the large Japanese corporation of the same last name:

"We are going to win and the industrial West is going to lose out; there's not much you can do about it because the reasons for your failure are within yourselves. Your firms are built on the Frederick Taylor model.

Even worse, so are your heads. With your bosses doing the thinking while the workers wield the screwdrivers, you're convinced deep down that this is the right way to run a business. For you, the essence of management is getting the ideas out of the heads of the bosses and into the hands of labor.

We are beyond your mindset. Business, we know, is now so complex and difficult, the survival of firms so hazardous in an environment increasingly unpredictable, competitive and fraught with danger, that their continued existence depends on the day-to-day mobilization of every ounce of intelligence."

It's not difficult to imagine how U.S. firms—most of which were run according to the Taylor mindset—lost all significant production of television sets and VCRs to electronics companies with Matsushita-like mindsets. In an industry such as electronics that requires local, swift problem solving supported by management, one can envision the impact of the top leader's assumptions in U.S. companies in the 1980s.

Questions Leaders Ask

Asking questions is a powerful technique in a leader's change arsenal. Good questions can direct attention, let people know what is important, and stimulate people's thoughts around an area they previously had not given much thought to. Great questions are ones that people start asking themselves long after the leader has left the room. This is one of the highest forms of leader effectiveness—getting people to change the way that they talk to themselves and to others.

In a slow-moving pharmaceutical company with stagnant growth and lackluster financial performance, I often heard a common reaction—at manager and director levels—to proposed process improvements. They would ask, "What will be the political impact of these proposed changes on our group and other groups involved?" If there would likely be any negative political fallout resulting from a proposed improvement, any one of the affected groups would kill the idea. When I questioned this practice, I was informed it was "a sign of respect to one's peers not to meddle in their area. And, by not meddling in others' areas a manager increases the likelihood that others will not meddle in his."

I believe this cycle of corporate civility and inaction significantly contributed to their substandard industry performance.

In contrast, at a large, fast-moving high-tech company with exponential growth and exceptional performance, I heard quite a different set of questions when someone suggested a process improvement. Directors and managers asked, "What will be the impact on our customers if we do this?" and "If we don't do this, will we become another IBM?" (This last question was asked prior to IBM's turnaround and referred to a situation in which a once market leader lost touch with the market and suffered financially.)

In many ways, a leader's questions are like chain letters in an organization—good or bad, they are passed on to lower levels and across departments. Leaders need to consider this impact when asking questions.

Rules Leaders Make

Another way leaders shape the way people think and interact (and subsequently perform processes) is by establishing rules that indicate what is acceptable behavior and what is not. When Jere Stead joined a division of AT&T as vice president shortly after they had been broken up, after being a monopoly for so long, he wanted to instill concern for the customer in all employees. To help drive home his message, he stated that if he was in a meeting and the external customer wasn't mentioned in the first ten minutes, he would leave. He left many meetings the first two weeks after his announcement, but soon people caught on that customers were extremely important to consider in all corporate discussions.

Technology That Assists Collaboration

There are many technological tools available that increase collaboration. Some tools help increase collaboration within the room, such as whiteboards that electronically capture and print documents from a brainstorming session and projection units that allow everyone equal access to spreadsheets and project the data on a screen for all to see. Other tools, such as videoconferencing, help collaboration among sites.

Since collaboration is crucial in an LSS/HPO, leaders need to allocate resources to and encourage intelligent uses of collaborative tools. In addition to helping the actual collaborative process, this spending also sends the message that collaboration is important.

Language Leaders Use That Shapes Peoples' Thoughts and Actions

It's been said that we use language to create our reality. This is an extremely powerful concept for leaders. Techniques for influence under this paradigm can range from the simple introduction of new words into the organizational lexicon to complex thoughts, concepts, and visions. Years ago, when the concept of "internal customer" was introduced, it had a powerful impact on how workers produced goods they would pass downstream. The thought that a downstream person was a "customer" made it more important to produce a higher quality part. And in today's environment leaders promoting the concept of "Six Sigma"—3.4 defects per million—fosters a mindset of near perfection.

Leaders can help make their case for improvement by making numbers "come alive" with language by using analogies and metaphors. In the early Motorola quality days, executive vice president Dave Melka once challenged an improvement team by saying, "For the scrap you have every day in your operation, I could drive a Lincoln Continental off a bridge every day."[5] This phrase stuck in people's minds more than, "Hey, everybody, you really need to get that scrap rate under control in your area."

Viewing work from the perspective of Type A, B, and C work can considerably impact the effectiveness of a leader in an LSS/HPO transformation because it can help a leader decide how to best spend time to improve organizational performance. Not all work, of course, needs to be Type C work. Improving processes—Type B work—is also important in an LSS/HPO. The important thing to remember is that when looking at alternative uses of a leader's time it is helpful for the leader to classify the potential uses in A, B, and C terms and to select the best combination of high leverage C and B work.

Great LSS/HPO leaders make distinctions that less experienced ones do not. This chapter provided four useful distinctions that leaders can use to increase their leverage. To trained LSS/HPO leaders these distinctions help them wisely allocate their time and mobilize organizational resources to achieve exceptionally high performance.

Notes

1. See PeopleSmartLSSHPO.com. This course, tailored to address the unique requirements of interpersonal and team interactions in an LSS/HPO environment, is based on the widely acclaimed PeopleSmart course series and books.

2. Adapted from Silberman, M., and Hansburg, S. (2000). *PeopleSmart: Developing your interpersonal intelligence.* San Francisco: Berrett-Koehler.

3. Heifetz, R. (1994). *Leadership without easy answers.* Boston, MA: Belknap Press.

4. Pascale, R. (1991). *Managing on the edge: How smart companies use conflict to stay ahead.* Carmichael, CA: Touchstone Books.

5. Personal conversation with Mike Carnell on November 25, 2002.

7

Leader's Basic Toolkit

The solution should be as simple as it can be, but no simpler.

Albert Einstein

AUDACIOUS GOALS REQUIRE LARGE-SCALE CHANGE. And let's face it, large-scale change is challenging work. This section presents four robust, time-tested, highly effective tools to help navigate the often murky waters of integrating Lean Six Sigma and HPOs. While it would be ideal to have just one tool that would fit all change situations, large-scale change is a complex issue not easily addressed by just one tool. Just as you can't build a house by using only a hammer, you can't successfully implement LSS/HPO with just one tool. A multi-faceted view is needed to execute a successful improvement initiative that is so wide-reaching in scope and depth. There are very few simple yes or no answers in LSS/HPO leadership. Paradoxes such as freedom versus control, innovation versus discipline, and team versus individual efforts need to be addressed frequently. F. Scott Fitzgerald once commented that the test of a first-rate intelligence was the ability to hold two opposed ideas in mind at the same time and still retain the ability to function. The tools in this chapter help build leader intelligence and provide essential perspectives that, considered together, dramatically increase a leader's chance of LSS/HPO success.

When seeking dramatic changes to the status quo, as with an LSS/HPO initiative, three key areas require serious attention. A simple tool for each and its associated strategy appear in Table 7.1.

Table 7.1. Key Tools by Areas Requiring Attention

Key Area Requiring Attention	Tool	Tool Strategy
The interaction of key performance factors such as business processes, HR practices, and organizational structure	Performance Framework	Use a visual map of high-leverage performance factors to develop congruent change plans among the performance factors; monitor progress; debate alternative courses of action; and conduct lessons learned analyses to continuously improve large-scale change efforts.
Human interactions within and among organizational levels and groups	Top/Middle/Bottom Space Analysis	Develop powerful change actions and communications by understanding a leader's own interaction optimization options and how targeted change audiences will react to proposed improvements; interpret communications about upcoming changes; and seek to optimize human interactions with other levels and groups in the organization.
Project management of the improvement effort	Leader's Integrated Work Plan Shaping and Quality Assurance Guide	Ask a set of questions to ensure high quality plans exist; the right people are involved but not overloaded; and the right things are scheduled at the right times.

Each of these tools will be used in all the stages from Initiation to Operations and Continuous Improvement (Section 2 of this part of the book). In this chapter, we will cover the basic premises for each tool, elements of the tool, and coaching tips on how to use it.

While there are other tools presented in this book that can help a leader along the transformation path, the three in this chapter form the basics leaders need to address the major issues in an LSS/HPO transformation.

The Performance Framework Tool

Major change is a major challenge. The most successful change efforts are those that address change on multiple fronts. For example, an improvement initiative that only provides total quality tools to people will not be as successful as one that provides people with quality tools and training; changes the culture so people have time and peer support to apply them; formally incorporates continuous improvement into the strategy; supports the deployment of the tools through the organizational structure; and changes HR practices to reward continuous improvement behavior.

Addressing multiple performance factors instead of just one is critical. The Performance Framework (see Figure 7.1) is a visual tool that helps leaders plan and implement changes that are congruent among an organization's key performance factors.

In addition to facilitating a more effective change effort, the Performance Framework helps reduce workforce resistance to change. People resist change when they perceive that top management sends inconsistent messages about the change and management's support of it. This tool helps leaders align change messages and change actions. Leaders can use the tool to explain the reason for change, the key factors involved, and upcoming events on the change horizon.

Basic Premises

Initiating major changes in the way people work is not easy. While there are key performance levers to pull, it's important to keep in mind that leaders must deal with a complex, interrelated *web* of performance factors. A change in one

Figure 7.1. Performance Framework Tool

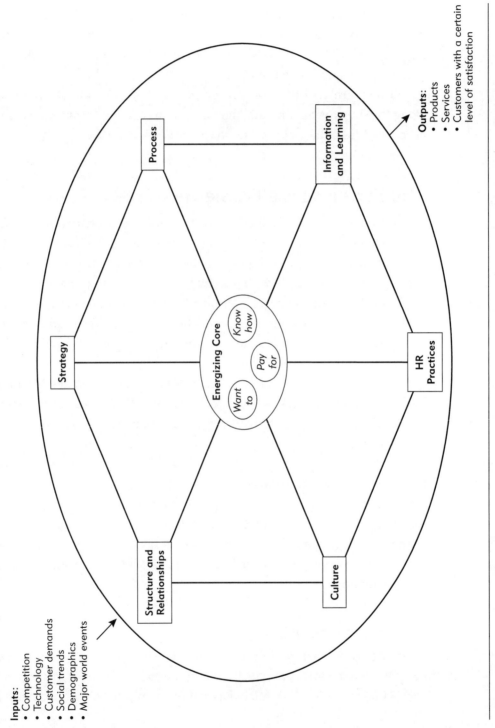

Inputs:
• Competition
• Technology
• Customer demands
• Social trends
• Demographics
• Major world events

Strategy

Process

Structure and Relationships

Energizing Core

Want to

Pay for

Know how

Information and Learning

Culture

HR Practices

Outputs:
• Products
• Services
• Customers with a certain level of satisfaction

factor will affect the others. It's unwise to change just one part of the web without considering whether the change is consistent with other transmitted messages and desired behaviors. Inconsistencies result in a confused workforce who bemoan time-worn change platitudes like, "I wish management could get their act together," "How can they expect us to do X when they just told us we're supposed to be doing Y?", and perhaps the most damaging, "If we just wait this one out, it'll pass just like the others." For these reasons it is important to identify the key performance factors and their interrelationships. The Performance Framework presents a visual, pragmatic way to do this.

Other models similar to the Performance Framework explain organizational performance, typically considering five to eight factors drawn as an interrelated web like the Performance Framework. The seven factors of the twenty-two-year-old McKinsey 7S model is one example.[1] Jay Galbraith's Star Model[2] shows key variables to consider in organization redesigns. Other models help explain change and performance in a variety of situations. However, I believe the Performance Framework is best suited for planning, charting, and managing performance in the implementation of and operation of LSS/HPOs. It was developed over a period of fifteen years based on my experience with over two hundred companies and contains some special targeted information especially relevant to LSS/HPOs:

- *The culture factor.* Culture can be defined as the shared beliefs and assumptions that determine behavior in the workplace. An organization's culture can be either an effective roadblock to or an enabler of change. Unlike the other models, the Performance Framework addresses culture because of its importance in an LSS/HPO transformation.

- *The information and learning factor.* Personal experience and research[3] show change can be dramatically accelerated by (1) providing relevant information to those who need it when they need it and (2) creating an infrastructure and motivation for learning at the individual, team, and organizational levels.

- *A monetary aspect.* It's common sense that organizations should consider financial implications of major changes. Oddly enough, this factor is often absent in performance models. Money is included here as an input to allocating resources to projects and as a way of evaluating improvement project success.

- *Human motivation factor.* People may know *what* they need to do to improve performance. They may even understand the theory behind *why* the need to do it. But unless they *want* to make the change, improvement will be limited and sustainability will be unlikely.

An underlying principle for the Performance Framework Tool is that all elements are aligned for peak performance. Misalignment of two or more elements will yield suboptimal results. Consider the case of a Michigan-based manufacturing company where senior management declared they would implement Six Sigma. Five months into the initiative, employees noticed people doing Six Sigma were working sixty-hour weeks because they were doing all their regular work *plus* Six Sigma; no structure was established to guide and allocate scarce resources to Six Sigma activities; middle managers had daily turf wars over people, projects, and daily production work; and four of the people who were working sixty-hour weeks each saved the company $850,000, yet received no additional compensation or recognition for their hard work.

Understandably, this Six Sigma initiative fizzled out within eight months of inception. Talented Black Belts left their project positions and returned to operations. Projects stalled. Some of the best people left the company. A brief look at the Performance Framework reveals alignment problems in multiple areas:

- The company was not structured to implement the strategy;

- The Human Resources Department did not reward extra efforts put forth for the new Six Sigma program; and

- The "want to" core element of performance waned as a result of the above points.

The combination of these three factors brought the project to a screeching halt. In my experience, people will tolerate one of the elements being out of alignment for a short time, but three will sound the death knell for a newly initiated LSS/HPO effort.

Elements of the Tool

Three major elements of the Performance Framework are

1. An external environment that depicts what's happening outside the organization;

2. Six performance bases that represent key performance factors leaders can influence; and

3. The energizing core that provides fuel for the desired changes.

Each of these segments is influenced by the others.

External Environment

Internal changes are nearly always affected by external factors. Examples of the major factors that can affect an improvement effort include a major economic downturn in demand (recession); a corporate acquisition; competitors implementing Six Sigma; or an unexpected change in the market (a competitor with a new product, failure to get regulatory approval of a new drug, a sudden finding that a product is not safe and effective).

All these can cause ripple effects on the organization. The outputs of the organization (shown in the lower right-hand corner of the model) are impacted by how well all the elements within the framework work together. For example, in 1974 Motorola lost television set production to Matsushita. In the 1974 board meeting, top management firmly stated that they would not lose another business like they did the television business, especially for reasons of quality.[4] Motorola launched cycle time reduction programs, team programs, and Six Sigma that dramatically changed their "performance bases" and "energizing core."

Not all organizational interactions with the external environment need be negative or spawn from an "it's being done to us" perspective. By periodically scanning the environment and learning from it, many organizations find they can influence the external environment. In a *Business 2.0* 2002 interview, Michael Dell, CEO of Dell Computer, talked about how Dell's revenues remained flat while those of IBM, Sun, and HP were reeling. Dell listed three reasons the company had weathered the terrible 2002 computer decline:

- "We talk early and often with our customers.

- Our strategy is the same now as it has always been: We stay focused on our customers.

- We never rest."

These points show how Dell's scanning the external environment helps keep Dell on top, even in bad times. Michael Dell finished the interview by sharing a philosophy that most companies don't have, which might also explain Dell's success. He said, "Keep raising the bar, for the industry and for yourself."

Six Performance Bases

The performance factors or "bases" in the organization's internal environment are

1. *Strategy.* Strategy represents the organization's direction. It delineates the organization's offerings of products and services, the markets they serve, and the channels they use to serve them.[5]

2. *Process.* A process is a collection of activities and decisions that produces an output for an internal or external customer. Processes often span departmental or group boundaries. Examples include new product development and order fulfillment.

3. *Information and Learning.* Information flow is critical to any improvement effort. It may be transactional information, such as the number of cars going through a toll booth, or it may be tacit knowledge, such as lessons learned from the last new product development launch. For information to be useful it has to be disseminated to the people who need it. The dissemination of information and creation of a learning environment positively impact the speed and effectiveness of improvement efforts.[6]

4. *Human Resources Practices.* Policies and activities of the HR function enable certain behaviors and limit others. When looking at alignment with other performance levers, it is critical to evaluate HR areas such as compensation, rewards, recognition, performance appraisals, training, retention, hiring, and firing.

5. *Culture.* Culture can be defined as the shared beliefs and assumptions that determine behavior. Although typically acknowledged as important, culture is usually not actively managed in large-scale changes. In successful LSS/HPO transformations, leaders seek to understand the difference between the current and the required culture and set a course to close the gap. Once closed, leaders still need to actively manage the culture, or the culture will manage them.

6. *Structure and Relationships.* Structure is the formalized pattern of how people interact within an organization, most often depicted as lines and boxes on an organization chart. But lines and boxes don't govern all the ways that people interact and relate to one another. Examples of behav-

iors and actions not governed by the formal structure include collaboration levels, ways people compensate informally for barriers, location of management tasks such as planning and goal setting in the hierarchical structure, the nature of supervision, and the clarity of organizational roles and responsibilities.

All Performance Framework bases influence each other. Very strong relationships, such as the Strategy-Structure and Relationships, and Strategy–Process connections are depicted by lines connecting the performance factors. Other influence connections such as the Process-Culture connection and the Information and Learning-Structure and Relationships connections are depicted as being connected through the energizing core. Additional information can be found in the Reference section of the Appendix.

The Energizing Core

The core three elements of the Performance Framework provide the energy for the remaining elements of the model. They are

1. *"Know how"*—knowledge that people have about what needs to be done, the process by which they are to do it, and the reason they are doing it.
2. *"Want to"*—motivation to perform a task.[7]
3. *"Pay for"*—the financial implications of (a) launching or not launching an improvement effort or (b) selecting one improvement project over the other based on benefits and costs.

Without knowledge, motivation, and funding few plans will come to successful fruition. The following questions all flow naturally from the energizing core of the Framework.

- Does the project team have the know-how to attack the problem?
- Are they and the people they must get the data from motivated to participate? and
- Will the financial return justify the time and resources invested in improving the process?

Outputs

The external environment, the six bases, and the energizing core combine to produce outputs. Key outputs the model focuses on include products and services from which a certain level of customer satisfaction is derived.

Coaching Tips

There are many uses for the Performance Framework. Senior managers and change agents have successfully used this framework for planning, assessment, alternative evaluation, and communication purposes throughout the LSS/HPO implementation lifecycle. Table 7.2 lists some recommended minimum uses of the Performance Framework in an LSS/HPO and also some optional, but nevertheless highly effective uses. The "mini-case" below provides an industry example of the first type of use.

Table 7.2. Potential Uses for the Performance Framework Tool

	Use
Recommended minimum uses in an LSS/HPO	Senior managers analyze their organization's current state and articulate their desired state using the Performance Framework
	Change leaders use the Performance Framework to prepare detailed plans at the start of each major change stage
	Executives use the Performance Framework to kick off and explain the entire upcoming large-scale change effort
	Change leaders use the Performance Framework to conduct an assessment and lessons learned analysis at the end of each change stage
Optional, but effective uses in an LSS/HPO	Communicate upcoming changes using the six performance bases and energizing core
	Diagnose organizational problems and develop internally consistent solutions within the context of the Performance Framework
	Evaluate potential actions in the context of the all the Performance Framework elements

Mini-Case

The senior management team for a Massachusetts-based electronics manufacturer met offsite to understand current organizational performance issues and develop an agreed-on future direction using the

Performance Framework. They began by posting a flip chart of the Performance Framework and then discussed the current state of all elements. They documented observations, facts, concerns, and trends, using three to five bullet points recorded in blue next to each topic heading.

They then looked for factors that were not in alignment, such as having a Structure consisting of teams but using HR Practices that only rewarded individuals, and noted those in blue on a convenient place on the chart. After completing the current state analysis for each of the factors they discussed the future state for each of the framework elements. They recorded highlights of their future state discussions in green adjacent to the topic heading. They then checked to ensure all future state elements were aligned and, if not, modified the descriptions so they would be. The group agreed to use this chart to explain the need for change to the workforce, develop tasks for their improvement work plan based on the gaps between the current and future states, and track progress throughout the project using the current state as a baseline.

A derivative tool of the Performance Framework is the Transformation EKG (Figure 7.2). This tool graphically depicts the status of each performance base and core element for each stage. The number shows energy expended relative to the baseline of 0 for each factor at the transformation start. Upon completion of a stage, participants—usually key change leaders from several areas—gather and assign scores to the level of activity expended in each stage and compare that to what was planned.

Managing the Performance Framework elements is not the exclusive responsibility of senior management. In an LSS/HPO, leadership responsibilities are distributed, and these elements become the responsibility of leaders at all levels. Although initiation of change may start at the top, the middle and the bottom need to embrace and lead the new ways of thinking and acting around each of the performance factors.

Figure 7.2. Transformation EKG

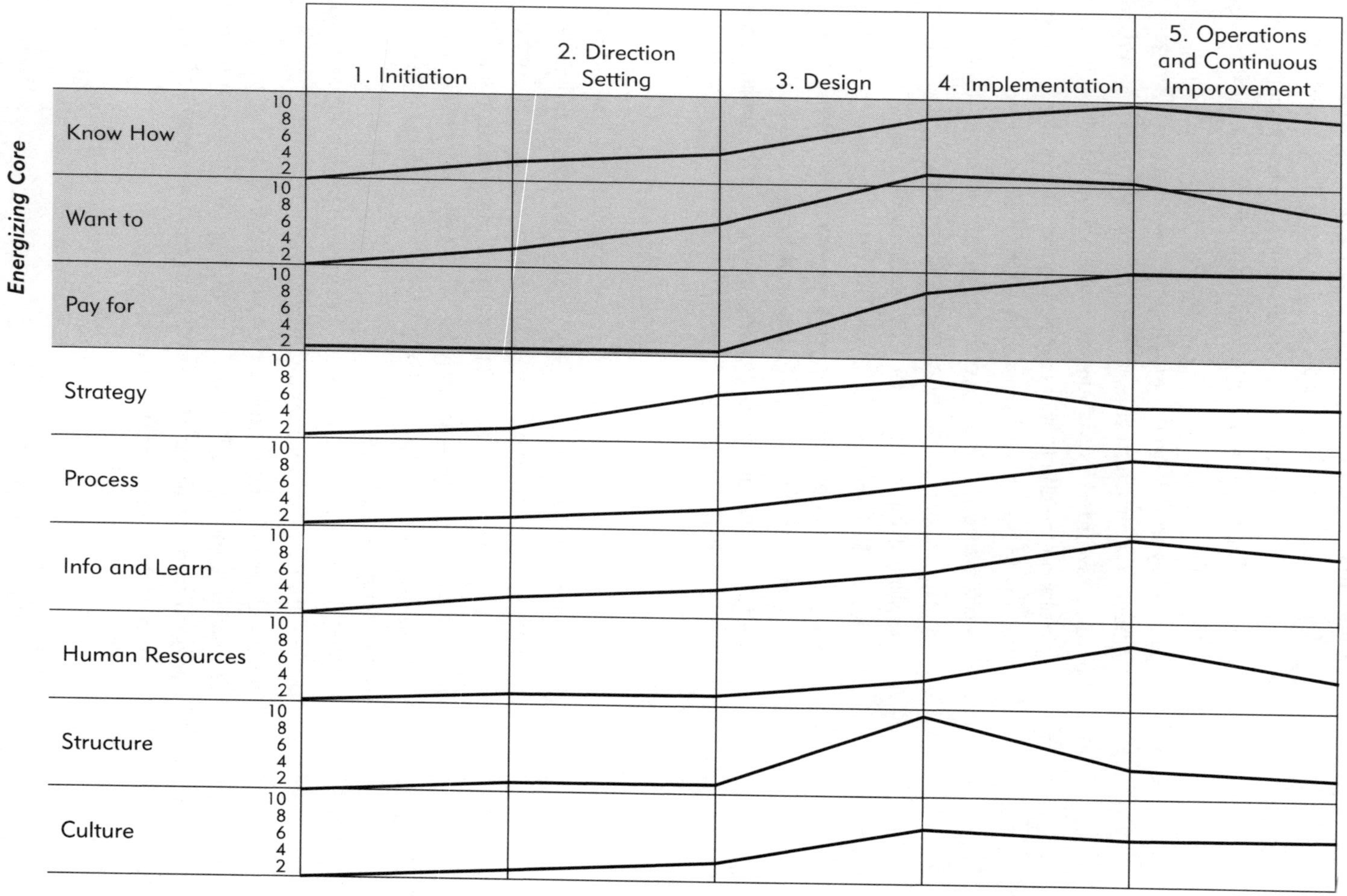

Top/Middle/Bottom Space Analysis Tool

Where a person is in the organization—the Top, Middle, or Bottom—has an associated set of conditions and likely performance traps. Barry Oshry began studying this phenomenon over thirty-five years ago and I have found his research particularly useful for leaders in LSS/HPO transformations. Based on the Oshry research, I have developed an "optical tool kit" consisting of two items that help leaders see the world from the perspectives of the Top, Middle, and Bottom organizational spaces.[8] The following section contains some of the Oshry theory and its translation into LSS/HPO tools for leaders. For a more in-depth study of the research I highly recommend each of the Oshry references listed in the resource section of this book.

I find it helpful at this early point in the discussion to bring up the use of the term "Bottoms." Absolutely no disrespect is intended in the use of the word. The term simply denotes the location of the organizational space that is under the Top and Middle levels and produces most of the products and services. Those who prefer terms such as "associates" or "front-line workers" can mentally replace the word "Bottoms" when encountered in the text.[9]

The items in the "optical toolkit" can be used to look at oneself and at others with greater organizational space clarity.

Basic Premises

There are six major premises of this tool:

1. One reason organizational improvement initiatives fall short of their goals is because people don't fully understand the organizational systems of which they are a part. Specifically, there is often a lack of understanding and appreciation for the conditions associated with being at the organizational Top, Middle, or Bottom and how these spaces can best interact for the organizational good.[10]

2. Once the conditions and performance traps are known, people can develop ways out of the traps (see Figure 7.3).[11]

3. By understanding the organizational spaces—both their own and others'—leaders can increase their leverage within their organizational system and achieve much better outcomes.

4. For the organizational system to perform better, all the parts must perform better. This means the Tops, Middles, and Bottoms must learn and execute ways out of their respective performance traps.

Figure 7.3. Organizational Spaces

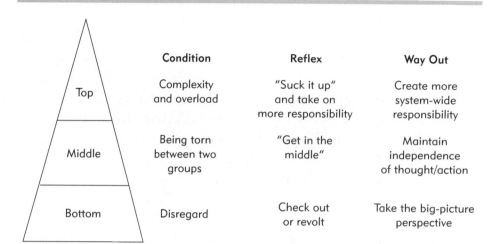

	Condition	Reflex	Way Out
Top	Complexity and overload	"Suck it up" and take on more responsibility	Create more system-wide responsibility
Middle	Being torn between two groups	"Get in the middle"	Maintain independence of thought/action
Bottom	Disregard	Check out or revolt	Take the big-picture perspective

5. Often what we think is personal really is not; it's related to organizational space.

6. Often what we think is situational really is not; it also is related to organizational space.[12]

To illustrate the last two points here are three examples:

Example 1. A junior engineer attended a conference on reengineering the new product development process. He came back excited, prepared a fifty-page summary of the conference, and presented it to the CEO. The CEO, coming from the Top space, saw this as more complexity and overload in his life and summarily rejected the idea. The engineer was shocked, thinking, "Why wouldn't the head of the company want to improve the way we develop products?"

Example 2. On an airplane a CEO read about a way to reengineer the new product development process. She came back and announced to the engineers and manufacturing people who would be involved how they would reengineer their process. The Bottoms heavily resisted, feeling once again that something was being thrust upon them without consultation or consideration of their local work conditions. The CEO was puzzled, wondering, "Why wouldn't people want a better way to work?"

Example 3. A CEO announced a new cafeteria-style insurance plan to the workforce that dramatically increased their total benefits as well as their choices. After his presentation at the town hall meeting, the CEO couldn't believe his ears when he overheard people at the water cooler grumbling about

"Just one more thing that company management is doing to us," and "It'll be a while before we figure out the catch, but I'm sure they're sticking it to us somehow!" The CEO, not thinking in terms of organizational space issues, was confused at the reaction of people working in the Bottom space.

Masters of the concepts of organizational space would not have been surprised at any of the above because the pull of the space conditions and natural reflex is so strong it can override apparent logic, make actions appear "personal" when they're not, and cause people to attribute outcomes to the specific situation when the underlying cause is in fact space-related.

There is a subtle, but important nuance in this model: organizational *space* may or may not be directly related to a *position* in an organization. In organizational space parlance, a "Top" has overall responsibility for the organizational system, and a "Middle" manages and integrates the work of "Bottoms," who are the primary producers. When considering a situation from an organizational space perspective (versus a position perspective), we can understand how it is possible for a junior analytical chemist to be a Bottom in the morning when she is doing lab tests and a Top in the afternoon when she is heading up a project team. In another example, the CEO may be Top in his staff meeting but a Middle when he is meeting with the board of directors and must deliver their mandate to the rest of the organization. Our tools for organizational spaces are determined by *conditions*, not *positions*.

Armed with this grounding in the Top/Middle/Bottom theory, it's now time to examine its application in the form of two toolkit items.

Elements of the Tool

Two items comprise this optical kit: (1) a *mirror* for self-examination and determination of high leverage actions based on the organizational space one finds oneself in at the moment, and (2) *lenses* for looking at the conditions, biases, and natural tendencies of others based on their organizational space and determining the best way to communicate with and influence them. Leaders can use each item for self-reflection and self-coaching.

Coaching Tips

It would be helpful for leaders to look at the mirror and the lenses at least one time during each stage of the transformation. This will help them prepare for one-on-one conversations about the upcoming changes in the next phase, as well as for large group communications like town hall meetings. Referring to these diagrams and checklists can increase a leader's personal leverage through an understanding of where people are coming from and how best to approach them.

The first item in the Top/Middle/Bottom optical kit is a mirror. When we find ourselves in a particular organizational space, it's time to look at ourselves in that space, reflect on our condition, and consider what high leverage actions might be beneficial for ourselves and for the entire organizational system. Figure 7.4 shows key questions for leaders when they find themselves in the Top, Middle, and Bottom organizational spaces.

Figure 7.4. Organizational Space Mirror

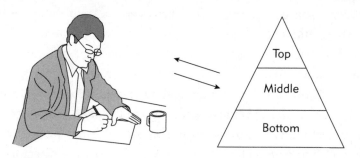

When I'm a	I need to consider
Top	Am I taking on more responsibility than I need to?
	Can I find some way to distribute my workload to others so I can think and act more strategically?
	How can I develop others in the organization so that in the future they can take more work from me?
Middle	Am I getting stuck in the middle in a political tug of war between the Tops and the Bottoms? Between one group and another in the organization?
	Have I been asked to pass down information or policies from the Tops to the Bottoms that I know may cause revolt? (If so, have I informed the Tops before passing the information down? Have I coached Tops to craft messages and strategies that Bottoms will accept?)
	Am I staying independent by coaching Bottoms on how to talk to Tops when they are seeking to influence Tops?
Bottom	Am I proposing plans that benefit the entire organizational system, instead of just me or my area?
	Am I constantly looking for how the consequences of my actions affect the organization's big picture and, if necessary, modifying my actions?
	Am I avoiding being a victim that things are "done to" and instead seizing the initiative to make things better?

Questions to consider were adapted from B. Oshry and T. Devane. (1999). Organization workshop. In P. Holman and T. Devane (Eds.), *The change handbook: Group methods for shaping the future.* San Francisco: Berrett-Koehler.

The second item in the Top/Middle/Bottom optical toolkit is a set of lenses. Just as different lenses on a camera provide different perspectives, so do organizational space lenses. When a leader finds himself dealing with someone in another space he should try looking at the other person's situation through the Top/Middle/Bottom lenses and take the action suggested in Figure 7.5.

Figure 7.5. Lenses for Interacting with Other Organizational Spaces

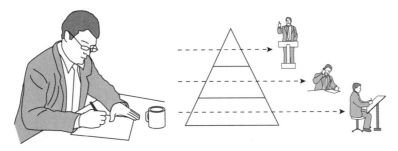

When you're dealing with	consider that they	and you might want to
Tops	Are up to their eyeballs in complexity and overload	Condense or summarize the information you're about to give Be responsible for following up so the Top won't have to Avoid just dumping problems on Tops' desks, and instead provide a briefing of problems, options, and implications for discussion Determine whether the Top likes to read new information before discussing, or vice versa, and then appeal to the Top's natural style to reduce complexity Be responsible for executing some of the tasks so the Top has fewer action items
Middles	Are often torn between having to side with the Tops sometimes and the Bottoms sometimes; in addition they often are caught in the middle of conflicts they should not be involved with	Propose that the Middle facilitate a direct conversation between you and the other party, thus not placing him "in the middle" Ask for coaching from the Middle on how to approach the other party so you can do it without the Middle's direct participation

Figure 7.5. Lenses for Interacting with Other Organizational Spaces, Cont'd

When you're dealing with	consider that they	and you might want to
Bottoms	Feel that they have good, workable solutions, but that they are usually disregarded; often Bottoms have a strong collective sense of "We" and tend to view interactions with management as We-They confrontations or negotiations	Acknowledge valuable contributions the Bottom has made recently Provide a forum for collecting improvement suggestions from Bottoms Recognize and celebrate Bottom contributions (both individual and collective) Coach Bottoms on how best to interact with Tops, if you know both parties involved Encourage Bottoms to take a "big picture" perspective when proposing solutions, thus making it more likely their solutions will be accepted

Getting out of the natural traps of the organizational spaces is not easy. At the heart of the effectiveness of this tool is the need for Tops, Middles, and Bottoms to commit to new ways of thinking and acting. There are *individual* commitments and *collective* commitments that each can make to enhance the success of an LSS/HPO. A summary of these commitments appears in Table 7.3.

Table 7.3. Individual and Collective Commitments to Success of an LSS/HPO

	Individual Commitment	Collective Commitment
Top	Create responsibilities in others	Understand each others' jobs and interfaces among functions to form a better Top team[i]
Middle	Coach parties on each side of them to interact more productively, while simultaneously maintaining independence of thought and action	Meet with other Middles to share information, solve problems, and plan for the future[ii]
Bottom	Be responsible for their personal condition and for the condition of the whole organizational system	Challenge the "we are victims" mentality that often surfaces in Bottom groups and strive instead to collectively make a difference for themselves and for the system

[i]Oshry, B. (1999). *Leading systems.* San Francisco: Berrett-Koehler.
[ii]Oshry, B. (1993). *In the middle.* Boston, MA: Power & Systems.

By making these commitments seriously, not just verbally, a leader opens the door to a wide variety of behaviors that support the new commitment. Some starter tips for each organizational space appear in each of the upcoming chapters dedicated to the respective LSS/HPO transformation stages. However, to get the highest leverage it is best to combine these starter tips with one's own ideas on how to live the commitment and then continually discover and self-reflect to reach ever-increasing levels of performance.

In addition to these tools for understanding conditions of and high leverage actions for Tops, Middles, and Bottoms, there is a powerful experiential exercise called an "Organization Workshop" that enables people to internalize some of these principles and practices. Lonnie Thomas, a senior manager at Boeing reports:

> In the Strategic Leadership Seminar taught at the Boeing Leadership Center, a segment is dedicated to understanding the Top, Middle, and Bottom spaces and associated high leverage actions. The group is taken through a learning experience where roles are assigned as a few Tops, some Middles, and the remaining class members as Bottoms. I was a Bottom. This experience left a profound learning with me. In a few short hours the senior managers assigned as Bottoms were transformed. We felt unimportant, not listened to, and had tremendous distrust of the Tops and Middles. We even formed a union and proposed a work stoppage until our needs were met. I highly recommend this workshop for people going through an LSS/HPO transformation as described in this book.

An excellent place for one or a series of Organization Workshops is in the Implementation stage. Some organizations also choose to run a short variation of the Organization Workshop for middle managers in the Design stage prior to the redesign of the organization into HPTs. To find out more about how Organization Workshops are tailored and used specifically for LSS/HPO transformations, refer to the website TopMiddleBottomLSSHPO.com.

The Leader's Integrated Work Plan Shaping and Quality Assurance Guide Tool

All important, time-consuming efforts in an organization, such as an LSS/HPO transformation, require a work plan that specifically articulates what needs to get done, who is going to do it, and when it needs to be done. In LSS/HPO efforts it's important to have just one master Integrated Work Plan that contains all the required activities. The trap that some organizations have run into is having one work plan for Six Sigma, another for HPOs, and perhaps yet another for change management activities. This approach is a recipe for disaster and holds the potential for overloading key people, scheduling important events on the same day, and making one work plan less important than the others, thus reducing the likelihood of people executing those tasks when time is tight. (Most often the change management work plan is slighted in these cases.) For these reasons an Integrated Work Plan is a necessity.

Basic Premises

The three fundamental premises for this tool are that (1) top leaders *don't* need to concern themselves with the development of the details of the Integrated Work Plan; (2) top leaders *do* need to be concerned that the Integrated Work Plan is of the highest possible quality since it will be driving the activities of the organization toward an LSS/HPO; and (3) it can be difficult for a leader to determine whether an Integrated Work Plan for LSS/HPO contains the necessary elements required for success, especially if the leader has not been through such an effort before.

The tool provides leaders with a set of questions to help shape the development of the Integrated Work Plan and perform periodic quality assurance checks throughout the LSS/HPO effort.

Elements of the Tool

Two types of questions are contained in this tool:

- Questions that leaders can ask that universally apply to all the stages, and

- Questions that leaders can ask that apply to a specific stage.

The universal questions appear in the top portion of the checklist, while the stage-specific questions appear in the bottom portion.

Coaching Tips

Leaders should convene project review sessions at the start of every stage and periodically within each stage. In these sessions it is helpful to ask the questions in Table 7.4 of the project manager or of the project team if it is a team effort.

Table 7.4. Questions to Ask of Project Managers

	Leader's Shaping and QA Questions
Universally applicable questions	Are the major deliverables and tasks in the work plan consistent with the organization's strategy at this point in time?
	Are the best people assigned to the tasks?
	Are any groups or individuals overloaded or at risk of burning out?
	Are celebrations of small wins as well as major financial gains scheduled?
	Is the project on schedule and on budget? If not, what are the plans for correction?
	Is the quality of work at this point in time sufficient to help the organization reach our overall goals?
	Is the project structured so that teams are collectively accountable for results (instead of individuals being accountable)?
	The activities that people are working on may be a *good* use of their time, but is it the *best* use of their time?
	Has anything changed since the start of the project that might cause us to cancel any portion of it?
	What have we learned about planning and executing the project so far, and how can we use that to improve future work?
Stage-specific questions	Questions unique for each stage appear in the Tools Application chapter for that stage.

Some of these questions seem like just plain common sense and a leader could be tempted to ignore them. But ask them anyway. In my experience sometimes the gap between common sense and common practice is huge. It's not unusual for day-to-day pressures, department crises, and organizational space biases to get in the way of even the best project manager's detailed work planning. Often all it takes is a gentle shaping question from a Top in a project review session to get the plan back on track. Table 7.4 shows questions that can help leaders shape the development and execution of an Integrated Work Plan. Stage-specific questions appear in the Tool Application chapter for each stage.

The leadership tools presented in this chapter will help leaders advance LSS/HPO objectives in four critical areas that need to be addressed. By using the Performance Framework Tool, leaders can plan and implement change strategies that are congruent among a number of interrelated performance factors. Leaders, of course, will have to deal with employees at all levels during the transformation. The Top/Middle/Bottom Space Analysis Tool helps leaders maximize their own potential in their space and also helps them in crafting messages and actions that will affect other levels. The last tool presented, the Leader's Integrated Work Plan Shaping and Quality Assurance Guide, will help leaders stay at the appropriate high level when discussing project progress and resourcing.

Notes

1. Pascale, R., and Athos, A. (1981). *The art of Japanese management.* New York: Simon & Schuster.

2. Galbraith, J. (2002). *Designing organizations.* San Francisco: Jossey-Bass.

3. Mohrman, S. (2002). The organizational level of analysis: Consulting to the implementation of new organizational designs. In R. Lowman (Ed.), *The California school of organizational studies handbook of organizational consulting psychology: A comprehensive guide to theory, skills, and techniques.* San Francisco: Jossey-Bass.

4. Personal conversation with John Lupienski on December 5, 2002.

5. LSS/HPO practices are not, of course, the sole or primary method for determining strategy. For organizations that have neglected strategic planning as a discipline, however, it can be helpful to use the LSS/HPO tools as a place to start. Used in conjunction with the Performance Framework, an organization can get a good start on understanding key external trends affecting it, as well as the interplay of its strategy, business processes, and structure.

   The methods outlined here are not a panacea for all that ails an organization. For example, they won't fix a poor marketing plan or poor market segmentation. The LSS/HPO planning methods should not be construed as a substitute for a comprehensive strategy development process. Excellent strategy books are available that cover the topic in detail. Some of my personal favorites are works by Gary Hamel and Henry Mintzberg, listed in the reference section of this book.

6. Mohrman, S. (2002). The organizational level of analysis: Consulting to the implementation of new organizational designs. In R. Lowman (Ed.), *The California school of organizational studies handbook of organizational consulting psychology: A comprehensive guide to theory, skills, and techniques.* San Francisco: Jossey-Bass.

7. This motivation may take the form of a supervisor breathing down an employee's neck, an external consultant threatening to expose an employee's inadequacies to his manager, a large bonus if a particular task is accomplished, or the intrinsic desire to make a contribution to the organization's strategic goals. While these motivations are quite different, each is valid, and for now we will not concern ourselves with the distinctions. Suffice it to say that some sort of motivation is required, and later chapters will draw key distinctions and provide practical implementation tips around the concepts of extrinsic and intrinsic motivation.

8. The Oshry research also discusses the organizational space of customers. For LSS/HPO transformations I have limited the discussion to organizational members experiencing the Top, Middle, and Bottom conditions. For an excellent introduction to all four spaces please see B. Oshry. (1986). *The possibilities of organization.* Boston, MA: Power & Systems.

9. Curiously enough, when researchers talk with Bottoms, they rarely have a problem with the term. In fact, to them it makes perfect sense and seems an appropriate way to describe their condition. Middles and Tops seem to have more of a problem with the term.

10. Oshry, B., and Devane, T. (1999). Organization workshop. In P. Holman and T. Devane (Eds.), *The change handbook: Group methods for shaping the future.* San Francisco: Berrett-Koehler.

11. Oshry, B., and Devane, T. (1999). Organization workshop. In P. Holman and T. Devane (Eds.), *The change handbook: Group methods for shaping the future.* San Francisco: Berrett-Koehler.

12. The final three bullet points and the adapted diagram, Organizational Spaces, are from B. Oshry and T. Devane (1999). *Collaborating for change booklet series: Organization workshop.* San Francisco: Berrett-Koehler.

8

Stage 1: Initiation
Activity Map and Leader To Do List

The journey of a thousand miles begins with a single step.

Confucius

IN THE INITIATION STAGE senior leaders take initial steps toward an LSS/HPO transformation. Most often sources triggering the need for major change are external to the organization and represent a sudden "call to arms," such as a new competitor, unfavorable benchmarking data, an FDA warning letter threatening to close a pharmaceutical plant, loss of government funding, or a merger. The call to arms may also be positive, such as a previously unexploited new market niche opening up that the company has unique core competencies to address.

But it's not always external forces that trigger change. Sometimes internal forces, such as a CEO deciding the organization requires dramatic improvement to survive or an internal company Six Sigma zealot conducting small, successful pilots, might launch the top leadership team into Initiation.

This chapter provides a preview of what's ahead for leaders in this stage. An Activity Map presents a picture of the sequence of major stage activities and milestones. The Leader To Do List presents a list of high leverage tasks that enable leaders to guide the LSS/HPO transformation smoothly along.

Activity Map

The Activity Map (Figure 8.1) shows major blocks of activity and their relative placement within the Initiation stage. Each of the three rows contains both LSS and HPO activities. The top row—LSS/HPO together—represents a strong

Figure 8.1. Activity Map for Initiation

LSS/HPO Combination	Stage 1: Initiation	Stage 2: Direction Setting	Stage 3: Design	Stage 4: Implementation	Stage 5: Operations and Continuous Improvement
LSS/HPO Together	A	A	A	A	A
Predominantly HPO Activities		B	B	B D	
Predominantly Lean Six Sigma Activities		C	C	C	

Duration	1–2 months	1–3 months	1–4 months	4–9 months	ongoing
Cumulative time	1–2 months	2–5 months	3–9 months	7–18 months	8–19+ months

Block	Key Milestones and Activities
A	Top management evaluates the appropriateness of LSS/HPO for the organization. Top leaders discuss this decision among themselves and may consult with other top leaders in different organizations or other outside expertise. If the decision to move in the LSS/HPO direction is deemed desirable, then top leaders form a coalition of enthusiastic supporters, develop communications about the change, and begin preparatory work for the next stage. The human resources group and top leadership evaluate the internal capabilities of the HR group to act as a strategic partner in the transformation.

combination of LSS and HPO activities and unfolding conditions. The second and third rows indicate a predominance of one discipline over the other, even though LSS and HPO elements appear in each.

Leader To Do List

In each stage there are high leverage actions leaders can take to influence transformation success. Throughout the transformation there are many demands for leaders' time, so it becomes important to organize and prioritize items most deserving of leader attention. A framework called the Transformation Grid ("Grid" for short) organizes Leader To Dos into six categories that provide focus for high leverage activities. Figure 8.2 shows a Grid with sample activities for Initiation. Leaders may wish to modify the content and activity placement in the sample to tailor the Grid for unique organizational situations.[1]

Activity descriptions for each high leverage category appear in the following sections.

Key Shaping Actions

During the Initiation stage there are four key shaping actions leaders can take to position the organization for the highest quality outcomes. The following section describes each of them.

Ensure a Business Case Is Made for Implementing an LSS/HPO

If leaders want the support of the workforce, it is essential they make a case about why the proposed upcoming change is needed. Based on lessons learned from a variety of industries, Exhibit 8.1 contains my short list of what a business case for change should contain.

Organize a Coalition That Supports the LSS/HPO Transformation

After the business case for change has been made, the next step is to organize a coalition for the change. Potential candidates should:

- Command a high degree of respect from peers and subordinates within the organization;

- Hold a position in at least the top three levels of the organization (starting a large-scale initiative like this will require wielding some formal power); and

- Be strongly in favor of the change.

Figure 8.2. Transformation Grid for Initiation

High Leverage Category	Stage 1: Initiation	Stage 2: Direction Setting	Stage 3: Design	Stage 4: Implementation	Stage 5: Operations and Continuous Improvement
Key Shaping Actions					
Participative Planning					
Process Awareness					
High Participation Restructuring					
Leadership Development					
Support					

	Stage 1: Initiation
Key Shaping Actions	Ensure a business case is made for implementing an LSS/HPO Organize a coalition that supports the LSS/HPO transformation Model open and direct communication with other senior managers, and have senior managers model it in staff meetings Develop a compelling change message
Participative Planning	Not applicable in this stage
Process Awareness	Ensure top management understands what a process is and its importance in an LSS/HPO
High Participation Restructuring	Not applicable in this stage
Leadership Development	Gain an understanding of the disciplines and transformation principles necessary to lead a successful LSS/HPO transformation Network with outsiders to obtain missing job or LSS/HPO knowledge Begin building self-observation, self-reflection, and self-correction skills Assign roles of internal champion to top leaders for a particular element of the transformation
Support	Develop a two-way, informal feedback system among change proponents and the rest of the organization Elevate role of HR to "strategic partner" and consider impacts on existing resources

Exhibit 8.1. A Business Case for Change Checklist

- ☐ The reason for the change
- ☐ The data and facts of the current situation that support the need for change
- ☐ Why the change is needed now
- ☐ What will happen of no change is made
- ☐ A stated belief that the change is possible
- ☐ Clear expectations for areas where possible (for example, financial position, competitive position, cultural changes)
- ☐ A vision of the future and what the change will look like (as specifically as possible, even though all details may not yet be available)

Although it may be difficult to resist the temptation, top leaders should *not* initially invite members of the senior management team who do not support, and may actively resist, the change. They can be brought into the coalition later, but initially the effort will need staunch supporters, and detractors can really slow or even kill the process before it gets off the ground.

Organizing a coalition can be a daunting task if only one member of the senior management team sees the organization's reality as dismal and has the vision to introduce radical improvements. It's easier if the person who wants the change is the top person in the organization (see Exhibit 8.2), although it is still possible to initiate and implement LSS/HPO if it is not the top person. Whoever the initiator is, he or she has to (1) help others to see the reality of the bad situation, (2) establish conditions for them to care about fixing it, and (3) have them participate in planning how to move forward.

Establishing an initial coalition of those dedicated to the change is an essential early step in creating energy for the change.

Model Open and Direct Communication with Other Senior Managers and Have Senior Managers Model It in Staff Meetings

Once a coalition of senior managers is formed, the coalition can begin one of the most important transformation tasks—reshaping cultural operating norms. One of the most important new cultural norms that must emerge is open and direct communication. By being honest and not dancing on the periphery of a key issue, leaders can get to the heart of a matter quickly. Such openness encourages others to behave similarly and break old speech and interaction patterns that may have existed a long time. Ray Alvarez did an excellent job of modeling these practices when he stepped in as general manager at Honeywell Micro Switch (see Exhibit 8.2).

Exhibit 8.2. A Pivotal Point in Organizational History

Ray Alvarez encountered a difficult situation when he moved from being general manager at Honeywell Keyboards Group to be general manager at Honeywell Micro Switch in Freeport, Illinois. A cursory review of the situation revealed slowing sales growth, customer defections to Japanese competitors, declining profits, and a dwindling customer base. After a tour of one of the three local Micro Switch plants, he was appalled at the loud, poorly lit environment that housed antiquated machines and air so thick with machine oil particles that Ray couldn't see more than ten yards in front of him. Talks with the workers indicated a demoralized workforce. When asked what he thought about the place, one worker replied, "I'm really thankful to have a job." The workforce was not exactly sitting atop Maslow's hierarchy of needs and primed for a fiery, grass roots, massive turnaround effort.

Ray surmised the current management team was out of touch with reality, complacent, or just hesitant to take decisive action to improve. He made it his short-term objective to show them the ugly reality of the situation. After that, he communicated that the transformation needed to start with the executives in charge. If the executives did not change their ways, he made it clear they would be asked to leave.

This account comes from J. Duck (2001), *The change monster.* New York: Crown Business.

All too often I have witnessed the following top management behavior. In a meeting leaders sit quietly, nod their heads yes, agree to high-level action plans, and then go back to their departments and do whatever is in their own self-interest, irrespective of commitments made in the meeting. Consultant Daniel Goleman dubbed this behavior "superficial congeniality."[2] Since LSS/HPOs are about speed, collaboration, and more effective business practices, superficial congeniality has no place in an LSS/HPO environment. This counterproductive behavior has to stop in the executive boardroom because executives set the example for workforce behaviors. Often top leaders can improve their behavior on their own through self-reflection, trying new things, and soliciting feedback. Sometimes tailored courses and coaching are needed to supplement individually paced learning. Such assistance may come from internal organization development sources or external third parties specializing in top management development.[3]

Develop a Compelling Change Message

Leaders need to develop a clear, succinct, motivating, easily communicated message about why the organization must change and management's commitment to making it happen. Having a logical, well-thought-out business case for change is only the first 20 percent of the communication effort to mobilize the organization to change in the Initiation stage. The remaining 80 percent consists of combining that logical element with an emotional appeal and making it clear to people that holding onto the status quo is not an option. Such a message is often called a "burning platform for change." The origin of the term came from Andy Mochan, who in 1988 faced certain death if he remained on a burning oil rig platform in the North Sea or possible survival if he jumped fifteen stories into the freezing water below amidst burning oil and debris and was rescued within twenty minutes.[4] He jumped and survived, and the term "burning platform" became an embodiment of the need to select one choice over another and the total resolve that is needed to back up that choice. In crafting the burning platform message, senior managers have found it helpful to consider the checklist in Exhibit 8.3.

Exhibit 8.3. Checklist for Communicating the Burning Platform for Change

☐ Use metaphors, similes, and visual images to help convey the message.

☐ Tell a story to get the message across.

☐ Appeal to people's logic *and* emotions regarding why the change is necessary.

☐ Include all the elements of the business case in the message.

☐ Talk about a few key possibilities of the future—not the numerous problems of today— to create conditions for motivation to change. (It's been said that it is easier to pull people into the future than it is to push them out of the past.)

☐ Include numbers and details people can relate to. Jack Welch's "Be number one or two in the business or risk being sold" got people's attention. Years ago Motorola senior managers set the goal of 10x improvement over a five-year period. After achieving that goal recently, Motorola set the goal of 10x improvement over just a two-year period.[i] Leaders need to consider that setting audacious stretch goals is fine, but they need to be achievable.[ii]

☐ Make it clear that management has the resolve to carry the change through and that staying the same is not an option for any member of the workforce.

☐ Develop a 90-second or less version of the message (sometimes called an "elevator speech" because it can be delivered quickly in the short span of an elevator ride).

[i]Personal conversation with John Lupienski of Motorola.

[ii]Collins, J., and Porras, J. (2002). *Build to last: Successful habits of visionary companies.* New York: HarperBusiness.

Getting many people interested in and actively participating in the transformation effort will be critical to its success. Businessman and consultant Marvin Weisbord contrasts the performance improvement efforts of years gone by: "We used to ask 'What's the problem, and how can we fix it?' Now people are starting to ask, 'What's possible and who cares?'"[5] This represents a significant mindset shift. While problem solving is still important, it's not the primary emphasis as organizations set to kick off an improvement initiative and do Direction Setting (stage 2). Early in the project it's more important to create energy about what's possible. In the Design and Implementation stage there are plenty of opportunities to address problems and useful Lean Six Sigma tools to do so. But early in the effort, a primary objective is getting people involved and energized around the effort. The development of a compelling change message is the start of that process.

The four key shaping actions for Initiation are important, but leaders also need to understand the concept of "process" as is an important foundation element for improvement.

Process Awareness

It is important that top management understand what a process is and its importance in an LSS/HPO. The concept of process is central in an LSS/HPO transformation. In each stage the organization needs to dedicate time to understanding, improving, and managing processes.

Since processes are so key to LSS/HPO success, top managers must be up-to-speed with at least the basics. Sources might include an external seminar, references in the back of this book, or conversations with peers at other organizations who have been through a similar transformation. Until leaders obtain more information, Exhibit 8.4 gives a solid grounding in the concepts.

Exhibit 8.4. Ten Process Fundamentals for Leaders

1. A process is a set of interconnected activities and decisions that transform inputs into outputs for a customer. Customers may be "internal customers" who work within the organization or "external customers" who pay the organization for goods and services provided.

2. Processes exist within a department, or may span departmental boundaries. In those that span departmental boundaries there are often great opportunities for improvement.

3. Maximizing one silo's performance often adversely affects other silos and the process outputs for a customer. For example, design engineers tend to like to design feature-rich products that may be difficult and expensive to manufacture. The problem: optimizing part of a process within a functional silo, instead of seeking to optimize the entire process that spans department silos and delivers value to a customer.

Exhibit 8.4. Ten Process Fundamentals for Leaders, Cont'd

4. Examples of processes in a manufacturing environment include production, new product development, order processing, strategic planning, and customer service. Examples of non-manufacturing processes, often called transactional or service processes, include loan origination, reservations, cash application, investigation report processing, on-site repair and service, clinical trials prior to drug approval, and software development.

5. Following in the footsteps of quality gurus Juran and Deming, leaders need to "blame the process, not the person." Juran asserted that 85 percent of workplace problems are in the processes that workers must follow. The remaining 15 perform are attributable to the people who perform the work. Deming believed the true figure was closer to 96/4.[i]

6. A bad process will beat a good person nearly every time. For this reason people at all levels of the organization need to be alert for broken processes. Good people showing up to execute bad processes every day not only affects the balance sheet and income statement, but also negatively affects employee motivation to perform, improve, and be accountable for results.

7. Processes that span functional silos are often invisible, fragmented, and consequently not managed.[ii]

8. All processes contain variation, and reducing unintended variation for key variables is an important LSS/HPO objective.

9. Processes contain two types of variation, common cause variation and special cause variation. Common cause variation is variation one might naturally expect from a process, for example, "the elevator in our building usually comes within one minute of pushing the call button, plus or minus ten seconds." Special cause variation is outside this typical variation, for example, "I pushed the call button three minutes ago and we only have a two-story building—something must be wrong."

10. Teams of people usually begin their understanding of a process by drawing process maps, graphical representations of the flow of activities and decisions within a process. Often great cycle time improvements are possible with this simple tool and related analysis.

[i]Scholtes, P., Joiner, B., and Streibel, B. (1996). *The team handbook.* Madison, WI: Oriel, Inc.
[ii]Hammer, M. (2001). *Reengineering the corporation.* New York: HarperBusiness.

Leadership Development

In each stage leaders need to continuously develop their leadership skills as they become "analyze-and-energize" leaders. In this stage leaders need to focus on the following for developmental purposes:

- Gaining an understanding of the disciplines and transformation principles necessary to lead a successful LSS/HPO transformation;

- Networking with outsiders to obtain missing information the leader needs to perform his or her job or specific LSS/HPO knowledge;

- Building self-observation, self-reflection, and self-correction skills; and
- Assuming the role of internal champion for a particular element of the LSS/HPO transformation.

Support

The support function provides additional leverage and benefits for the previous Grid categories, such as key shaping actions, participative planning, and process awareness. That support includes items such as communication, HR processes, and information technology support.

Develop a Two-Way, Informal Feedback System Among Change Proponents and the Rest of the Organization

Feedback on how the improvement effort is going, what people are feeling, and other key pieces of information will be critical for the leaders to increase their chances of a successful implementation. Effective ideas from previous successful efforts include:

- Conducting large group town hall meetings in which people can give reactions to messages delivered by senior management;
- Establishing a communication team and setting them up for two-way communications—the senior management message and people's reaction to it; and
- Setting up anonymous electronic or manual surveys to collect feedback.

Elevate Role of Human Resources to "Strategic Partner" and Consider Impacts on Existing Resources

If LSS/HPO is to be successful, there has to be a significant amount of strategic support from the HR function. Top leaders should assess whether or not existing HR personnel are capable of undertaking such a role and focusing more on "organization development" activities than on administrative and compensation design activities.

In 1986 collaborative research partners Columbia University, the Alfred P. Sloan Foundation, Carnegie Mellon University, and the World Bank conducted a study of human resource and economic practices in organizations. The study included 495 organizations and reached the following conclusions, all relevant to the role that HR will need to play in the upcoming transformation:

- Companies that share profits and gains with employees have significantly better financial performance than those that do not;

- Companies that share information broadly and that have broad programs of employee involvement (the researchers defined involvement as area of intellectual participation) perform significantly better than do companies that are run autocratically;

- Flexible work design (flexible hours, rotation, and job enlargement) is significantly related to financial success;

- Training and development have a positive impact on business financial performance; and

- Two-thirds of the bottom-line impact was due to the combined effect of group economic participation, intellectual participation, flexible job design, and training and development.

As if members of the research team anticipated skepticism about their findings, they went a step further, using statistical techniques to identify causal relationships between human resource practices and bottom-line performance. Thus, their conclusions demonstrate that not only do such practices affect bottom-line performance, but that they actually help to cause it.[6]

HR may need to play an entirely different role than in the past. If it is determined that there is insufficient internal capability to meet the new demand, a search should be initiated immediately to hire or contract with resources that can help in these key strategic areas.

 In the Initiation stage, leaders need to focus their efforts on the big picture that was provided by the Activity Map and on key day-to-day tasks, as suggested in the Leader To Do List. Leaders learned how to use the Transformation Grid to plan their activities for the upcoming work in the stage and monitor those activities to ensure adequate progress is being made.

Notes

1. For further information on uses of the Grid and content updates see TransformationGrid.com.

2. Goleman, D. (1997). *Emotional intelligence.* New York: Bantam Books.

3. The website www.PeopleSmartLSSHPO.com provides tips and learning sessions for open and direct communication skills tailored to LSS/HPO transformation efforts.

4. Conner, D. (1992). *Managing at the speed of change.* New York: Random House.

5. Weisbord, M. (1991). *Productive workplaces.* San Francisco: Jossey-Bass.

6. Maslow, A. (1998). *Maslow on management.* New York: John Wiley & Sons.

CHAPTER 9

Stage 1: Initiation

Tools Application

A man who dares waste one hour of time has not discovered the value of life.

                                                    Charles Darwin

IN THE PREVIOUS CHAPTER leaders learned about the major blocks of activities and specific high leverage actions leaders could take during the Initiation stage. This chapter presents key leader challenges and a set of tools to address them in a fast, efficient manner. During Initiation top leaders face the following challenges:

- Determining whether or not change is necessary;

- Crafting a message that can motivate others to change;

- Avoiding the natural tendency to postpone a major transformation effort because the top leaders' world is one of complexity and overload; and

- Establishing a general idea of timeframes and key people to head up various critical segments of the change.

Each of the tools described in this chapter will help leaders address the above challenges.

Performance Framework

During Initiation, the Performance Framework helps leaders:

- Analyze the organization's current state and articulate the desired state in the context of the performance factors (a large gap indicates a change to current plans is necessary);

- Prepare detailed plans at the start of each major change stage;

- Kick off and explain the entire upcoming large-scale change effort; and

- Conduct an assessment and lessons learned analysis at the end of each change stage.

In each instance above, leaders:

1. Convene a meeting and post a large Performance Framework flip chart on a wall;

2. Facilitate discussions about each performance element and key element interrelationships;

3. Record participant comments on the flip chart near the related performance factor being discussed; and

4. Ensure that meeting notes and action items are typed and distributed.

In addition, the tool can be used to illustrate which factors are addressed in this stage. Figure 9.1 shows the primary factors addressed during Initiation. Italicized comments appear adjacent to the factors addressed and describe how leaders address them in this stage. During Initiation the factors are primarily addressed through questions top management poses and discusses. Exhibit 9.1 describes how two leaders made a difference by taking decisive action using Performance Framework elements.

Figure 9.1. Performance Framework for Initiation

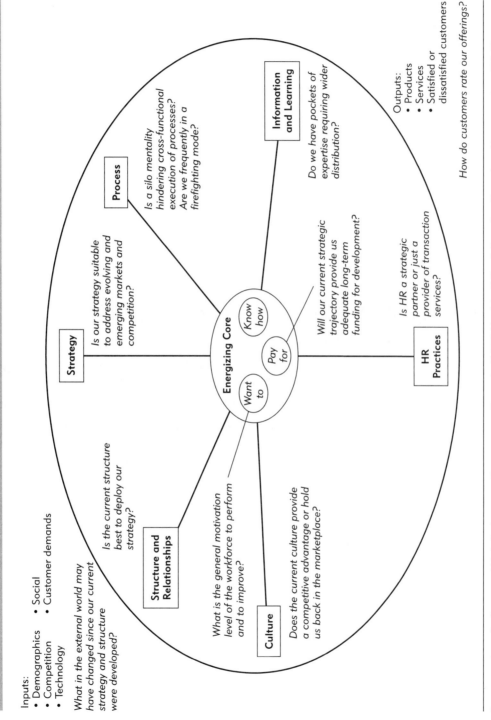

Inputs:
- Demographics
- Competition
- Technology
- Social
- Customer demands

What in the external world may have changed since our current strategy and structure were developed?

Strategy

Is our strategy suitable to address evolving and emerging markets and competition?

Structure and Relationships

Is the current structure best to deploy our strategy?

Culture

Does the current culture provide a competitive advantage or hold us back in the marketplace?

What is the general motivation level of the workforce to perform and to improve?

Energizing Core

- Know how
- Pay for
- Want to

Process

Is a silo mentality hindering cross-functional execution of processes? Are we frequently in a firefighting mode?

Information and Learning

Do we have pockets of expertise requiring wider distribution?

HR Practices

Is HR a strategic partner or just a provider of transaction services?

Will our current strategic trajectory provide us adequate long-term funding for development?

Outputs:
- Products
- Services
- Satisfied or dissatisfied customers

How do customers rate our offerings?

Integrating Lean Six Sigma and High-Performance Organizations. Copyright © 2004 by John Wiley & Sons, Inc. Reproduced by permission of Pfeiffer, an Imprint of Wiley. For more information, please contact the author at tdevane@mindspring.com.

Exhibit 9.1. Pivotal Points in Organizational History

Like other providers to the semiconductor industry, Credence Systems' test equipment business is subject to wild swings based on semiconductor market cycles. Some internal processes had problems that resulted in firefighting, and historically, large-scale process improvements remained elusive. In a downturn there was no money for process improvements, and in an upturn people were too busy.

Two visionary leaders, in Manufacturing and Finance, decided to break this cycle. During a major business upturn, they allocated time for the workforce to do process improvement, assisted by an external consultant. Within five weeks, output in a key area rose 90 percent. Because they addressed three Performance Framework elements—process (a bottleneck), "pay for" (cash for external help and ability to absorb a temporary production dip in exchange for sustainable long-term gain), "want to" (the desire to improve and accept short-term heat), the result was a resounding, long-lasting success for several semiconductor cycles.[i]

[i]Personal conversation with Mike Deal, senior director of product operations at Credence Systems.

Top/Middle/Bottom Space Analysis

The Top/Middle/Bottom Space Analysis helps leaders address two key Initiation challenges: communicating new mindsets and practices and managing reactions to increased participation. While the previous Performance Framework tool focused on performance factors, this tool focuses on people. It shines the light on where they are in the organization, their perceptual filters, and how they might best be influenced to enthusiastically participate in improving performance. By understanding the Top, Middle, and Bottom[1] organizational spaces, leaders can dramatically improve their leverage and accelerate the LSS/HPO implementation. This section contains an organizational analysis and recommendations for leaders based on the Organization Space concepts. The three topic areas presented here are (1) an *involvement profile*, which depicts the spaces' relative involvement in this stage; (2) *coaching for this stage*, which presents stage-specific insights for each space; and (3) *tool use*, which describes tool usage to address space issues.

Involvement Profile

The participation of the three position-based spaces are shown by shaded areas in Figure 9.2.

Figure 9.2. Participation During Initiation

LSS/HPO
Participation

The Involvement Profile shading indicates that not all Tops are yet actively engaged in the potential change effort. Some may not even feel the need to change. Gaining consensus on the need to change is a primary Top task in this stage.

Coaching for This Stage

Understanding leads to insight. This section provides tips on dealing with issues and interactions for each space.

What's Going on for the Tops in This Stage

The Initiation stage can be a turbulent, gut-wrenching time for Tops. To help Tops understand how to be the best they can be and also how to deal with someone in a Top position in this stage, this section contains organizational space concerns and issues, items for consideration, and practical tips.

Space Concerns and Issues   Tops feel a bit overwhelmed at having to make such a major decision. Implementing an LSS/HPO will require a lot of effort, especially from Tops who don't feel they have time to spare. There may be a tendency for Tops to say, "We have too much on our plates right now. We should postpone any major upheaval to the organization until things quiet down for us as a management team."

Items for Consideration   Things rarely quiet down for a Top management team. It's easy to get into "analysis paralysis" and stall making a decision for a quarter or two. That can be precious time lost for capturing additional market share and increasing profitability if the ultimate decision is to implement LSS/HPO. Senior management needs to decide, relatively quickly, whether such a transformation is really needed. If so, they need to initiate the change. Questions that can help Tops decide appear in Figure 9.1.

Practical Tips   Tops may want to contact Tops at other organizations, particularly connections they have in their own industry, and find out current industry thinking about Lean Six Sigma and HPOs. It can also be helpful to contact Tops in *other* industries and determine whether being the first to import LSS/HPO practices and performance would be beneficial.

What's Going on for the Middles in This Stage

Often Middles are engaged heavily in "firefighting" activities. Middles find themselves addressing problems that could have been prevented if they had had time, but there never seems to be enough time. There are too many fires that have to be tended to. Often Middles are frustrated because Tops override Middle authority and go directly to Bottoms when there is a problem. However, Middles are not yet involved in the transformation effort. Typical conditions and reflex actions are described in Chapter 7.

What's Going on for the Bottoms in This Stage

Many Bottoms feel they have some great solutions to workplace problems, but they are never listened to. Bottoms react differently to this condition. It creates frustration in some people, but causes others to "check out" and not care anymore about wanting to make workplace improvements. Bottoms are not yet involved in the transformation effort. Typical conditions and reflex actions are described in Chapter 7.

Tool Use

The Organization Space Analysis toolkit contains two tools: the Organizational Space Mirror and the Organizational Space Lenses. These practical tools, and the theory behind them, can be found in Chapter 7. The Organizational Space Mirror provides reflective insights into high leverage actions leaders can take based on an understanding of their space.

The Organizational Space Lenses help leaders consider space factors when dealing with others. The lenses provide insights into others' motivations, filters they use to perceive change events, and natural tendencies based on the space occupied.

By using the Organizational Space Analysis toolkit, leaders can sharpen their self-reflection skills as well as positively influence individuals and groups in the organization.

Integrated Work Plan Questions for Leaders

While previous tools focused on performance factors and people's filters and behaviors, the final tool in the leader's toolkit shines the spotlight on the approach to transformation. The Integrated Work Plan is the central document that ensures that activities for training, improvement activities, workshops, and meetings are properly scheduled. While the Transformation Coordination Team is typically responsible for developing and managing this document and related activities, Top leaders provide a very important quality assurance (QA) function by ensuring the plan is of high quality and can be executed.

This tool, explained in detail earlier, contains two sets of questions for leaders to ask: questions applicable for all stages and stage-specific questions.

Some questions may seem to be common sense, but often common sense is not common practice during high levels of activity and with multiple project priorities in an LSS/HPO transformation. By periodically asking the questions shown in Exhibit 9.2, leaders can gently guide the transformation along a swift and productive path.

Exhibit 9.2. Leader's Integrated Work Plan Shaping and QA Guide for Initiation

	Leader's Shaping and QA Questions
Universally Applicable Questions	Are the major deliverables and tasks in the work plan consistent with the organization's strategy at this point in time?
	Are the best people assigned to the tasks?
	Are any groups or individuals overloaded or at risk of burning out?
	Are celebrations of small wins as well as major financial gains scheduled?
	Is the project on schedule and on budget? If not, what are the plans for correction?
	Is the quality of work at this point in time sufficient to help the organization reach our overall goals?
	Is the project structured so that teams are collectively accountable for results (instead of individuals being accountable)?

**Exhibit 9.2. Leader's Integrated Work
Plan Shaping and QA Guide for Initiation, Cont'd**

	Leader's Shaping and QA Questions
	The activities that people are working on may be a *good* use of their time, but is it the *best* use of their time?
	Has anything changed since the start of the project that might cause us to cancel any portion of it?
	What have we learned about planning and executing the project so far, and how can we use that to improve future work?
Stage 1: Initiation— Specific Questions	Do all senior managers agree on the desired outcomes that will drive the next phase of work plan development?
	Who are the likely candidates at the next lower level to drive the improvement and restructuring efforts?
	Do we need to free people up entirely from their daily work to help drive LSS/HPO, or can the initial improvement driving team consist of part-timers?
	What is a reasonable end date, subject to revision after looking at activities in the Integrated Work Plan, for LSS/HPO to be implemented in this organization in consideration of the changing external forces affecting the organization, our competition, our customers, and the status of internal capabilities?
	Of the three typical project management tradeoff items—cost, time, and quality—do Top leaders agree which are the one or two most important for the organization (so that if tradeoffs must be made the Transformation Co-ordination Team and everyone else is clear on criteria selection for options)?

In the Initiation stage top leaders decide whether or not LSS/HPO would benefit their organization. If they decide it will, they embark on a path that will significantly impact people's ideas about accountability, performance, organizational culture, and day-to-day work. The tools supplied in this chapter enable leaders to make best use of their time and quickly achieve quality results.

The Performance Framework helps top leaders assess current and desired states of nine different performance factors, such as strategy, structure, and business processes. With the Top/Middle/Bottom Spaces Analysis leaders can examine their own and others' motivations toward change. Using the Integrated Work Plan Questions for Leaders, leaders can make sure they ask the right questions about the LSS/HPO approach.

The tools presented in this chapter, in conjunction with the pragmatic tips listed in the next chapter, provide leaders with an arsenal of ways to tackle the big issues that most commonly arise during Initiation.

Note

1. This model is based on over thirty-five years of research by Barry Oshry of organizational "spaces." An excellent introduction to the theory appears in B. Oshry. (1986). *The possibilities of organization.* Boston, MA: Power & Systems.

CHAPTER 10

Stage 1: Initiation
Pragmatic Tips

I must create a system, or be enslaved by another man's.

William Blake

THE INITIATION STAGE IS A TIME of strategic decisions. In the previous chapter leaders learned tools to help address Initiation challenges. Those tools can help shorten stage duration, enhance the quality of the stage outcomes, and reduce complexity for leaders. But tools alone are not enough. When leaders combine those tools with the pragmatic tips in this chapter, they can achieve truly superior performance. The contents of this chapter will help leaders "peer around the corner" and see what's ahead in the upcoming stage. By knowing common problems and high leverage opportunities in advance, a leader can plot a course of action at the start of a stage instead of having to react to events as they occur.

The key outputs and deliverables section of this chapter lets leaders know early in the stage what they should expect. Once leaders have started with the end in mind, they can direct their own and others' attention by means of some thought-provoking questions. While asking people questions is one effective way to engage them, increasing their participation is another. The next section presents a minimal set of gatherings—both small and large—in which people generate work products for the LSS/HPO transformation. In addition to generating high quality work products, these gatherings reduce resistance to change by eliciting genuine commitment through participation.

There is no single path to LSS/HPO excellence. To stimulate a leader's creative juices on how to adapt the material in this book to his or her situation, the next section presents some optional activities. While there is admittedly no single path to excellence, there are definitely common traps during this stage, which appear next.

For many leaders, LSS/HPO leadership is quite different from non-LSS/HPO leadership. In fact, some LSS/HPO mindsets and behaviors may seem downright counterintuitive viewed from "traditional leadership" thinking. This next section presents some of the more prevalent counterintuitive leadership elements and how to think differently in an LSS/HPO. As a final help to leaders in this stage, there is a leadership checklist of important items to consider throughout and upon completion of the Initiation stage.

Key Outputs and Deliverables

The list below shows what leaders should expect by the end of this stage. If sufficient progress is not being made on these items throughout the stage, top leaders must ask that the people responsible direct their attention to them immediately. Key outputs and deliverables for this stage are

- A decision—based on facts and analysis—by senior management to proceed with the move toward LSS/HPO;

- A guiding coalition has been formed and is beginning to enlist support of others for the change; and

- The burning platform for change, including logical reasons, emotional reasons, and a statement of management's resolve.

Important Questions to Ask

Instead of *telling* people what to think about and do, great leaders achieve organizational objectives by *asking key questions* that provoke thought and direct people's attention. Here are some important questions leaders should ask themselves and others during this stage.

Ask of Self

- Am I objectively looking at what's best for the organization, or am I taking a narrow view based on self-interest?

- What can I contribute that will significantly affect the performance and the results of the institution I serve?[1]

- In the long run, will what's best for the organization be best for me? If the answer is no, what choices do I have, and what am I prepared to do?

- Am I willing to bide my time until retirement, a steward of the inevitable, or do I want my presence at this company to have made a difference?

- If we decide to embark on this effort, will any personal transformation be required of me, specifically in the areas of leadership style and personal objectives within the organization?

- If the answer to the above question is yes, might this change be difficult for me personally, and if so, how might it be managed?

Ask of Others

- What does the organization really need in this phase of its development?

- Do we have a silo-based mentality? If so, is it hurting us?

- Would our organization benefit from increased collaboration in the areas of rapid decision making and generation of innovative ideas?

- Are Lean Manufacturing and Six Sigma becoming standards of process improvement in our industry?

- Are HPOs becoming a standard for organizing and creating an execution focus in our industry?

- If the answers to the above two questions are yes, should we consider implementing both Lean Six Sigma and HPOs simultaneously to gain competitive advantage?

In Initiation, top leaders benefit spending time in groups discussing their answers to the questions below. Their answers reveal assumptions about the workforce and affect leader behavior in the future. There are two reasons to explore these questions early in the process: (1) leaders need to know the governing assumptions of their peers to better interact with them during the transformation and (2) a preponderance of "no" answers would suggest that the organization *not* attempt to implement the HPO component of an improvement program.

Ask of the Senior Management Team

- Do you believe people are trustworthy?
- Do you believe that people seek responsibility and accountability?
- Do you believe that people seek meaning in their work?
- Do you believe that people naturally want to learn?
- Do you believe that people don't resist change but they resist being changed?
- Do you believe that people prefer work to being idle?[2]

These questions, first posed over a half century ago by Abraham Maslow and Douglas McGregor, form a great starting point for healthy, heated debates and dialogue about the workforce and subsequent approach to the change effort. Fortunately, leaders do not need to decide whether these are true for the entire human race—just for the majority of people in their organization.

While the HPO element of an LSS/HPO can raise organizational performance to extremely high levels and promote sustainability, this is only true if the leaders lean toward positive responses to the questions above. While some members of the top leadership team may change negative answers to positive ones over time, it is helpful if a majority answers the questions in the affirmative during Initiation.

Large-Group Interventions and Key Meetings

Getting groups of people to work together on critical LSS/HPO tasks is an excellent way to simultaneously accomplish four objectives:

1. Develop high quality work products for the implementation because of the diverse perspectives provided;

2. Achieve high levels of understanding among all participants about the topics discussed;

3. Increase energy and commitment regarding decisions made resulting from participation; and

4. Build leaders for the future by involving people in important discussions who might not normally be involved.

Large group interventions (LGIs) are methods for engaging large groups of people for a specific purpose. They typically involve over twenty people, a number far too high to utilize traditional meeting management and small group dynamics rules. LGIs are explained in greater detail in the Appendix. In addition to LGIs there are key meetings that are also important in advancing LSS/HPO and generating enthusiasm and commitment. Figure 10.1 depicts a sample sequence of LGIs and key meetings. Table 10.1 provides a brief description of each entry on Figure 10.1. Leaders can use the sample sequence as provided or develop another, more tailored approach.

Interesting Options

While LSS/HPO transformations will vary from organization to organization, successful ones are principle-based. Here are some optional approaches, based on the principles in this book, that some organizations have found to be successful. These are not mutually exclusive options. Leaders should feel free to use these or other custom-developed options to address unique local requirements.

Option 1: Dialogue

One interesting option for Initiation is to conduct a large-group intervention called "dialogue" with the senior management team. The word "dialogue" typically conjures up images of people talking about something in a give-and-take manner. This common use of the word should not be confused with the more structured LGI template called Dialogue (see the Appendix) in which participants use specific ground rules and principles to gain a shared understanding of a complex issue.

Figure 10.1. Large-Group Interventions and Key Meetings Map for Initiation

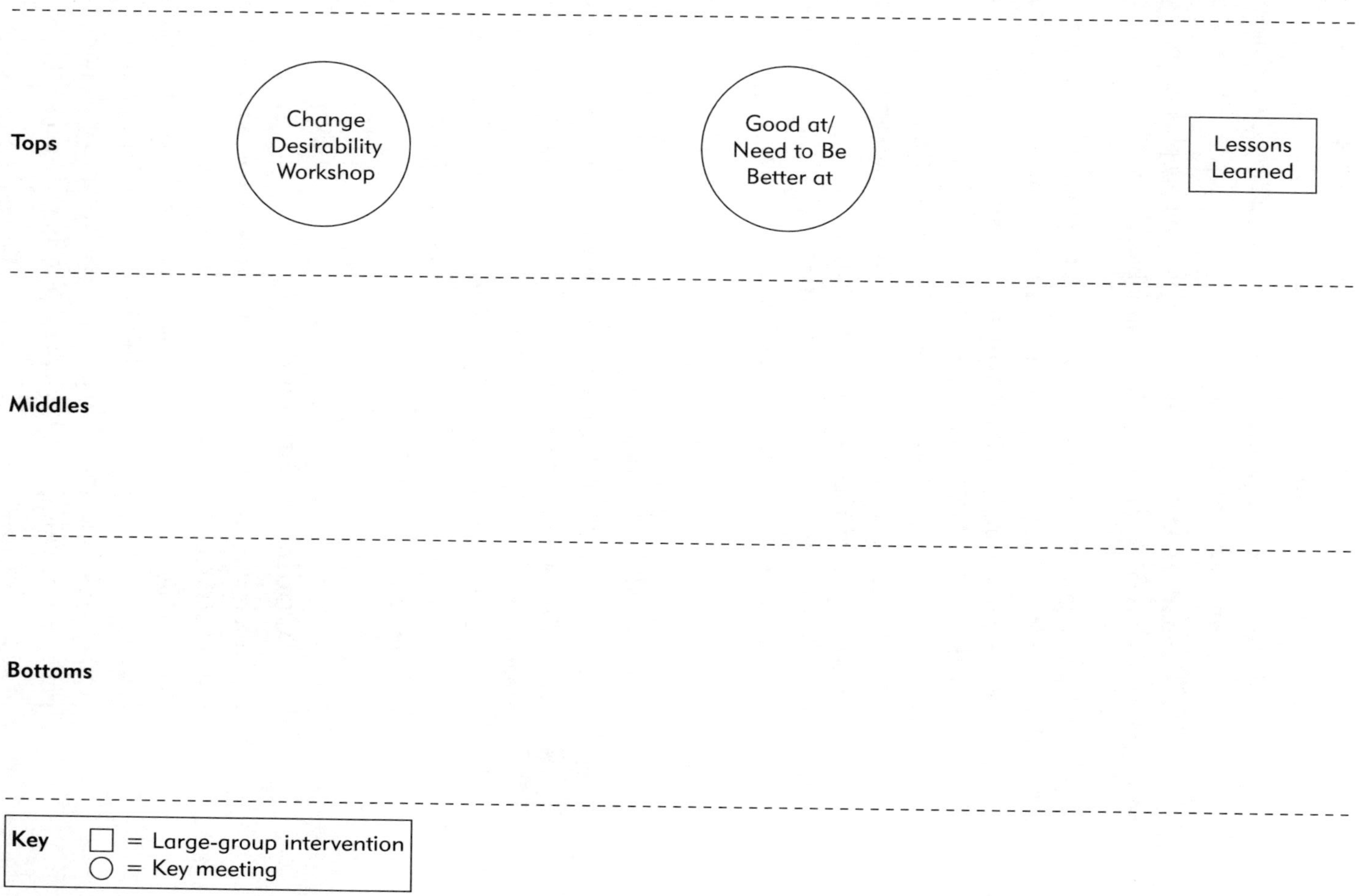

Tops

Change Desirability Workshop

Good at/ Need to Be Better at

Lessons Learned

Middles

Bottoms

Key   □ = Large-group intervention
       ○ = Key meeting

Table 10.1. Large-Group Interventions and Key Meetings for Initiation

Name	Gathering Type	Description of Key Elements
Change Desirability Workshop	Meeting	Senior managers meet to determine if the organization requires a radical business change that could be accomplished through LSS/HPO. The team identifies the organization's strengths, weaknesses, opportunities, and threats on separate flip charts and then looks for patterns or trends among the four lists. The team then challenges the validity of the organization's current assumptions about the organization's environment, the organization's mission, and the core competencies needed to accomplish the mission.[i] Collectively the team then develops answers to the following questions:
		1. Based on our current trajectory of where the organization is headed and what's happening in the external world, will we be where we need to be in three to five years with our current business practices and culture?
		2. Would we benefit from a more data-driven and execution-oriented environment?
		3. Is the pain of remaining the same greater than the pain of changing?
Good at/Need to Be Better at	Meeting	The senior management team meets to develop two lists: (1) what the organization is currently good at and (2) what the organization needs to become better at if it is to survive and thrive. These lists can later be used as starter lists for discussion when engaging other top and middle leaders.
Lessons Learned	LGI	The senior management team gets together at the end of the stage to identify (1) what went well in this stage and (2) what the senior management team might do differently in the future.

[i]These three challenges are adapted from P. Drucker. (1994). The theory of business. *Harvard Business Review*, September/October, 1994, pp. 96–104.

Option 2: Where Unions Exist, Involve Them Early

Additional advice includes:

1. The union needs clear goals that help define what they want. These should come from local union leadership and should be related to what the organization wants. Without a clear idea up-front, there will be problems sustaining commitments to joint work.

2. Delegates and shop stewards need to know how the upcoming changes will benefit the rank-and-file workers.

3. The workforce needs to understand the organization's economics, business issues, and external environmental pressures.

4. The union needs to know how the union strategy for change relates to the business the company is in and also relate that to the importance of what workers need.

5. Union leadership needs to be freed up to manage the change process alongside a management person being freed up. Rank and file members need to be paid to participate in problem solving and design team work.

6. Great results occur when the change process is conceived of and developed jointly.[3]

Option 3: Teams of Top Leaders Research Different Improvement Disciplines

Top—and sometimes middle—leaders would organize into teams responsible for researching different improvement disciplines such as Lean Manufacturing, Six Sigma, and HPOs. The research focus would be on results achieved by each method, foundation principles, culture required, and leadership actions required to maximize returns from each. Research teams would then present their research results, which would not contain detailed tools of the disciplines, but only the leader topics listed above, to the other top leaders, with organization implications for their organization.

Common Traps

Although no two implementations of LSS/HPO are exactly alike, some common traps exist. The ones most often found in Initiation are

- *Blindly accepting LSS/HPO without considering the organization's true strategic needs for change.* If the real issue could not directly benefit from an LSS/HPO (such as is incorrect segmentation of customer markets or a poor marketing plan), then LSS/HPO should not be considered.

- *Rejecting LSS/HPO because it looks like too much work for senior management.* The fact is that, by combining LSS and HPO, senior management will spend significantly less time supporting the effort after the Direction Setting stage than if the effort were either strictly a Lean Six Sigma or an HPO implementation. This is because the *motivation to achieve* is driven into the entire organization using HPO principles and the *methods to improve* are driven in using LSS tools and principles.

- *Rejecting LSS/HPO because it looks like too much work for the organization.* While there may initially be some additional activities required as people become skilled in problem-solving methods and better group dynamics, this time is soon recaptured as people begin to accomplish more in a day than previously possible because of better processes and improved collaboration. Productivity gains of 20 percent to 50 percent over a four-month period are not uncommon, which most senior managers believe is well worth the initial investment.

- *Avoiding or delaying LSS/HPO because it appears the payback period will be too long.* By incorporating Lean Manufacturing practices of process mapping and non-value-added analysis, the organization can find some initially *significant* gains quickly, usually in five weeks or less!

- *The top person trying to move ahead—even it it's the right idea—before there is a coalition of supporters.* In 1983 some senior managers at Xerox wanted to initiate a massive quality improvement effort.[4] One vice president wanted an immediate decision, while others favored waiting. They waited nine months to announce the program, and it proved extremely beneficial. By that time they were able to lobby to get the support of key opinion leaders in major business units and unions, and the effort proceeded smoothly and successfully.

- *Once a CEO states the organization is moving to LSS/HPO, others assume it is being done.* As Peter Drucker once commented, "At some point in time all great ideas need to degenerate into work." Great things just don't happen as the result of an announcement. There needs to be an integrated work plan that specifically states who is responsible for doing what by when and a mechanism in place to ensure accountability.

- *Deciding to simultaneously implement LSS/HPO across all locations in a large, global organization.* Not all CEOs should try to change an entire organization as Jack Welch or Larry Bossidy did. Organizations can see excellent results by implementing the same large-scale change one division at a time, or one large organizational unit at a time. Becton, Dickinson and Company, a $4 billion medical technology company, does not dictate improvement programs from corporate headquarters. Instead, divisions have a great deal of autonomy, which many insiders believe contributes to their excellent profitability. Some divisions now are implementing Six Sigma, some are implementing Lean Manufacturing, some are implementing the principles of HPO, and some are implementing combinations of the above. Although divisions are highly autonomous, the company has built a strong infrastructure for cross-divisional learning, and consequently best practices spread quickly.[5] This is an implementation template organizations may wish to strive for, instead of the "all at once with the standard approach" way of implementing a large-scale change.

Counterintuitive Elements

 Leadership in an LSS/HPO looks different than it does in traditional organizational structures. However, some of those differences are keys to LSS/HPO success. Table 10.2 shows three such elements often encountered during Initiation.

Table 10.2. Counterintuitive Elements in the Initiation Stage

Traditional Thinking	Counterintuitive LSS/HPO Reality
"Our people are busy making products and delivering services. I would be remiss in my duty as a leader if I pulled them away from the things that make the company money to do other things."	Time spent in learning process improvement, restructuring into HPTs, and designing an execution-based culture is an investment, not an expense. The returns are significant, from 35 percent to 300 percent—for organizations that implement LSS/HPO successfully. Without LSS/HPO, one reason people may seem busy is that they're spending excessive time on non-value-adding activities, for example, fixing defects, performing redundant activities, firefighting, and waiting to be told what to do.

Table 10.2. Counterintuitive Elements in the Initiation Stage, Cont'd

Traditional Thinking	Counterintuitive LSS/HPO Reality
"I want an improvement program that will slash cycle times in half and triple productivity so we can put ourselves far ahead of the competition. However, I don't want to disrupt the current organization in doing so."	Organizations don't get dramatic gains without dramatic, systemic change. Period. Leaders who think they'll reap radical, sustainable savings and revenue improvement by merely focusing on one leverage area, such as training a few people in process improvement techniques, are delusional. For big changes that last, leaders will need to carefully plan and implement changes to multiple performance factors such as the organization's processes, structures, compensation system, and culture so that all factors are aligned and each factor supports the improvement objectives of others. Historical experience and recent documented research show that organizations that implement large-scale change that addresses multiple performance factors perform better financially than those experiencing incremental or no change.[i]
"We're a services firm. We don't have huge amounts of inventory sitting around, so we wouldn't benefit from process improvement efforts."	Although services don't have inventory, they certainly do have their fair share of things that stack up. Paper. Requisitions. Reports. And they also have queue times. LSS/HPO principles and tools are extremely useful in non-manufacturing environments. Some situations are more complex, so service organizations benefit even more. For example, in the service industry, the customer is often also the supplier. The real value-added provided by a service company, such as a financial institution, is manipulation of information and then a return of that data to the supplier (now the customer). This is a much more complex relationship to manage than many manufacturing firms have.[ii]
"Putting in two large efforts such as Lean Six Sigma and HPO simultaneously will take an incredibly long time to get benefits. It would be better to do one, do it well, and then do the other."	In fact doing both simultaneously will require a shorter time to get benefits than the time required to implement both sequentially. The HPO component instills intrinsic motivation and an execution focus. The Lean Six Sigma component provides a discipline and set of tools that helps employees gain insights into difficult problems. Implemented together there is a synergy, and total implementation time decreases.

[i]Waclawski, J. (2002). Large-scale organizational change and performance: An empirical examination. *Human Resources Development Quarterly, 13*(3).
[ii]Personal interview with Rob Tripp of Six Sigma Consultants.

Leadership Checklist for Proceeding to the Next Phase

 Before the organization can move to the next stage of an LSS/HPO transformation, top leaders should check to ensure the items in Exhibit 10.1 have been completed. It can also be helpful for top leaders to refer to this list as the stage is unfolding to ensure that activities are started on time to produce the desired results before the stage completion. All Leadership Checklist items for the Initiation stage are the responsibility of top leaders. Other levels of leadership become involved in Stages 2 through 5.

Exhibit 10.1. Leadership Checklist for the Initiation Stage

By the end of this stage, top leaders have

☐ Examined the multiple factors of organizational performance using the Performance Framework Tool and developed a preliminary analysis and improvement recommendations for each of the factors, and the alignment of the factors

☐ Received a basic education in principles and best practices of LSS/HPO

☐ Conducted a high-level strengths/weaknesses/opportunities/threats (SWOT) analysis to determine the appropriateness of proceeding to the next step of implementing LSS/HPO

☐ Formed a coalition of people enthusiastically committed to the new change

☐ Gone through the exercise of asking what they personally really want and what the organization really needs

☐ Begun to identify sources of expertise for Lean Six Sigma and HPOs (perhaps an internal person who has experience, an external consultant, or an individual to be hired away from another organization)

☐ Initiated personal processes for self-observation, self-reflection, and self-correction; feedback from others is also included in this process

☐ Begun to practice and model open and direct communication so that they can successfully demonstrate this critical, emerging operating norm to the workforce

The pragmatic tips presented in this chapter can help leaders anticipate potential problems and exploit opportunities that arise in the Initiation stage. By understanding the key outputs and deliverables, leaders know what people should be working on throughout the stage and can suggest mid-course corrections if needed. The sample thought-provoking questions provided will help leaders and others think about important transformation issues.

Public gatherings and collective decision making are key elements of successful LSS/HPOs. In any large group setting it's important that the group becomes productive as fast as possible. To accomplish that, leaders can call on some standard templates called large-group interventions to help people be productive quickly and accomplish the objectives as quickly as possible. The large-group interventions and key meetings listed will help advance LSS/HPO objectives by quickly delivering high quality work products and generating enthusiasm and commitment to LSS/HPO objectives.

The path to a successful LSS/HPO is guided by principles and a flexible approach, not a cast-in-concrete process. This chapter presented some optional activities that have been successful for other practitioners. By studying the common traps presented, leaders can choose to plan for, instead of react to, problems others have encountered. To help ease the transition to new leadership practices, this chapter presented the most common counterintuitive leadership practices that appear during this stage. As a final help to leaders, there is a leadership checklist of important items leaders need to consider throughout and upon completion of Initiation.

Notes

1. Drucker, P. (1985). *The effective executive.* New York: HarperBusiness.
2. Maslow, A. (1998). *Maslow on management.* New York: John Wiley & Sons.
3. Personal conversation with Peter Lazes.
4. Nadler, D. (1998). *Champions of change: How CEOs and their companies are mastering the skills of radical change.* San Francisco: Jossey-Bass.
5. Personal conversation with Valerie Larson, corporate manager of organizational development, and Derek Wendelken, vice president of human resources, at Becton, Dickinson and Company.

CHAPTER 11

Stage 2:
Direction Setting

Activity Map and Leader To Do List

Everyone thinks about changing the world, but no one thinks of changing himself.

Tolstoy

DURING THE DIRECTION SETTING STAGE, the organization develops the details of its strategy, specifics of how it will achieve its strategy, articulates the transformation effort guidelines and boundaries, and charts a course for the development of senior managers into an effective top team.

This chapter provides a preview of what's ahead for leaders in the Direction Setting stage. An Activity Map presents a picture of the sequence of major stage activities and milestones. The Leader To Do List presents a list of high leverage tasks that enable leaders to guide the LSS/HPO transformation smoothly along.

Activity Map

The Activity Map (Figure 11.1) shows major blocks of activities and their relative placement within this stage. Each of the three rows contains both LSS and HPO activities. The top row, LSS/HPO together, represents a strong combination of LSS and HPO activities and unfolding conditions. The second and third rows indicate a predominance of one discipline over the other, even though LSS and HPO elements appear in each.

Figure 11.1. Activity Map for Direction Setting

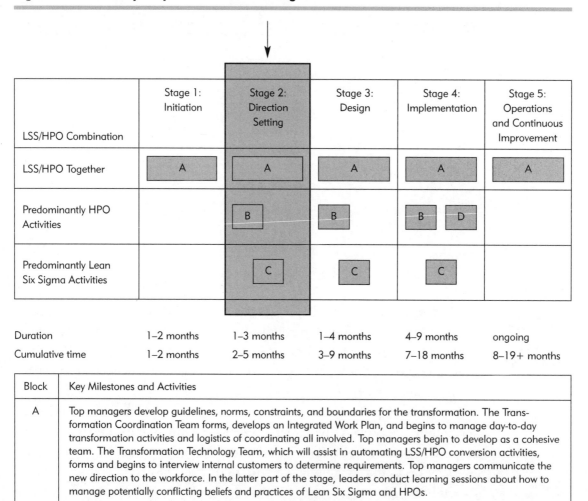

	Stage 1: Initiation	Stage 2: Direction Setting	Stage 3: Design	Stage 4: Implementation	Stage 5: Operations and Continuous Improvement
LSS/HPO Combination					
LSS/HPO Together	A	A	A	A	A
Predominantly HPO Activities		B	B	B D	
Predominantly Lean Six Sigma Activities		C	C	C	

Duration	1–2 months	1–3 months	1–4 months	4–9 months	ongoing
Cumulative time	1–2 months	2–5 months	3–9 months	7–18 months	8–19+ months

Block	Key Milestones and Activities
A	Top managers develop guidelines, norms, constraints, and boundaries for the transformation. The Transformation Coordination Team forms, develops an Integrated Work Plan, and begins to manage day-to-day transformation activities and logistics of coordinating all involved. Top managers begin to develop as a cohesive team. The Transformation Technology Team, which will assist in automating LSS/HPO conversion activities, forms and begins to interview internal customers to determine requirements. Top managers communicate the new direction to the workforce. In the latter part of the stage, leaders conduct learning sessions about how to manage potentially conflicting beliefs and practices of Lean Six Sigma and HPOs.

Figure 11.1. Activity Map for Direction Setting, Cont'd

Block	Key Milestones and Activities
B	Participative planning sessions set the direction for the organization's strategy, vision, and approach to implement the strategy. By expanding the circle of participation in planning sessions beyond the traditional "inner circle" of the organization, there is more widespread understanding, buy-in, and commitment to implementation. The Initial Restructuring Team forms and receives training to facilitate the organization in converting to HPTs and coaching HPT members and managers. Selected members of the Initial Restructuring Team receive training in LSS principles and statistical methods.
C	Employees close to customers create customer profiles that include customer characteristics, expectations, challenges customers face, and customer behaviors. Middle managers develop high-level process maps and Value Stream Maps™. Top management reviews the customer profiles, process maps, Value Stream Maps™, and industry trends and then evaluates candidate process improvement projects. Top management selects Champions who wield formal organizational power to help process improvement teams meet their goals. Top management selects Black Belts—those who will become expert practitioners of analytical and advanced statistical tools—to lead process improvement teams. Black Belt training begins. Selected Black Belts receive training in facilitating HPT design and coaching HPTs.

Leader To Do List

In each stage there are high leverage actions leaders can take to influence transformation success. Because there are many demands for leaders' time throughout the transformation, it becomes important to organize and prioritize items most deserving of leader attention. The Transformation Grid ("Grid" for short) organizes Leader To Dos into six categories that provide focus for high leverage activities. Figure 11.2. shows a Grid with sample activities for Direction Setting. Leaders may wish to modify the content and activity placement in the sample to tailor the Grid for unique organizational situations.[1]

Activity descriptions for each high leverage category appear in the following sections.

Key Shaping Actions

During the Direction Setting stage there are seven key shaping actions leaders can take to position the organization for the highest quality outcomes.

Figure 11.2. Transformation Grid for Direction Setting

High Leverage Category	Stage 1: Initiation	Stage 2: Direction Setting	Stage 3: Design	Stage 4: Implementation	Stage 5: Operations and Continuous Improvement
Key Shaping Actions					
Participative Planning					
Process Awareness					
High Participation Restructuring					
Leadership Development					
Support					

	Stage 2: Direction Setting
Key Shaping Actions	Understand and address forces that support and undermine successful LSS/HPO implementations Narrow the big picture focus to three to five areas Develop, communicate, and model new culture expectations Identify key first wave people Broaden participation in the change Deal with top leaders who are not with the program Communicate intentions numerous times through a variety of channels
Participative Planning	Select appropriate topics and timeframes for planning Scan the external environment and plan to adapt to and influence it
Process Awareness	Develop customer profiles that contain key customer characteristics Conduct process training for planning participants Begin using the word "process" in conversations daily Develop a Value Stream Map™ depicting a high level flow of materials and information for each product family Identify potential first wave projects
High Participation Restructuring	Not applicable in this stage

Figure 11.2. Transformation Grid for Direction Setting, Cont'd

Leadership Development	Begin to practice self-awareness and authenticity Conduct a formal leadership skill assessment to establish relevant development plans Obtain education in LSS/HPO concepts and leadership principles Model and expand the practice of open and direct communication
Support	Ensure training plans exist and begin for process improvement, HPTs, and leadership Ensure a communication plan exists and execution begins Ensure a sound, high level integrated work plan is developed Ensure a high level resource plan exists to compensate for the best people potentially being removed temporarily from current jobs Develop a strategic human resources plan that links key HR processes and functions tosupport LSS/HPO

Understand and Address Forces That Support and Undermine Successful LSS/HPO Implementations

Leaders and change agents can use a tool called a Force Field Analysis that illustrates forces that drive *toward* implementing LSS/HPO, and that work *against* it. Figure 11.3 shows part of a Force Field Analysis conducted for a financial institution considering LSS/HPO.

Figure 11.3. Force Field Analysis to Evaluate Ease of Implementation

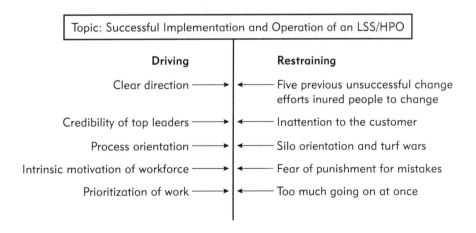

Topic: Successful Implementation and Operation of an LSS/HPO

Driving	Restraining
Clear direction →	← Five previous unsuccessful change efforts inured people to change
Credibility of top leaders →	← Inattention to the customer
Process orientation →	← Silo orientation and turf wars
Intrinsic motivation of workforce →	← Fear of punishment for mistakes
Prioritization of work →	← Too much going on at once

Narrow the Big Picture Focus to Three to Five Areas

When employees have more than five important concerns, energy is dissipated and results are diluted. Leaders may replace metrics once goals have been achieved each year, but for a particular year it's best to focus on three to five high-level organization goals, such as inventory reduction, zero defects, and improved customer satisfaction scores. These can then cascade down to HPTs, where they establish and monitor local congruent goals.

Develop, Communicate, and Model New Culture Expectations

Top and Middle leaders must actively shape and manage the new culture. Whenever possible they should talk about new culture expectations and model them. The workforce will always pay more attention to what top management does than what they say. Exhibit 11.1 provides an illustration.

Exhibit 11.1. Pivotal Point in Organizational History

In a process improvement workshop for an electronics assembly company, middle managers asserted that senior managers weren't "walking the talk" of quality. The four senior managers were truly shaken. They asked the middle managers if they really believed the senior managers wanted poor quality products shipped to customers. The seven middle managers, practicing open and direct communication, unanimously replied "Yes. In the past—and currently—we don't see any commitment to quality on the part of senior managers to ship quality products out the door."

The senior managers weren't sure how to respond, other than, "We do too care about quality!" As the facilitator, I asked the middle managers to consider "what commitment would look like" and then asked for a break so people could cool down and collect their thoughts.

When the middle managers returned, they had a list of five items, but by far the most important was the item at the top of their list: "Don't ship products if there are known quality defects." In the past there had been pressure to "ship the product no matter what." The VPs had talks with all their directors and changed this incorrect understanding. Within one month four products—each worth over $800,000 in sales—were held up and not shipped, causing the plant to miss its monthly forecast. Senior managers allowed time for problem-solving activities and were careful not to lay blame on individuals, but rather on the process. These departures from historical behavior sent a strong message to middle managers and lower levels that this time senior management was serious about quality. Quality levels and revenues steadily rose together in subsequent months.

Identify Key First Wave People

Top leaders select the first wave of Black Belts, the Transformation Coordination Team, Initial Restructuring Team, and Transformation Technology Team. The eyes of the organization are upon this first selected group of individuals so it is important that top leaders send the right message by selecting role models for LSS/HPOs.

Broaden Participation in the Change

To increase buy-in for the proposed new ways at this point, leaders include additional members in direction setting sessions. Most come from the Middle ranks of the organization, but occasionally there is some participation from front-line workers.

Deal with Top Leaders Who Are Not with the Program

In this stage it is important to bring top managers who are not in the coalition in. After some coaching, if they refuse to accept the LSS/HPO direction, they should be removed from leadership positions in the organization. Notorious holdouts of the old system are frequently human resources and finance departments. Their support is absolutely critical, so they must be supportive of LSS/HPO, or removed. This is far less painful for everyone if it is done sooner rather than later during the implementation. In 1986, then CEO of Motorola Bob Galvin made several requests of a successful Austin, Texas, division vice president to implement Motorola's new Participatory Management Program. The VP continued to refuse. Galvin relieved him of his duties. In addition to finding someone who would focus on increasing employee participation in decisions that affect them locally in this division, Galvin sent a strong message that employee participation was an important emerging cultural norm.[2]

Questions to consider in determining whether or not a senior management team member should continue on the top team include (1) Is he or she in favor of LSS/HPO? and (2) Can he or she be coached to co-lead the change and contribute? This should not become a personality contest or a search for the "right" leadership traits. Regarding characterizations of good leaders, management sage Peter Drucker asserts, "'Leadership personality,' 'leadership style,' and 'leadership traits' do not exist. Among the most effective leaders I have encountered and worked with in a half century, some lock themselves in their office and others were ultra-gregarious." In an interview with *Forbes,* Drucker goes on to contrast leaders with different styles and traits who were all highly effective. He concluded, "The one and only one personality trait the effective ones I have encountered did have in common was something they did *not* have: they had little or no 'charisma' and little use either for the term or for what it signifies."[3]

As he often does, Drucker makes a great point that seems to run counter to traditional thinking. This especially rings true for LSS/HPOs. A top leader with charisma is neither a necessary, nor sufficient condition for high performance. But if an LSS/HPO has a top leader who is charismatic, it can be very beneficial. It's a great plus, like having a patent in a niche market that no one else is in. A key strategy for that leader would be to focus on developing organization capability and improving performance for the long term without creating dependence on charisma. But lack of a charismatic top leader will not deter, nor will it adversely affect, LSS/HPO success. In searching for a final top team to implement LSS/HPO, focus on execution ability instead of a list of leadership traits.

Communicate Intentions Numerous Times Through a Variety of Channels

Senior managers should communicate an important message from five to eight times and through more than one communication channel. Exhibit 11.2 provides some thoughts for how leaders might communicate new messages.

Exhibit 11.2. Checklist of Communication Channels for Leaders

One-Way Information Sharing

☐ The company newsletter (paper or electronic)

☐ Brief voice-mail messages from top leaders when significant events happen that affect the organization

☐ E-mails to the general workforce

☐ Videotapes on key topics of interest

☐ Postings to the organization's intranet site

Information Sharing with Opportunities for Feedback and Dialogue

☐ Town hall meetings

☐ "Breakfast/lunch with the CEO" meetings

Exhibit 11.2. Checklist of Communication Channels for Leaders, Cont'd

☐ Kick-off sessions for participative planning events

☐ An intranet site dedicated to the LSS/HPO effort with posting capabilities for all, with options for both signed and anonymous postings.

☐ Meetings in which employees set goals for projects or teams

☐ One-on-one meetings

☐ An open door policy that encourages drop-ins from different levels of the organization

☐ Top leaders dropping in on training sessions and being available for questions and discussions

☐ Top leaders responding to employee e-mails

☐ A river cruise or other departmental event away from the office

☐ Lunch and learn sessions in which employees bring their lunches (or on some occasions the company may provide lunch) and listen to topics of interest, usually introduced by a top leader

Participative Planning

Because people tend to be more committed to something they have helped create, it makes imminent business sense to involve more people than just a handful of top leaders in planning the future of an organization. In addition to building a wider base of initial commitment, such increased involvement provides four additional benefits:

1. A greater variety of experiences and perspectives to draw on for developing plans;

2. The opportunity for developing mid-level leaders so they become involved earlier than they might normally be in strategic issues facing the organization;

3. A demonstration of confidence in mid-levels of leadership, thereby feeding the next generation of leaders; and

4. Modeling the emerging norm of collaboration in the organization.

Top leaders, of course, need to guard against people developing plans that make little economic or high level strategic sense. As Tops of the organization, these leaders most often have a big picture view of the market and external conditions that lower levels of the organization do not have. For this reason it's important that senior managers establish boundaries and guidelines for the participative planning sessions and allow people to plan within those boundaries. For example, a CEO of a software development firm established the pre-planning session boundary "To keep our scarce resources focused for the next three years we will continue to address our current market niches and not expand into other growth areas such as cable and telecommunications." This focused the attention of the participants and kept them from straying into areas the CEO knew would provide minimal value for the firm at that time. There are two participative planning activities on the Leader's To Do List in the Direction Setting stage.

Select Appropriate Topics and Timeframes for Planning

Participative planning events create energy and generate high quality products resulting from participant diversity. Three topics that typically benefit from participative planning events are developing transformation guidelines, developing transformation activity details, and developing strategic focal points and action plans for the direction of the organization.

Scan the External Environment and Plan to Adapt To and Influence It

Today's fast-paced business environment has mandated that the nature of strategic planning needs to change. Whereas previously organizations tried to predict the future and how they would fit into it, rapid rates of change now dictate that organizations must develop the ability to sense what is occurring in the external environment and quickly respond.[4] Planning sessions in this stage do that. And for organizations bold enough to attempt it, they can sense and even try to shape the direction of their entire industry, as Dell, Wal-Mart, and Microsoft have.

Process Awareness

As mentioned in Chapter 8, the concept of a business process is a cornerstone of a successful LSS/HPO transformation. In fact, the central theme of a process appears in Lean Six Sigma efforts implemented independently of HPO efforts and in HPO efforts implemented independently of Lean Six Sigma efforts. The five Leadership To Do items for Process Awareness are described in this section.

Develop Customer Profiles That Contain Key Customer Characteristics

Use interviews and past data to create customer profiles that include items such as customer characteristics, expectations, customer challenges, purchasing patterns, and customer behaviors. Many organizations use their business processes as a starting point to examine customer requirements. I advocate the reverse order. Existing processes may require elimination, not improvement. Or processes may need to be created to address emerging customer needs. Teams rarely reach such radical conclusions if existing processes are taken as "givens." By first developing customer profiles and then evaluating processes in that context, organizations can save time trying to improve processes that perhaps should not exist at all, or that should be so dramatically changed that a "blank sheet of paper" approach is the best place to start.

Conduct Process Training for Planning Participants

As the concept of process is an integral part of LSS/HPO performance, leaders need to ensure that all participants in planning sessions understand the basics of analyzing, improving, and managing business processes.

Begin Using the Word "Process" in Conversations Daily

When Bob Nardelli moved from General Electric to become CEO of The Home Depot, he brought along many concepts and tools to improve profits of the ailing retailer. Repetition of terms was one way he put his message across. "Told that Home Depot execs in meetings with Nardelli are counting the number of times that he says 'process,' Nardelli chuckles. 'Well, if you're hearing that,' he says, 'my message is getting across.'"[5]

Develop a Value Stream Map™ Depicting a High Level Flow of Materials and Information for Each Product Family

A great tool for identifying waste and reducing cycle time for key production processes is a Lean tool called a Value Stream Map,™[6] a visual depiction of the flow of materials and information required to build a family of like products. The results of a Value Stream Analysis and an analysis of the organization's high level process maps provide input to the selection process for first wave projects and also provide inputs for restructuring into HPTs.

Identify Potential First Wave Projects

During the Direction Setting stage, leaders need to select an initial set of improvement projects—often referred to as the "first wave"—that will address performance challenges. Critical performance areas will vary by organization, but in general include customer satisfaction, speed, cost, revenue enhancement, and internal quality. Leaders can use the checklist in Exhibit 11.3 to help evaluate improvement projects. In this stage it is important to bring people from the finance function in to help with the payback analyses. Leaders should not limit initial projects to cost reductions in production processes. Revenue processes can provide extremely high leverage returns. As Raytheon found out, there can also be hidden opportunities in less noticeable processes such as supply chain management, intellectual property, and human resources processes.[7]

Exhibit 11.3. Checklist for Evaluating and Selecting Improvement Projects

☐ Amount of payback

☐ Contribution to the organization's strategic goals

☐ Speed of payback

☐ Capability of improvement team members in the areas of:

- Process improvement

- Project management

- Change management

- Motivation of team members

☐ Availability of potential team members with necessary skills and knowledge

☐ Ease of containing the project within the initial scope

☐ Place on the ladder of problem complexity

☐ Availability of data

☐ Probability of success

☐ Publishability of results (the organization may not want sensitive data published)

Leadership Development

In each stage leaders need to continuously develop their leadership skills as they become "analyze-and-energize" leaders. In this stage leaders need to focus on the following four topics for developmental purposes.

Practice Self-Awareness and Authenticity

One of the most important things a leader needs to do is understand his or her own strengths, weaknesses, and personal objectives. Extensive research in the area of emotional intelligence supports the importance of such an introspective look.[8] Leaders seldom take time for this, however. According to Warren Bennis, leaders need to take advantage of their strengths and make their weaknesses irrelevant. The senior management team at Mary Kay Cosmetics has gone so far as to formally assess and discuss the strengths and weaknesses of every senior management team member, so they can capitalize on their strengths and cover for one another's weaknesses.[9]

Being authentic is essential to a leader's credibility. For leaders who find authenticity difficult, Exhibit 11.4 presents some very simple, but highly effective tactics for increasing leader credibility and trust.

Exhibit 11.4. Tips for Increasing Credibility and Trust

- ☐ If you're pleased with someone's work, say so
- ☐ If you're upset at something, express that
- ☐ If you're sorry something turned out the way it did, let the other person know
- ☐ If you're angry, say so and say why
- ☐ If you don't know something, admit it and say you'll find out and get back to people, or enlist the other's help and recommend that you figure it out together

Conduct a Formal Leadership Skill Assessment to Establish Relevant Development Plans

Formal skill assessments of the top and middle leadership teams can help target the greatest areas of need for training, coaching, and job rotation assignments. Using an electronic or web-based assessment tool can help accelerate the process.[10] There should also be post-training and post-coaching assessments that assess knowledge of the material, new behaviors, and business impacts.

Obtain Education in LSS and HPO Concepts and Leadership Principles

For Top leaders to ignite the fires of change and subsequently fan them effectively, they will require two types of training in LSS and HPOs: (1) the fundamentals of the disciplines and (2) questions leaders should ask of improvement teams and middle managers. Leaders should avoid courses that teach details of tool usage, as leaders will likely not be using detailed tools.

Model and Expand the Practice of Open and Direct Communication

Open and direct communication is the linguistic bedrock for increased levels of trust, healthy collaboration, and more rapid decision making in an LSS/HPO. In this stage, leaders should model open communication in order to create safe conditions for others to practice these new skills. Helena Dolny, managing director of the Land Bank of South Africa, did just this at the kickoff meeting for their strategic transformation initiative. In one segment of the workshop, each of the five subgroups was asked to draw the animal they felt most closely resembled their experience with the Land Bank.

> "One group drew a rhinoceros standing in water with small fish swimming between its legs. Their rational was that, first of all, it was an African animal that dates back a long while, but hasn't evolved greatly. It was like the Bank in that it had a thick skin—impervious to criticism; its small ears represented the Bank as short on listening skills. The other features were: poor eyesight/narrow vision, demarcates its area, a limited diet, a threatened species, and moves very slowly, except when angry. The numerous small fish represented a staff who currently felt they could not make any real impact on the behavior of the rhinoceros."[11]

Other animals selected were an ostrich and a tortoise. Each group report-out had an equally insightful, amusing, honest, and self-critical set of observations. Dolny commended the group for their honesty and engaged them in determining what to do about turning around the current situation. The new norm of open and direct communication began to make its way throughout the organization.

Support

The support function provides additional leverage and benefits for the previous Grid categories: key shaping actions, participative planning, and process awareness. That support includes items such as communication, HR processes, and information technology support. In this section there are no support activities for which top leaders are directly responsible. Rather, top leaders need to ensure that the following five support activities are happening.

Ensure Training Plans Exist and Begin for Process Improvement, HPTs, and LSS/HPO Leadership

It will be important for the identified audiences to receive this training immediately before they will use it. It's acceptable for external consultants to train Black Belts, but I recommend an organization's Black Belts or Master Black Belts provide all training for Green Belts. This strategy causes Green Belts to turn to internal Black Belts and Master Black Belts as the trusted experts, instead of turning to outside consultants. The members of the Initial Restructuring Team, those who will be leading the workshops to design HPTs and initially teach new team members how to work in HPTs, will require five to eight days of training, plus one or two apprenticeship sessions. This training is typically provided by external consultants or by internal people experienced in HPT design and management.

Ensure a Communication Plan Exists and Execution Begins

In the Direction Setting stage, it is critical that top leaders communicate the upcoming changes to the workforce. The best way to ensure that key messages are delivered to the appropriate people at the right time using the optimal communication channels is to have a communication plan. A sample template appears in Table 11.1.

Table 11.1. Communication Plan Template

	Message	Responsibility	Channels	Frequency	Measure of Success	Date(s)	Feedback
1.							
2.							
3.							
4.							
5.							
6.							
7.							
8.							

CEOs need to help communicate key messages and set the tone for open communication. Some may balk at this because of other high-priority tasks, but these responsibilities can not be delegated. Sun Microsystems CEO Scott McNealy receives, reads, and answers e-mails from employees at all levels of the organization. Unlike at many large organizations, such communications are not discouraged. Sometimes McNealy will even circulate certain employee messages around the senior leadership that are of particular interest to him. In addition, once a month McNealy interviews customers, employees, and analysts live on "The McNealy Reports," an in-house radio talk show available on Sun's Intranet.[12] The result is a culture that places a high value on communication and openness, and a workforce that feels in touch *daily* with the strategy of the organization. Few organizations can boast that kind of communications excellence.

Another important item that must be developed is an Integrated Work Plan.

Ensure a Sound, High Level Integrated Work Plan Is Developed

Many activities and resources are required to raise an organization's performance through an LSS/HPO, and these all require coordination. The Integrated Work Plan provides that coordination. (A detailed description of the Integrated Work Plan is in Chapter 7.) Top leaders need to ensure that the Transformation Coordination Team prepares one integrated plan to coordinate all transformation tasks.

Develop a High Level Resource Plan to Compensate for the Best People Potentially Being Removed Temporarily from Current Jobs

The organization will be taking some of the best people out of their current jobs and most often there will be no backfill. In this stage the HR group typically develops plans for how to remove these people with as little disruption to operational performance as possible.

Develop a Strategic Human Resources Plan That Links Key HR Processes and Functions to Support LSS/HPO

In this stage the HR group must identify the processes that will be used to support the new high performance environment. In addition to identifying the processes, it's important to articulate the interrelationships of these processes and other key factors. For example, Operational Management International, Inc. (OMI), a 2000 Baldrige Award winner involved in water treatment and types of environmental protection, has developed a model that articulates the relationship of the corporate strategy; associate performance; training needs assessment; job description; recognition, compensation, and bonuses; training plan; assessment and succession; and continuous improvement activities.[13]

Such a model is extremely important for preparing the human resources support necessary for the upcoming changes.

 In the Direction Setting stage leaders need to focus their efforts on the big picture that was provided by the Activity Map and on key day-to-day tasks as suggested in the Leader To Do List. Leaders learned how to use the Transformation Grid tool to plan their activities for the upcoming work in the stage and monitor those activities to ensure adequate progress is being made.

Notes

1. For further information on uses of the Grid and content updates see TransformationGrid.com.

2. Personal conversation with John Lupienski of Motorola, December 5, 2002.

3. Peter Drucker, quoted in G. Rifkin (1996, April 8), Leadership: Can it be learned? *Forbes.*

4. Haekel, S. (1999). *Adaptive enterprise: Creating and leading sense-and-respond organizations.* Boston, MA: Harvard Business School Press.

5. Sellers, P. (2001, March 19). Exit the builder, enter the repairman. *Fortune.*

6. Rother, M., and Shook, J. (1999). *Learning to see: Value stream mapping to create value and eliminate mud.* Brookline, MA: The Lean Enterprise Institute.

7. Personal interview with Mike Grimm, Six Sigma Expert at Raytheon in Tucson, Arizona.

8. Goleman, D. (1997). *Emotional intelligence.* New York: Bantam Books.

9. Jick, T., and Allen, N. (1987). Mary Kay Cosmetics No. 2: Question and answer session with second year MBA students [Video]. Boston, MA: Harvard Business School.

10. For assessment tools, please see LSSHPOAssessments.com.

11. Dolny, H. (2001). *Banking on change.* London: Penguin.

12. Personal conversation with David Adrian of Sun Microsystems, December 4, 2002.

13. Personal conversation with Gary Hunt, vice president of HR, administration, and MIS at OMI.

CHAPTER 12

Stage 2: Direction Setting

Tools Application

A good plan violently executed right now is far better than a perfect plan executed next week.

General George Patton

IN THE PREVIOUS CHAPTER leaders learned about the major blocks of activities and specific high leverage actions they could take during the Direction Setting stage. This chapter presents key leader challenges and a set of tools to address them. Because of the activities on multiple, varied fronts, this stage poses some unique challenges for leaders:

- *Combining quality direction and speed.* If the direction for the business and the transformation are not well-defined, serious problems will result. Two key future activities—process improvement projects and restructuring into high-performance teams—are based on the directions set in this stage. However, leaders need to balance development of a "good plan" with "over-planning."

- *Communicating the direction.* The workforce must share a common understanding or people may work toward conflicting goals.

- *Managing workforce reactions to increased participation in planning.* Early stages of an LSS/HPO transformation offer opportunities for middle managers and even lower levels of the organization to participate in activities traditionally thought of as "senior management" activities. Reactions will range from caution to skepticism.

- *Ensuring the overall game plan is not missing key elements.* The Integrated Work Plan is the master guide of what needs to be done. The plan must be sound.

Each of the tools described in Chapter 11 will help leaders address the above challenges.

Performance Framework

 During Direction Setting, the Performance Framework helps leaders accelerate the development of plans by providing a way to ensure all key performance elements have been addressed; communicate the comprehensiveness of plans to the workforce, thereby increasing buy-in likelihood; and gain insights during a lessons learned analysis at stage completion.

For each, leaders must:

1. Convene a meeting and post a large Performance Framework flip chart on a wall;

2. Facilitate discussions about each performance element and about interrelationships of key elements;

3. Record participant comments on the flip chart near the related performance factor being discussed; and

4. Ensure that meeting notes and action items are typed and distributed.

In addition, the tool can be used to illustrate which factors are addressed in this stage. Figure 12.1 shows the primary factors addressed during Direction Setting. Italicized comments appear adjacent to the factors and describe how they are addressed in this stage.

Figure 12.1. Performance Framework for Direction Setting

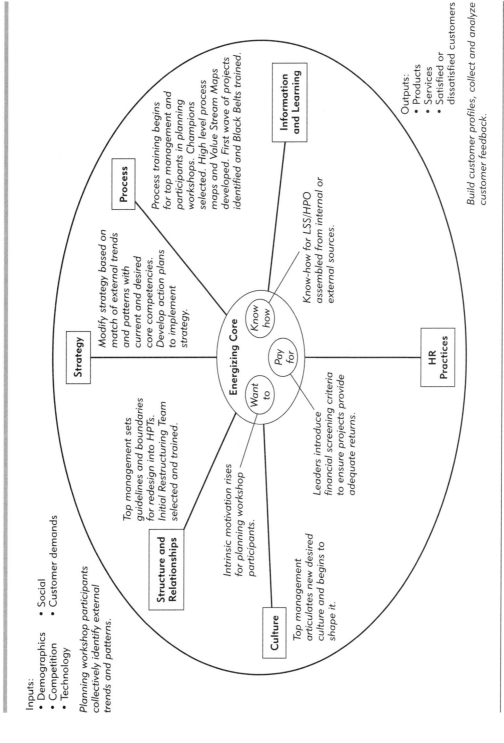

Inputs:
- Demographics
- Competition
- Technology
- Social
- Customer demands

Planning workshop participants collectively identify external trends and patterns.

Strategy

Modify strategy based on match of external trends and patterns with current and desired core competencies. Develop action plans to implement strategy.

Process

Process training begins for top management and participants in planning workshops. Champions selected. High level process maps and Value Stream Maps developed. First wave of projects identified and Black Belts trained.

Information and Learning

Know-how for LSS/HPO assembled from internal or external sources.

Outputs:
- Products
- Services
- Satisfied or dissatisfied customers

Build customer profiles, collect and analyze customer feedback.

Energizing Core

Know how

Pay for

Want to

Structure and Relationships

Top management sets guidelines and boundaries for redesign into HPTs. Initial Restructuring Team selected and trained.

Intrinsic motivation rises for planning workshop participants.

Culture

Top management articulates new desired culture and begins to shape it.

Leaders introduce financial screening criteria to ensure projects provide adequate returns.

HR Practices

Integrating Lean Six Sigma and High-Performance Organizations. Copyright © 2004 by John Wiley & Sons, Inc. Reproduced by permission of Pfeiffer, an Imprint of Wiley. For more information, please contact the author at tdevane@mindspring.com.

Top/Middle/Bottom Space Analysis

The Top/Middle/Bottom Space Analysis helps leaders address two key Direction Setting challenges: (1) communicating new mindsets and practices and (2) managing reactions to increased participation. While the previous Performance Framework tool focused on performance factors, this tool focuses on people. It shines the light on where they are in the organization, their perceptual filters, and how they might best be influenced to participate enthusiastically in improving performance. By understanding the Top, Middle, and Bottom[1] organizational spaces, leaders can dramatically improve their leverage and accelerate the LSS/HPO implementation. This section contains an organizational analysis and recommendations for leaders based on the organization space concepts presented earlier, the *involvement profile*, which depicts the spaces' relative involvement in this stage; *coaching for this stage*, which presents stage-specific insights for each space; and *tool use*, which describes tool usage to address space issues.

Involvement Profile

The participation of the three position-based spaces is shown by the shaded area in Figure 12.2. The Involvement Profile shows that nearly all Tops are actively engaged in LSS/HPO at this point. Middles are involved in both, although more Middles are involved in HPO activities such as participative planning. Some Bottoms may be involved in participative planning, although no Bottoms are yet involved in LSS activities.

Figure 12.2. Participation During Direction Setting

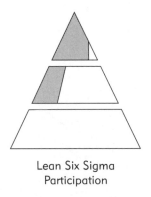

Lean Six Sigma
Participation

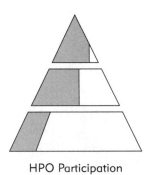

HPO Participation

Coaching for This Stage

Understanding leads to insight. This section provides tips on dealing with issues and interactions for each space.

What's Going on for the Tops in This Stage

Direction Setting can be a hectic, rapid-paced time for Tops. To help leaders understand how to be the best Top one can be and also how to deal with someone in a Top position in this stage, this section contains organizational space concerns and issues, items for consideration, and practical tips.

Organizational Space Concerns and Issues   There is a lot to plan, and it must be done quickly to initiate and sustain momentum. Tops must demonstrate active commitment. Among Tops there is an understanding that they are on the cusp of a major direction change (one executive described it to me as "like jumping out of a plane").

Items for Consideration   Early in the transformation the organization needs the most support from the Tops of the organization. As the LSS/HPO migration proceeds, less Top time is required.

Practical Tips   Some practical tips for Tops during Direction Setting are listed below:

- Use large-group forums, such as town hall meetings, to reach the maximum number of people at once. Follow-up small group discussions and one-on-ones can be pursued to reinforce the messages from the large group.

- Ensure that conditions exist for development of a good vision and strategy. Subsequent stages will require solid direction.

- Meet with key implementation groups such as the Transformation Coordination Team (TCT), Black Belts (BBs), and Initial Restructuring Team (IRT) to ensure these groups understand Tops' vision and boundaries.

- Gain cooperation from Middles, which is absolutely critical for success in the Design and Implementation stages. Meet with many Middles, seek their advice, and share selected information about upcoming events.

- It can also be helpful to engage in a hobby outside of work to relax and take one's mind off the day's activities. One of the most successful Tops I know regularly participated in t'ai chi sessions twice a week after work at the height of the transformation to regain inner calmness.

What's Going on for the Middles in This Stage

The Direction Setting stage can be a confusing time for Middles and an emotional roller coaster. To help you understand how to be the best Middle one can be and also how to deal with someone in a Middle position in this stage, here are some organizational space concerns and issues, items for consideration, and practical tips.

Organizational Space Concerns and Issues   In the Direction Setting stage Middles are torn between the Tops who have announced the upcoming change and the Bottoms who are skeptical that anything will change. Many Bottoms have already lived through numerous large-scale attempts at change, only to see them lose energy in nine to twelve months.

At this time Middles may also feel a bit schizophrenic in that the Tops certainly look like they want this to happen and seem to have their collective act together. On the other hand, Bottoms are right that the past few attempts at large-scale change failed. It's not uncommon for a Middle in this phase to feel like LSS/HPO will be wildly successful after a meeting with Tops in the morning, and then to feel the depths of change despair in the afternoon after meeting with Bottoms.

Items for Consideration   Middles are an important piece of the transformation puzzle. Without Middle support, Tops' transformation messages never reach the required critical mass of Bottoms. Unfortunately, Middles often feel threatened by any change because they perceive they have the most to lose. Decisions will be moved down from Middles in the new structure. Black Belts will be coming into Middles' areas and fixing things that may have been broken for years. HPTs will challenge the very identify of Middles as HPTs take on more managerial responsibilities such as goal setting, scheduling, work coordination, budgeting, and problem solving.

Practical Tips   It is extremely helpful if Middles convene several times before the Design stage to discuss the above issues and how they might best address them individually and as a collective group. It can also be time for Middles to invest in relationships with others at all levels of the organization, as they will need a large web of interrelationships for success in future stages.

What's Going on for the Bottoms in This Stage

Early in the Direction Setting stage, Bottoms will hear something about the potential changes, but there are no tangible points of contact with the change effort or people driving it. By the end of the stage, Bottoms will have an idea that something may indeed be different about this change effort. To understand how to be the best Bottom one can be and also how to deal with someone in a Bottom position in this stage, here are coaching tips for leaders.

Organizational Space Concerns and Issues Organizational skepticism is high. Upon hearing about a new change effort, Bottom reactions range from vocal cynicism to laughter. Water cooler conversations manifest themes such as "We'll see how far this change effort will get" "Don't worry, this too shall pass" or "When this new program is part of my goals, I'll begin to think seriously about it."

Items for consideration It's a natural reflex of the Bottom space to hold higher-ups responsible for the current poor state of affairs.[2] Unfortunately, usually the most negative people are the most vocal. In my experience, a typical profile of an organization's readiness for change is

- 20 percent are enthusiastic about the change;

- 20 percent openly or covertly oppose it; and

- 60 percent are on the fence and could go either way.

For Tops and Middles it is critical to get that 60 percent swing vote. Understanding the Bottom perspective and space pressures is an excellent place to start.

Practical Tips Bottoms should try to keep an open mind with regard to the chances of LSS/HPO success. The combination of improvement principles, statistical tools, HPTs, and increased job satisfaction greatly increases the likelihood of successful change. Bottoms should also begin to think about what they would personally want out of a major change like LSS/HPO. In the subsequent Design stage, Bottoms will have a voice and some power to restructure their local working environment.

When dealing with Bottoms in the Direction Setting stage, Top and Middle leaders should not invest a lot of time in telling Bottoms how great life will be in the LSS/HPO world. Significant talk not followed quickly by associated action will, in fact, only fuel the fires of skepticism. For Bottoms to commit to and support the proposed changes, they will need to see three things: (1) that something is actually going to change, (2) that Bottoms can have an impact, and (3) that changes will benefit Bottoms. These happen in the next stage, Design.

Tool Use

The Organization Space Analysis toolkit contains two tools: the Organizational Space Mirror and the Organizational Space Lenses (each tool and relevant theory appear in Chapter 7). The Organizational Space Mirror provides reflective insights into high leverage actions leaders can take based on an understanding of their space. The Organizational Space Lenses help leaders consider space factors when dealing with others. The lenses provide insights into others' motivations, the filters they use to perceive change events, and their natural tendencies depending on the space they occupy.

By using the Organizational Space Analysis toolkit, leaders can sharpen their self-reflection skills as well as positively influence individuals and groups in the organization.

Integrated Work Plan Questions for Leaders

While previous tools focused on performance factors and people's filters and behaviors, the final tool in the Leader's toolkit shines the spotlight on the approach to transformation. The Integrated Work Plan is the central document that ensures activities for training, improvement activities, workshops, and meetings are properly scheduled. While the Transformation Coordination Team is typically responsible for developing and managing this document and related activities, Top leaders provide a very important quality assurance (QA) function by ensuring that the plan is of high quality and can be executed.

This tool, explained in detail in Chapter 7, contains questions applicable for all stages and stage-specific questions. Some questions may seem to be common sense, but often common sense is not common practice when activity levels are high and multiple projects cause conflicting priorities during an LSS/HPO transformation. By periodically asking the questions in Exhibit 12.1, leaders can gently guide the transformation.

Exhibit 12.1. Leader's Integrated Work Plan Shaping and QA Guide for Direction Setting

	Leader's Shaping and QA Questions
Universally Applicable Questions	Are the major deliverables and tasks in the work plan consistent with the organization's strategy at this point in time?
	Are the best people assigned to the tasks?

**Exhibit 12.1. Leader's Integrated Work Plan
Shaping and QA Guide for Direction Setting, Cont'd**

	Leader's Shaping and QA Questions
	Are any groups or individuals overloaded or at risk of burning out?
	Are celebrations of small wins as well as major financial gains scheduled?
	Is the project on schedule and on budget? If not, what are the plans for correction?
	Is the quality of work at this point in time sufficient to help the organization reach our overall goals?
	Is the project structured so that teams are collectively accountable for results (instead of individuals being accountable)?
	The activities that people are working on may be a *good* use of their time, but is it the *best* use of their time?
	Has anything changed since the start of the project that might cause us to cancel any portion of it?
	What have we learned about planning and executing the project so far, and how can we use that to improve future work?
Stage 2: Direction Setting— Specific Questions	Is there a general work plan in place that outlines major milestones, key deliverable dates, assigned resources, and high level activities?
	Are there activities in the work plan that adequately collect customer requirements and how we are doing in meeting them?
	Who are potential Black Belts for improvement projects and Initial Restructuring Team members for HPT redesigns?
	For purposes of generating buy-in and minimizing resistance, are there adequate numbers of people participating in setting direction?
	Does the work plan address establishing two-way feedback mechanisms between senior management and the workforce?

The Direction Setting stage is important because it lays the groundwork for the success of the remainder of the project. By using the tools supplied in this chapter leaders can ensure that high quality directions are established.

The Performance Framework helps top leaders consider different performance factors such as strategy, structure, and business processes as they create conditions for effective group planning. With the Top/Middle/Bottom Space Analysis, leaders can examine their own and others' motivation for change. By using the Leader's Integrated Work Plan Shaping and QA Guide for Direction Setting, leaders can ask the right questions about the LSS/HPO approach.

The tools presented earlier in this chapter, in conjunction with the pragmatic tips listed in the next chapter, provide leaders with an arsenal of ways to tackle the big issues that most commonly arise during Direction Setting.

Notes

1. This model is based on over thirty-five years of research by Barry Oshry of organizational "spaces." An excellent introduction to the theory appears in B. Oshry (1986), *The possibilities of organization*. Boston, MA: Power & Systems.

2. Oshry, B. (1986). *The possibilities of organization*. Boston, MA: Power & Systems.

CHAPTER 13

Stage 2: Direction Setting

Pragmatic Tips

The difference between a dream and a goal is a plan.

Unknown

THE DIRECTION SETTING STAGE CHARTS THE COURSE for a successful LSS/HPO transformation. In the previous chapter leaders learned to use some tools to help them address Direction Setting challenges. Those tools can help shorten the stage, enhance the quality of the outcomes, and reduce complexity for leaders. But tools alone are not enough. When leaders combine the tools with the pragmatic tips in this chapter, they can achieve truly superior performance. The contents of this chapter will help leaders "peer around the corner" and see what's ahead. By knowing common problems and high leverage opportunities in advance, a leader can plot a course of action instead of reacting to events as they occur.

The key outputs and deliverables section of this chapter lets leaders know early in the stage what they should expect. Once leaders have started with the end in mind, they can direct their own and others' attention through a set of thought-provoking questions. While asking questions is one effective way to engage people, increasing their participation is another. The next section presents a minimal set of gatherings—both small and large—in which people generate work products for the LSS/HPO transformation. In addition to generating high quality work products, these gatherings reduce resistance to change by eliciting genuine commitment through participation.

To stimulate a leader's creative juices on how to adapt the material in this book to his or her situation, the next section presents some optional activities. While there is admittedly no single path to excellence, there are definitely common traps during this stage, which appear next.

For many leaders, LSS/HPO leadership is quite different from non-LSS/HPO leadership. In fact, some LSS/HPO mindsets and behaviors may seem downright counterintuitive viewed from "traditional leadership" thinking. This next section presents some of the more prevalent counterintuitive leadership elements and how to think differently in an LSS/HPO. As a final help to leaders in this stage, there is a leadership checklist of important items to consider throughout and upon completion of the Direction Setting stage.

Key Outputs and Deliverables

The list below shows what leaders should expect by the end of this stage. If sufficient progress is not being made on these items throughout the stage, leaders need to request that the people responsible for them work on them immediately. Key outputs and deliverables for this stage are

- A customer profile that contains key customer characteristics and critical requirements;
- High level process maps of the organization's five to ten key processes;
- Value Stream Maps™ for each product or service family showing the flow of material and information as well as key information such as cycle time, wait time, inventory build-ups, staffing levels, and value-added versus non-value-added activity designations;
- Guidelines and constraints—sometimes called "minimum critical specifications"—for the redesign into a team-based organization;
- A communication plan;
- An integrated work plan with a greater level of detail for near-term activities;

- A list of Initial Restructuring Team members who will facilitate the workshops for HPT redesign;
- A list of Champions and their associated areas of responsibility;
- A preliminary list of improvement projects;
- A list of Black Belts and Green Belts to work on selected improvement processes; and
- A greater number of people who begin to care about the success of the organization.

This last point is extremely important. The Direction Setting stage begins to broaden the circle of involvement and of caring about organizational success beyond those at the very top of the organization. This is critical to the success of any transformation. Consultant and business professor Richard Pascale sheds some light on the successes and failures of improvement programs:

> The problem is not the programs, some of which have worked wonders. The problem is that the whole burden of change typically rests on so few people. In other words, the number of people *at every level* who make committed, imaginative contributions to organizational success is simply too small. More employees need to take a greater interest and a more active role in the business. More of them need to care deeply about success. Companies achieve real agility only when every function, office, strategy, goal, and process—when every person—is able and eager to rise to every challenge.[1]

As mentioned above, a critical output of the Direction Setting stage is an increased number of people who care about and are committed to the transformation.

Important Questions to Ask

Instead of *telling* people what to think about and do, great leaders achieve organizational objectives by *asking key questions* that provoke thought and focus people's attention. Here are some important questions leaders should ask themselves and others during this stage.

Ask of Self and Others

- What are the behaviors and values we desire in the new environment, and how can we showcase them in the upcoming participative planning sessions?

- Are the projects selected truly the best ones to start with, or do some represent a political bias?

- Will the Black Belts and Green Belts we selected be the best ones to work on this improvement project?

- What are some opportunities to provide meaningful participation in order to grow the "circle of participation"?

- Are there any high talent people whose names have not been offered as Black Belts (some managers may attempt to hide their best people so they don't lose them for the typical eighteen-month Black Belt commitment)?

- Are a few of the initial projects targeted at improving processes close to customers?

Large-Group Interventions and Key Meetings

Getting groups of people to work together on critical LSS/HPO tasks is an excellent way to simultaneously accomplish four objectives:

1. Develop high quality work products for the implementation because of the diverse perspectives provided;

2. Achieve high levels of understanding among all participants about the topics discussed;

3. Increase energy and commitment regarding decisions made resulting from participation; and

4. Build leaders for the future by involving people who might not normally be involved.

Large group interventions (LGIs) are methods for engaging large groups of people for a specific purpose. They typically involve over twenty people, a number far too high to utilize traditional meeting management and small group dynamics rules. LGIs are explained in greater detail in the Appendix. In addition to LGIs there are key meetings that are also important in advancing LSS/HPO and generating enthusiasm and commitment. Figure 13.1 depicts a sample sequence of LGIs and key meetings. Table 13.1 provides a brief description of each entry on Figure 13.1. Leaders can use the sample sequence as provided or develop another, more tailored approach. Appendix Exhibit A.1 provides an example of a Large Group Intervention template used for Direction Setting and Action Planning purposes.

Figure 13.1. Large-Group Interventions and Key Meetings Map for Direction Setting

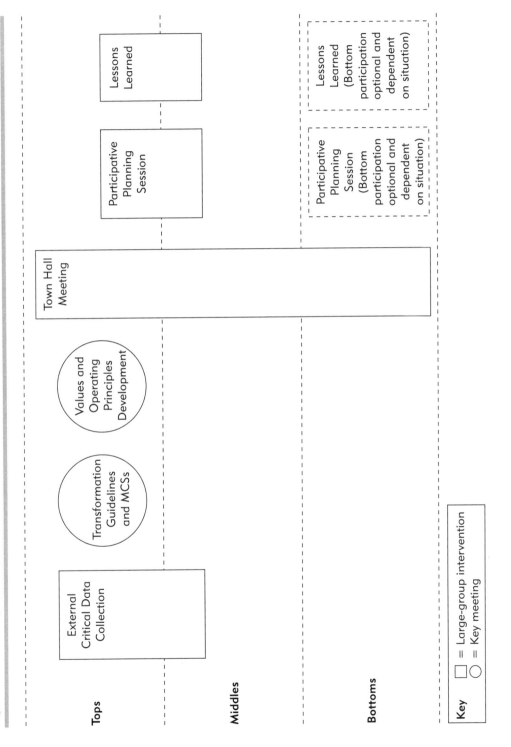

Table 13.1. Large-Group Interventions and Key Meetings for Direction Setting

Name	Gathering Type	Description of Key Elements
External Critical Data Collection	LGI	A group gathers key external data about markets, demographic shifts, best practices in process improvements and organizational redesign, changing customer requirements and technological advances that will be useful inputs to the upcoming participative planning session(s) in this stage. (Intel and Hewlett-Packard use these before embarking on participative planning sessions because the amount of data to consider is so great it is unlikely that participants will come to the participative planning session with all the necessary knowledge in their heads.)
Transformation Guidelines and MCSs	Meeting	Senior management develops a short list of guidelines—often called "minimum critical specifications" (MCSs)—for the transformation and the upcoming restructuring sessions. Examples of some MCSs: Increase client base by 20 percent within two years, no increases in operating costs, and the designs must be cost-effective.
Values and Operating Principles Development	Meeting	Senior management develop the values and operating principles for the new environment. These will be important elements of the new culture.
Town Hall Meeting	LGI	Provide an opportunity for two-way conversations between senior managers and the workforce regarding organizational strategy, the burning platform for change, and the LSS/HPO transformation approach.
Participative Planning Session	LGI	Involve a group of 20+ people to scan and analyze patterns, trends, and data external to the organization that affect the organization; critically examine the current organizational conditions for performance; develop a set of "strategic focal points" that articulate crisp, compelling elements of the strategy; and collectively develop action plans for advancing the organization to higher levels of performance. Based on the number of people involved in the planning, there may be more than one participative planning session.
Lessons Learned	LGI	A group of people involved in the transformation convenes at the end of the stage to identify (1) what went well during this stage; (2) what they might do differently in the future; and (3) how the group can make their learning accessible to people who need this information in the future.

The next to last LGI in the table—the participative planning session—is usually a pivotal turning point for the organization. Several important things occur:

- More than the "inner circle" receive first-hand exposure to and experience with the organization's strategies, strategic tradeoff analyses, and decisions.

- People beyond the inner circle begin to feel they have had a voice and can have an impact. They feel more trusted, begin to own the change, and tend to take on more responsibility and initiative to fix things.

- The organization sets the stage for a shorter implementation time because people other than the inner circle know the plan and have energy around achieving it.

The Appendix contains a sample LGI template for a participative planning session called a "search conference."[2]

An important point for leaders to consider and to convey to the workforce is that these events are very engaging. They are highly visible. They generate a lot of energy in the moment. Consequently, people often have the impression that the only time change happens in the organization is during large-group events. After a major event, many participants think, "Well, that was a great event and we got some good change areas addressed—now let's get back to work." Leaders need to dispel that myth and take care that they themselves do not fall into that trap. Continuous transformation activities such as modeling new behaviors and asking questions like "What's your data to support that conclusion?" need to occur daily.

Interesting Options

While LSS/HPO transformations will vary from organization to organization, successful ones are principle-based. Here are some optional approaches—based on the principles in this book—that some organizations have found to be successful. These are not mutually exclusive options. Leaders should feel free to use these or other custom-developed options to address unique local requirements.

Option 1: Consider Naming the Transformation Something Other than "LSS/HPO"

Creating a local, unique organizational theme can create buy-in for the project. I've seen titles ranging from goal-oriented descriptions like "The 10x Challenge" and "20x in 5 years" to titles that are a bit whimsical such as "Legend 2000" for a company seeking legendary performance in the year 2000 (the project was initiated in 1998).

Option 2: Address Special Issues Presented by Unions Early

If unions are involved, there are some special issues that require early attention during the Direction Setting stage. Jane Savage of Cornell University's School of Industrial Labor Relations suggests that decision-making boundaries be established before going into any joint planning session with union members and management. Often discussions will get to a point and can go no further without input from the rank and file. To prevent this frustrating occurrence, Savage recommends that everyone going into the planning session be very clear about what decisions the union attendees can make and what decisions they cannot make. In some cases it may even be possible for the rank and file to authorize planning session attendees to have considerable amounts of decision-making authority, but these arrangements would need to be negotiated in advance, and many would still need to later go through a ratification process.

Option 3: Conduct an LGI Called Dialogue with the Planning Session Participants Prior to the Event

This sequence can help participants gain an in-depth understanding of each other's perspectives and assumptions prior to planning together. A Dialogue overview appears in the Appendix in Table A.1.

Common Traps

 Although no two implementations of LSS/HPO are exactly alike, some common traps exist. The ones most often found in Direction Setting are

- *Assuming there has been enough communication.* Members of the workforce are busy doing "their real jobs" and often screen out transformation messages. Research shows that important messages need to be communicated five to eight times before the receiver hears them.

- *Selecting a bad portfolio of projects for the first wave.* To build momentum it is critical that the first set of improvement projects yield significant gains in increased profits, decreased cycle time, or improved quality. Some quick results are highly desirable. Top leaders must ensure that people are not funding their pet projects or just selecting projects that are "safe" with low risk and returns. In addition to top managers reviewing potential projects, J.F. DeBetz of StorageTek, a $2 billion manufacturer of storage devices, advises companies starting out to have a finance person involved at the start and all the major evaluation points along the way to assist in cost/benefit analyses.

- *Selecting only Black Belts who have old values and an old results orientation.* The eyes of the organization are on this first graduating class of Black Belts. The not-so-subtle message to the organization is, "These people are examples of what the organization values going forward." Nonparticipative, command-and-control Black Belts who bully their teams into producing results in short time frames and provide no team recognition or rewards send the absolute wrong message. Leaders must be cautious about selecting "successful" people from the old environment who may not be able to exhibit the new values and behaviors.

- *Not publicly demonstrating that senior management is on board.* The workforce needs to hear that senior management is 100 percent behind the new initiative. When General Electric sent top executives to the "Green Belt for Champions" program, it sent a strong message that Six Sigma was a new part of the company's business.

- *Targeting only production operations in the first wave.* Often significant improvements are possible in nonproduction work. Johnson & Johnson has been highly successful in targeting marketing, sales, quality, documentation, environmental monitoring, and facilities areas for Lean Six Sigma improvement. Karl Schmidt, Johnson & Johnson vice president of process excellence, formerly a VP of Environmental Affairs, reports that using Lean and Six Sigma methods in pollution prevention yielded $87 million in 2000 and in $55 million 2001. This was achieved through clearly defining metrics, identifying areas of waste, and putting projects in place to improve. These huge sums were a combination of cost avoidance and hard dollar savings, resulting from lower raw material costs and reduced waste disposal.[3]

- *Not providing a picture of what operating in the new environment might look like.* Before the next stage, the workforce will need a general idea of what it will be like for them and others once improvement projects begin and teams are formed. Leaders need to provide their vision of what this will look like and be open to discuss it. For ideas about what a high-performance environment looks like, leaders might want to take a look at an article about the General Electric plant in Durham, North Carolina, that builds some of the world's most powerful jet engines. I highly recommend this article, which is available in *Fast Company*'s online archives.[4]

- *Failing to have some areas of stability for the workforce during times of great change.* John Lupienski of Motorola states, "If you don't change you'll die. People know that here. People eat that up. But we also recognize that we need to have some point of stability when we are asking people to make big changes. At Motorola one of the points of stability in our automotive division has been the need to drive customer loyalty. We constantly ask 'How long have they been with us?' 'How happy are they?' 'Are we satisfying them?' Total Customer Satisfaction is Motorola's main objective." Even though Motorola's tactical goals may change and the methods they use to get there may change, the Total Customer Satisfaction objective is a constant that people can count on, even in times of great change.[5]

- *Not removing or relocating senior managers who will not support LSS/HPO midway through the Direction Setting stage.* A recent study found that replacement of key personnel who resisted transformation characterized 50 percent of the businesses studied that achieved successful transformation, but only 17 percent of those who were unsuccessful.[6] As painful as it may be, and as much as these managers may have contributed to previous success, they have no place as *leaders* of the new organization. In my experience with hundreds of large-scale change efforts, delaying the decision to remove non-supporters only makes it more difficult in later stages for everyone involved.

- *Not recognizing the importance of top team continuity for the change effort.* When the computer industry entered a serious downturn in 2000, Sun Microsystems CEO Scott McNealy agressively began to challenge the way things were done at Sun. *Sun Sigma,* launched in June, 1999, based on McNealy's hearing about Six Sigma benefits from golf partner Jack Welch, would play an important part. McNealy understood the value of top team continuity for a major change initiative. He asked that members of his senior management team stay on for the duration of the change effort.[7] Some top leaders left. This wisely ensured that McNealy would have a consistent top team of players, all enthusiastically dedicated to the success of the upcoming dramatic changes.

In an effort to appear participative, Top leadership sometimes fails to make important strategic decisions about the organizational structure. Not all restructuring decisions are given to the general workforce. Before people start redesigning into HPTs in the next stage, Top leaders need to make "macro design decisions" they deem necessary. These high-level, strategic structural decisions are then presented as "givens" that are not open to redesign by lower levels. For example, within six weeks after Bob Nardelli joined The Home Depot, he removed an entire layer of management that his predecessor had implemented. Those VPs were not consulted nor involved in the decision. If the decision were left up to those VPs, it is highly unlikely they would have taken that action. As Nardelli saw it, that additional hierarchical level wasn't useful for quick response and customer satisfaction, so he made the strategic decision to remove it.[8]

Counterintuitive Elements

 Leadership in an LSS/HPO looks different than it does in traditional organizational structures. However, some of those differences are keys to LSS/HPO success. Table 13.2 shows eight such elements often encountered during Direction Setting.

Table 13.2. Counterintuitive Elements in the Direction Setting Stage

Traditional Thinking	Counterintuitive LSS/HPO Reality
Senior management can't tell the workforce if the company is in trouble.	Leaders must tell people bad news that may ultimately affect them. Telling the truth enhances leader credibility. If credibility alone isn't a good enough reason, leaders have to consider that, with today's widespread availability of information, people will find out anyway. People will question the leaders' competency or integrity if they hear bad news elsewhere. Max DePree says one of a leader's most important jobs is to help people see reality.[i] Great leaders can even use bad news as a way to generate energy for improvement (see Exhibit 13.1).
If this is to be a participative enterprise, we need to involve all the members of the workforce in that decision.	The decision to move to a more participative work structure such as an HPO belongs to the top leaders of the organization. This is an important strategic decision, just like what products to offer and which markets to be in. Top leaders may choose a strategy of gradually introducing the concepts and selling the idea to the workforce, but ultimately the decision belongs to top management.
Senior management must keep a positive attitude, especially when talking among themselves. If one vice president's area is having problems, the culture prohibits bringing it up.	When top leaders only talk to each other about positive things, even if bad things are going on, this sets a bad example for the organization. This practice—sometimes called "Happy Talk"—must be replaced with open and direct communication. Leaders definitely need to be positive and display optimism for the workforce. But they also need to be honest about negative events.
Leaders need to show a lot of progress in the first couple of months of a large-scale change effort.	Sometimes you need to go slow to go fast. "It's better to take more time at the beginning to make sure everybody's on board than to rush it," says Henry Schacht, who, as CEO, led highly successful change at Lucent Technologies and, before that, at Cummins Engine. I'm a great believer that if you don't have everybody on board, you're not going to get there. You're pushing a boat through the water sideways. You're far better off to get the boat turned around, get everybody pulling the oars, and then go like hell."[ii]
People require extensive team building and interpersonal skills training to prepare for operating in teams.	People absorb new knowledge and skills more when they request it, not when it's mandated. Most organizations find early training in these areas is counterproductive and must be repeated. Experience shows teams are thirsty for these skills sixty to ninety days after the initial HPT redesign.
The human resources department needs to administer a change readiness assessment to see whether the workforce is ready for change.	A lengthy readiness assessment is not required if leadership does a good job of introducing the change, articulating the burning platform, showing what's in it for the workforce, and quickly moving to some participative events to demonstrate things are really changing.

Table 13.2. Counterintuitive Elements in the Direction Setting Stage, Cont'd

Traditional Thinking	Counterintuitive LSS/HPO Reality
If top leaders permit lower levels to participate in planning efforts and redesign themselves into teams, a lot of control will be lost.	Control is an important issue. It needs to be present or organizations can quickly damage customer relationships, lose market share, or have costs go sky high as people work on the wrong things. Control is especially important in government agencies, where there is sometimes decreasing funding from year to year, but expectations that service levels will remain the same. Janet Bubnis, who manages the HPTs in the the U.S. District Court for the Western District of Washington, makes an interesting point about control and HPTs. She states, "I believe there is more control in the system now that we have gone to self-managing teams. Now control is distributed among many people who can watch what's happening. Before HPTs, when I was the sole person responsible for control, I could only realistically watch a few things at a time."
Historically problematic employees will most likely remain that way and need to be closely monitored and controlled.	Employees who caused problems in the past sometimes appeared difficult because they were fighting the old processes and culture. Often these "problem employees" from the past in fact turn out to be star performers in the new environment. Instead of monitoring and controlling them initially, a wiser strategy is to challenge them to dream, motivate them to perform, and then decide whether they are still problematic.

[i]DePree, M. (1990). *Leadership is an art.* New York: Dell Publishing Company.
[ii]Mercer Delta white paper, "Managing the dynamics of change," p. 11.

Exhibit 13.1. A Missed Opportunity in Organizational History

A telecom VP was brought to a site to either close it down or turn it around in two years. The problem was that he didn't want to say this for fear of demotivating the employees. The site had been around for over fifty years, and a huge entitlement mentality existed. In my view, it would have been far more effective for him to have declared, "I'm Ron, and I've been brought here to close this place down or turn it around in two years. If it's closed down, everyone loses a job. If we turn it around, you keep jobs, variable pay goes up, and this becomes a better place to work for everyone. I need your help. I don't have all the answers, but I have some key strategic and market points you may not know about. I will share what I know, and hope you will also and that you'll work with me to get this place profitable in two years. Can I count on your support?" Talk about creating a burning platform that had strong emotional as well as logical buy-in! Might some good people have left once informed about the potential shutdown? Possibly. But the energy of the remaining workforce would have been a positive force in a turnaround effort. But the VP never told the workforce his mission, thus never got a preponderance of support for process improvement, and the site was closed two and one-half years after he arrived.

Leadership Checklist for Proceeding to the Next Phase

Before the organization can move to the next stage of an LSS/HPO transformation, top leaders should check to ensure the items in Exhibit 13.2 have been completed. It can also be helpful for top leaders to refer to this list as the stage is unfolding to ensure activities are started on time to produce the desired results before the stage completion.

Exhibit 13.2. Leadership Checklist for the Direction Setting Stage

☐ Strategy, mission, and values all fully defined, developed, and communicated

☐ Leaders publicly demonstrate at least three top leader behaviors have changed that support the desired new environment

☐ Public announcement of LSS/HPO is made to interested stakeholders (Some leaders believe this demonstrates strong leader resolve and makes it more difficult to kill the program once started[i])

☐ "Minimum critical specs" that provide guidelines and boundaries for the redesign into High-Performance Teams have been completed and clearly communicated

☐ A high level integrated work plan exists for implementing LSS/HPO

☐ A communication plan exists

☐ Leaders send, reinforce, and reinforce again the following key messages

- The customer is extremely important and people ask of their work, "How will this affect the customer?"

- We will be a process-oriented organization focused on the design and execution of reliable, repeatable processes that provide value to customers

- Open and direct communication is emerging as a new norm

- In the new organization teams will be the basic performing unit

☐ Begin to replace command-and-control leadership with analyze-and-energize leadership

[i]Interestingly enough, as of the writing of this book, many companies' stock still goes up when an announcement is made to Wall Street that the company will implement Six Sigma.

The pragmatic tips presented in this chapter can help leaders anticipate potential problem areas and exploit opportunities that arise in the Direction Setting stage. By understanding the key outputs and deliverables, leaders know what people should be working on throughout the stage and can suggest mid-course corrections as needed. The sample thought-provoking questions provided will help leaders and others think about important transformation issues.

Public gatherings and collective decision making are key elements of successful LSS/HPOs. In any large group setting it's important that the group become productive as fast as possible. To accomplish that, leaders can call upon some standard templates called large-group interventions to help people become productive quickly and accomplish the objectives as quickly as possible. The large-group interventions and key meetings listed will help advance LSS/HPO objectives by quickly delivering high quality work products and generating enthusiasm and commitment to LSS/HPO objectives.

The path to a successful LSS/HPO is guided by principles and a flexible approach, not a cast-in-concrete process. This chapter presented some optional activities that have been successful for other practitioners. By studying the common traps presented, leaders can choose to plan for, instead of react to, problems others have encountered. To help ease the transition to new leadership practices, this chapter presented the most common counterintuitive leadership practices that appear in this stage. As a final help to leaders, there is a checklist of important items they need to consider throughout and upon completion of Direction Setting.

Notes

1. Pascale, R., et al. (1997, November/December). Changing the way we change. *Harvard Business Review*, pp. 125–139.

2. The objective of providing the sample is to familiarize leaders with the types of agenda items contained in such a template, not to make leaders experts in the template application.

3. Personal conversation with Karl Schmidt of Johnson & Johnson.

4. http://www.fastcompany.com/magazine/28/ge.html.

5. Personal conversation with John Lupienski of Motorola.

6. Beer, M., Eisenstadt, R.A., and Spector, B. (1990). *The critical path to corporate renewal.* Boston, MA: Harvard Business School Press.

7. Personal interview with David Adrian, organization development manager at Sun Microsystems in Boulder, Colorado.

8. Sellers, P. (2001, March 19). Exit the builder, enter the repairman. *Fortune.*

CHAPTER 14

Stage 3: Design
Activity Map and Leader To Do List

The perfect is the enemy of the good.

Voltaire

IN THE DESIGN PHASE members of the organization begin process improvement efforts for selected processes and develop a structure consisting of High-Performance Teams (HPTs). In this stage top leaders focus their attention on creating conditions for the organization to succeed in an LSS/HPO environment. Specifically, top leaders ensure the workforce knows the strategy, has been trained in a standard approach to process improvement, understands the principles of designing HPTs, and has a motivated, skilled core of mid-level and lower-level leaders directing the first wave of improvements and HPT redesigns.

This chapter provides a preview of what's ahead for leaders in the Design stage. An Activity Map presents a picture of the sequence of major stage activities and milestones. The Leader To Do List presents a list of high leverage tasks that enable leaders to guide the LSS/HPO transformation smoothly along.

Activity Map

The Activity Map (Figure 14.1) shows major blocks of activity and their relative placement within this stage. Each of the three rows contains both LSS and HPO activities. The top row represents a strong combination of LSS and HPO activities and unfolding conditions. The second and third rows indicate a predominance of one discipline over the other, even though LSS and HPO elements appear in each.

Figure 14.1. Activity Map for Design

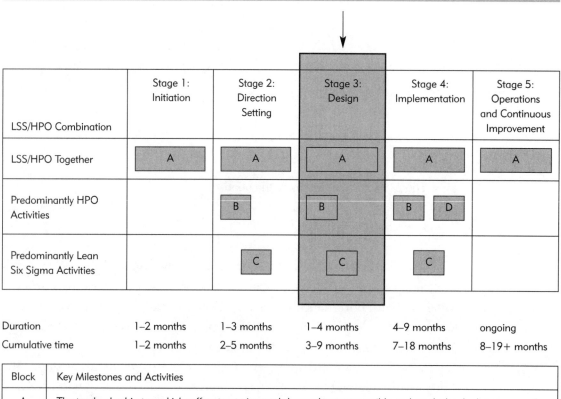

	Stage 1: Initiation	Stage 2: Direction Setting	Stage 3: Design	Stage 4: Implementation	Stage 5: Operations and Continuous Improvement
LSS/HPO Combination					
LSS/HPO Together	A	A	A	A	A
Predominantly HPO Activities		B	B	B D	
Predominantly Lean Six Sigma Activities		C	C	C	
Duration	1–2 months	1–3 months	1–4 months	4–9 months	ongoing
Cumulative time	1–2 months	2–5 months	3–9 months	7–18 months	8–19+ months

Block	Key Milestones and Activities
A	The top leadership team kicks off restructuring workshops whenever possible and sends the dual messages of process improvement and culture change to the workforce. The top leadership team conducts learning sessions around managing in the new LSS/HPO environment because many of the required skills and attitudes are quite different from the previous environment. The Transformation Technology Team begins to deliver automated solutions to Black Belts and the Initial Restructuring Team, such as a lessons learned database and a system for tracking HPT goals. Information technology specialists provide access to teams that was previously only accessible by managers. Throughout Design leaders communicate the new messages and mindsets of LSS/HPO in group settings and one-on-ones.

Figure 14.1. Activity Map for Design, Cont'd

Block	Key Milestones and Activities
B	Top management guidelines and high level process maps from previous LSS activities provide input into HPT restructuring workshops. In these tightly facilitated one- to two-day workshops, fifteen to two hundred people at a time redesign segments of the organization into HPTs. HPTs are appropriate where a collective work effort is required to achieve a goal. Nearly all lower levels are organized into HPTs. Middle levels and the Top level are organized into HPTs if there is true interdependence in nearly all their daily work. Otherwise, they remain as individuals on the organization chart, instead of being teams. All participate in redesign workshops, which are facilitated by one or two trained members of the Initial Restructuring Team. In these workshops HPTs set local goals, identify needed skills, articulate the team's performance challenge, establish full-time and part-time team membership, and set team boundaries. All these workshop outputs are negotiated with the manager(s) to whom the team reports to ensure strategic alignment. By moving down some simple decisions and information to the teams from what was formerly the responsibility of higher management, team intrinsic motivation levels rise as they see they can positively impact their local work environment. LSS influence is present in the team redesigns as all teams must have at least two goals associated with process improvement as well as with process execution. Teams are also granted permission to improve their local work. This permission is critical for quickly increasing motivation and job satisfaction, as many lower level team members will not have an opportunity to participate in the Black Belt-assisted improvement efforts in the first improvement wave.
C	Champions from senior management develop a business case for each improvement project and work with the Black Belts to define the project's scope and objectives clearly. Training for Green Belts begins so they can work with the Black Belts on projects. After the required initial training, the first wave of improvement projects is launched. HPO concepts of new cultural norms for interaction, meeting ground rules, collective accountability, and HPT goal setting are included in LSS process improvement sessions. Throughout the improvement project, champions ensure that the proper resources are allocated to the effort, coach the Black Belts, and remove roadblocks to success. Black Belts form learning groups, called communities of practice, to share best practices and lessons learned from their improvement efforts. Top management establishes regular meetings at which progress on all improvement projects is reported. From the conception of a project to its completion, there are financial reviews to ensure it is providing an adequate return.

Leader To Do List

In each stage there is a set of high leverage actions leaders can take to influence transformation success. Because there are many demands for leaders' time throughout the transformation, it becomes important to organize and prioritize items most deserving of leader attention. The Transformation Grid ("Grid" for short) organizes Leader To Dos into six categories that provide focus for high leverage activities. Figure 14.2. shows a Grid with sample activities for Design. Leaders may wish to modify the content and activity placement in the sample to tailor the Grid for unique organizational situations.[1]

Figure 14.2. Transformation Grid for Design

High Leverage Category	Stage 1: Initiation	Stage 2: Direction Setting	Stage 3: Design	Stage 4: Implementation	Stage 5: Operations and Continuous Improvement
Key Shaping Actions					
Participative Planning					
Process Awareness					
High Participation Restructuring					
Leadership Development					
Support					

	Stage 3: Design
Key Shaping Actions	Establish conditions for successful restructuring to HPTs Establish conditions for successful process improvement Use language to help shape new thought Set expectations for evaluation based on results and desired new behaviors Develop new culture management mechanisms Ensure there is a visible infrastructure for measuring results
Participative Planning	NA in this stage
Process Awareness	Conduct a primer on process management and its impact on organizational design and results management
High Participation Restructuring	Ensure that team goals are aligned with strategy Ensure that teams set SMART goals that are outcome-based Ensure that design tradeoffs are identified and addressed Satisfy the six criteria for productive work[i] in team designs
Leadership Development	Practice "analyze-and-energize" leadership Solicit feedback on how well leadership skills are developing
Support	Communicate strategic organization direction Initiate required changes to information systems Communicate transformation principles and approach

[i]These six criteria are elbow room, variety, learning, mutual support and respect, whole product view, and desirable future.

Activity descriptions for each high leverage category appear in the following sections.

Key Shaping Actions

During the Design stage there are six key shaping actions leaders can take to position the organization for the highest quality LSS/HPO outcomes. This section describes each.

Establish Conditions for Successful Restructuring to HPTs

In LSS/HPOs leaders focus heavily on creating conditions for high performance and continuous improvement. For many, this is a considerable change from traditional responsibilities such as problem solving, supervising, and actually performing technical work. In the Design stage leaders create conditions for a successful redesign into HPTs by

- Establishing guidelines and boundaries for the individual redesign sessions so that Middle and Bottom workers know precisely where to focus their energies (for an example, see Exhibit 14.1);

- Having a top leader personally kick off restructuring sessions whenever possible;

- Developing a "macro" design, if necessary, that specifies high level design decisions made by top management that are not open for redesign at lower levels. One example would be Citibank's reorganization from geographic-based teams to customer-based teams.[2] This element was non-negotiable, but teams had latitude to design details and ways to operate within that decision. Generally speaking, there should be as few of these macro design elements as possible;

Exhibit 14.1. Sample Guidelines and Constraints for HPT Redesign Sessions

- Increase clients by 15 percent over three years
- Be cost effective
- No increase in operational costs
- Multi-skilled self-managing teams
- Branch and team empowerment

- Removing blocks to "intelligent empowerment," described in Chapter 5; and

- Moving people around the organization to provide them with a fresh start (for example, in one financial organization the top leader moved command-and-control leaders from their current branch to other parts of the organization. This helped leaders practice and continually learn the new leadership principles without subordinates reacting to them personally and judging them based on their old behaviors. This worked exceptionally well, as some of the most reputed command-and-control leaders became some of the best analyze-and-energize leaders).

Establish Conditions for Successful Process Improvement

As with the initial work for restructuring to HPTs, leaders need to create conditions for effective improvement by chartering improvement teams, ensuring that LSS/HPO logistics and "administration" tasks are adequately resourced, establishing project review meetings with standard agendas and milestone reviews, and ensuring that there is a visible infrastructure for measuring both operating results and improvement results.

Use Language to Help Shape New Thought

Language is a powerful shaper of people's thoughts and resultant actions. It has been said that "we use language to create reality." Through language leaders can change the ways that people talk to themselves and to one another. For example, if top leaders start asking, "How will this proposed change impact the end customer?" soon people will begin to think they had better consider the end customer in all their improvement efforts.

Set Expectations for Evaluation
Based on Results and Desired New Behaviors

Even before Six Sigma became a driving force at GE, Jack Welch laid the groundwork to address the cultural aspect of improved performance by introducing the Results/Values Matrix (Figure 14.3). After several rounds of coaching, people would be moved if they didn't both get results and exhibit the new values. Welch demonstrated how serious he was at his annual meeting of top GE vice presidents in Boca Raton by calling attention to the VPs not present who had been fired because they did not exhibit the new desired values.[3]

Figure 14.3. Results/Values Matrix

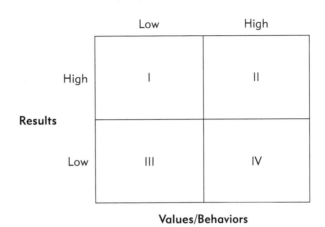

Values/Behaviors

Develop New Culture Management Mechanisms

Leaders need to actively manage culture in an LSS/HPO. Incorporating a results/values matrix in a company's formal performance evaluation system is one way to manage culture. Another way is to have managers coach team members and peers in culture-related aspects of work instead of just performance-related aspects. Yet another way some companies have had success is by establishing a group of top managers who listen to observations from lower organizational levels about manager behavior. After deliberating, this group decides whether the manager needs coaching and whether or not the culture infraction need to be rectified.

Ensure There Is a Visible Infrastructure for Measuring Results

People need to know what the organization really wants them to pay attention to. It is necessary to have top to bottom visibility so each team and each person can see how they fit in to the big picture and that all goals are aligned. John Lupienski, who has implemented Six Sigma at many Motorola sites, describes a measurement infrastructure and its importance clearly:

In trying to drive any strategic initiative the company must have a micro and a macro measurement system that is visible to everyone. The micro level shows what's happening in the front lines. The macro level shows overall company performance in relation to past performance, to the competition, and to the overall market.

Top management needs to drive the implementation of this infrastructure and drive measurement within it. People need to see it, and they need to see that it isn't going to go away. Teams are measured against their goals and their achievements are posted. All team goals and achievements are rolled up to the plant manager level for all to see.

Organizations need to take care not just to report current results within the reporting infrastructure. A good measurement infrastructure shows the current results for the reporting period; historical trends and patterns; helpful internal intra-company comparisons, and comparisons of internal results to external touch points such as competitor performance, customer demands, and shifting market requirements.

Often key results such as the above are reported on a "dashboard" that displays the critical results as well as relevant trends and patterns. There may be a dashboard of critical metrics at the top level of the organization, and those may break down into greater detailed dashboards at successively lower levels of the organization. Metrics on each dashboard would support the higher level metrics.

In the Design stage top leaders need to ensure that such an infrastructure is created and that mechanisms are in place to ensure that measurement infrastructure activities occur.

Process Awareness

The concept of process is central to any LSS/HPO transformation. In each stage the organization needs to dedicate time to understanding, improving, and managing processes. In the Design stage, the understanding of process must be expanded beyond the top leaders and initial planning group to the general workforce.

Conduct a Primer on Process Management and Its Impact on Organizational Design and Results Management

Black Belts, members of the Initial Restructuring Team, and middle managers receive training on what a process is, how to improve it, and how to manage its results for sustainability of gains once the improvement has occurred. It is important that members of the Initial Restructuring Team attend these sessions so they can understand the impact of processes on the organization's redesign to HPTs.

High-Participation Restructuring

In the Design stage members of the organization restructure their current organizational units into HPTs. Each redesign session is led by one to three trained facilitators who do the following:

- Provide briefings to participants on how to develop good designs;

- Ensure that participants produce high-quality workshop products such as team goals, a listing of skills needed, required information technology, a strategy for how they will manage and improve what they do, and clearly articulated responsibilities among and within teams;

- Provide coaching assistance on design points if the participants appear "stuck";

- Keep participants on schedule so they have a high-quality work product at the end of the one- to two-day redesign session; and

- Monitor and, if necessary, intervene in unproductive group dynamics.

For a sample agenda of one of these redesign sessions, please consult Exhibit A.2 in the Appendix in the Large-Group Interventions section under the topic "Participative Design Workshop."

It is often helpful to have a sample of what before and after designs might look like. Figures 14.4 and 14.5 provide before and after examples from the Land Bank in South Africa. Figures 14.6 and 14.7 provides before and after examples of a high-tech manufacturer of recording devices. In Figure 14.7, solid lines are direct reporting interfaces. Dotted lines are negotiated cross-team deliverables. Each team negotiates these as required. Cross-team deliverables change as work changes over time.

Figure 14.4. Traditional Structure of a Financial Institution

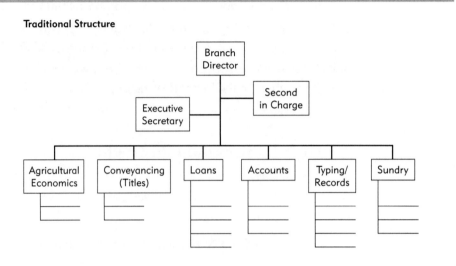

Figure 14.5. HPO Redesign of a Financial Institution

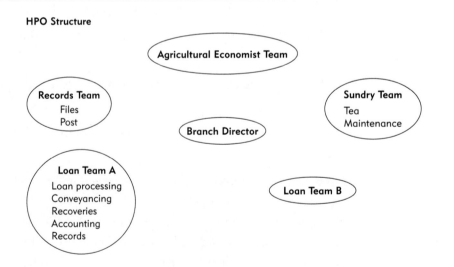

Figure 14.6. Traditional Structure of a Manufacturing Organization

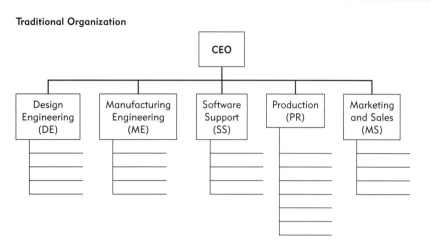

Figure 14.7. HPO Redesign of a Manufacturing Organization

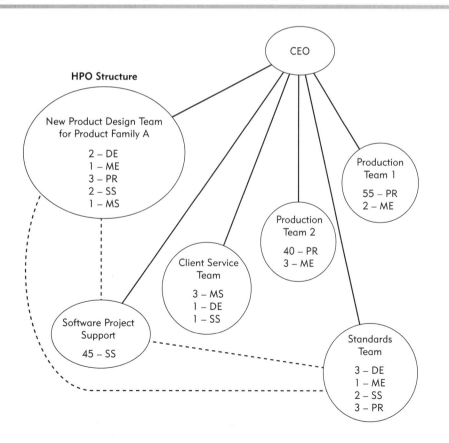

Within these redesign sessions there are four important areas for leaders to consider, presented below. These are also the items for the facilitators to consider when leading the sessions after discussing these with top leaders to gain their perspectives.

Ensure That Team Goals Are Aligned with Strategy

Leaders must exercise caution and not just turn teams loose and permit them to set their own goals. The same sequence for restructuring into teams applies to goal setting, namely, Tops set direction, Bottoms set goals and negotiate with Middles, and Middles set their goals and negotiate with Tops. Motorola is one of many companies that has had great success with this sequence:

> The senior management team articulates the strategies and high level goals, and shortly afterward the people on the front lines bubble up ideas from the bottom. Front-line goals are negotiated with middle managers, and then approved. Goals are then shared with the next level up. There is a clear path from top to bottom of the organization and it's obvious how the goals are linked and aligned. Motorola then adds one additional step in keeping with the culture. There are individual goals, which are linked to team goals, which are linked to department goals, which are linked to the overall business. All goals are linked from bottom to top, *and* to the customer.[4]

Ensure That Teams Set SMART Goals That Are Outcome-Based

When people can set their own goals, their motivation to perform increases.[5] Leaders can ensure the best possible results by having teams set SMART goals that focus on outcomes. A SMART goal is specific, measurable, achievable, relevant, and time-bound.[6]

Goals also need to focus on outcomes instead of activities. For example, "Cut purchasing costs by 18 percent" is preferable to "Attend five meetings to discuss purchasing opportunities."

Finally, teams should set more than just financial goals. The "Balanced Scorecard Approach"[7] can help teams consider multiple perspectives that indicate overall performance and also build for the future. A Balanced Scorecard might address customer needs, financial needs, internal process needs, and learning and innovation needs.

Ensure That Design Tradeoffs Are Identified and Addressed

Every organizational design—even a *great* design—accomplishes some objectives at the expense of others. For example, organizing around functional disciplines can mean sacrificing the quality of cross-functional activities for customers. On the other hand, organizing based on processes can provide great customer focus and quality, but over a long period of time people's skills tend to degrade as they spend time on cross-functional teams instead of remaining current with their functional specialties. It is important for leaders to keep design tradeoffs in mind and to help teams be aware of them too.

Satisfy the Six Criteria for Productive Work in Team Designs

Research and personal experience have shown that the following factors increase levels of productive work within an organization: autonomy for making local decisions, variety, learning, mutual support and respect, a whole product view, and a desirable future.[8] Teams should reference these during their redesign process and afterward to ensure that scores stay high.

Facilitators, and later top and middle leaders, need to ensure that the previous four items have been adequately addressed in the redesign sessions. After the sessions, the teams will negotiate their goals with their manager. Most of the time goals remain as initially designed, but occasionally a manager must provide additional information to a team and have them revise a goal to ensure it is congruent with strategy.

Leadership Development

In each stage leaders need to keep developing their leadership skills as they become "analyze-and-energize" leaders. In this stage leaders need to focus on the following:

Practice "Analyze-and-Energize" Leadership

In the Design stage leaders should receive training on analyze-and-energize leadership and practice the skills in a safe environment.

Solicit Feedback on How Well Leadership Skills Are Developing

To continuously improve, leaders require performance feedback. It's often helpful for them to solicit feedback from peers, superiors, subordinates, and customers. For organizations that have many leaders, automated systems that score and analyze results of questionnaires can be helpful. For an example of online leadership skill development and management, see LSSHPOAssessments.com.

Support

The support function provides additional leverage and benefits for the previous Grid categories, such as communication, HR processes, and information technology support.

Communicate Strategic Organization Direction

Strategy is important to all redesign and process improvement activities. The individual or team responsible has to communicate the strategy clearly and make it available to everyone through a variety of channels.

Initiate Required Changes to Information Systems

Teams typically will need more information than any one member needed before the redesign effort. Information technology teams should begin work on altering user access profiles so that (1) teams have access to much of the information that only their managers previously had access to and (2) teams have access to other teams' information. Getting the right information to the teams is critical for their success. Research shows that by improving the quality and timeliness of the information people receive, their performance can improve by as much as 20 percent to 50 percent.[9]

Communicate Transformation Principles and Approach

In advance of the redesign workshops, the organization needs to hear about and read about the principles and approach that will be used for the transformation to LSS/HPO.

In the Design stage leaders need to focus their efforts on the big picture in the Activity Map and on key day-to-day tasks as suggested in the Leader To Do List section. In the Leader To Do List section, leaders learned how to use the Transformation Grid tool to plan their activities for the upcoming work and how to monitor those activities to ensure adequate progress.

Notes

1. For further information on uses of the Grid and content updates, see TransformationGrid.com.

2. Galbraith, J. (2002). *Designing organizations.* San Francisco: Jossey-Bass.

3. Welch, J. (2001). *Jack: Straight from the gut.* New York: Warner Books.

4. Personal conversation with John Lupienski of Motorola on December 6, 2002.

5. Macy, B., and Izumi, H. (1991). "Organizational change, design and work innovation: A meta-analysis of 131 North American field studies—1961–1991." In R. Woodman and W. Pasmore (Eds.), *Research in organizational change and development,* vol. 7. New York: JAI Press.

6. Over time many words have been attributed to the SMART acronym. Other words for A include acceptable, agreed-on, attainable, and actionable. Another for R is realistic. Others for T include Timely, Timed, and Timeframe. Use whatever combination of these best fits your organization.

7. Kaplan, R., and Norton, D. (1996). *The balanced scorecard approach: Translating strategy into action.* Boston, MA: Harvard Business School Press.

8. Emery, F., and Thorsrud, E. (1976). *Democracy at work: The report of the Norwegian industrial democracy program.* Leiden, The Netherlands: Martinus Nijhoff Social Sciences Division.

9. Boyett, J., and Boyett, J. (1998). *The Guru guide: The best ideas of the top management thinkers.* New York: John Wiley & Sons.

15

Stage 3: Design
Tools Application

One can never consent to creep when one feels the impulse to soar.

Helen Keller

IN THE LAST CHAPTER, leaders learned about the major blocks of activities and specific high-leverage actions they could take during Design. Key challenges and tools to address them are presented in this chapter of the Design stage. Because of the major cultural shifts introduced and launching the first round of process improvements, this stage poses some unique challenges for leaders:

- Ensuring the new organizational structure and improvement teams directly support the organization's strategy;

- Managing potential skepticism and withdrawal of front-line workers based on the high level of workforce participation required in LSS/HPO redesign activities; and

- Synchronizing design activities for organizational restructuring and process improvement teams to reduce burnout of key talent, ensure proper sequencing of activities, and avoid scheduling key activities in the same timeframe.

Each of the tools presented in this chapter will help leaders address the above challenges.

Performance Framework

During Design, the Performance Framework helps leaders:

- Articulate specific links between the key performance elements of strategy, structure, and process;

- Give the workforce a big picture understanding of the transformation direction; and

- Gain insights during a lessons learned analysis at completion.

In each use above, leaders follow these four steps:

1. Convene a meeting and post a large Performance Framework flip chart on a wall;

2. Facilitate discussions about interrelationships among performance elements and core elements;

3. Record participant comments on the flip chart near the related performance factor being discussed; and

4. Ensure that meeting notes and action items are typed and distributed.

In addition, the tool can be used to illustrate which factors are addressed in this stage. Figure 15.1 shows the primary factors addressed during Design. Italicized comments appear adjacent to the factors addressed and describe how they are addressed in this stage.

Figure 15.1. Performance Framework for Design

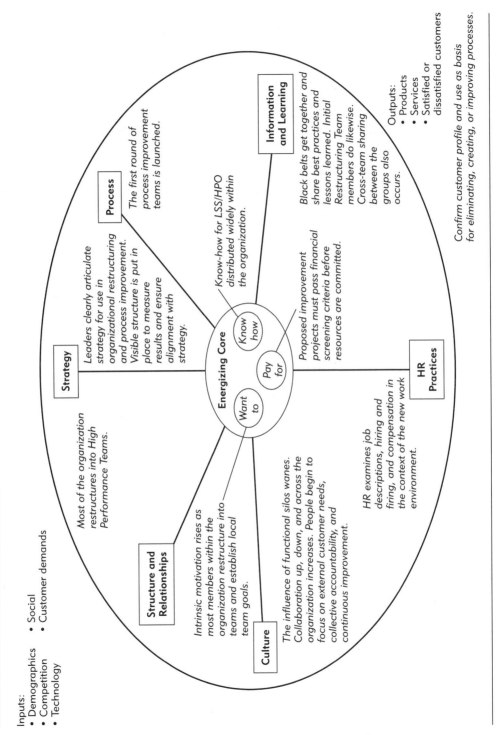

Inputs:
- Demographics
- Competition
- Technology
- Social
- Customer demands

Strategy

Leaders clearly articulate strategy for use in organizational restructuring and process improvement. Visible structure is put in place to measure results and ensure alignment with strategy.

Most of the organization restructures into High Performance Teams.

Process

The first round of process improvement teams is launched.

Information and Learning

Black belts get together and share best practices and lessons learned. Initial Restructuring Team members do likewise. Cross-team sharing between the groups also occurs.

Energizing Core
- Know how
- Pay for
- Want to

Know-how for LSS/HPO distributed widely within the organization.

Proposed improvement projects must pass financial screening criteria before resources are committed.

HR Practices

HR examines job descriptions, hiring and firing, and compensation in the context of the new work environment.

Structure and Relationships

Intrinsic motivation rises as most members within the organization restructure into teams and establish local team goals.

Culture

The influence of functional silos wanes. Collaboration up, down, and across the organization increases. People begin to focus on external customer needs, collective accountability, and continuous improvement.

Outputs:
- Products
- Services
- Satisfied or dissatisfied customers

Confirm customer profile and use as basis for eliminating, creating, or improving processes.

Top/Middle/Bottom Space Analysis

The Performance Framework tool in the previous section presented a way of looking at key performance factors such as Strategy, Process, and Structure and how they combine to determine organizational performance in the Design stage. The Top/Middle/Bottom Space Analysis focuses leaders' attention on people—where they are in the organization, what their perceptual filters are about the upcoming opportunity, and how they might best be influenced to enthusiastically join in the LSS/HPO transformation. By understanding the Top, Middle, and Bottom organizational spaces, leaders can dramatically improve the leverage of their actions and accelerate the advancement of the organization to an LSS/HPO. This section is organized into three topic areas: (1) an *involvement profile,* which depicts the involvement of the Top, Middle, and Bottom positions in the LSS/HPO transformation; (2) *coaching for this stage,* which presents stage-specific insights into what each organizational space is experiencing during this part of the LSS/HPO transformation; and (3) *tool use,* which outlines the tools in the organization space toolkit.

Involvement Profile

This segment contains an organizational analysis and recommendations for leaders based on the organization space concepts presented in Chapter 7. For a quick review of those concepts, please refer to that section. The participation of the three position-based spaces, shown by shaded areas, is shown in Figure 15.2.

Figure 15.2. Participation During Design

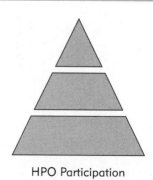

Lean Six Sigma
Participation

HPO Participation

The Involvement Profile shows that in the Design stage nearly all the Top leaders are actively engaged in the LSS/HPO elements of the upcoming transformation. By the end of this stage Top leaders not fully engaged will either have to join the effort or find other options inside or outside the organization. Middles are involved in both, although more Middles are involved in the HPO activities than in the Lean Six Sigma activities. Some Bottoms will be involved in the first wave of improvement projects, and all Bottoms will be involved in transforming the organization to HPTs.

Coaching for This Stage

Understanding leads to insight. This section provides tips on dealing with issues and interactions for each space.

What's Going on for the Tops in This Stage

The Design stage can be a traumatic time for Tops. HPTs are being formed and decisions are beginning to flow from the top of the organization to the bottom. The first wave of process improvement projects, which absolutely must succeed, is beginning. To help understand how to be the best Top one can be and also how to deal with someone in a Top position in this stage, here are some coaching tips.

Organizational Space Concerns and Issues   Tops begin to struggle with the clarity of their individual and collective roles as a Top team. When should an issue become the property of one Top, and under what conditions? When should they behave as a collective Top team, and when should they behave as individuals who head up their respective areas? All these issues add to the pressure Tops feel mounting as the organization moves through the Design stage. Especially unnerving for many Tops can be the perception of "loss of control" that will soon be brought on by a series of participative workshops in which Bottoms and Middles redesign their organizational structures into HPTs and pull down responsibilities under the guidelines of intelligent empowerment. Although it all looked so logical on paper, when the final hour countdown begins, high levels of Top anxiety are not uncommon.

Items for Consideration   At this point in the transformation, the Tops' world is increasing in complexity and they are overloaded as they prepare to push down selected decision-making power in the organization and charter key improvement projects. It looks to Tops as if they will have to watch more and more areas closely as they distribute decisions.

But in fact there is more control throughout the organization than Tops initially think. Tops don't just give a high level direction and then let teams do whatever they want. Specifically, there are six points of control, as shown in Exhibit 15.1.

Exhibit 15.1. How Control Is Addressed in an LSS/HPO

1. Tops provide two key inputs into the HPT redesign sessions:
   - The strategy, which the teams use to articulate performance challenges and develop structures, and
   - Transformation guidelines, which establish boundaries and set stretch objectives.
2. Teams need to negotiate goals with Middle managers to ensure they satisfy the strategy and do not obviously conflict with other team goals.
3. Because most people understand the strategy, they serve as control points on teams where team members may be about to stray. Since a team's pay is based on meeting goals that are aligned with strategy, everyone on a team is concerned about this, not just those in managerial ranks.
4. Team members monitor other team members' behaviors and provide appropriate coaching and corrective counseling as needed.
5. Managers monitor team metrics to ensure teams are meeting objectives and provide support if they are not.
6. Other teams provide corrective counseling to a team that is not producing what the other teams need, as defined by inter-team agreements.

Tops are distributing not only *decisions,* but also *control* throughout the organization.

Practical Tips   Here are some tips for Tops during Design:

- Ensure that the six points in Exhibit 15.1 exist;
- Distribute responsibility wherever possible;
- Help teams and Middles define and finalize goals for later fine-tuning;
- Create and coach teams for special projects to develop experience in process improvement and LSS/HPO leadership;

- Follow the discipline of analyze-and-energize leadership and coach others whenever possible; and

- Attend kick-off sessions for process improvement projects to demonstrate the importance of the improvement work.

Leaders must quickly grasp new LSS/HPO leadership mindsets and begin to get all Tops and Middles up-to-speed on them. To do this quickly, it will not be possible to have Tops learn first and then cascade knowledge down the organization. Learning forums for new leadership might include Tops, the Transformation Coordination Team, Black Belts, and the Initial Restructuring Team.

Now is the time to begin the evolution of the "Top team." Tops will rarely operate 100 percent as a team because their outputs do not all require interdependent and collective action. But some performance challenges require a Top team effort. At this time the Top team should start to figure out what they need to do together and what they should do separately.

What's Going on for the Middles in This Stage

In this stage Middles' natural feelings of being disenfranchised and isolated begin to heighten. They see that Bottoms will soon be assuming more responsibilities that used to be theirs. Their identity as managers is in a state of flux, and they are not sure how they will contribute to the new order of things. To help understand how to be the best Middle one can be and also how to deal with someone in a Middle position in this stage, here are coaching tips on organizational space concerns and issues, items for consideration, and practical tips.

Organizational Space Concerns and Issues   Black Belts present two concerns for Middles at the start of the Design stage. The first is that a Middle's star player may be selected as a Black Belt and be removed from a high contribution position for eighteen months or perhaps even longer. A second concern regarding Black Belts is that a Black Belt may be assigned to an improvement project in a Middle's area and find some really serious problems that will soon become known by all in the organization. Middles perceive that each of these situations could seriously weaken a Middle's effectiveness in the new LSS/HPO. Until the culture changes to one in which there is a greater penalty for hiding process problems than for addressing them, many Middles will continue to be concerned about turf issues and protection from embarrassment.

The HPTs that will be designed in this stage raise three major concerns for Middles. They wonder:

- What is my new role after teams assume many managerial activities?
- Will the reorganization make many of my business relationships formed over the years irrelevant?
- I understand I'm supposed to integrate the work of teams reporting to me, but what does that mean, and will I be competent at this new role?

A final space concern for Middles is that they may feel torn between Tops, who are excited about upcoming changes, and Bottoms, who are skeptical or resistant to them. It will be a difficult emotional time for Middles as sometimes they feel compelled to side with Tops for the sake of the organization's future, and sometimes they feel more connected to the initial Bottom reluctance to venture into the unknown.

Items for Consideration   The natural pressures and conditions of the Middle space cause Middles to look primarily upward and downward in the organization. They look up to see what their manager wants and down to coordinate the activities of their direct reports. Middles rarely spend time in high leverage interactions with other Middles. This isolationist behavior, although it may be innocent, contributes to Middles' feelings that they don't get along with other Middles. This feeling in turn reinforces the practice of being isolated from other Middles.[1] A vicious cycle escalates that increases Middles separation and closes the door on high leverage Middle integration necessary in an LSS/HPO environment.

Practical Tips   Middles need to be proactive in defining their new roles in the new environment. Middles will take on more of an integration role for the teams reporting to them. Middles will have to be prepared to spend more time developing those reporting to them and less time supervising them.

In the Design stage Middles should strive to develop strong lateral bonds with peers. When they get together, useful topics of conversation would be their new roles in an HPT structure, specific business problems that other Middles could provide coaching for, and high leverage ways that Middles can interact with Black Belts who may be assigned for their operations. In addition, because of their unique position in the structure, Middles should continue to add value to the transformation by:

- Continuing to share high quality information with Tops and Bottoms about what's going on in the others' respective worlds;

- Creating opportunities for dialogue between parties that disagree or that passionately are pursuing one avenue to the exclusion of others;

- Requesting one or more information sharing sessions with Tops that would paint a general picture of the new operating environment and guidelines for leaders operating within it;

- Understanding and helping to reinforce that there are no penalties for having a broken process as long as it is being addressed with continual improvement projects;

- Coaching Tops for what they feel will be palatable transformation messages and approaches for Bottoms; and

- Coaching Bottoms on ways to present their story and objections to Tops in a way that Tops can listen and understand.

By taking these actions Middles can begin to assume their new important roles in the LSS/HPO management structure.

What's Going on for the Bottoms in This Stage

Bottoms face a crisis of perception in the Design stage. The natural Bottom organizational space condition is to feel like no one listens. However, in this stage they are offered a genuine opportunity to have a significant impact on their local work conditions. They assume some managerial responsibilities that formerly belonged to their supervisor. After the redesign into HPTs, they are also able to improve workflow and work practices within the team. An additional empowering element for Bottoms is the possession of data. With it they can challenge managers and even vice presidents who don't have data. A new world opens up to Bottoms that is dramatically different from the pre-HPT world.

Organizational Space Concerns and Issues   In the Design stage Bottoms begin to get a steady flow of communication about the redesign process and the basics of Lean Six Sigma objectives and tools. Before the redesign workshop they are skeptical. Sometimes skepticism blocks out key parts of leadership communications, so leaders need to communicate the same ideas numerous times. Once Bottoms get the idea that major change is coming, their natural condition of vulnerability begins to increase.

Items for Consideration   The workshops that design the organization into HPTs dramatically change Bottoms' feelings of vulnerability. The new concept of "intelligent empowerment" begins to feel very real. For many Bottoms this is exhilarating—but for others, scary.

Practical Tips   Bottoms need to begin to take a big picture perspective with respect to solutions they propose and actions they take. That is, a Bottom should not just think of him- or herself or team, but should instead take a "big picture" view when recommending new structures and process improvements. After the redesign workshops have been completed and the organization is operating under a new set of rules and cultural norms, Bottoms should feel comfortable challenging behaviors of Bottoms and of other levels that are not consistent with the new desired state. For example, if a manager publicly berates a direct report in a large group, any Bottom should be able to pull the manager aside after the meeting and gently suggest that the behavior was not consistent with the organization's new value of "respect for the individual" (if this had been an articulated new value). If there is no change in manager behavior, Bottoms may avail themselves of other escalation methods, such as bringing issues to a high-level group concerned with the new organizational values or collectively approaching a manager's boss if they have approached the manager and have seen no behavioral changes. In this stage it is important that Bottoms use their new powers and co-determine their boundaries for action with their managers.

Tool Use

The Organization Space Analysis toolkit contains two tools: the Organizational Space Mirror and the Organizational Space Lenses (each tool and relevant theory appear in Chapter 7). The Organizational Space Mirror provides reflective insights into high leverage actions leaders can take based on an understanding of their space. The Organizational Space Lenses help leaders consider space factors when dealing with others. The lenses provide insights into others' motivations, the filters they use to perceive change events, and their natural tendencies depending on the space they occupy.

By using the Organizational Space Analysis toolkit, leaders can sharpen their self-reflection skills as well as positively influence other individuals and groups in the organization.

Integrated Work Plan Questions for Leaders

During this busy phase the Integrated Work Plan Questions (Exhibit 15.2) will help top leaders ask the key questions that can prevent over-burdening key resources and ensure that key activities are placed in the proper time sequence. The Integrated Work Plan is the central document that ensures that time-phased activities for Lean Manufacturing, Six Sigma, HPO, and change management activities are scheduled at the right time in the transformation. While the Transformation Coordination Team is typically responsible for developing and managing this document and related activities, top leaders provide a very important quality assurance (QA) function.

This tool, explained in detail in Chapter 7, contains two sets of questions for leaders to ask: questions applicable for all stages and stage-specific questions.

Some questions may seem to be common sense, but often common sense is not common practice when there are high levels of activity and multiple project priorities in an LSS/HPO transformation. By periodically asking the questions in Exhibit 15.2, leaders can gently guide the transformation along a swift and productive path.

Exhibit 15.2. Leader's Integrated Work Plan Shaping and QA Guide for Design

	Leader's Shaping and QA Questions
Universally Applicable Questions	Are the major deliverables and tasks in the work plan consistent with the organization's strategy at this point in time?
	Are the best people assigned to the tasks?
	Are any groups or individuals overloaded or at risk of burning out?
	Are celebrations of small wins as well as major financial gains scheduled?
	Is the project on schedule and on budget? If not, what are the plans for correction?
	Is the quality of work at this point in time sufficient to help the organization reach our overall goals?
	Is the project structured so that teams are collectively accountable for results (instead of individuals being accountable)?
	The activities that people are working on may be a *good* use of their time, but is it the *best* use of their time?
	Has anything changed since the start of the project that might cause us to cancel any portion of it?

**Exhibit 15.2. Leader's Integrated Work Plan
Shaping and QA Guide for Design, Cont'd**

	Leader's Shaping and QA Questions
	What have we learned about planning and executing the project so far, and how can we use that to improve future work?
Stage 3: Design— Specific Questions	Does the work plan assign tasks and dates to individuals for evaluating candidate improvement projects according to established financial criteria?
	Has the work plan included management processes that will ensure that teams have adequate time to negotiate goals with the next higher level up?
	Is adequate lead time provided for training internal restructuring facilitators and improvement specialists before key deadlines? Are apprenticeship programs designed into the work plan to accelerate learning curves for new Black Belts and Initial Restructuring Team members?
	Is the Transformation Technology Team having adequate interaction with their internal customers, or are they working in isolation?
	Are people in human resources assigned to evaluate alternate pay processes that support the new LSS/HPO practices?

In the Design stage the blueprints for the organization's success are drawn up. By using the tools supplied in this chapter, leaders ensure that the design for the organization's structure and for the process improvement infrastructure are of the highest quality, are understandable, and are straightforward to implement.

The Performance Framework tool helps leaders assure that the new organizational designs support the organization's strategy and are aligned with the other performance elements. By viewing middle manager and front-line work actions through the Top/Middle/Bottom Spaces Analysis, leaders can introduce changes that have the highest likelihood of being accepted. And finally, by using the Leader's Integrated Work Plan Shaping and QA Guide for Design, they can minimize schedule overlaps of key events and attempt to minimize the all-too-often occurrence of burnout in key personnel in the first wave of process improvements.

Note

1. Oshry, B. (1992). *Possibilities of organization.* Boston, MA: Power and Systems.

16

Stage 3: Design
Pragmatic Tips

Try? There is no try! There is only do, or not do.
> Yoda in Star Wars, responding when Luke Skywalker
> says he will "try" to use a newly learned Jedi skill.

THE DESIGN STAGE IS A TIME OF COMMITMENT. The organization commits to continuous improvement and to organizing into High-Performance Teams (HPTs). In the previous chapter leaders learned tools to help address Design challenges. Those tools can help shorten stage duration, enhance the quality of the stage outcomes, and reduce complexity for leaders. But tools alone are not enough. When leaders combine those tools with the pragmatic tips in this chapter, they can achieve truly superior performance. The contents of this chapter will help leaders "peer around the corner" and see what's ahead in the upcoming stage. By knowing common problems and high leverage opportunities in advance, a leader can plot a course of action at the start of the stage instead of having to react to events as they occur.

The key outputs and deliverables section of this chapter lets leaders know early in the stage what they should expect. Once leaders have started with the end in mind, they can direct their own and others' attention through a set of thought-provoking questions. While asking people questions is one effective way to engage them, increasing their participation is another. The next section presents a minimal set of gatherings, both small and large, in which people generate work products for the LSS/HPO transformation. In addition to generating high quality work products, these gatherings reduce resistance to change by eliciting genuine commitment through participation.

To stimulate a leader's creative juices on how to adapt the material in this book to a situation, the next section presents some optional activities. While there is admittedly no single path to excellence, there are definitely common traps during this stage, which appear next.

For many leaders, LSS/HPO leadership is quite different from non-LSS/HPO leadership. In fact, some LSS/HPO mindsets and behaviors may seem downright counterintuitive viewed from "traditional leadership" thinking. This section presents some of the more prevalent counterintuitive leadership elements encountered in this stage and explains how to think differently in an LSS/HPO. As a final help to leaders in this stage there is a leadership checklist of important items to consider throughout, and on completion of the Design stage.

Key Outputs and Deliverables

The list below shows what leaders should expect by the end of this stage. If sufficient progress is not being made on these items throughout the stage, leaders need to request that the people responsible for them direct their attention to them immediately. Key outputs and deliverables for this stage are

- A first wave of process improvement projects that have passed the financial hurdle rate and are underway;

- An organizational structure consisting primarily of High-Performance Teams (HPTs);

- An integrated work plan that includes more details for the Design, Implementation, and Operations and Continuous Improvement stages than were available before;

- The organization's strategy is driven down to the lowest level via the goal-setting process in the redesign workshops;

- Permission, training, and encouragement for members of HPTs to improve their local work (local improvement projects within a team, as contrasted to the larger, Black-Belt-assisted improvement projects included in the first wave of improvements, more likely to address more complex, cross-team and cross-organizational issues); and

- An increase in worker motivation and job satisfaction resulting from local goal setting, team formation, and the ability to improve local work.

Important Questions to Ask

Instead of *telling* people what to think about and do, great leaders achieve organizational objectives by *asking key questions* that provoke thought and direct people's attention. Here are some important questions leaders should ask themselves and others during this stage.

Ask of Self

- Am I continually improving as a leader?

- What three things will I do in the next month to try to establish and manage the new culture?

- What else could I be doing to push down responsibility in the organization?

Ask of Others

- Have you maintained the appropriate balance between empowerment of others and control of the organization's assets?

- Where does the potential improvement project fit on a grid that would map the two variables of ease of implementation and impact?

- Is the scope of this proposed improvement project too big?

- Do we have a balance of long-term and short-term operation and improvement goals?

- Do we have a balanced portfolio of performance goals, not just financial? For example, have we included other performance measurement categories, such as customer, process, innovation, and learning?

Large-Group Interventions and Key Meetings

Getting groups of people to work together on critical LSS/HPO tasks is an excellent way to simultaneously accomplish four objectives:

1. Develop high quality work products for the implementation because of the diverse perspectives provided;

2. Achieve high levels of understanding among all participants about the topics discussed;

3. Increase energy and commitment regarding decisions made resulting from participation; and

4. Build leaders for the future by involving people in important discussions who might not normally be involved.

Large group interventions (LGIs) are methods for engaging large groups of people for a specific purpose. They typically involve over twenty people, a number far too high to utilize traditional meeting management and small group dynamics rules. LGIs are explained in greater detail in the Appendix. In addition to LGIs there are key meetings that are also important in advancing LSS/HPO and generating enthusiasm and commitment. Figure 16.1 depicts a sample sequence of LGIs and key meetings. Table 16.1 provides a brief description of each entry on Figure 16.1. Leaders can use the sample sequence as provided or develop another, more tailored approach. Exhibit A.2 in the Appendix provides an example of a Large-Group Intervention template used in restructuring to High-Performance Teams.

Leaders need to be prepared for new depictions of organizational structures generated in the restructuring workshops. Team designs may no longer look like the traditional straight lines and boxes of an organizational chart. Instead, they are more likely to contain circles, other geometric shapes, and arcs to represent the new lateral flows of information and materials. Figure 16.2 provides a graphic representation of what leaders might expect.

Figure 16.1. Large-Group Interventions and Key Meetings Map for Design

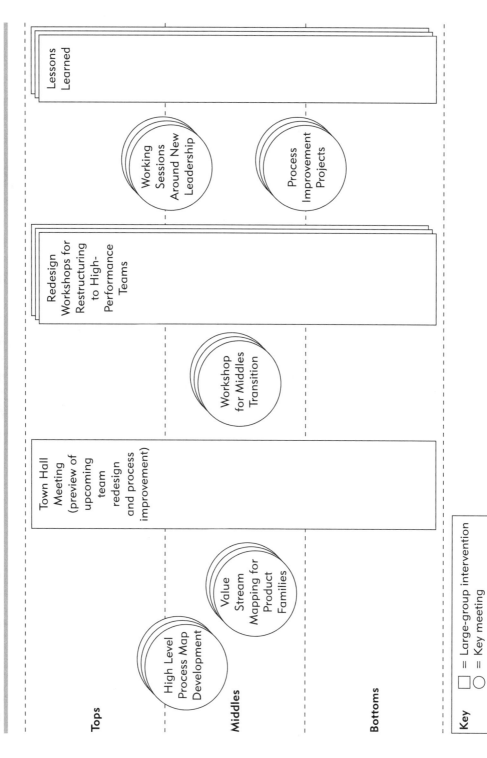

Table 16.1. Large-Group Interventions and Key Meetings for Design

Name	Gathering Type	Description of Key Elements
High Level Process Map Development	Meeting	Eight to twelve people who have knowledge of a process develop high level flows of activities and key decisions.
Value Stream Mapping™ for Product Families	Meeting	Managers develop a visual representation of the flow of information and materials as they are combined to produce a family of products or services. In addition to the picture of the flow, participants document information about how long the work in process is at each operation, amount of changeover time required, resources applied to each operation, an assessment of whether or not a particular step adds value to the customer, and places where inventory (of parts, paper, or other items) accumulate.
Town Hall Meeting (Preview of Upcoming Team Redesign and Process Improvement)	LGI	Provide an opportunity for two-way conversations between senior managers and the workforce regarding lessons learned from the previous Direction Setting Stage, the organizational strategy, a reiteration of the burning platform for change, and the approach to transforming to an LSS/HPO. Top management also provides a preview of the approach that consists of redesigning to HPTs and launching process improvement teams.
Workshop for Middles Transition	Meeting	An Initial Restructuring Team member convenes a session in which middle managers discuss the following questions and develop action plans to address concerns: (1) What excites you about the upcoming changes? (2) What concerns you about the upcoming changes? and (3) What needs to be done to make the new environment the best it can be for Middles and the entire organization? Middles often find it is helpful to invite an outsider who has been through a similar experience to this session to provide some best practices and answer questions about Middles' new roles.
Redesign Workshops for Restructuring to HPTs	LGI	Convene a session in which fifteen to two hundred participants reorganize a segment of the organization into one that consists primarily of HPTs. While there may still be some individual contributors whose work is not interdependent with others, most of the organization will be structured into HPTs that highly value goal setting and process execution. Whenever possible, top leaders should show up and kick off a redesign session. A sample template for a redesign LGI called a Participative Design Workshop appears in the Appendix.
Process Improvement Projects	Meeting	Black Belts lead the analysis and application of improvement methods and tools to processes that do not meet desired standards of cost, cycle time, or quality. Tools range from simple cycle time reduction tools to complex statistical methods.
Working Sessions Around New Leadership	Meeting	New leaders convene and discuss challenges of leading in the new environment and collectively develop better ways to do so.
Lessons Learned	LGI	A group of people involved in the transformation convenes at the end of the stage to identify (1) what went well in this stage; (2) what they might do differently in the future; and (3) how the groups can make their learning accessible to people in the future who need this information.

Figure 16.2. Examples of Traditional and HPO Structures

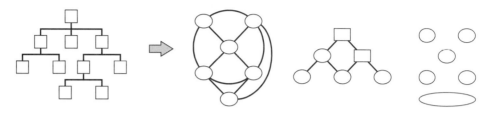

From . . .

Traditional structure
of lines and boxes
representing individuals
and reporting relationships.

To . . .

New High-Performance Team designs with elipses
representing teams, boxes representing individuals, and
lines representing information flow. In some LSS/HPO
designs, lines may be absent, representing the ad hoc
nature of negotiated information flow and lateral
relationships required to achieve team goals.

Interesting Options

While LSS/HPO transformations from organization to organization will vary, successful ones are principle-based. Here are some optional approaches—based on the principles in this book—that some organizations have found to be successful. These are not mutually exclusive options. Leaders should feel free to use these or other custom-developed options to address unique local requirements.

Option 1: Plan and Execute a Five-Day Rapid Process Redesign

Process improvement projects will often span months with people committed to the project for two to four hours per week. However, some successful organizations put a team of about ten people on a process full-time for an entire week and complete the analysis and process redesign. Leaders may wish to look for critical processes that may benefit from such an approach.

Option 2: Have Top and Middle Leaders Fill Out Responsibility Charts

Clarity of responsibilities is a hallmark of high-performing organizations. A simple mapping of individuals to responsibilities can be a significant step toward eliminating task confusion and can help the speed and quality of task execution. A simple tool called a RACI matrix, shown in Figure 16.3, is often used when front-line workers develop the HPT designs to clarify team responsibilities, but it's not often used by top-level leaders. Such a tool can be extremely helpful, as top leaders are often quite unclear about responsibilities related to departmental handoffs necessary to accomplish a process. People's names go across the top of the matrix, and roles, responsibilities, and knowledge areas are documented on the left-hand side. The specific relationship between the two is denoted by an R for primary (R)esponsibility, A to indicate (A)pproval is required, C to indicate that a person must be (C)onsulted, or I to indicate that a person needs to be (I)nformed.

Figure 16.3. Example of a RACI Chart

Responsibility Charting Tool

Roles/Resp	People		
	Peter	Paul	Mary
Run assay 203	R	A	I
FDA submissions	A	R	
Write lyrics to "Blowin' in the Wind"		R	

Key
R = Primary Responsibility
A = Approval
C = Consult
I = Inform

Critical Steps
1. List all people involved.
2. List key roles and responsibilities.
3. Negotiate RACI assignments in group.
4. Periodically review and revise.

Option 3: Get People Used to Lateral Communication and Collaboration Before Moving to HPTs

Lily Ruppe, head of organization development for Johns Manville in their Denver headquarters facilities, expressed a concern: people accustomed to hierarchical silos—particularly in non-production or knowledge work—for many years may have a difficult time quickly adjusting to an environment made up entirely of teams. To get people to break out of a silo mentality and work well cross-functionally, the company established a matrixed environment organized by function and by process with very clearly defined roles and responsibilities. This proved to be a successful first step in helping people to think cross-functionally[1] on their way toward more team-based structures.

Option 4: Establish an LSS/HPO Steering Group or Council

Some organizations have chosen to have a special group monitor the progress of improvement projects and of the redesign activities. The benefit of this is that it can focus attention on—through the use of senior management resources—the new ways of doing things. Eventually, though, this group should disband as LSS/HPO becomes a way of life, not a separate project to be managed. For this reason, many organizations do not opt to have a special group like this, but opt to have the regular middle and top management meetings track progress, ask questions, and resolve resource conflicts.

Option 5: Incorporate Other Improvement Disciplines Under the LSS/HPO Umbrella if There Is Internal Expertise

It makes little sense to discard an existing improvement method, particularly if it has yielded excellent results. For example, an organization may wish to incorporate the theory of constraints into the training programs for Black Belts and in improvement projects. This improvement approach, which focuses on identifying and removing constraints, can be rapidly grasped by reading the original work on the topic, *The Goal*.[2] It's a quick read because it's written like a novel, and the principles can be implemented shortly after.

Option 6: Use Formal Service Level Agreements Between Teams and Outside Entities

Between teams and with outside entities such as customers and suppliers some organizations find such a formal document useful. The document typically includes targets for time, cost, and quality. Many also include reporting requirements and a process for resolving disputes.

These six options have worked well for some organizations.

Common Traps

Although no two implementations of LSS/HPO will be exactly alike, there are some common traps that organizations encounter. Those most often found in the Design stage are

- *Having specific organizational design recommendations in mind but not expressing them, resulting in having to overturn team redesign decisions.* This results in decreased morale and a diminished employee desire for continuous improvement. If top leaders believe that a recommendation is what's truly needed, then they should list it as a "minimum critical specification" not open for redesign by lower levels in the organization. An example would be the decision to have international teams organized by customer, instead of by geographic region.

- *Being overly optimistic for the duration of an improvement project because the data are not yet available.* Since a new organizational imperative is to manage by data, it's an absolute requirement that adequate time be allowed to collect and analyze it and then develop recommendations.[3]

- *Forcing people to be on a team, even though their work is not interdependent.* People belong in teams only if they depend on each other to achieve an objective. People work as individual contributors in the structure if their work can be done independently, although today's complex world typically calls for more collective effort. Forcing people into a team if their work is truly not interdependent is a drain of time and energy.

- *Failing to develop links among processes.* Many organizations that move from function-based organizations to process-based organizations make the mistake of establishing processes as the primary basis of organization, and stopping there. It is also important for a process team or process owner to communicate across processes as needs arise. For example, if the recruiting process at a consulting firm changes, someone in that recruiting process needs to notify others in affected processes such as project management and customer relations. If such lateral coordination is not designed in, the organization runs the risk of moving from function silos to process silos and still retaining "fiefdoms" that act independently to optimize their own goals, irrespective of others.' Cross-unit coordination needs to be designed in, irrespective of the primary organizing theme—such as functional specialty, process, or geography—for truly high performance.

- *Overeducating in early stages.* Experience shows that it's best not to try to cram every possible statistical tool into the first round of Black Belt training. The train-do-train-do cycle will be more beneficial after a starter set of tools is presented and applied.

- *Disregarding the cultural aspect of the change effort and focusing only on the tools.* It's necessary to have cultural change goals and measurements as well as goals like "reduce the defect per million opportunities for the stamping process by 40 percent."

- *Telling people that teams are "just an experiment, a pilot; if it doesn't work we'll change it."* The director of a research laboratory moving to HPTs said it best when he said, "If I told them it was an experiment, they might get the idea we'd go back to the old way of doing things. They can't think that way if this transformation is going to work."

- *Failing to consolidate improvement efforts, such as Baldrige, selected reengineering projects, and so on, under a new change effort.* After consolidating these projects, it is beneficial to publicly recognize their previous good work.

- *Being too specific about top level goals for the organizational unit about to redesign.* Teams have to feel they have some latitude so they can contribute. Honeywell CEO Jim Renier's instruction to Ray Alvarez was "Make Micro Switch competitive for the 21st century." From this simple instruction, Alvarez figured the transformation would require a new strategy, a refined business model, revamped processes, adoption of new technologies, entry into new markets, a new manager team, new team-based work in the factory, and retraining of the workforce.[4]

- *Assuming that teams always have to be multi-skilled from the start.* Although multi-skilling is highly desirable for HPOs, it's acceptable to first move to a team-based structure without combing different functional departments in the first redesign. Hewlett-Packard in Greeley, Colorado, first designed teams of the same functional discipline and then later moved to multi-skilled teams. In this design strategy the departments of production, engineering, and purchasing first organized from a department into teams and learned how to operate as teams first; then after six months they formed multi-functional teams.[5]

- *Letting teams develop their own goals and not having managers review and negotiate them.* Teams may have missed an important part of the strategy that was not evident to them. In this case it is a necessary control to conduct a manager-team negotiation to align team goals and organization strategy.

- *Not ensuring that lower organizational levels don't pull down more managerial capability than they can handle.* Usually responsibilities such as goal setting, internal coordination and control, work scheduling, peer quality reviews, and preparation of preliminary budgets are in the first wave of responsibility downloads from higher-ups. Later, after appropriate training, more advanced managerial tasks such as hiring, disciplinary actions, and firing can also be downloaded.

- *Allowing the human resources function to remain in a transaction-oriented role, instead of a strategic role.* From this stage out, HR people can no longer just focus on mundane personnel-related tasks. They need to be strategic partners as they evaluate new ways of compensating people, rewarding teams, and formally evaluating new behaviors. Recently, top executives are paying more attention to the benefits of an excellent HR person in a transformation. When Bob Nardelli left GE to become CEO of The Home Depot, he quickly hired Dennis Donovan, an HR executive who worked with Nardelli at GE Power Systems. In 2001, Donovan was the second highest paid person at Home Depot, with a $21.5 million pay package (Nardelli was the highest paid with $24 million).[6] In 2002 Home Depot was the fastest growing retailer (even outpacing Wal-Mart) and Nardelli proudly claimed, "We open a new store every forty-three hours." He also forecast moving from a $50 billion company to a $100 billion company in 2007. People are the key to success in a large-scale change like LSS/HPO, and HR can help enlist people and direct their attention to the new ways of doing things.[7]

- *Assuming top-level and mid-level managers should always be a part of and behave as teams.* There are bona fide tasks that require individual action instead of interdependent action. Leadership teams that try do everything as a team will cause themselves and the organization significant problems.

Counterintuitive Elements

 Leadership in an LSS/HPO looks different than it does in traditional organizational structures. Some of those differences are keys to LSS/HPO success. Table 16.2 shows eleven such elements often encountered during Design.

Table 16.2. Counterintuitive Elements in the Design Stage

Traditional Thinking	Counterintuitive LSS/HPO Reality
We can't start an LSS/HPO conversion until we have a well-defined strategy.	Although having a great strategy helps immensely, some organizations have made the conversion successfully and let strategic details emerge. Hewlett-Packard's Santa Clara Division successfully went to an HPO structure before revamping their strategy.[i]
Having a few people on a "design team" that develops new organizational structures will save time.	Once in place, peers view the design team as outsiders, removed from day-to-day work details. Consequently, the design team must "sell" solutions to the larger group. The result: multiple iterations result in a longer implementation, and only a few people understand redesign principles for future redesigns.
People can't redesign their own work. It takes HR departments and consulting groups to do complex things like that.	Time and again it has been shown that with minimal input—about two days in a redesign workshop—workers can learn the principles of HPT redesign and implement learning systems that enable them to continuously improve.
We can't spare the time for nearly 100 percent of the people in the workforce to participate in the organizational redesign. They have to get product out the door.	The benefits far exceed the costs. The workshop for converting to an HPO takes only one to two days per person. For large organizations this workshop time can be staggered for various organizational units so that products and services still are provided to customers. Participation in this restructuring process helps drive the strategy down through local goal setting, generate energy for achieving goals, and increases job satisfaction that results in motivation for continuous improvement. Over the course of a year or two, leaders need to consider whether the lack of the above conditions costs at least two days of lost productivity. Usually the answer is a resounding, Yes.
HPT members may get the first design wrong, since they don't do it for a living. The result: serious problems.	Steve Rosselli, a Weyerhaeuser finance director, was apprehensive about team self-design. But he found when teams did it, they truly owned the design and worked hard to make it succeed. After identifying possible improvements, his teams even redesigned two more times within the first year and delivered superior results.
Every team must have one designated leader.	Many teams work best when the leadership rotates based on the task at hand. Al West, CEO of the highly successful SEI Investments says, "We call it fluid leadership. People figure out what they're good at, and that shapes what their roles are. There's not just one leader. Different people lead during different parts of the process."[ii] This strategy affords more people the opportunity to think strategically, gain a sense of accomplishment, and develop leaders at multiple levels. Some teams may require just one leader, but this is a design decision during the redesign workshop for special situations, not the default.

Table 16.2. Counterintuitive Elements in the Design Stage, Cont'd

Traditional Thinking	Counterintuitive LSS/HPO Reality
We need to squelch the views of naysayers against the change.	Giving dissidents a voice can actually help surface some key issues that can then be visibly resolved. At Honeywell's Technical Instruments Division in 1994 there was a major change effort underway, with many initial naysayers. They published the "Honeywell TID Grapevine," containing rumors and attacks on the change effort. The president dealt openly with the issues and the paper ceased to exist after three printings.
We can't just eliminate layers in the hierarchy; those layers are doing something now.	As HPTs take on more responsibilities of those above them, there becomes much less of a need for numerous intermediate levels of supervision and coordination. Middle layers don't disappear, but there are fewer.
Learning new things is all that's important.	The workforce must unlearn many things to operate effectively in LSS/HPO. Gregory Bateson once remarked that in periods of major change what most people need isn't a good pencil, but a good eraser.
If we're going to more participative management, why do Tops get to make a lot of the key up-front decisions, like moving to an LSS/HPO, which projects are in the first wave, and initial restructuring decisions?	Tops often know more about external forces and strategy than the rest of the organization. Such initial decisions have far-reaching implications. Since Tops have ultimate responsibility for the organization, these initial decisions belong to them.
Authoritarian leaders cannot be converted to the new analyze-and-energize leadership style, so they should be removed.	Authoritarian leaders can change if they have the desire, the willingness to try practices that may feel initially uncomfortable, and coaching. In my experience, such leaders need to be given a chance because they may become some of the best new leaders.

[i]Zell, D. (1997). *Change by design.* New York: ILR Press.
[ii]Kirsner, S. (1998, April). Total teamwork: SEI Investments. *Fast company, 18,* p. 130.

Leadership Checklist for Proceeding to the Next Phase

 Before the organization can move to the next stage of an LSS/HPO transformation, top leaders should check to ensure the items in Exhibit 16.1 have been completed. It can also be helpful for top leaders to refer to this list as the stage is unfolding to ensure that activities are started on time to produce the desired results before the stage is complete.

Exhibit 16.1. Leadership Checklist for the Design Stage

☐ Communicated the objectives and direction of the LSS/HPO transformation at least five times to the entire workforce

☐ Visited some redesigned HPTs to solicit feedback about how it's going, and demonstrate Top management interest in the redesign process and outcomes

☐ Set expectations that both results and culture will be managed in the new LSS/HPO environment

☐ Checked with individual managers and teams of managers at lower levels to ensure the negotiated goals at all organizational levels are consistent with the organization's strategic intent

☐ Conducted a personal reflection of performance in the current stage and personal leadership objectives for the next stage

☐ Set the tone for creating a learning environment

☐ Personally discussed objectives and details of selected improvement projects in a public forum

The pragmatic tips presented in this chapter can help leaders anticipate potential problem areas and exploit opportunities that arise in the Design stage. By understanding the key outputs and deliverables, leaders know what people should be working on throughout the stage and can suggest mid-course corrections as needed. The sample thought-provoking questions provided will help leaders and others think about important transformation issues.

Public gatherings and collective decision making are key elements of successful LSS/HPOs. In any large group setting it's important that the group become productive as fast as possible. To accomplish that, leaders can call on some standard templates called large-group interventions to help people be productive quickly and accomplish the objectives as quickly as possible. The large-group interventions and key meetings listed will help advance LSS/HPO objectives by quickly delivering high quality work products and generating enthusiasm and commitment to LSS/HPO objectives.

The path to a successful LSS/HPO is guided by principles and a flexible approach, not a cast-in-concrete process. This chapter presented some optional activities that have been successful for other practitioners. By studying the common traps presented, leaders can choose to plan for, instead of react to, problems others have encountered. To help ease the transition to new leadership practices, some of which may appear counterintuitive to traditional leadership thinking, this chapter presented the most common counterintuitive leadership practices that appear in the Design stage. As a final help to leaders, there is a leadership checklist of important items leaders need to consider throughout and upon completion of Design.

Notes

1. Personal conversation with Lily Ruppe of Johns Manville.

2. Goldratt, E. (1992). *The goal: A process of ongoing improvement.* Great Barrington, MA: North River Press.

3. Senior leaders often don't understand that, so it warrants a bit of a warning here. A simple tool called a "run chart" that collects data points over time should have twenty-five or more points to be able to draw conclusions. A picture of the distribution of a set of data points—called a "histogram"—should have 50 to 100 points to be reliable. In some cases data might only be able to be collected every three days because of the process cycle under study. This would be bad news if the senior sponsor believed he was going to have results in two months for a process that required a histogram with no previous data collection! It's a common error to become excited about an improvement project and promise it in what seems to be a reasonable amount of work time, but beware the data collection time.

4. Duck, J.D. (2001). *The change monster.* New York: Crown Business.

5. Personal conversation with Walt Grady of Hewlett-Packard.

6. Sellers, P. (2002, June 9). Home Depot: Something to prove. *Fortune.*

7. Nardelli, R. (2002). An address to the Terry College of Business alumni. ww.terry.uga.edu.news/releases/2002/ttt_nardelli.html.

CHAPTER 17

Stage 4: Implementation

Activity Map and Leader To Do List

To produce quality, you must have a system to improve it.

Thomas Edison

IN THE DESIGN STAGE, the organization designed the new structure consisting primarily of High-Performance Teams (HPTs) and the infrastructure to support process improvement. In the Implementation stage, some first-wave improvement teams complete their projects and the organization begins to see improved profits, reduced cycle time, and fewer defects. Simultaneously, new cultural norms become anchored and job satisfaction and intrinsic motivation increase. As the process unfolds, people have increased positive feelings toward LSS/HPO and are willing put more time into its activities. During Implementation senior managers work on improving their effectiveness as individuals and as a Top team. In this stage they will face new challenges in the areas of activity prioritization and resource allocation.

This chapter provides a preview of what's ahead for leaders in the Implementation stage. An Activity Map presents a picture of the sequence of major stage activities and milestones. The Leader To Do List presents a list of high leverage tasks that enable leaders to guide the LSS/HPO transformation smoothly along.

Activity Map

The Activity Map in Figure 17.1 shows major blocks of activity and their relative placement within the Implementation stage. Each of the three rows contains both LSS and HPO activities. The top row—LSS/HPO together—represents a strong combination of LSS and HPO activities and unfolding conditions. The second and third rows indicate a predominance of one discipline over the other, even though LSS and HPO elements appear in each.

Figure 17.1. Activity Map for Implementation

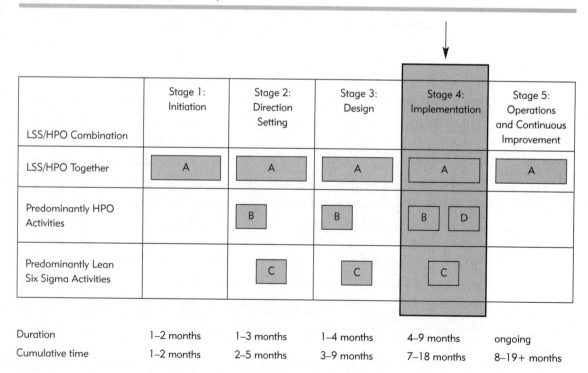

	Stage 1: Initiation	Stage 2: Direction Setting	Stage 3: Design	Stage 4: Implementation	Stage 5: Operations and Continuous Improvement
LSS/HPO Combination					
LSS/HPO Together	A	A	A	A	A
Predominantly HPO Activities		B	B	B D	
Predominantly Lean Six Sigma Activities		C	C	C	
Duration	1–2 months	1–3 months	1–4 months	4–9 months	ongoing
Cumulative time	1–2 months	2–5 months	3–9 months	7–18 months	8–19+ months

Figure 17.1. Activity Map for Implementation, Cont'd

Block	Key Milestones and Activities
A	While the organization sees benefits in performance indicators, employees feel benefits in increased control over their work environment and the ability to make a difference in improvement and performance areas. These factors fuel the spread of improvement tools and a continuous improvement culture. More decisions and responsibilities flow to HPTs from above as teams receive training in technical skills, process improvement principles, statistical tools, managerial skills, and team skills. Publicized process improvement successes spur teams on to develop informal cross-team mentoring programs in simple improvement tools and team skills. Throughout Implementation, leaders communicate messages and reinforce new mindsets of LSS/HPO in group settings and one-on-ones. Top leaders examine their dual roles of individual and Top team contributors and develop action plans for improvement.
B	Intrinsic motivation levels continue to rise and teams become very execution-focused to meet the goals they developed during the redesign workshops. Groups of middle managers begin to meet and form middle management groups that discuss issues facing middle managers and collective ways to address them. Groups called "communities of practice" and "centers of excellence" emerge in importance as they keep technical skills honed for those who are primarily in process-based teams and who do not frequently interact with functional peers. Some teams often restructure into more process-based structures resulting from breakthroughs from the first wave of Black Belt improvement projects. Leaders provide encouragement and support to teams and individuals in the new ways of thinking and acting.
C	Many first wave improvement teams complete their projects and financial benefits begin to appear. A "dashboard" of critical metrics is developed for the overall organizational unit and possibly for major processes or departments. Leaders use the dashboard to prioritize and de-prioritize projects, as well as to run the business. Celebrations are conducted. Continuous improvement and customer focus begin to be institutionalized in the culture. New Black Belts and Green Belts are trained for second and third improvement waves. Process managers and process-based teams begin to emerge as the concept of business process becomes a cornerstone for excellence. De-prioritization of improvement projects becomes important as key resources become stretched. The demand for improvement principles and tools is accelerated by HPTs desiring ways to meet and exceed their goals.
D	Based on experience with operating as an HPT, some HPTs or groups of HPTs restructure themselves again during the latter part of the Implementation stage. The human resources group studies and begins to implement compensation and reward systems that fit with the new continuous improvement philosophy and team structures and culture.

Leader To Do List

In each stage there is a set of high leverage actions leaders can take to influence transformation success. Because there are many demands for leaders' time throughout the transformation, it becomes important to organize and prioritize items most deserving of leader attention. The Transformation Grid ("Grid" for short) organizes Leader To Dos into six categories that provide focus for high leverage activities. Figure 17.2. shows a Grid with sample activities for Implementation. Leaders may wish to modify the content and activity placement in the sample to tailor the Grid for unique organizational situations.[1]

Figure 17.2. Transformation Grid for Implementation

High Leverage Category	Stage 1: Initiation	Stage 2: Direction Setting	Stage 3: Design	Stage 4: Implementation	Stage 5: Operations and Continuous Improvement
Key Shaping Actions					
Participative Planning					
Process Awareness					
High Participation Restructuring					
Leadership Development					
Support					

	Stage 4: Implementation
Key Shaping Actions	Continually seek to push down decisions, information, skills, and rewards Hold teams collectively accountable for results Hold management accountable for results and behaviors Actively manage the measurement conflicts that often become problematic in this stage Use senior management operations review meetings to help shape and manage culture Protect and defend HPTs from non-LSS/HPO units outside the LSS/HPO boundary Foster leadership learning networks
Participative Planning	NA in this stage
Process Awareness	Include project reviews in senior management operations review meetings Use a data-driven process to identify improvement projects Prioritize and de-prioritize improvement projects to meet organizational goals Publicize improvement projects' progress and results Foster process improvement learning networks
High Participation Restructuring	*Optional, based on need:* Encourage and provide support for any necessary restructuring
Leadership Development	Continue self-assessment and self-reflection activities Allot time for middle manager meetings Coach other leaders toward higher levels of performance

Figure 17.2. Transformation Grid for Implementation, Cont'd

Support	Focus on problem solving, process improvement, technical and leadership training, and related developmental activities
	Initiate revision of the new hire process, job descriptions, and compensation to reflect new directions and desired behaviors
	Automate selected HR functions and make HR more of a strategic partner
	Standardize evaluation forms and clearly state the expected behaviors

Activity descriptions for each high leverage category appear in the following sections.

Key Shaping Actions

During the Implementation stage there are seven key shaping actions leaders can take to position the organization for the highest quality outcomes. The following section describes each.

Continually Seek to Push Down Decisions, Information, Skills, and Rewards

Leaders should continue the "intelligent empowerment" started in the Design stage. Leaders need to remember that pushing these elements down is only one part of a high-performance equation. Another important part is holding teams accountable for results.

Hold Teams Collectively Accountable for Results and Behaviors

Holding teams *collectively* accountable is essential for building the team's energy and sense of a collective "we." This applies to *all* standing work teams, special project teams, and management teams for both operations and process improvement.

Hold Management Accountable for Results and Behaviors

In an LSS/HPO, Middle accountability is critical. Tops hold Middles accountable for integrating HPT work and providing appropriate resources to HPTs. There is also downward accountability, in that HPTs hold Middles accountable for their promises, behaviors, and general HPT support.

Actively Manage the Measurement Conflicts That Often Become Problematic in This Stage

With all HPTs setting goals, it is likely some goals may conflict. While some conflicts are discovered in the Design stage when HPTs negotiate goals with their managers, some conflicts may not be so apparent until Implementation. Classic conflicts such as the sales group wanting a warehouse full of inventory and the warehouse manager seeking low inventory levels may not be uncovered at first. Middle managers, a concerned corporate citizens group, or an internal quality function should review all goals to ensure alignment. For goal conflicts that cannot be resolved at lower levels, there must be an escalation process for elevating the issue to higher organizational levels.

Use Senior Management Operations Review Meetings to Help Shape and Manage Culture

People watch Top leader behavior in the meetings to determine what is appropriate cultural behavior, so these meetings can be an important forum for shaping and managing the new culture. Changes to the format and style of the meeting, such as discarding the old "king holding court" one-way flow of information and replacing it with a forum for debate and discussion, sends a powerful message about new interaction patterns. And when senior managers ask questions about the impact of proposed changes on customers and process variation, it helps to reinforce the new norms.

Protect and Defend HPTs from Non-LSS/HPO Units Outside the LSS/HPO Boundary

When changing the culture and operating practices of a division or plant within a larger company, those outside units that interact with the changed unit will try to interact as they always have before. Outsiders will make demands such as "I don't want to talk with a team about my problem, I want to talk to the manager!" when, in fact, there is no manager because the teams perform the old manager's job as well as the technical work. The head of the LSS/HPO—as the person with some high level organizational clout—must inform outsiders of the new environment and enforce their interacting with the LSS/HPO in a manner consistent with the new culture and practices. Gerry FitzPatrick, a director of a highly successful LSS/HPO that started in 1995 at StorageTek, puts it well:

People outside the group were used to dealing with us in the old ways. This was tough on the team, and tough in the new culture we were trying to create. The culture change needed to be nurtured and protected. It was like something in a dish that you didn't want people messing with until it was fully developed. The head of the LSS/HPO has to rise to the challenge and defend the boundaries and new practices.[2]

Foster Leadership Learning Networks

Because leaders will encounter many challenges they have not yet seen, it will be important for leaders at all levels to convene, reflect, and discuss best practices in leadership throughout the organization. One of the best ways to do this is a leaders' learning group that discusses issues and develops action plans for personal and group improvement.

Process Awareness

The concept of process is central to any LSS/HPO transformation. In each stage the organization needs to dedicate time to understanding, improving, and managing processes. In the Implementation stage, all in the workforce need to understand how to analyze, improve, and monitor processes.

Include Project Reviews in Senior Management Operations Review Meetings

Organizations have two primary choices for review of process improvement projects: holding stand-alone improvement review meetings or including the review as a part of regularly scheduled operations review meetings. I recommend the latter because it sends a strong message that improvement is now part of the normal operation of the business, instead of being a stand-alone, separate activity. I've found this tactic has the added benefit of making the progress report-outs shorter.

Use a Data-Driven Process to Select Improvement Projects

Some candidate projects in the first wave are obvious "no brainers" for selection. But as the low-hanging fruit is plucked in early projects, it becomes less obvious where best to next apply resources. Black Belts and change agents may choose to develop their own method or reference an excellent tool developed by Mike Carnell and Shree Nanguneri that will be published on isixsigma.com in 2003.

Prioritize *and* Deprioritize Improvement Projects to Meet Organizational Goals

In the Implementation phase the list of potential projects will begin to grow exponentially as more people are trained and a "buzz" is created around process improvement. To avoid overloading key talent and to ensure that projects are completed in a timely fashion, leaders will need to continually determine whether or not projects should be reprioritized.

Publicize Improvement Projects' Progress and Results

Celebrate successes and publicly praise deserving teams. Consider having a president's award for quality, and focus this award on the process of quality improvement. About twenty years ago when the topic of quality was growing in importance, the president of Matsushita, a multi-billion-dollar global enterprise with locations on nearly every continent, gave the annual president's quality award to the women who served tea in one of the company dining rooms. The two implicit messages were significant: no job is trivial in the overall scheme of Matsushita's business, and process improvement is important everywhere.

Foster Process Improvement Learning Networks

As has been mentioned several times in this book, establishing a network of learners substantially accelerates the rate of change and also increases levels of performance. The Transformation Technology Team can greatly help teams here by helping to build and use a database that captures lessons learned from process improvement and restructuring efforts. Leaders need to keep in mind that active discussion about the elements that go into the database is just as critical as the technology.

High-Participation Restructuring

In the Design stage members of the organization restructured their current organizational units into HPTs. In some cases teams wish to do this again as early as the Implementation stage based on what they've learned about operating as a team or based on changed external conditions. Since one key principle is that teams can reconfigure the organization when necessary, leaders need to support this and ensure that teams affected renegotiate goals with their manager and other teams affected by the proposed restructuring.

Leadership Development

In each stage leaders need to continuously develop their leadership skills as they become "analyze-and-energize" leaders. In this stage leaders need to focus on continuing self-assessments and reflections and also on helping other leaders improve their levels of performance.

Continue Self-Assessment and Self-Reflection Activities

Although things get hectic in the Implementation stage, leaders need to take stock of any personal performance issues that may have arisen and correct them. By this time leaders have identified what the new leadership looks like and are often capable of closing gaps between desired and actual behaviors.

Allot Time for Middle Manager Meetings

As presented in the context of the Top/Middle/Bottom model, it is important for middle management groups to gather and do activities such as share issues that other Middles may be able to provide coaching on, jointly engage in problem solving, and develop plans for the future. Unless Tops specifically give permission to do this (or Middles are really daring), this may fail to happen. So much is going on that Middles think, "Oh, the Tops would never let us spend time on that." The message to Tops is to specifically allot time for Middles to meet. High leverage results appear in the form of lateral information sharing across the middle of the organization and improved coordination of HPT activities below. An additional benefit is that Middles can pull down more Top responsibilities, freeing up Tops' time for more strategic issues.

Coach Other Leaders Toward Higher Levels of Performance

During Implementation leaders need to rely heavily on each other to increase levels of leadership awareness and performance. This will be instrumental for future leadership development as leaders form relationships that enable the giving and receiving of honest feedback and make time to do so.

Support

The support function provides additional leverage and benefits for the previous Grid categories. That support includes items such as communication, HR processes, and information technology support. There are four important support processes for the Implementation stage.

Focus on Problem Solving, Process Improvement, Technical and Leadership Training, and Related Developmental Activities

Teams and managers need to continue along their development path. Leaders need to ensure that appropriate training exists and that teams receive it.

Initiate Revision of the New Hire Process, Job Descriptions, and Compensation to Reflect New Directions and Desired Behaviors

Human resource people become very active in this phase to get HR systems and policies in line with the new ways of thinking and acting. A starter list of HR activities includes:

- Screening job applicants for culture fit as well as technical capabilities;
- Modifying job descriptions to reflect new team responsibilities;
- Modifying performance appraisals to include results, behaviors, and development of interpersonal and team skills; and
- Training team members in legal and EEOC guidelines as they assume hiring, discipline, and firing responsibilities.

Automate Selected HR Functions and Make HR More of a Strategic Partner

Consider implementing aspects of electronic HR functions on the organization's intranet (sometimes called "eHR") to administer routine, repetitive HR functions such as new employee orientation, competency descriptions, and training planning and scheduling. This strategy will free up HR resources to spend more time supporting strategic organization objectives while also making the HR performance element visible for all in the organization to access, understand, and use.

Standardize Evaluation Forms and Clearly State the Expected Behaviors

When The Home Depot was transforming to a higher performance organization, the HR department pared down the existing 157 appraisal forms for 295,000 employees to two forms. In addition, salaried associates, from the CEO on down, are rated by co-workers, above and below, on identical criteria such as "gets results," "develops people," "drives change", and "displays character." Graded on overall performance from A (outstanding) to D (improvement required), they're paid based on how well they score.[3] And recently Home Depot has begun to pay "success sharing" bonuses that pay groups of people for achievements, in addition to individual compensation.

The important support functions of training and modifying HR practices begin to gain momentum in the Implementation stage and carry through into the next stage.

In the Implementation stage leaders need to focus their efforts on the big picture that was provided by the Activity Map and on key day-to-day tasks as suggested in the Leader To Do List section. In this chapter leaders learned how to use the Transformation Grid tool to plan their activities for the upcoming work in the stage and monitor those activities to ensure that adequate progress is being made.

Notes

1. For further information on uses of the Grid and content updates, see TransformationGrid.com.

2. Personal conversation with Gerry FitzPatrick, director of business operations, Information Storage at StorageTek.

3. Sellers, P. (2002, June 9). Home Depot: Something to prove. *Fortune.*

18

Stage 4:
Implementation

Tools Application

Life is not the way it's supposed to be. It's the way it is. The way you cope with it is what makes the difference.

Unknown

IN CHAPTER 17, LEADERS LEARNED about the major blocks of activities and specific high leverage actions they could take during the Implementation stage. This chapter presents key leader challenges and a set of tools to address them. Because of the major cultural shifts introduced and launching the first round of process improvements, the Implementation stage poses some unique challenges for leaders. Specifically, in this stage leaders face the following:

- Preventing leaders' time from becoming scattered as mini-crises and new situations present themselves, all seeming to demand immediate attention;

- Making sure the first wave of process improvement teams progress as they should and deliver benefits promised;

- Ensuring High-Performance Teams are supporting the organization's strategy;

- Actively managing the culture by focusing on desired behaviors as well as results;

- Keeping the workforce motivated to perform in the new execution-oriented and improvement-oriented environment; and

- Ensuring process improvement teams are doing high quality work quickly.

Each of the tools described in this chapter will help leaders address the above challenges.

Performance Framework

 During Implementation, the Performance Framework helps leaders:

- Avoid becoming scattered by focusing attention on key performance factors;

- See how the new culture is related to the other performance factors and managing the new culture accordingly;

- Give the workforce a big picture understanding of the transformation direction; and

- Gain insights during a lessons-learned analysis at stage completion.

In each use above, leaders:

1. Convene a meeting and post a large Performance Framework flip chart on a wall;

2. Facilitate discussions about each performance element and key element interrelationships;

3. Record participant comments on the flip chart near the related performance factor being discussed; and

4. Ensure meeting notes and action items are typed and distributed.

In addition, the tool can be used to illustrate which factors are addressed in this stage. Figure 18.1 shows the primary factors addressed during Initiation. Italicized comments appear adjacent to the factors addressed and describe how they are addressed.

Figure 18.1. Performance Framework for Implementation

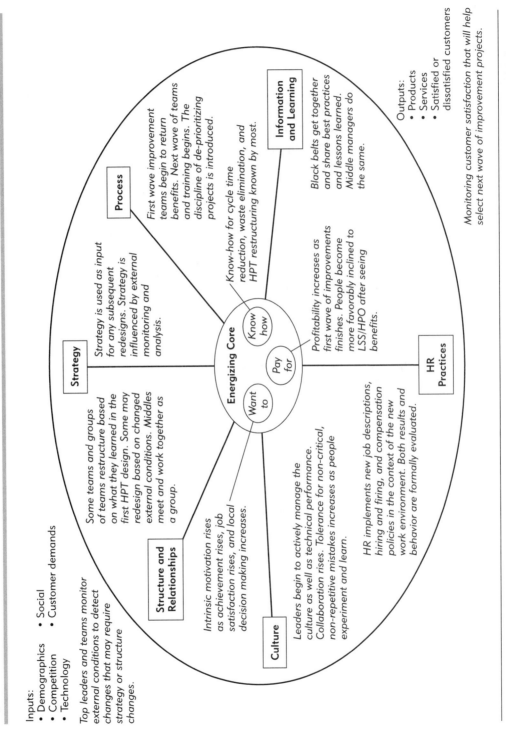

Inputs:
- Demographics
- Competition
- Technology
- Social
- Customer demands

Top leaders and teams monitor external conditions to detect changes that may require strategy or structure changes.

Strategy

Strategy is used as input for any subsequent redesigns. Strategy is influenced by external monitoring and analysis.

Structure and Relationships

Some teams and groups of teams restructure based on what they learned in the first HPT design. Some may redesign based on changed external conditions. Middles meet and work together as a group.

Intrinsic motivation rises as achievement rises, job satisfaction rises, and local decision making increases.

Culture

Leaders begin to actively manage the culture as well as technical performance. Collaboration rises. Tolerance for non-critical, non-repetitive mistakes increases as people experiment and learn.

HR implements new job descriptions, hiring and firing, and compensation policies in the context of the new work environment. Both results and behavior are formally evaluated.

Energizing Core
- Know how
- Pay for
- Want to

Process

First wave improvement teams begin to return benefits. Next wave of teams and training begins. The discipline of de-prioritizing projects is introduced.

Know-how for cycle time reduction, waste elimination, and HPT restructuring known by most.

Information and Learning

Black belts get together and share best practices and lessons learned. Middle managers do the same.

Profitability increases as first wave of improvements finishes. People become more favorably inclined to LSS/HPO after seeing benefits.

HR Practices

Outputs:
- Products
- Services
- Satisfied or dissatisfied customers

Monitoring customer satisfaction that will help select next wave of improvement projects.

Top/Middle/Bottom Space Analysis

The Performance Framework tool in the previous section presented a way of looking at key performance factors such as Strategy, Process, and Structure and how they combine to determine organizational performance in the Implementation stage. The Top/Middle/Bottom Space Analysis focuses leaders' attention on people—where they are in the organization, what their perceptual filters are about the upcoming opportunity, and how they might best be influenced to enthusiastically join in the LSS/HPO transformation. By understanding the Top, Middle, and Bottom organizational spaces, leaders can dramatically improve the leverage of their actions and accelerate the advancement of the organization to an LSS/HPO. This section is organized into three topic areas: (1) an *involvement profile,* which depicts the involvement of the Top, Middle, and Bottom positions in the LSS/HPO transformation; (2) *coaching for this stage,* which presents stage-specific insights into what each organizational space is experiencing during this part of the LSS/HPO transformation; and (3) *tool use,* which outlines the tools in the organization space toolkit.

Involvement Profile

This segment contains an organizational analysis and recommendations for leaders based on the organization space concepts presented in Chapter 7. For a quick review of those concepts, please refer to that section. This participation of the three position-based spaces, shown by shaded area, is shown in Figure 18.2.

Figure 18.2. Participation During Implementation

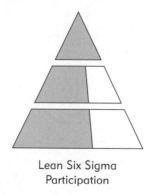

Lean Six Sigma
Participation

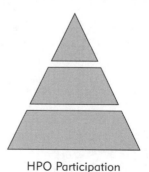

HPO Participation

As shown in the figure, in the Implementation stage all Top leaders are actively engaged in the LSS/HPO elements of the upcoming transformation. Ones who would not support the effort were offered a severance package or moved to a non-leadership position in the organization. Middles are involved in both, although more Middles are involved in the HPO activities than in the Lean Six Sigma activities. More Bottoms receive training in process improvement principles and techniques, and all Bottoms remain vigilant about early recognition of the need to redesign the organizational structure.

Coaching for This stage

This section provides insights into what's going on for each organizational space. By understanding the typical LSS/HPO forces affecting each of the organizational spaces, leaders can gain insight on how to best deal with issues affecting them, as well as gain insight into how to best interact with people based on the space that others are in.

What's Going on for the Tops in This Stage

During Implementation Tops begin to reap the rewards of seeds sown in earlier stages. HPTs identify and implement quick improvements because they now have the authority to act on things they have known were broken for years, but never had the authority to fix. The first wave of process improvement yields some spectacular results. A major challenge for Tops in this stage is to offload more tasks to Middles than their comfort level might permit. To help understand how to be the best top one can be, and also how to deal with someone in a Top position in this stage, here are coaching tips on organizational space concerns and issues, items for consideration, and practical tips.

Organizational Space Concerns and Issues   The immortal words of Charles Dickens, "It was the best of times, it was the worst of times" ring true for Tops in the Implementation stage. Great things are starting to happen for the organization, but there are also numerous areas requiring their attention. They evaluate progress in improvement projects, gently steer teams toward supporting the organization's strategy, and help reshape and solidify new cultural norms. At this point if Tops have done a good job of building responsibility at lower levels, they can begin to slightly decrease their involvement in the change effort and focus more on the strategic operation of the business. And Tops' world of complexity continues. As process improvement teams begin to apply advanced statistical methods, Tops need to ask them questions about team progress and technical improvements, without having had the advantage of the six weeks of training Black Belts have had.

Items for Consideration   Tops don't need to have all the answers to LSS/HPO leadership. Using their unique positional space as Tops, they can create conditions for leadership to develop in the organization by sponsoring leadership forums. Tops do not need to understand advanced statistical methods. They do need to make sure that team efforts are supporting the strategy and that the teams are operating on schedule and within budget. And finally, Tops don't need to be able to predict all the new problems and opportunities that appear. By having helped create and maintain an adaptive organizational system, they have ensured that the combined abilities of the organization's members, working together, can address even the toughest challenges that appear. In this stage life should become a bit less hectic for Tops because the rest of the organizational system has quite a bit of energy in it for high performance and continual improvement.

Practical Tips   Here are some tips for Tops during Implementation:

- Measure and critically discuss improvement projects at operations review meetings;

- Become more accessible to Middles and Bottoms in this stage. If Tops are going to distribute some of their responsibilities, they must involve others in addressing strategic questions and learning how to think strategically;

- Allow time and space for leadership forums in which people explore leadership skills and discuss successes and other learning points;

- Challenge yourself to push down more responsibility, and challenge Middles to accept and seek more responsibility;

- Identify what to do with newfound time. Some sample high leverage activities include strategic planning, customer visits, personal development, networking, and benchmarking;

- Become skilled at asking questions about statistically advanced improvement projects, while not having to learn the statistical details.

What's Going on for the Middles in This Stage

Bottoms have begun to assume responsibilities that used to belong solely to Middles. Middles are supposed to start taking on some responsibilities that have been held by Tops. In addition to distributing responsibilities to those below and taking on responsibilities from above, Middles continue to find themselves pulled in different directions by the needs of Tops and Bottoms. To help understand how to be the best Middle one can be and also how to deal with someone in a Middle position in this stage, here are insights on organizational space concerns and issues, items for consideration, and practical tips.

Organizational Space Concerns and Issues   In addition to being torn between Tops and Bottoms, Middles are torn between the old ways and the new. The expectation is that every day Middles will use the new analyze-and-energize leadership, but this represents such a stark departure from historical ways that sometimes it's quite difficult, so occasionally Middles revert back to the old behaviors.

Items for Consideration   Structurally speaking, Middles are the primary interface between the Tops and Bottoms. Because of the structural position they occupy, Tops and Bottoms will often make requests on Middles based on unreasonable expectations they have of the Middle position. Other spaces interacting with Middles typically expect Middles to take their side when dealing with others.

Practical Tips   Here are four high leverage strategies for Middles in this stage:[1]

1. *Seize Top responsibility whenever possible.* For example, instead of asking permission to get project team members together for a four-hour lessons-learned session (a decidedly Middle approach), a Middle should call the meeting, collect the lessons-learned data, and take responsibility for a high quality output (a definite Top action).

2. *Facilitate productive interactions between Tops and Bottoms and between any other two groups.* Middles can coach Tops on how to communicate with Bottoms and coach Bottoms on how to communicate with Tops. Black Belts often find themselves in a Middle condition when the manager of an operations areas tells the Black Belt, "You'll just have to tell senior management that our process isn't capable of those cycle time reductions

they want." A suboptimal Middle action would be trot down to the executive suite and relay the message (with the high likelihood of being sent back and forth several times). A well-trained, effective Black Belt, however, will immediately think, "Oh no, you're not putting me in the middle on this one" and say "Let's get together and I'll show you how to present the data we have to date to senior management. They may want to chat with you about this directly."

3. *Get together with other Middles and collectively explore the new LSS/HPO business operating environment.* Middles can gain power and substantial learning just by allocating one to two hours per week to discuss Middle issues and how Middles are approaching them.

4. *Try some of the analyze-and-energize behaviors, even if you may not initially agree with them.* This may seem odd advice in the face of the earlier advice to "be authentic." However, a better principle here is that sometimes it's easier to act your way into a new way of thinking than it is to think yourself into a new way of acting.[2] It's not necessary for a Middle to believe in the new leadership behaviors for them to work. Noted psychologist Abraham Maslow highlights the key difference of *being* something versus *trying to be* something. Maslow points out that a transition state of trying to be something is necessary and helpful to adopting new behaviors and becoming adept at them.[3] He suggests it is beneficial, even though initially a person may feel self-conscious, artificial, not spontaneous, and even phony. However, it is a necessary phase to go through on the road to being able to practice the new behaviors naturally. I have seen this "try it" approach work for numerous previously command-and-control style managers whom others had deemed "unsalvageable" in the new LSS/HPO environment.

By implementing these practical tips, Middles can be instrumental in shaping the new cultural norms and performance.

What's Going on for the Bottoms in This Stage

By the time Bottoms enter the Implementation stage, most have assisted in redesigning their local work conditions and setting up their teams. Most have a feeling of empowerment and an increased execution focus resulting from the team goal-setting process, sense of achievement, and increased job satisfaction.

Organizational Space Concerns and Issues   The two primary negative conditions of the Bottom space—vulnerability and invisibility—become less of an issue. Although Bottoms still are vulnerable to high level policies and decisions made by Tops, they have greater control over their local work conditions and how they interact within their team and with other teams. This greater degree of local control, as long as it is supported and nurtured by Middles above, provides a sense of ownership and elicits greater commitment toward the strategy.

Items for Consideration   Bottoms can increase their organizational power substantially. By producing more, which becomes easier in an HPT where intelligent empowerment is practiced and where Black Belts are leading process improvements designed to achieve significant results, Bottoms earn a stronger voice with Middles and Tops regarding what goes on at local Bottom levels.

Practical Tips   Bottoms should be on a constant lookout for ways to improve processes in their areas that benefit the entire organization. Bottoms do not need to wait to be on one of the officially chartered major improvement projects. They may initiate changes in their local area, as long as the impact of the changes is relatively contained in their area. Not only will this result in higher bonus payouts (in an LSS/HPO bonuses for improvement are paid out at all levels, not just the senior management level), but also in the increased ability to have a say over local work conditions. Generally speaking, the higher the performance of Bottom teams, the more responsibility will be given to them.

Tool Use

The Organization Space Analysis toolkit contains two tools: the Organizational Space Mirror and the Organizational Space Lenses (each tool and relevant theory appear in Chapter 7). The Organizational Space Mirror provides reflective insights into high leverage actions leaders can take based on an understanding of their space. The Organizational Space Lenses help leaders consider space factors when dealing with others. The lenses provide insights into others' motivations, the filters they use to perceive change events, and their natural tendencies depending on the space they occupy.

By using the Organizational Space Analysis toolkit, leaders can sharpen their self-reflection skills as well as positively influence other individuals and groups in the organization.

Integrated Work Plan Questions for Leaders

The final tool in the Leader's toolkit for the Implementation stage, the Integrated Work Plan Questions (Exhibit 18.1), is designed to help leaders ensure that the right activities have been planned and that they are adequately staffed. While the Transformation Coordination Team is typically responsible for developing and managing the Integrated Work Plan and related activities, top leaders provide a very important quality assurance (QA) function by ensuring the plan is of high quality and can be executed. One important new concept that appears in question 12 in the exhibit is the "tollgate" concept. This facilitates rapid, high quality improvements by requiring that the team meet a specified set of deliverables before moving from one step to the next in the DMAIC improvement process.

This tool, explained in detail in Chapter 7, contains two sets of questions for leaders to ask: questions applicable for all stages and stage-specific questions.

Some questions may seem to be common sense, but often common sense is not common practice when there are high levels of activity and multiple project priorities in an LSS/HPO transformation. By periodically asking the questions in Exhibit 18.1, leaders can gently guide the transformation along a swift and productive path.

Exhibit 18.1. Leader's Integrated Work Plan Shaping and QA Guide for Implementation

	Leader's Shaping and QA Questions
Universally Applicable Questions	Are the major deliverables and tasks in the work plan consistent with the organization's strategy at this point in time?
	Are the best people assigned to the tasks?
	Are any groups or individuals overloaded or at risk of burning out?
	Are celebrations of small wins as well as major financial gains scheduled?
	Is the project on schedule and on budget? If not, what are the plans for correction?
	Is the quality of work at this point in time sufficient to help the organization reach our overall goals?
	Is the project structured so that teams are collectively accountable for results (instead of individuals being accountable)?

Exhibit 18.1. Leader's Integrated Work Plan Shaping and QA Guide for Implementation, Cont'd

	Leader's Shaping and QA Questions
	The activities that people are working on may be a *good* use of their time, but is it the *best* use of their time?
	Has anything changed since the start of the project that might cause us to cancel any portion of it?
	What have we learned about planning and executing the project so far, and how can we use that to improve future work?
Stage 4: Implementation— Specific Questions	Is training for improvement principles, restructuring principles, and interpersonal team skills going according to plan?
	Do project teams need to pass through "tollgates" before moving from one step of an improvement project to the next?
	Does the work plan contain a section on capturing, codifying, and disseminating lessons learned from improvement projects?
	Is human resources tasked with determining whether Black Belts and other key talent and key contributors are being adequately rewarded (relative to industry practices outside the company)?
	Does the work plan allow for the collection of and processing of employee feedback regarding the status of the recent culture changes and employee morale?

During the Implementation stage, significant benefits of LSS/HPO begin to materialize. Many of the first wave of process improvement teams complete their DMAIC cycle and improve profitability, cycle times, and quality. High-Performance Teams have high levels of motivation to meet and exceed their goals. It is important for leaders to keep the momentum going and to fan the fires of motivation for improvement.

By using the Performance Framework, leaders can manage results and behaviors using a systemic approach that considers the interrelationship of nine key performance factors. With the Top/Middle/Bottom Space Analysis, leaders can anticipate potential Implementation problems and address them before they become serious. The Leader's Integrated Work Plan Shaping and QA Guide helps leaders ensure that the progression to successful LSS/HPO is proceeding in a rapid, high quality fashion.

Notes

1. This section is adapted from B. Oshry (1992), *Possibilities of organization*. Boston, MA: Power & Systems.

2. Pascale, R., Millemann, M., and Gioja, L. (2000). *Surfing the edge of chaos: The laws of nature and the new laws of business*. New York: Three Rivers Press.

3. Maslow, A. (1998). *Maslow on management*. New York: John Wiley & Sons.

CHAPTER 19

Stage 4: Implementation

Pragmatic Tips

God is in the details.

Ludwig Mies van der Rohe, architect

THE IMPLEMENTATION STAGE is a time of high energy and numerous improvement activities. Process improvement teams aggressively pursue their objectives. High-Performance Teams (HPTs) have increased enthusiasm and commitment, as they have taken on more responsibility and have more control over managing and improving their local work environment. Managing the details in Implementation becomes extremely important.

In the previous chapter leaders learned tools to help address Implementation challenges. Those tools can help shorten stage duration, enhance the quality of the stage outcomes, and reduce complexity for leaders. But tools alone are not enough. When leaders combine those tools with the pragmatic tips in this chapter, they can achieve truly superior performance. The contents of this chapter will help leaders "peer around the corner" and see what's ahead in the upcoming stage. By knowing common problems and high leverage opportunities in advance, a leader can plot a course of action at the start of the stage instead of having to react to events as they occur.

The key outputs and deliverables section of this chapter lets leaders know early in the stage what they should expect. Once leaders have started with the end in mind, they can direct others' attention and their own attention through a set of thought-provoking questions provided. While asking people questions is one effective way to engage them, increasing their participation is another. The next section presents a minimal set of gatherings—both small and large—in which people generate work products for the LSS/HPO transformation. In addition to generating high quality work products, these gatherings reduce resistance to change by eliciting genuine commitment through participation.

There is no single path to LSS/HPO excellence. To stimulate a leader's creative juices on how to adapt the material in this book to his or her situation, the next section presents some optional activities. While there is admittedly no single path to excellence, there are definitely common traps during this stage, which appear next.

For many leaders, LSS/HPO leadership is quite different than non-LSS/HPO leadership. In fact, some LSS/HPO mindsets and behaviors may seem downright counterintuitive viewed from "traditional leadership" thinking. This next section presents some of the more prevalent counterintuitive leadership elements encountered in this stage, and how to think differently in an LSS/HPO . As a final help to leaders in this stage, there is a leadership checklist of important items to consider throughout and on completion of the Implementation stage.

Key Outputs and Deliverables

The list below shows what leaders should expect by the end of this stage. If sufficient progress is not being made on these items throughout the stage, leaders need to request that the people responsible for them direct their attention to them immediately. Key outputs and deliverables for this stage are

- Projects begin to return benefits;

- A set of critical metrics is included in a "dashboard" that is used to provide a quick status of the business health of an organization, division, major process, or department;

- Control charts and pull systems begin to appear in many parts of the organization;

- Successive waves of training and improvement begin;

- Teams become multi-skilled on technical knowledge, management, and collaboration topics and may seek external course assistance to accelerate learning;[1]

- Teams and groups of teams restructure their HPT structures as needed;

- Intrinsic motivation rises as HPT teams meet their goals and process improvement teams meet their goals;

- Cross-team mentoring for simple improvement tools (such as process maps, Pareto analyses, and waste removal) begins; and

- HR begins to modify job descriptions, hiring, firing, and compensation policies to fit with new LSS/HPO performance and behavior expectations.

Important Questions to Ask

Instead of *telling* people what to think about and do, great leaders achieve organizational objectives by *asking key questions* that provoke thought and direct people's attention. Here are some important questions leaders should ask themselves and others during this stage.

Ask of Self

- How might I personally be unwittingly reinforcing the past?

- How might I, collectively with the group of leaders around me, be unwittingly reinforcing the past?

- What else could I be doing as a leader to push down responsibility into lower levels of the organization?

- Am I "managing the culture" as I must to make key principles stick, or am I just focusing on the "hard stuff" like new tools because they're easier to see and talk about?

Ask of Others

- What does the organization really need in this phase of its development?

- How might we collectively be unwittingly reinforcing the past?

- Is this really a project that requires advanced statistical tools, or can we obtain a lot of benefits by just using process maps?

- Are the appropriate mechanisms/processes in place to provide feedback to leaders if leaders are not holding true to the new values? If not, what would they look like?

Large-Group Interventions and Key Meetings

Bringing groups of people to work together on critical LSS/HPO tasks is an excellent way to simultaneously accomplish four objectives:

1. Develop high quality work products for the Implementation because of the diverse perspectives provided;

2. Achieve high levels of understanding among all participants about the topics discussed;

3. Increase energy and commitment regarding decisions made resulting from participation; and

4. Build leaders for the future by involving people in important discussions who might not normally be involved.

Large group interventions (LGIs) are methods for engaging large groups of people for a specific purpose. They typically involve over twenty people, a number far too high to utilize traditional meeting management and small group dynamics rules. LGIs are explained in greater detail in the Appendix. In addition to LGIs there are key meetings that are also important in advancing LSS/HPO and generating enthusiasm and commitment. Figure 19.1 depicts a sample sequence of LGIs and key meetings. Table 19.1 provides a brief description of each entry on Figure 19.1. Leaders can use the sample sequence as provided or develop another, more tailored approach.

Figure 19.1. Large-Group Interventions and Key Meetings Map for Implementation

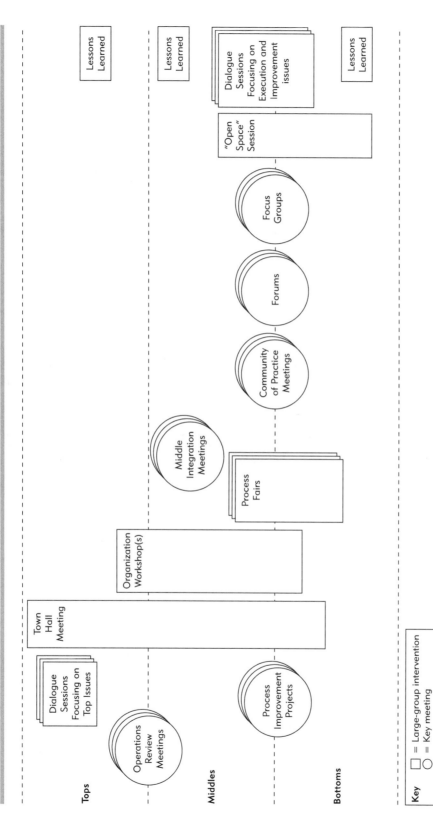

Table 19.1. Large-Group Interventions and Key Meetings for Implementation

Name	Gathering Type	Description of Key Elements
Operations Review Meetings	Meeting	Middle leaders and Black Belts update Top leaders on process improvement efforts and general organizational performance. Occasionally an entire process improvement team may attend.
Process Improvement Projects	Meeting	Black Belts lead the analysis and application of improvement methods and tools to processes that do not meet desired standards of cost, cycle time, or quality. Tools range from simple cycle time reduction tools to complex statistical methods.
Dialogue Sessions Focusing on Top Issues	LGI	Top leaders use ground rules and principles of the LGI template called Dialogue to surface assumptions and gain deeper understanding of LSS/HPO top leadership issues, such as leading cultural change, increasing accountability within the organization, and development of the senior management group into a "Top Team" as conditions require.
Town Hall Meeting	Meeting	Provides an opportunity for two-way conversations between senior managers and the workforce regarding lessons learned from the previous stage and the upcoming events in the current Implementation stage.
Organization Workshop(s)	LGI	An experience-based, principle-driven learning and action planning session in which participants discover common traps, reflex actions, and high leverage ways out of the Top, Middle, and Bottom organizational spaces. These sessions are used for developing awareness of the power that can be exercised at various levels of the organization.[i] The first workshop typically includes most members of the top management team as well as selected Middles. After this session, other workshops help roll out the concepts to the rest of the organization.
Process Fairs	LGI	Opportunities for process improvement teams to present and discuss their results and methods used to achieve those results. Such events are helpful for disseminating best practices in improvement and celebrating and recognizing achievements of teams that will most likely result in higher levels of commitment and intrinsic motivation.
Middle Integration Meetings	Meeting	Middle leaders convene and discuss the challenges of leading in the new environment and collectively develop better ways to do so. In addition, Middles integrate the work of their direct-report Bottoms with other Middles' areas. In these meetings Middles also expand their collaboration to include joint problem solving, joint planning, and forming coalitions of Middles who have a specific performance or improvement objective in mind that could benefit from a coalition being formed.
Community of Practice Meetings	Meeting	Gatherings in which people who share a common interest present and discuss emerging trends for their common interest as well as challenges, best practices, and ways to excel in that practice. A community of practice (COP) is typically a more formal gathering than a forum (see below) in that a COP has a defined membership as well as goals

Table 19.1. Large-Group Interventions and Key Meetings for Implementation, Cont'd

Name	Gathering Type	Description of Key Elements
		and a specific meeting schedule. For example, in a high-tech company all members of a Design Engineering Community of Practice might attend two briefings per year in best practices on designing high density, surface-mount integrated circuits.
Forums	Meeting	Gatherings in which participants present and discuss topics of interest. For example, a biotech organization might hold a forum on the topic of emerging industry practices for increasing the yields of fermentation reactions. Anyone interested could attend.
Focus Groups	Meeting	An independent facilitator interviews eight to fifteen members of an intact team or group of teams to identify barriers to breaking free of the current performance plateau and management best practices that are working well now. The independent facilitator provides the relevant manager(s) with focus group session results and then manager(s) prepare a list of action items that respond to focus group participants. The result of the action plan and the discussion is mutual accountability for results with an agreed-on timetable for implementation.
"Open Space" Session	LGI	A participative session that enables high levels of group interaction and productivity around areas of shared interest that provide a basis for enhanced organizational functioning over time. This method is helpful for teams—and entire organizations—to explore complex issues, disseminate information, create commitment to new directions, and develop action plans for the future.[ii]
Dialogue Sessions Focusing on Execution and Improvement Issues	LGI	Middle and Bottom leaders use ground rules and principles of the LGI template called Dialogue to surface assumptions and gain deeper understanding of LSS/HPO critical leadership issues such as implementing a culture that highly values execution, instilling and managing collective accountability, and managing change.
Lessons Learned	LGI	A group of people involved in the transformation convenes at the end of the stage to identify (1) what went well in this stage; (2) what they might do differently in the future; and (3) how the groups can make their learning accessible to people in the future who need this information.

[i]For an overview of the Organization Workshop method, please see B. Oshry and T. Devane. (1999). Organization workshop. In P. Holman and T. Devane (Eds.), *The change handbook: Group methods for shaping the future*. San Francisco: Berrett-Koehler. For a more detailed look please see B. Oshry. (2000). *Seeing systems*. San Francisco: Berrett-Koehler. I also recommend a intensive five-day exercise that explores Top, Middle, and Bottom issues called the Power Lab, designed by Barry Oshry. Find more out about the Power Lab at powerandsystems.com or fastcompany.com/magazine/10/camp.html. For Organization Workshops specifically tailored to meet the needs of an LSS/HPO, please see TopMiddleBottomLSSHPO.com.

[ii]For an overview of the Open Space method, please see H. Owen. (1999). Open space. In P. Holman and T. Devane (Eds.), *The change handbook: Group methods for shaping the future*. San Francisco: Berrett-Koehler. For a more detailed look please see H. Owen. (1998). *Open space technology: A user's guide*. San Francisco: Berrett-Koehler.

Interesting Options

While LSS/HPO transformations will vary from organization to organization, successful ones are principle-based. Here are some optional approaches—based on the principles in this book—that some organizations have found to be successful. These are not mutually exclusive options. Leaders should feel free to use these or other custom-developed options to address unique local requirements.

Option 1: Plan Novel Ideas for Celebrations and Rewards

Celebrations are important to demonstrate the value the organization places on successful execution and improvement. Top leaders can emphasize this point with novel celebration ideas such as cruises, local winery tours, family trips to the circus, and other activities.

Option 2: Introduce Innovation and Creativity Tools to Complement the Data-Driven Focus

In addition to new problem-solving tools, it is also important for leaders to provide tools and methods for innovation and creativity. Books and workshops by leaders in this field, such as Edward de Bono, Roger van Oeck, and Ronald Purser, would be helpful to organizations seeking a balance of structured problem-solving techniques and disciplined approaches to creativity and innovation.

Common Traps

Although no two implementations of LSS/HPO will be exactly alike, there are some common traps that organizations encounter. The common traps most often found in the Implementation stage are

- *People assume they know the voice of the customer and jump to solutions without adequate analysis.* In an effort to compress the improvement process sometimes teams neglect, or fail to devote the necessary time to, gathering and analyzing what customers actually need.

- *Improvement teams have too large a project scope.* While it's good that improvement teams choose stretch goals, it's also important to be realistic about what can be accomplished in a reasonable timeframe. Some project teams simply attempt to address too many problems, seeking to "boil the ocean" instead of trying to "boil a cup of water."

- *The wrong people are on improvement teams.* Steve Hollans from AlliedSignal reported that "An early barrier for us was selecting some people on the basis of their availability instead of people who were capable of being change agents."[2] Other characteristics that would qualify candidates as being the "wrong" people include those who are emotionally or financially tied to the old ways of doing things and those who lack skills or desire to improve the process.

- *Inadequate management of team problems and day-to-day teamwork.* LSS/HPO managers agree that one of the most difficult things to do is to let teams make mistakes. But teams learn from mistakes and mistakes increase team solidarity. Gerry FitzPatrick of StorageTek puts it succinctly, "It's a little like raising kids. You see they're about to make a mistake, but you have to let them make it so they know how to approach the situation in the future." FitzPatrick maintains that once a manager is comfortable letting teams make mistakes, a manager can engage in more strategic activities that have a greater impact, and the manager's job can become much more interesting.[3]

- *Opinions are used instead of data to make key decisions.* It's easy to fall into old patterns of thought, even for leaders who are trying their best to instill new ways of LSS/HPO thinking. Unfortunately, questions like "But we already know what's wrong and what needs to be done to fix it, why do we have to go through the entire DMAIC process?" still arise in improvement meetings in the Implementation stage. People can still use intuition, but leaders need to focus people on collecting data where possible. As Jack Welch once quipped, "If we're going to use opinions, I'd rather use mine."

- *A "hands-off" management style.* Some leaders misinterpret the principle of empowering HPTs and let teams do whatever they want once they have been formed and have developed goals. This type of management—called "laissez-faire"—is unacceptable in an LSS/HPO. Managers need to monitor team metrics, periodically check in, help teams and members develop, and ask teams what resources might be required to accomplish their goals.

- *Control charts being developed for low leverage variables.* In many organizations a sort of control charting mania seems to spread rapidly once teams become familiar with how to develop them. But control charts should only be set up to track variables that have a significant impact on meeting customer requirements.

- *Project team members and Black Belts opt to use advanced statistical methods instead of quick and simple improvement principles and tools.* All too often teams abandon easy to learn tools and principles like process mapping, cause-and-effect diagrams, and elimination of non-value-added activities in favor of the more quantitative tools. Such a strategy is foolish. "There are some real basic skills—TQM, Green Belt and Yellow Belt kinds of skills—that are going to fix a huge amount of your problems," says Mike Carnell, a Six Sigma expert who has worked with Motorola, General Electric, and AlliedSignal. "If you go and make everything a Six Sigma problem, you're going to constipate your system and waste a lot of resources."[4]

- *Waiting for new personnel evaluation forms to begin evaluating employees using results and behavior performance criteria.* Ideally, the official form would address employee performance in these areas. However, some HR departments, moving at glacial speed, make it difficult for managers to give formal feedback in the new environment. This should not preclude feedback about the new desired criteria in a general comments section until the new forms appear.

- *Compensating executives, but not teams, with variable pay for improvements.* The strategy of compensating *only* executives with variable pay demotivates Middle managers, lower levels of the organization, and talented Black Belts (who may leave because of current high demand). A practical solution is to pay out moderate, not huge, amounts of money to teams that meet their standing goals and improvement goals based on *verified financial benefits to the company.* This strategy is a win-win for all as the company gets money it wouldn't have received without the improvement effort, and teams see there is a "line of sight" between what management says they want, benefits the organization achieves, their efforts, and what management will reward people for.

- *Implementing solutions, such as control charts and pull systems, used for process management purposes before the process is stable.* If a process exhibits a lot of variability, it is necessary to *fix* it, not *manage* it. Six Sigma control charts and lean manufacturing pull systems are helpful in managing stable processes. Implementing them before a process is stable can lead to even worse performance and morale problems.

- *Not seeking opportunities to celebrate the new ways.* Even small successes require celebration. Certainly ones that support the new norms do. Every month Raytheon throws a party for people who have advanced from the initial "specialist" status (what some organizations call a Green Belt) to the "qualified specialist" status. About seventy-five qualified specialists and their managers attend the celebration. It's a fun event, and sweatshirts with the Raytheon logo and Six Sigma emblem are distributed to celebrate the rite of passage.[5]

- *Failing to have a process for tracking major process improvement efforts.* During Implementation projects will proliferate. Central tracking is necessary to avoid duplication of effort, project overlap, projects working at cross-purposes to each other, and over-utilization of constrained resources.

- *Failing to change HR systems to support the new ways of thinking and acting.* Practices such as rewarding teams, hiring for cultural fit, paying individuals for skills held, evaluating results and behaviors, sharing gains, collapsing pay bands so there are fewer bands and greater flexibility in work assignments, and providing capabilities for evaluations from peers, direct reports, and managers need to become part of the organization's standard procedures.

- *Forcing all improvement efforts to be a formal "Six Sigma–type" project.* There is a lot of overhead associated with convening a formal process improvement team, negotiating for full-time personnel already committed elsewhere, and collecting and analyzing the data required for a full-blown statistical analysis. Some simple improvements are best suited to be initiated within a standing HPT to address issues directly associated with that HPT. Sun Microsystems has instituted what they call "Sun Shots"— a modified version of General Electric's "Work-Out"™ improvement process that yielded quick results from candid, often heated, conversations between management and the workforce regarding worker-suggested changes. Potential process improvement projects are mapped onto a two-dimensional grid with impact on one dimension and complexity on the other. For high impact, low complexity projects people will use the Sun Shot approach instead of a more robust, lengthier Six Sigma improvement process (called *Sun Sigma* at Sun Microsystems).[6]

Counterintuitive Elements

 Leadership in an LSS/HPO looks different than it does in traditional organizational structures. However, some of those differences are keys to LSS/HPO success. Table 19.2 shows eight such elements often encountered during Implementation.

Table 19.2. Counterintuitive Elements in the Implementation Stage

Traditional Thinking	Counterintuitive LSS/HPO Reality
If we're going to have a participative work environment, we need to have everyone in the room who will be affected by a particular decision.	Getting everyone involved in every decision that affects them is a recipe for chaos and organizational inefficiency. In an LSS/HPO it is important to determine the purpose of the meeting and then decide who needs to be involved. In some early LSS/HPO events, such as the redesign sessions to HPTs and intra-team HPT meetings, 100 percent participation is desirable to encourage universal participation and build solidarity. For other meetings, invitees should be carefully selected.
For this to be a true LSS/HPO, in our first wave of improvement projects we need to have numerous quantitative tools and methods.	True LSS/HPOs focus on results, not on tools. If simple tools can yield exceptional results, it's best to use those. The complexity of the tool should match the complexity of the problem.
We should discourage rotating leadership within most teams. One person must be in charge or the team can't function.	In an LSS/HPO leadership is an activity, not a position. Some types of teams would benefit greatly from rotating the team leadership. This rotation may be based on the skill set needed, the particular time in the lifecycle of a product, or developmental opportunities for a particular person. Research by Katzenbach and Smith indicates truly high performing teams do not have a single designated leader; leadership rotates.[i]
The team nominates a representative to meet with management for a key issue.	All people on a team come to a meeting of important issues, such as reporting of improvements, celebrations, and disciplinary sessions. The rationale is that since they are managed as a unit, they need to appear as a unit. Under traditional management thinking, this seems like a waste of time. But it is essential for building team solidarity and a sense of collective responsibility and accountability, especially in early stages of team development.

Table 19.2. Counterintuitive Elements in the Implementation Stage, Cont'd

Traditional Thinking	Counterintuitive LSS/HPO Reality
An LSS/HPO leader should be popular and well-liked.	They need to do what's necessary for the long-term benefit of the work system for which they are responsible and for the development of the people within that system. At times this may result in being unpopular.
A Top or Middle leader needs to totally believe in the new LSS/HPO analyze-and-energize leadership style before trying it.	Years ago noted psychologist Abraham Maslow observed that for truly significant changes it is sometimes necessary to try the behavior first, even if there is not a full belief in it, so that it becomes part of a new pattern. Stanford professor and consultant Richard Pascale asserts that it is often easier to act ourselves into a new way of thinking than it is to think ourselves into a new way of acting. Peer support networks are helpful in developing new leadership skills that go beyond the old command-and-control mindsets.
Since we know that people pay attention to pay, we should put in a new compensation and reward system immediately after the Design stage is completed.	Research shows that it is better to redesign pay systems after HPTs have been operating for a while. The reason is that if the pay system is changed before the new organization is designed and operating, the organization will be paying based on old performance paradigms and criteria. This would necessitate yet another round of pay system changes.
As a lower level person, I can't challenge a higher level person's decisions or reasoning.	In an LSS/HPO environment, data is more important than positional authority. If there is an argument between two people, the person with the data wins, irrespective of organizational level. Karl Schmidt, a vice president at Johnson & Johnson, says, "Data is the great leveler. A manager or a staff person can challenge senior management and usually win the argument if they have data to support their position and senior management doesn't. This is part of management by fact and our culture. Everybody understands and honors this practice."[ii]

[i]Katzenbach, J., and Smith, D. (1993). *The wisdom of teams*. Boston, MA: Harvard Business School Press.
[ii]Personal conversation with Karl Schmidt, vice president of process excellence for Johnson & Johnson.

Leadership Checklist for Proceeding to the Next Phase

 Before the organization can move to the next stage of an LSS/HPO transformation, top leaders should check to ensure the items in Exhibit 19.1 have been completed. It can also be helpful for top leaders to refer to this list as the stage is unfolding to ensure that activities are started on time to produce the desired results before the stage completion.

Exhibit 19.1. Leadership Checklist for the Implementation Stage

☐ Ensure that inherent measurement conflicts among teams are resolved; push the decision down to the teams for resolution before intervening

☐ Continually seek to push down decisions, information, skills, and rewards

☐ Ensure process improvement projects are continually evaluated and appropriately prioritized and de-prioritized in consideration of strategic objectives

☐ Celebrate improvement team successes

☐ Watch for project scope creep

☐ Make public examples of rewards for those who live the new values and achieve good results and punishments for those who are not living according to the new cultural norms

☐ Make at least two visible demonstrations of the commitment to establishing a learning and continuous improvement environment

☐ Ensure HR system changes are underway, such as evaluation of compensation alternatives, including new results and behaviors in formal employee evaluations, new hiring policies, job descriptions that reflect the new competencies and values, and rewards for the new environment

☐ Ensure that knowledge management systems are established to capture and disseminate learnings on improvement efforts and HPT operation

The pragmatic tips presented in this chapter can help leaders anticipate potential problem areas and exploit opportunities that arise in the Implementation stage. By understanding the key outputs and deliverables, leaders know what people should be working on throughout the stage and can suggest mid-course corrections as needed. The sample thought-provoking questions provided will help leaders and others think about important transformation issues.

Public gatherings and collective decision making are key elements of successful LSS/HPOs. In any large group setting it's important that the group becomes productive as fast as possible. To accomplish that, leaders can call on some standard templates called large-group interventions. The large-group interventions and key meetings listed will help advance LSS/HPO objectives by quickly delivering high quality work products and generating enthusiasm and commitment to LSS/HPO objectives.

The path to a successful LSS/HPO is guided by principles and a flexible approach, not a cast-in-concrete process. This chapter presented some optional activities that have been successful for other practitioners. By studying the common traps presented, leaders can choose to plan for, instead of react to, problems others have encountered. To help ease the transition to new leadership practices, some of which may appear counterintuitive to traditional leadership thinking, this chapter presented the most common counterintuitive leadership practices that appear in the Implementation stage. As a final help to leaders there is a leadership checklist of important items leaders need to consider throughout and upon completion of Implementation stage.

Notes

1. The website www.PeopleSmartLSSHPO.com provides tips and courses for interpersonal and collaboration skills tailored to LSS/HPO transformation efforts.

2. Hollans, S. (1998). Success with six sigma often an elusive goal. *Aviation Week and Space Technology, 139*(20), p. 53.

3. Personal conversation with Gerry FitzPatrick, director of business operations, information storage at StorageTek on May 19, 2003.

4. Drickhamer, D. (2002, May 1). Best practices—where lean meets six sigma. *Industry Week.*

5. Personal interview with Mike Grimm, Six Sigma Expert at Raytheon in Tucson, Arizona.

6. Personal interview with David Adrian, organization development manager, Sun Microsystems in Boulder, Colorado.

Stage 5: Operations and Continuous Improvement

Activity Map and Leader To Do List

Experiment, make it your motto day and night.

Cole Porter

DURING THE IMPLEMENTATION STAGE the organization begins to reap the benefits of structured process improvement efforts and High-Performance Teams (HPTs). In the Operations and Continuous Improvement stage, the organization focuses on sustaining gains from the previous stages. Prior to the Operations and Continuous Improvement stage, many people in the organization believed continuous improvement activities were something they had to do in addition to their "real jobs." From this stage forward nearly everyone in the organization understands continuous improvement is part of everyone's job. The challenge from this point on will be for leaders to keep the momentum going and keep the focus on execution. The challenge of Top, Middle, and Bottom organizational spaces will always be there, but the problems tend to become more interesting and the solutions move people to higher performance levels as an organization evolves in its LSS/HPO lifecycle.

This chapter provides a preview of what's ahead for leaders in the Operations and Continuous Improvement stage. An Activity Map presents a picture of the sequence of major stage activities and milestones. The Leader To Do List presents a list of high leverage tasks that enable leaders to guide the LSS/HPO transformation smoothly along.

Activity Map

The activity map (Figure 20.1) shows major blocks of activity and their relative placement within this stage. Each of the three rows contains both LSS and HPO activities. The top row—LSS/HPO together—represents a strong combination of LSS and HPO activities and unfolding conditions. The second and third rows indicate a predominance of one discipline over the other, even though LSS and HPO elements appear in each.

Figure 20.1. Activity Map for Operations and Continuous Improvement

	Stage 1: Initiation	Stage 2: Direction Setting	Stage 3: Design	Stage 4: Implementation	Stage 5: Operations and Continuous Improvement
LSS/HPO Combination					
LSS/HPO Together	A	A	A	A	A
Predominantly HPO Activities		B	B	B D	
Predominantly Lean Six Sigma Activities		C	C	C	

Figure 20.1. Activity Map for Operations and Continuous Improvement, Cont'd

	Stage 1	Stage 2	Stage 3	Stage 4	Stage 5
Duration	1–2 months	1–3 months	1–4 months	4–9 months	ongoing
Cumulative time	1–2 months	2–5 months	3–9 months	7–18 months	8–19+ months

Block	Key Milestones and Activities
A	Successive waves of training and process improvement occur. LSS and HPO merge into one as a way of doing business each day. As Black Belt and Green Belt populations grow, more people are able to perform advanced process improvement analyses, and financial gains multiply. When there are dramatic changes in the external or internal environment, high performance teams in a segment of the organization restructure that segment as needed to respond to and capitalize on the changes. Selected team members become more financially savvy as they apprentice with finance department personnel and begin to take on responsibilities of project selection, project statusing, and benefit measurement as part of an overall effort to equip teams with multiple skill sets. Top and Middle leaders design and conduct "leadership forums" in which leaders identify a contemporary topic of interest, research it, write a case about it, and help other leaders learn about the topic. Top and Middle leaders convene a "leadership summit" meeting in which organization and non-organization members discuss leadership best practices in an offsite setting and develop action plans for improved leadership. Teams actively seek and obtain training in interpersonal skills and team skills such as communication, negotiation, and conflict management.

Leader To Do List

In each stage there are a set of high leverage actions leaders can take to influence transformation success. Since throughout the transformation there are many demands for leaders' time, it becomes important to organize and prioritize items most deserving of leader attention. A framework called the Transformation Grid ("Grid" for short) organizes Leader To Dos into six categories that provide focus for high leverage activities. Figure 20.2 shows a Grid with sample activities for Operations and Continuous Improvement. Leaders may wish to modify the content and activity placement in the sample to tailor the Grid for unique organizational situations.[1]

Activity descriptions for each high leverage category appear in the following sections.

Figure 20.2. Transformation Grid for Operations and Continuous Improvement

High Leverage Category	Stage 1: Initiation	Stage 2: Direction Setting	Stage 3: Design	Stage 4: Implementation	Stage 5: Operations and Continuous Improvement
Key Shaping Actions					
Participative Planning					
Process Awareness					
High Participation Restructuring					
Leadership Development					
Support					

	Stage 5: Operations and Continuous Improvement
Key Shaping Actions	Monitor organizational health Demonstrate ongoing top management support for the new ways Utilize productive conflict to move to higher levels of performance Begin to focus the organization on another major improvement initiative Consider having multiple units and cultures for multiple purposes Challenge people to abandon products and processes Extend LSS/HPO up and down the organization's industry supply chain
Participative Planning	Develop strategic plans in a participative fashion with multiple perspectives Continually scan the external environment to enhance the quality of planning
Process Awareness	Teach advanced improvement tools and methods to more employees in subsequent waves of improvement Help shape process and team goals each year by cycling target improvement goals in and out
High Participation Restructuring	Restructure the organization as external and internal demands necessitate Guard against the rise of the team at the expense of the organization
Leadership Development	Engage in self-reflection and self-correction. Solicit evaluations from peers, superiors, customers, and direct reports
Support	Redesign the compensation and reward system as new skill and behavior norms emerge Periodically revisit scores for the six criteria for productive work and assess for needed changes Emphasize team rewards, but don't allow individuals to get lost within the team

Key Shaping Actions

During the Operations and Continuous Improvement stage there are seven key shaping actions leaders can take to position the organization for the highest quality outcomes. They are described below.

Monitor Organizational Health

In this final, sustaining stage leaders need to ensure that the organization remains healthy. To accomplish this, there has to be a visible set of metrics, a process for periodic review, and any required corrective actions.

Demonstrate Ongoing Top Management Support for the New Ways

Top leaders need to show, on an ongoing basis, what is important to the organization by both their words *and* their actions. For example, Motorola introduced customer satisfaction teams fifteen years ago. The best teams from each Motorola group would compete with each other annually. They underwent a very intensive and systematic scoring by the CEO and the CFO. This meant that each year Bob Galvin, the number-one person at Motorola, personally spent one entire day reviewing the results of twenty-four problem-solving teams. This also meant that managers in semiconductors, communications, automotive, and so on spent their time scoring team performance before the finalists reached Bob Galvin.[2] Being the winning team meant a lot. There was no additional cash bonus awarded to the team. No stock options were granted. The reward was intrinsic. The results were long-lasting. And the overall benefits of the process to Motorola were immeasurable.

Another way top leaders lend support for the new ways is by providing resources to lower levels to perform their work. Workers lose motivation quickly when they don't feel they have the tools and other resources necessary to perform at their best. Leaders must make it a point to find out what workers need and provide it within budget or find another way.

Utilize Productive Conflict to Move to Higher Levels of Performance

Good LSS/HPO leaders resonate with Thomas Crum's assertion that "Conflict is neither good nor bad, it just is."[3] LSS/HPO leaders can harness conflict productively to generate options that people truly care about. Leaders can utilize people's energy to craft a solution that incorporates multiple viewpoints to improve performance. Conflict management resources appear in this book's Reference Material section.

Begin to Focus the Organization
on Another Major Improvement Initiative

LSS/HPO should not be the end of an organization's quest for excellence. A benefit of launching another improvement initiative after a successful LSS/HPO is that it is often easier after LSS/HPO. Members of the organization are tightly interconnected through the goal-setting process and vertical and lateral negotiation of goals. New ideas travel quickly. There is a "stronger" culture, as Collins and Porras would describe it, meaning the culture is widespread and people share the same basic organizational values.[4] One post-LSS/HPO logical choice would be innovation. Excellent innovation references include Drucker's *Innovation and Entrepreneurship*[5] and Hamel's *Leading the Revolution.*[6]

Consider Having Multiple Units
and Cultures for Multiple Purposes

Advanced organizational design practices suggest it may be necessary to have separate organizational units for research and production functions. Excellent, thought-provoking books, such as Tushman's *Winning Through Innovation* and Christensen's *The Innovator's Dilemma,* argue forcefully that the assumptions, behaviors, and practices of people in research are clearly different from those of people in production. Therefore, leaders may wish to create separate organizational units with separate practices and cultures for each.

Challenge People to Abandon Products and Processes

Peter Drucker advises organizations to periodically strive to abandon products that are no longer good for customers or profitable for the organization.[7] I would recommend doing the same for processes.

Extend LSS/HPO Up and Down the
Organization's Industry Supply Chain

Once an organization has its own house in order, it may wish to spread the principles of LSS/HPO to customers and suppliers. If the scope of large-scale improvement is limited to only the organization's boundaries, hand-offs may be costly, slow, unpredictable, and ineffective. Benefits of extending LSS/HPO upstream and downstream would include improved forecasts, easier material planning, and lower overall costs resulting from better coordination.

Participative Planning

High levels of participation in planning and restructuring in earlier stages have set expectations for high levels of participation in the future. Leaders need to continue to keep the workforce involved in strategic planning, local planning, and restructuring. The nature of planning has changed, as outlined below.

Develop Strategic Plans in a Participative Fashion with Multiple Perspectives

While including more people provides the obvious benefit of them understanding and supporting the plan, the additional benefit is having a variety of perspectives contribute to the plan, which enhances its quality. Using multiple levels in the organization can also be helpful. MIT researcher Henry Mintzberg asserts that strategic planning should be part of what line management does, not something done separately.[8] In an LSS/HPO many people participate in planning.

Continually Scan the External Environment to Enhance the Quality of Planning

One key difference for LSS/HPOs will be the frequency with which strategic plans are developed and revised. With today's fast-paced changes in technology and markets, organizations can no longer afford to plan once a year and wait until the following year to think about strategy again. World-class organizations establish sensors to detect changes in the external environment that may call for mid-year changes in strategy, or at least tactics to execute the strategy. These sensors may be in front-line workers who have direct contact with customers, such as counter clerks in retail stores, or they may be technology-enabled sensing and pattern recognition programs in a back room that collect and analyze data from a variety of sources. In the future LSS/HPO environment, great planning will be a combination of deliberate forecasting, action plan development, and emergent strategies that adapt to the external environment.

Process Awareness

By this stage, redesigning, optimizing, and managing processes is becoming second nature to all workforce members. In this stage and beyond, all levels begin to identify and seize opportunities for process improvement.

Teach Advanced Improvement Tools and Methods
to More Employees in Subsequent Waves of Improvement

Leaders must ensure that there are advanced classes for the more technical tools that require a longer time to learn. However, leaders should keep in mind that the current benchmarking standard is to have only about 2 to 3 percent of the organization trained as Black Belts or Master Black Belts. The reality is that there are a limited number of complex projects that require advanced tools and so it is better to have people focusing on other areas, such as creativity or innovation.

Help Shape Process and Team Goals Each Year
by Cycling Target Improvement Goals in and out

Each year top leaders should focus the organization on three to five areas in which to excel. Some areas, such as safety, may be carried over from year to year just to remind people they continually need to be thinking about that topic. But once some targets are met it makes sense for the organization to replace them with new ones.

High-Participation Restructuring

During the Design stage, all or nearly all members of the organization participated in workshops that restructured their current organizational units into HPTs. One of the key principles presented in the workshops was that at any point the organization could be reconfigured into a design.

Restructure the Organization as External
and Internal Demands Necessitate

Leaders must encourage teams to redesign as external patterns and events unfold that make the existing structure irrelevant. Before teams redesign, leaders should provide them with the most current version of the strategy because teams primarily redesign to support strategy.

Guard Against the Rise of the Team
at the Expense of the Organization

HPTs, especially those that are relatively self-contained and have all the skills necessary to produce a product or service, have a tendency to form a strong solidarity. This can lead to isolation from other teams, failure to take time to align goals with other teams, and failing to share information across team boundaries. Leaders can take three steps to guard against these problems:

1. Openly state that it is expected that teams will learn and collaborate across boundaries in support of the strategy;

2. Increase inter-team collaboration by having two teams share one or two common goals; and

3. Reward cross-boundary collaboration and information sharing.

As the teams continue to restructure and develop in the Operations and Continuous Improvement stage, so do the leaders.

Leadership Development

Leaders must continuously develop their leadership skills as they become "analyze-and-energize" leaders. In this stage leaders need to focus on the following for developmental purposes.

Engage in Self-Reflection and Self-Correction

From time to time leaders need to pause and ask themselves questions such as, "What's been going well that I want to continue?" and "What hasn't been going well that I would like to change?" If leaders do take the time to ask questions, a high percentage of the time they will be able to diagnose problems and develop a correction plan. However, even the best leaders can have blind spots. For that reason it is important to solicit evaluations from others.

Solicit Evaluations from Peers, Superiors, Customers, and Direct Reports

Evaluations from people above, below, and beside in the organizational hierarchy—often called 360-degree evaluations—can be extremely helpful in surfacing unnoticed areas for improvement. Research shows that the respondents are most honest when the evaluation is for developmental purposes only. If the evaluation is the basis for a raise, bonus, or promotion, the evaluators may have reasons to be less than honest in the ranking. This process is much easier to administer if the data is collected electronically, such as through an Internet-based service or the company's intranet. There are excellent software packages available that electronically collect, interpret, and detect patterns for useful feedback to leaders. For an example of how an electronic scoring and interpretation package functions, see LSSHPOAssessments.com. Typically, specific comments are not attributed to an individual, and such feedback is often provided by a person trained in evaluative feedback.

Support

The support function provides additional leverage and benefits for the previous Grid categories through items such as communication, HR processes, and information technology support. There are three important support processes for the Operations and Continuous Improvement stage.

Redesign the Compensation and Reward System as New Skill and Behavior Norms Emerge

Over time an organization's core competencies and the desired behaviors may require change. Often organizations neglect this fact and retain old performance evaluation forms and systems years after they are relevant. Leaders at all levels need to guard against this and notify HR leaders and Top leaders if the current evaluation process and criteria are becoming outdated.

Periodically Revisit Scores for the Six Criteria for Productive Work and Assess for Needed Changes

In the workshops in which employees redesigned themselves into HPTs there was a segment in which each individual scored each of the six criteria that lead to high performance. Periodically the organization should have individuals complete these scorings again. This may be done in the form of a survey from which general trends and patterns could be analyzed or within intact HPTs in which individuals discuss how their scores might be raised. Such a conversation would also support an important LSS/HPO norm: talking not only about the technical tasks, but also about how people work together.

Emphasize Team Rewards, but Don't Allow Individuals to Get Lost Within the Team

Leaders need to focus heavily on rewarding teams as a unit to help build solidarity, but occasional individual awards help remind people of their individuality. For example, while a team may receive a team bonus, individuals on the team may have quite different compensation packages based on skills they hold. Operational Management International, Inc. (OMI), winner of the Baldrige award in 2000, has an interesting set of reward practices that focus attention on the importance of teams, reward for outstanding individual efforts, and simultaneously spread folklore and reinforce culture. Each year OMI presents the presidential teamwork award in the form of a cash bonus. All but one of the rewards at OMI go to teams. That award to an individual is called the Rock Award. It is so named because years ago two highly competitive managers were on a long hike on the Appalachian Trail, and one of the managers—being very competitive—put a huge rock in the backpack of the other manager. Turns out the manager with the rock still made it to the top first. Each year the Rock Award is given to people who deliver superior performance in spite of the burdens placed on them. This award strategy focuses attention on teams, but doesn't lose sight of individuals in the organization. (And it's a great way to continue building a strong culture by reinforcing company folklore.)[9]

In the Operations and Continuous Improvement stage, leaders need to focus their efforts on the big picture that was provided by the Activity Map and on key day-to-day tasks as suggested in the Leader To Do List section. Leaders learned how to use the Transformation Grid tool to plan their activities for the upcoming work in this stage and monitor those activities to ensure adequate progress is being made.

Notes

1. For further information on uses of the Grid and content updates, see TransformationGrid.com.
2. Personal conversation with John Lupienski.
3. Crum, T. (1998). *The magic of conflict.* Carmichael, CA: Touchstone Press.
4. Collins, J., and Porras, J. (2002). *Built to last: Successful habits of visionary companies.* New York: HarperBusiness.
5. Drucker, P. (1985). *Innovation and entrepreneurship.* New York: HarperBusiness.
6. Hamel, G. (2000). *Leading the revolution: How to thrive in turbulent times by making innovation a way of life.* Boston, MA: Harvard Business School Press.
7. Drucker, P. (1999). *Management challenges for the 21st century.* New York: HarperBusiness.
8. Mintzberg, H. (1994). *The rise and fall of strategic planning.* New York: The Free Press.
9. Personal conversation with Gary Hunt, vice president of HR, Administration, and MIS at OMI.

Stage 5: Operations and Continuous Improvement

Tools Application

If you have accomplished all that you have planned for yourself, you have not planned enough.

Edward Everett Hale

IN THE PREVIOUS CHAPTER leaders learned about the major blocks of activities and specific high leverage actions they could take during the Operations and Continuous Improvement stage. This chapter presents key leader challenges and a set of tools to address them. Specifically, in this stage leaders face the following challenges:

- Actively managing the culture consistent with the desired strategy, the new structure, and new leadership paradigm;

- Ensuring that training in advanced improvement topics occurs, both for the technical content and to support an environment of learning;

- Keeping all levels of the organization engaged in finding better ways to do things and seizing the initiative to identify potential improvement efforts; and

- Addressing the danger that people's energy for superior performance and continuous improvement will wane once the LSS/HPO transformation is "complete."

Each of the tools described here will help leaders address the above challenges.

Performance Framework

During Operations and Continuous Improvement, the Performance Framework helps leaders:

- Avoid becoming scattered by focusing attention on key performance factors;

- See how the new culture is related to the other performance factors and manage the new culture accordingly;

- Give the workforce a big-picture understanding of the direction of the transformation; and

- Gain insights during lessons-learned analyses.

In each use above, leaders:

1. Convene a meeting and post a large Performance Framework flip chart on a wall;

2. Facilitate discussions about each performance element and interrelationships among them;

3. Record participant comments on the flip chart near the related performance factor being discussed; and

4. Ensure meeting notes and action items are typed and distributed.

In addition, the tool can be used to illustrate which factors are addressed in this stage. Figure 21.1 shows the primary factors addressed during Operations and Continuous Improvement. Italicized comments appear adjacent to the factors addressed and describe how they are addressed in this stage.

Figure 21.1. Performance Framework for Operations and Continuous Improvement

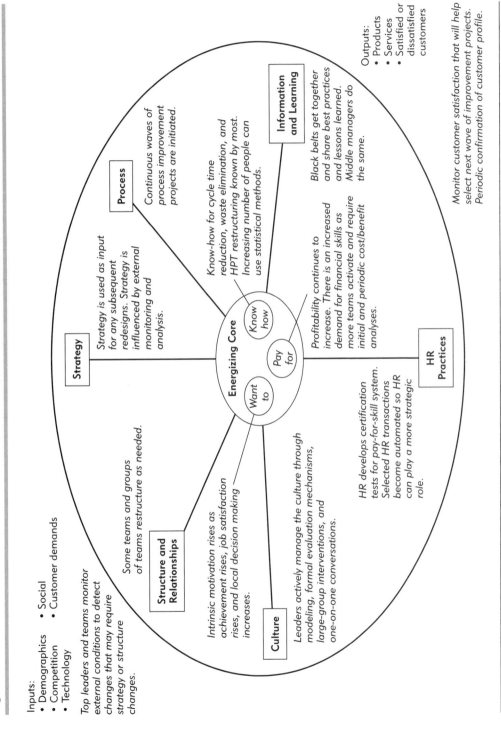

Inputs:
• Demographics   • Social
• Competition   • Customer demands
• Technology

Top leaders and teams monitor external conditions to detect changes that may require strategy or structure changes.

Strategy

Strategy is used as input for any subsequent redesigns. Strategy is influenced by external monitoring and analysis.

Structure and Relationships

Some teams and groups of teams restructure as needed.

Intrinsic motivation rises as achievement rises, job satisfaction rises, and local decision making increases.

Culture

Leaders actively manage the culture through modeling, formal evaluation mechanisms, large-group interventions, and one-on-one conversations.

Energizing Core
- Know how
- Pay for
- Want to

Process

Continuous waves of process improvement projects are initiated.

Know-how for cycle time reduction, waste elimination, and HPT restructuring known by most. Increasing number of people can use statistical methods.

Information and Learning

Black belts get together and share best practices and lessons learned. Middle managers do the same.

Profitability continues to increase. There is an increased demand for financial skills as more teams activate and require initial and periodic cost/benefit analyses.

HR Practices

HR develops certification tests for pay-for-skill system. Selected HR transactions become automated so HR can play a more strategic role.

Monitor customer satisfaction that will help select next wave of improvement projects. Periodic confirmation of customer profile.

Outputs:
• Products
• Services
• Satisfied or dissatisfied customers

Top/Middle/Bottom Space Analysis

The Performance Framework tool in the previous section presented a way of looking at key performance factors such as Strategy, Process, and Structure, and how they combine to determine organizational performance in the Operations and Continuous Improvement stage. The Top/Middle/Bottom Space Analysis toolkit focuses leaders' attention on people, where they are in the organization, what their perceptual filters are, and how they might best be influenced to enthusiastically join in the LSS/HPO operation. By understanding the Top, Middle, and Bottom organizational spaces, leaders can dramatically improve the leverage of their actions and accelerate the advancement of the organization. This section is organized into three topic areas: (1) an *involvement profile,* which depicts the involvement of the Top, Middle, and Bottom positions in the LSS/HPO transformation; (2) *coaching for this stage,* which presents stage-specific insights into what each organizational space is experiencing during this part of the LSS/HPO transformation; and (3) *tool use,* which outlines the tools in the organization space toolkit.

Involvement Profile

This segment contains an organizational analysis and recommendations for leaders based on the Organization Space concepts presented in Chapter 7. For a quick review of those concepts, please refer to that section. The participation of the three position-based spaces, shown by shaded area, is shown in Figure 21.2. Participation is shown in one pyramid because by this stage workforce members do not view LSS and HPO as separate disciplines having different tool sets.

Figure 21.2. Participation During Operations and Continuous Improvement

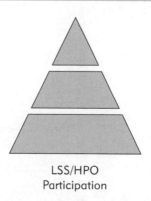

LSS/HPO
Participation

The Involvement Profile shows the relative involvement of each positional level for this stage. In ongoing efforts all levels are actively involved in LSS and HPO activities.

Coaching for This Stage

This section provides insights into what's going on for each organizational space. By understanding the typical LSS/HPO forces affecting each of the organizational spaces, leaders can gain insight on how to best deal with issues affecting them, as well as how to best interact with people based on the space that others are in. It is important to note here that just because an organization has successfully implemented LSS/HPO, the natural conditions, reflex actions, and common traps for each of the spaces do not go away. Those things still exist because of the structural interrelationships of Tops, Middles, and Bottoms. In a successful LSS/HPO there is in fact much more variety in the number of conditions a person may experience in the course of a week, making it even more important to be on the lookout for space conditions and how to manage them.

A few examples make this point. At times Black Belts will be Tops when applying statistical methods and problem-solving principles to process problems. At other times Black Belts will be Middles when reporting status of project teams to Tops. And sometimes Black Belts will be Bottoms when being given assignments and being told the compensation policies that apply to them. Space conditions also shift for others.

What's Going on for the Tops in This Stage

With overall responsibility for the performance of the organization, senior management is feeling pretty good going into Stage 5 in a well-implemented LSS/HPO. By this time several successful large-scale process improvement efforts have yielded great savings, lower cycle times, and higher quality. The energy level of the general workforce is high, as is commitment to the strategy because of the high levels of intelligent empowerment. In this ongoing stage, Tops need to remain ever vigilant of organizational space traps and help the organization steer clear of them.

Organizational Space Concerns and Issues   The complexities and overload conditions that characterize Top space persist, even though the organization is functioning at a higher level of performance. Paul O'Beirne, a Top of a Microsoft group that had implemented HPTs, once remarked that the group's problems didn't go away once they implemented HPTs. But they did have problems of a higher order that were much more interesting and had greater leverage opportunities. Process improvement opportunities require strategic prioritization and consistent application of financial screening guidelines.

Tops need to continue efforts to enhance their Top team performance, even though they may still primarily operate as individuals, especially in an organization of highly specialized functional disciplines. Tops need to ask themselves, "What performance challenge can we best address collectively that we cannot address separately?"

Items for Consideration   Immediately after the first and second waves of improvement there is a tremendous amount of energy in the organizational system for high performance and continual improvement. Tops need to walk a fine line between becoming so involved in efforts that others feel ownership dissipate, and being involved enough to ensure the organization's strategic objectives are being served. Successfully walking this fine line will ensure the proper balance between energy and control in the system.

Practical Tips   To maximize their effectiveness and the effectiveness of the overall organizational system for which they are responsible, Tops must

- Ensure that new people coming on board are educated on improvement methods and teaming.

- Increase proficiency at guiding people and simultaneously developing them by asking good questions, like "Is this still the right problem? Should we limit it? Should we expand it? Should we somehow contract it to finish it faster and get a quicker payback? Should we finish up on this project and start anew on another, higher issue? Has the team thought through both the short-term and long-term implications of the proposed solution?"

- Solicit participation from other Tops and Middles in important strategic decisions to (1) gain a variety of perspectives to reach a higher quality decision and (2) build internal capability in strategic thinking.

- Seek measurement results from a variety of sources to see a true "big picture" of improvement efforts and overall performance. Information from quality groups and improvement teams provides a good process orientation, while an internal audit group or HPT team member trained in finance provides a more financially sophisticated picture. A combination is excellent to have, but in the early stages of an LSS/HPO organizations rarely find one person who can do both tasks well.

- Implement adequate sensors in the organization so Tops know when it is necessary to intervene in team decisions or suboptimal performance that is detrimental to the organization.

What's Going on for the Middles in This Stage

Although Middles occupy important leverage positions in an LSS/HPO, they continue to be torn between the various groups they work with. Tops still want to make sure Bottoms are producing and that the "right" process improvement projects are selected. Bottoms will occasionally—although not as often as in pre-LSS/HPO days—feel they are being victimized by higher-ups in the system and want Middles to intervene.

To help understand how to be the best Middle one can be and also how to deal with someone in a Middle position in this stage, here are coaching tips on organizational space concerns and issues, items for consideration, and practical tips.

Organizational Space Concerns and Issues   Even after the initial conversion to an LSS/HPO occurs, it is still a busy time for Middles. Tops are at Middles' doorsteps asking for the next list of high impact improvement projects and simultaneously demanding performance of Middles and the HPTs that report to them. Bottoms are at Middles' doorsteps wanting more training so they can ratchet up their goals, receive greater bonuses, and increase their sense of achievement. Peers and Tops are evaluating Middles' performance on improvement projects. Middles also find themselves being evaluated by their direct reports in 360-degree evaluations.

Items for Consideration   Occasionally Middles will need to be unpopular and say *No* to the groups they are dealing with. Even though Tops are demanding higher levels of performance, Middles sometimes need to let Tops know that performance will worsen before it improves because there is a learning curve associated with doing things a new way. And while Bottoms may all want training in advanced process improvement techniques so they can meet and exceed their goals, everybody can't be trained on every tool. Finally, the tearing at Middles from Tops and Bottoms make it difficult for Middles to engage in one of their truly highest leverage activities, Middle integration.

Practical Tips   Although Middles, by definition, find themselves between two groups that each want attention and want Middles to do their bidding, Middles need to maintain their independence of thought and action.[1] They need to focus on intelligent empowerment for themselves and others. In addition to performing important functions for Tops and Bottoms, Middles also must integrate the work of the Middles. There are four different types of integration that Middles can do to increase the system power and their leverage at this point:[2]

1. Get together to talk about common problems, challenges, and issues;

2. Get together for joint problem-solving sessions;

3. Meet to do collective planning for the Middles and HPTs and individuals who report to them; and

4. Form a "power block" that acts as an informal de facto team that has goals and targets and wields some organizational power by virtue of its control of certain resources.

Stage 5 is a time of both opportunities and challenges for Middles, but with the understanding of organizational spaces and the exploration of leadership principles Middles can have an extremely positive impact on the organization's performance.

What's Going on for the Bottoms in This Stage

By the time Bottoms enter the Operations and Continuous Improvement stage, most have had very positive experiences in reshaping their local work conditions, increasing their sense of achievement, and receiving financial remuneration and recognition for their accomplishments. Most have a feeling of empowerment, and some may even have reorganized the initial HPT structure to optimize performance.

Organizational Space Concerns and Issues   Bottoms in this stage are in a high producing and high improvement state. The key challenges for Bottoms are (1) not to let the energy die out and (2) to maintain an enterprise perspective instead of a local perspective. Because Bottoms are on the lowest rung of the organizational ladder, they are subject to the policies and other decisions made at the levels above them, even though they have more control over their local work than before. Bottoms must keep involved in energizing activities to keep the spirit of execution and improvement alive. If Bottoms have not seen some attempt to change the compensation system by this stage, they will likely become impatient. Many will want more compensation for doing "more manager work" and for helping the organization achieve substantial gains in process improvement.

Items for Consideration   Bottoms can increase their organizational power substantially by continuing to meet and raise their goals and by participating in continuous improvement activities that benefit the entire organization.

Practical Tips   By virtue of their closeness to production capabilities and often to customers, Bottoms see many problems that need to be addressed. In the new spirit of LSS/HPO, Bottoms should seize the initiative and address these problems, while always keeping the big picture in mind. To do this they can ask questions such as, "Do we require input from any other groups? Does our solution affect any other groups that need to be consulted as we go through the DMAIC process?" and "Does what we are proposing support the organization's strategy?"

In addition, Bottoms need to have the mindset that the processes cause problems, not the people. This is especially important to keep in mind when one Bottom team finds that a second Bottom team is generating problems for the first group.

Tool Use

The Organization Space Analysis toolkit contains two tools: the Organizational Space Mirror and the Organizational Space Lenses (each tool and relevant theory appear in Chapter 7). The Organizational Space Mirror provides reflective insights into high leverage actions leaders can take based on an understanding of their space. The Organizational Space Lenses help leaders consider space factors when dealing with others. The lenses provide insights into others' motivations, the filters they use to perceive change events, and their natural tendencies depending on the space they occupy.

By using the Organizational Space Analysis toolkit, leaders can sharpen their self-reflection skills as well as positively influence individuals and groups in the organization.

Integrated Work Plan Questions for Leaders

The organizational space tools provide leaders with insights into views and behavior of the organizational spaces during a transformation. The final tool in the Leader's toolkit for the Operations and Continuous Improvement stage is the Integrated Work Plan and QA (Quality Assurance) Questions for leaders (Exhibit 21.1), designed to help leaders ensure that the right activities have been planned and that they are adequately staffed. The Integrated Work Plan is the central document that ensures that time-phased activities for Lean Manufacturing, Six Sigma, HPO, and change management activities are scheduled at the right time in the transformation. Work plans for key initiatives will continue long after the Operations and Continuous Improvement stage is finished, and top leaders will still provide a very important quality assurance (QA) function by ensuring the plan is of high quality and can be executed.

This tool, explained in detail in Chapter 7, contains two sets of questions for leaders to ask: questions applicable for all stages and stage-specific questions.

Some questions may seem to be common sense, but often common sense is not common practice when there are high levels of activity and multiple project priorities in an LSS/HPO transformation. By periodically asking the questions in Exhibit 21.1, leaders can gently guide the transformation along a swift and productive path.

Exhibit 21.1. Leader's Integrated Work Plan Shaping and QA Guide for Operations and Continuous Improvement

	Leader's Shaping and QA Questions
Universally Applicable Questions	Are the major deliverables and tasks in the work plan consistent with the organization's strategy at this point in time?
	Are the best people assigned to the tasks?
	Are any groups or individuals overloaded or at risk of burning out?
	Are celebrations of small wins as well as major financial gains scheduled?
	Is the project on schedule and on budget? If not, what are the plans for correction?
	Is the quality of work at this point in time sufficient to help the organization reach our overall goals?

Exhibit 21.1. Leader's Integrated Work Plan Shaping and QA Guide for Operations and Continuous Improvement, Cont'd

	Leader's Shaping and QA Questions
	Is the project structured so that teams are collectively accountable for results (instead of individuals being accountable)?
	The activities that people are working on may be a *good* use of their time, but is it the *best* use of their time?
	Has anything changed since the start of the project that might cause us to cancel any portion of it?
	What have we learned about planning and executing the project so far, and how can we use that to improve future work?
Stage 5: Operations and Continuous Improvement— Specific Questions	Has formal training in process improvement been scheduled for at least two additional "waves" of training participants?
	Are all standing teams that have not yet been scheduled for business literacy training on the schedule to receive such training?
	Has the organization scheduled times for meetings with key customers to determine the impact of the recent organizational changes on them and to solicit additional feedback on what might be improved?
	In keeping with the principle of external focus, are there tasks on the work plan that address benchmarking and sharing of best practices with other world-class organizations?
	Is there an activity on the work plan that evaluates the sustainability of the gains and structural changes made to date?

During the Operations and Continuous Improvement stage the organization begins to reap the dramatic benefits of LSS/HPO on an ongoing basis. The challenge for leaders is to continue to provide conditions for the workforce to have a fanatical customer-based execution mindset and a spirit and tools for continuous improvement. A common trap that many organizations fall into is thinking they are "done" once they complete the Implementation stage. Leaders need to be aware of this tendency and keep using analyze-and-energize leadership principles.

As organizations move beyond the five LSS/HPO stages, leaders will most likely develop their own set of leadership tools that are tailored to their own environment. This is highly desirable, since it provides ownership and relevance to local conditions. On an ongoing basis, leaders may also continue to use the tools used in earlier phases to focus attention and assist in mobilizing energy. Leaders may wish to select tools, principles, and large-group interventions from earlier stages to help in new improvement efforts.

The Performance Framework helps leaders plan for and manage results and behaviors using a systemic approach that considers the interrelationship of nine key performance factors. With the Top/Middle/Bottom Spaces Analysis leaders can anticipate potential implementation problems and address them before they become serious. The Leader's Integrated Work Plan Shaping and QA Guide helps leaders ensure that the progression to increasingly higher LSS/HPO performance levels is proceeding in an orderly fashion and that activities are included in the plan to ensure continued levels of energy and motivation towards superior performance and continuous improvement.

Notes

1. Oshry, B. (1992). *Possibilities of organization.* Boston, MA: Power & Systems.
2. Oshry, B. (1998). *In the middle.* Boston, MA: Power & Systems.

Stage 5: Operations and Continuous Improvement

Pragmatic Tips

Life can only be understood backwards; but it must be lived forwards.

Søren Kierkegaard

THE OPERATIONS AND CONTINUOUS IMPROVEMENT STAGE is a time for reflection on recent achievements and learnings. It also a time to look ahead to reaching even higher levels of performance. In the previous chapter leaders learned tools to help address Operations and Continuous Improvement challenges. Those tools can help shorten stage duration, enhance the quality of the stage outcomes, and reduce complexity for leaders. But tools alone are not enough. When leaders combine those tools with the pragmatic tips in this chapter, they can achieve truly superior performance. The contents of this chapter will help leaders "peer around the corner" and see what's ahead in the upcoming stage. By knowing common problems and high leverage opportunities in advance, a leader can plot a course of action at the start of the stage instead of having to react to events as they occur.

The key outputs and deliverables section of this chapter lets leaders know early in the stage what they should expect. Once leaders have started with the end in mind, they can direct others' and their own attention through a set of thought-provoking questions provided. While asking people questions is one effective way to get them engaged, increasing their participation is another. The next section presents a minimal set of gatherings—both small and large—in which people generate work products for the LSS/HPO transformation. In addition to generating high quality work products, these gatherings reduce resistance to change by eliciting genuine commitment through participation.

There is no single path to LSS/HPO excellence. To stimulate a leader's creative juices on how to adapt the material in this book to his or her situation, the next section presents some optional activities. While there is admittedly no single path to excellence, there are definitely common traps during this stage, which appear next.

For many leaders, LSS/HPO leadership is quite different from non-LSS/HPO leadership. In fact, some LSS/HPO mindsets and behaviors may seem downright counterintuitive viewed from "traditional leadership" thinking. This next section presents some of the more prevalent counterintuitive leadership elements encountered in this stage and explains how to think differently in an LSS/HPO. As a final help to leaders in this stage, there is a leadership checklist of important items to consider throughout and upon completion of the Operations and Continuous Improvement stage.

Key Outputs and Deliverables

The list below shows what leaders should expect by the end of this stage. If sufficient progress is not being made on these items throughout the stage, leaders need to request that the people responsible for them direct their attention to them immediately. Key outputs and deliverables for this stage are

- Successive waves of improvement;
- Multi-skilling of teams;
- HPTs restructuring as needed; and
- Training in team skills such as negotiation, communication, and conflict management.

Important Questions to Ask

Instead of *telling* people what to think about and do, great leaders achieve organizational objectives by *asking key questions* that provoke thought and direct people's attention. Here are some important questions leaders should ask themselves and others during this stage.

Ask of Self

- What should I be working on as a leader?
- How can others support my personal development, and I theirs?

Ask of Others

- In your view, what should I be working on as a leader?
- What can leaders do to inject more energy into the organization?

Large-Group Interventions and Key Meetings

Getting groups of people to work together on critical LSS/HPO tasks is an excellent way to simultaneously accomplish four objectives:

1. Develop high quality work products for the implementation because of the diverse perspectives provided;

2. Achieve high levels of understanding among all participants about the topics discussed;

3. Increase energy and commitment regarding decisions made resulting from participation; and

4. Build leaders for the future by involving people in important discussions who might not normally be involved.

Large-group interventions (LGIs) are methods for engaging large groups of people for a specific purpose. They typically involve over twenty people, a number far too high to utilize traditional meeting management and small group dynamics rules. LGIs are explained in greater detail in the Appendix. In addition to LGIs there are key meetings that are also important in advancing LSS/HPO and generating enthusiasm and commitment. Figure 22.1 depicts a sample sequence of LGIs and key meetings. Table 22.1 provides a brief description of each entry on Figure 22.1. Leaders can use the sample sequence as provided or develop another, more tailored approach.

Figure 22.1. Large-Group Interventions and Key Meetings Map for Operations and Continuous Improvement

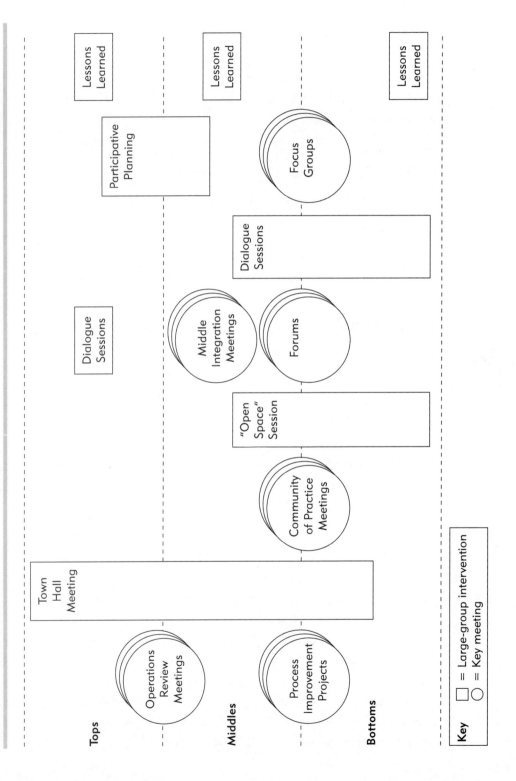

Key   ☐ = Large-group intervention
      ○ = Key meeting

Table 22.1. Large-Group Interventions and Key Meetings for Operations and Continuous Improvement

Name	Gathering Type	Description of Key Elements
Process Improvement Projects	Meeting	Black Belts lead the analysis and application of improvement methods and tools to processes that do not meet desired standards of cost, cycle time, or quality. Tools range from simple cycle time reduction tools to complex statistical methods.
Operations Review Meetings	Meeting	Middle leaders and Black Belts update Top leaders on process improvement efforts and general organizational performance. Occasionally an entire process improvement team may attend.
Town Hall Meeting	Meeting	Provides an opportunity for two-way conversations between senior managers and the workforce regarding lessons learned from the previous stages and upcoming events.
Community of Practice Meetings	Meeting	Gatherings in which people who share a common interest present and discuss emerging trends for their common interest as well as challenges, best practices, and ways to excel in that practice. A community of practice (COP) is typically a more formal gathering than a forum (see below) in that a COP has a defined membership as well as goals and a specific meeting schedule. For example, in a high-tech company all members of a Design Engineering Community of Practice might attend two briefings per year in best practices on designing high density, surface mount integrated circuits.
"Open Space" Session	LGI	A participative session that enables high levels of group interaction and productivity around areas of shared interest that provide a basis for enhanced organizational functioning over time. This method is helpful for teams—and entire organizations—to explore complex issues, disseminate information, create commitment to new directions, and develop action plans for the future.[i]
Dialogue Sessions Focusing on Top Issues	LGI	Top leaders use ground rules and principles of the LGI template called Dialogue to surface assumptions and gain deeper understanding of LSS/HPO top leadership issues such as leading cultural change, increasing accountability within the organization, and development of the senior management group into a "Top Team" as conditions require.
Middle Integration Meetings	Meeting	Middle leaders convene and discuss the challenges of leading in the new environment and collectively develop better ways to do so. In addition, Middles integrate the work of their direct-report Bottoms with other Middles' areas. In these meetings Middles also expand their collaboration to include joint problem solving, joint planning, and forming coalitions of Middles who have a specific performance or improvement objective in mind that could benefit from a coalition being formed.

Table 22.1. Large-Group Interventions and Key Meetings for Operations and Continuous Improvement, Cont'd

Name	Gathering Type	Description of Key Elements
Forums	Meeting	Gatherings in which participants present and discuss topics of interest. For example, a biotech organization might hold a forum on the topic of emerging industry practices for increasing the yields of fermentation reactions. Anyone interested could attend.
Dialogue Sessions Focusing on Execution and Improvement Issues	LGI	Middle and Bottom leaders use ground rules and principles of the LGI template called Dialogue to surface assumptions and gain deeper understanding of LSS/HPO top leadership issues such as implementing a culture that highly values execution, instilling and managing collective accountability, and managing change.
Focus Groups	Meeting	An independent facilitator interviews eight to fifteen members of an intact team or group of teams to identify barriers to breaking free of the current performance plateau and management best practices that are working well now. The independent facilitator provides the relevant manager(s) with focus group session results and then manager(s) prepare a list of action items that respond to focus group participants. The result of the action plan and the discussion is mutual accountability for results with an agreed-on timetable for implementation.
Participative Planning	LGI	Involve a group of 20+ people to scan and analyze patterns, trends, and data external to the organization that affect the organization; critically examine the current organizational conditions for performance; develop a set of "strategic focal points" that articulate crisp, compelling elements of the strategy; and collectively develop action plans for advancing the organization to higher levels of performance. Based on the number of people involved in the planning process, there may be more than one participative planning session.
Lessons Learned	LGI	A group of people involved in the transformation convenes at the end of the stage to identify (1) what went well in this stage; (2) what they might do differently in the future; and (3) how the groups can make their learning accessible to people in the future who need this information.

[i]For an overview of the Open Space method, please see H. Owen. (1999). Open space. In P. Holman and T. Devane (Eds.), *The change handbook: Group methods for shaping the future.* San Francisco: Berrett-Koehler. For a more detailed look please see H. Owen. (1998). *Open space technology: A user's guide.* San Francisco: Berrett-Koehler or at the web-site www.openspaceworld.org.

Interesting Options

While LSS/HPO transformations will vary from organization to organization, successful ones are principle-based. Here are some optional approaches, based on the principles in this book, that some organizations have found to be successful. These are not mutually exclusive options. Leaders should feel free to use these or other custom-developed options to address unique local requirements.

Option 1: Follow Through on the Innovation and Creativity Introduced in the Previous Stage

If an organization introduced innovation and creativity during a previous stage, leaders would continue to provide resources, guidance, and internal motivation to this effort.

Option 2: Consider Implementing Activity-Based Costing (ABC)

Many organizations that have implemented Lean and Six Sigma principles have found that traditional cost accounting tends to distort product costs once waste has been removed and variation is reduced. This has led them to implement ABC for increased reporting accuracy and targeting of improvement efforts so that costs can be traced to activities later consumed by products or services. It may not be necessary for an organization to run ABC forever. There can be great benefits in just running it once a year or every two years to analyze product/service profitability and customer profitability. ABC can also help identify opportunities for cost reduction based on the most costly activities reported from the ABC study. Two excellent sources of information about ABC are the website www.icms.net, developed by long-time ABC thought leader Tom Pryor, and the book *Activity-Based Cost Management: An Executive's Guide*[1] by Gary Cokins.

Option 3: Conduct a Periodic Formal Audit of LSS/HPO Operations

Many companies today use the Baldrige criteria and audit method to evaluate their organizational health. Many world-class companies such as Johnson & Johnson have an internally trained group that conducts audits across the globe.[2]

LSS/HPO practitioners may want to consider some sort of similar audit process or a modification of the Baldrige or other process to include LSS/HPO criteria. Such audits, followed by coaching activities, can help rejuvenate improvement attitudes.

Options 4: Move LSS/HPO Up and Down the Supply Chain

If an organization introduced LSS/HPO beyond its boundaries in a previous stage, during this stage leaders would continue to provide resources, guidance, and support.

Common Traps

Although no two implementations of LSS/HPO will be exactly alike, there are some common traps that organizations encounter. The ones most often found in the Operations and Continuous Improvement stage are

- *People thinking they're "done" when they complete Implementation.* The mindsets and practices of continuous improvement, collaboration, and execution need to persist far beyond Implementation. Other initiatives, such as innovation, may *add* to what people have learned about LSS/HPO, but should not *replace* it.

- *Managers and teams trying to improve results by tampering with processes.* By this stage nearly all LSS/HPO leaders know that process variation can lead to serious performance problems. Quality leader W. Edwards Deming recommended distinguishing between types of variation, and addressing variation outside the realm of expected variation—"special cause variation"—through improvement activities. Natural variation in every process—"common cause variation"—does not require corrective action. In fact, attempting to "fix" such situations wastes resources and may introduce more problems. Deming dubbed these ill-advised fixes "tampering."

- *People overselling and overusing statistical tools.* Unfortunately, many people tend to equate a good LSS/HPO program with the use of numerous, complex statistical tools. While advanced tools are certainly part of a good LSS/HPO toolkit, the use of such tools is not an indicator of success. The *true* indicator of success is the business results obtained. For many processes the use of simple process maps and elimination of waste will yield considerable benefits.

- *Talent focusing only on problems and not on opportunities.* Problematic areas need not be the sole focus of LSS/HPO tools and principles. Top leaders should also charter improvement teams to develop new markets, alternative revenue streams, and innovations in customer-facing processes such as sales, field service, and delivery.

- *The top leadership group devoting insufficient time to the improvement of teamwork capabilities.* Sometimes Top tasks require interdependent thought and action, and sometimes they do not. But too often Tops don't think of themselves as a "team." For those times when collective action is needed, Tops need to schedule dedicated conversation time—sometimes with outside assistance—to plan and act as a productive group.

- *People spending lots of time in DMA and not enough in IC.* In the improvement approach Define, Measure, Analyze, Improve, and Control (DMAIC), teams often devote a high percentage of time to the first three activities. The DMAIC process includes a linked set of measurement and analysis tools that are very engaging and provide a strong sense of accomplishment. However, since benefits aren't realized until the recommendations are implemented, leaders need to ensure that teams don't spend a disproportionate amount of time in the early activities.

- *Tracking accomplishments and missed targets, but not clearly articulating development needs.* It's easy to report what went well and what went poorly. However, organizations miss valuable opportunities if they do not take the next step and identify what *developmental work,* for example, training, coaching, internal knowledge dissemination, and external benchmarking, needs to occur.

- *Populating improvement teams with large numbers of people.* Mike Grimm, Six Sigma Expert at Raytheon, warns against oversized improvement teams. Even companies experienced with Six Sigma sometimes fall into the trap of inviting people because an issue may tangentially involve their areas or they have a general interest in the problem. Mike's advice: Just invite people who can help fix the problem.[3]

- *Not including project management training as part of overall Black Belt training.* A process improvement project requires coordinating multiple resources, developing a detailed work plan, preparing a budget, monitoring team member progress, implementing change, and influencing people who do not directly report to the project leader. For these reasons, Black Belts need to receive project management training.

- *Failing to recognize and reward the contributions of and marketability of good Black Belts and Master Black Belts.* A good Black Belt is a hot commodity during economic upturns and downturns. Average turnover for Black Belts is about 30 percent. Once they are trained, it makes economic sense to try to keep them through financial and non-financial rewards. At Becton, Dickinson and Company, Black Belts deliver well above the average annual financial return for a Black Belt. Yet Black Belt turnover is a surprisingly low 16 percent. How do they do it? They reward Black Belts and improvement teams with bonuses and generous stock options and provide excellent opportunities for rotation to see different parts of the business.[4] They believe the amount invested in keeping Black Belts and other key talent around is well worth the rewards. The company keeps rewarding people, and the people keep delivering at high levels. Everyone wins.

- *Letting others set expectations for the types of improvements that are possible.* Six Sigma consultant Rob Tripp reported that once the word got out that a securities custodian in the Northeast was doing Six Sigma, their customers demanded a 50 percent reduction in cycle time for the handling of account openings and certain types of inquiries. Managing customer expectations about outcomes is just as important as making the improvements.

- *Managers inappropriately intervening in team work and in team mistakes.* For truly high LSS/HPO performance, teams must be responsible for their work and be able to learn from their mistakes. When a manager at a higher level redirects a team's activities, a potential side effect is that the team owns less of the output. In addition, when a manager tries to save a team from making a mistake, the team feels less invested in the process and can begin to depend on that manager to rescue them in the future. There are most definitely cases that require manager intervention, but these should only be when the team's decision will drastically and negatively impact the business. In other instances it can be best for the team to figure out how to detect and correct errors. Janet Bubnis, a manager of HPTs in the United States District Court system, says she carefully considers each case where one of her teams is about to make a mistake and then decides whether or not she should intervene. Unwarranted team intervention is akin to a passer-by stooping to pick up a fledgling bird on the sidewalk as it struggles unsuccessfully to fly and placing it back in its nest. Without some struggling, hard lessons will not be learned and the necessary development will not occur.

Counterintuitive Elements

 Leadership in an LSS/HPO looks different than it does in traditional organizational structures. However, some of those differences are keys to LSS/HPO success. Table 22.2 shows three such elements often encountered during Operations and Continuous Improvement.

Table 22.2. Counterintuitive Elements During Operations and Continuous Improvement

Traditional Thinking	Counterintuitive LSS/HPO Reality
Top leaders have to continually drive changes toward higher performance levels	In an LSS/HPO much of the organizational power and energy are distributed throughout the organization. As a result, much less effort is required of top leaders than in traditional, non-LSS/HPO organizations. Support is necessary, but Tops "driving all changes" is not necessary.
With a bias towards action and execution, we need to quickly try to fix problems	It's important to obtain relevant data before making an important decision. Management by opinion needs to be replaced with data-driven analyses.
All improvements need to go through the formal process for identifying, screening, and chartering	Major improvement projects will most definitely need to proceed through the improvement cycle. However, there may be small improvements that one or more teams believe should be made that do not require significant resources and do not have an impact beyond those immediately solving the problem. In addition to not clogging up the main improvement process, such local efforts can energize groups to continuously improve and perform at high levels.
Conflict is a negative aspect of work that leaders should avoid and minimize when they encounter it	Leaders need to consider Steve Crum's assertion that "Conflict is neither good nor bad, it just is."[i] Whenever more than one person is involved in a situation, there most often will be more than one interest in the outcome. In LSS/HPOs, productive conflict can be quite helpful in getting out all the facts and emotions necessary to reach higher levels of performance. Conflict should be managed, not suppressed.

Table 22.2. Counterintuitive Elements During Operations and Continuous Improvement, Cont'd

Traditional Thinking	Counterintuitive LSS/HPO Reality
HPTs are part of a very participatory mode of operation. Therefore, HPTs need to be consulted regarding any decision that directly affects them.	In an LSS/HPO participation and collaboration are means to an end, but they are not the end. Leaders need to focus on the health of the overall organizational system and on the development of people within. For example, when an HPT in the U.S. District Court for the Western District of Washington was performing poorly, the manager, Janet Bubnis, assessed the situation and without any team collaboration took away the team's self-managing status for three months. The decision was initially viewed as a violation of the sacrosanct status of self-management by some outsiders. It was not. Within three months of Bubnis' coaching, the team was back to self-managing status and performing well. At times a leader must evaluate the situation and act unilaterally for the good of the entire organization.
People understand that they have the knowledge and authority to reconfigure their segment of the organization as external and internal needs dictate and all teams frequently avail themselves of this opportunity	Some teams do reorganize within about a ninety-day period after the first redesign session. However, it's not uncommon for teams to then settle down and develop such a strong sense of solidarity and like for working with each other that they are reluctant to redesign. Managers need to be on the lookout for this behavior, and make suggestions at appropriate times.
People have all been trained in process improvement tools, philosophies, and methods, so they will also take a rigorous approach to problem solving and decision making	At times, many people in an educated workforce will begin to search for shortcuts to problem solving by intuiting solutions and utilizing "educated guesses"—also known as opinions—instead of using the problem-solving rigor of DMAIC for large, complex problems. The "I'm-right-because-I'm-me" thinking returns, and leaders need to watch for and address it.

[i]Crum, S. (1998). *The magic of conflict*. Washington, DC: Touchstone Press.

Leadership Checklist for Proceeding to the Next Phase

 Before the organization can move to the next stage of an LSS/HPO transformation (or into a new transformation), top leaders should check to ensure the items in Exhibit 22.1 have been completed. It can also be helpful for top leaders to refer to this list as the stage is unfolding to ensure activities are started on time to produce the desired results as continuous improvement progresses.

Exhibit 22.1. Leadership Checklist for the Operations and Continuous Improvement Stage

☐ Celebrate and extensively publicize team successes

☐ Continually seek to push down decisions, information, skills, and rewards

☐ Work on improving the collective work products and team dynamics of the team at the top of the organization

☐ Seek innovative financial and non-financial ways to reward people who participated in a successful improvement project shortly after it is completed

☐ Change the old ways of strategic planning and organizational restructuring to incorporate the ability to adapt to and influence the external environment. A great strategic planning balance consists of "plan when you can" and "sense and respond." To accomplish this ensures that the organization builds in external environment sensors and grants HPTs the authority to reconfigure the structure when needed

☐ Ensure HR system changes are implemented, such as the evaluation of compensation alternatives, new hiring policies, and recognition and rewards for the new environment

☐ Continue using previous leadership tools such as the Performance Framework, Top/Middle/Bottom Space Analysis, Integrated Work Plan, Leader To Do List, Large-Scale Interventions, and the Leader's Guide for Analyze-and-Energize Leadership in the future to initiate and sustain other improvements

The pragmatic tips presented in this chapter can help leaders anticipate potential problem areas and exploit opportunities that arise in the Operations and Continuous Improvement stage. By understanding the key outputs and deliverables, leaders know what people should be working on throughout the stage and can suggest mid-course corrections as needed. The sample thought-provoking questions provided will help leaders and others think about important transformation issues.

Public gatherings and collective decision making are key elements of successful LSS/HPOs. In any large group setting, it's important that the group become productive as fast as possible. To accomplish that, leaders can call on some standard templates called large-group interventions to help get people productive quickly, and accomplish the objectives as quickly as possible. The large-group interventions and key meetings listed will help advance LSS/HPO objectives by quickly delivering high quality work products and generating enthusiasm and commitment to LSS/HPO objectives.

The path to a successful LSS/HPO is guided by principles and a flexible approach, not a cast-in-concrete process. This chapter presented some optional activities that have been successful for other practitioners. By studying the common traps presented, leaders can choose to plan for, instead of react to, problems others have encountered. To help ease the transition to new leadership practices, some of which may appear counterintuitive to traditional leadership thinking, this chapter presented the most common counterintuitive leadership practices that appear in this stage. As a final help to leaders there is a leadership checklist of important items leaders need to consider throughout the Operations and Continuous Improvement stage and beyond in other improvement efforts with LSS/HPO serving as the foundation.

Notes

1. Cokins, G. (2002). *Activity-based cost management.* New York: John Wiley & Sons.
2. Personal interview with Susan Conway of McNeil Consumer Products, a Johnson & Johnson Company, in February, 1996.
3. Personal conversation with Mike Grimm of Raytheon.
4. Personal conversation with Valerie Larson, Corporate Manager of Organizational Development, and Derek Wendelken, Vice President, Human Resources, at Becton, Dickinson and Company.

Conclusion

Certainty is generally illusion, and repose is not the destiny of man.
Oliver Wendell Holmes

THE DESIRE FOR PERFORMANCE IMPROVEMENT is here to stay. As long as companies are faced with intense competition and escalating customer demands, government organizations experience budget cuts and are asked to do more with less, and not–for–profits seek to attract volunteers with high energy who are committed to special projects and operate in a low cost mode, there will be a desire for improvements. Leaders need to remember six final things in their quest for performance improvement.

1. LSS/HPO Provides a Powerful Combination for Improvement

Leaders can use the complementary disciplines of LSS/HPO to implement dramatic, sustainable change. *Lean* principles are easy to learn and provide rapid improvements. Such early improvements pay for themselves and generate energy for continuing. *Six Sigma* contributes advanced statistical tools and formal ties to the management system. These longer-term benefits and links to reinforcement enable and encourage employees to go after bigger gains that may require more data collection and analysis. *High-Performance Organization* principles directly reshape the culture, organizational structure, and peoples' mindsets. By instilling a widespread attitude of ownership, execution, and continuous improvement, leaders can assure that their gains are sustainable. In combination, the three disciplines provide a fast, effective way for organizations to improve and keep on improving.

2. Teams Are Fast Becoming the Basic Unit of Organizational Performance

Teams can quickly pull together expertise from multiple disciplines to address a serious performance challenge. Teams can demolish an organization's silo mentality by having multiple silo members empowered to act as a single group. And teams provide an immediate coaching and peer feedback group of about ten team members, instead of just one boss in traditional structures. Although a departure from traditional organizational structures, an organization composed principally of teams is an extremely fast way to instill the cultural values required to quickly implement and sustain dramatic Lean Six Sigma improvements. Most people have experienced the great feelings of working on at least one high-performing team in their lives. The LSS/HPO approach takes this peak performance one step further by officially sanctioning and encouraging teams throughout the entire organization.

3. Leaders Have a Dramatic Impact on the Success of Any Improvement Effort

People initially look to leaders to determine how serious they are about a change effort. If leaders aren't taking the right actions, modeling the new behaviors, and rewarding new practices, the workforce is unlikely to embrace the proposed changes. Great leaders shape the way that people think by increasing contact with the general workforce in early transformation stages. They use the power of language—through new terms, repeated phrases, stories, and questions—to introduce and emphasize new ways of thinking and acting. In an LSS/HPO, leaders can—and, in fact, must—actively manage culture. Key new cultural characteristics include an environment of inquiry and dissatisfaction with the status quo, an infrastructure and motivation for learning, an emphasis on measurement and accountability, a fanatical focus on the external customer, and an attitude of continuous improvement in everybody. Such cultural aspects result in workforce members banding together and making the organization a more profitable, fun place to work.

4. Leaders May Have to Change Some of Their Own Behaviors

Leading an LSS/HPO is different from leading a traditional organization. In an LSS/HPO there is a concerted effort to blend the "hard" and "soft" aspects of change. Teams are the fundamental performance unit, rather than individuals. People are held collectively accountable for results and improvements. Culture is actively managed, instead of just happening. People are expected to continually improve, not just perform the technical tasks for which they are responsible. These differences, as well as a host of others, require leaders to think and behave differently. Often a skeptical leader—perhaps well-versed in the command-and-control school of management—will need to try some of the new behaviors before he or she is logically and emotionally convinced of their value. Such experimentation is encouraged, because questioning of new ideas is natural and experimentation is a critical step toward authentically using principles of the new "analyze-and-energize" leadership.

5. Principles and Tools Make a Leader's Job Easier

It can be difficult for a leader to "try on" new behaviors and ways of thinking. Fortunately, LSS/HPO provides a set of tools and principles that help ease that awkwardness and compress the cycle time for a successful transformation. A tool called the Performance Framework helps leaders plan, monitor, analyze, and explain what is happening based on a critical set of performance factors. The Top/Middle/Bottom Space Analysis tool focuses on human interactions.

It helps leaders understand perceptual filters and helps optimize interactions among groups within the organization. The Leader's Integrated Work Plan QA Checklist provides questions leaders can ask to direct the planning and execution of the transformation. And the checklists for analyze-and-energize leader behaviors help leaders approach problem situations from a different viewpoint. These, and other tools in the book, help guide leaders down a successful LSS/HPO path so that leaders can benefit from those who have gone before them.

6. Leadership Must Be Distributed Throughout the Organization

Highly successful organizations pay special attention to creating many leaders at all levels. This requires a cascading process of creating the *eligibility* and *capability* for leadership from the top of the organization to the bottom. Pushing important decisions down the hierarchy and rotating leadership among team members helps increase eligibility. Leadership training, personal reflection time, and feedback from a variety of sources help increase capability. Distributed leadership helps create ownership, an execution focus, and a spirit of continuous improvement. Leadership is like a muscle in that the more it is exercised, the stronger it becomes. And the more people who exercise it, the stronger an entire organization becomes.

The principles and tools of LSS/HPO can help a leader systematically move an organization toward higher performance. The path to LSS/HPO is a rewarding, and also challenging one. One of the most challenging, gut-wrenching decisions is whether or not to use LSS/HPO as a single vehicle for transformation, a system of management, and continuous improvement.

Because radical improvement and sustainability appear to be givens in today's environment, leaders must decide which discipline, or combination of disciplines, can address both those goals. Asking that question is a critical one for leaders who are seeking optimal organizational performance and who wish to leave a mark on their organization, their industry, and perhaps even society. What's keeping your leadership team from examining that question today?

Appendix

THERE ARE three sections for this Appendix:

1. A Glossary of terms;

2. A more complete examination of Large-Group Interventions; and

3. Reference Material.

Glossary

THE FOLLOWING PAGES CONTAIN A GLOSSARY of key terms for concepts central to leading an LSS/HPO. Definitions and explanations have been developed to be free of jargon and to be of the most practical use to leaders.

Adaptive Work System   An organization that can quickly change internal policies, structures, and practices in response to changing patterns and trends in the organization's external environment. In many cases an organization can alter the evolution of the external environment to the organization's advantage. Effective adaptive systems have good sensors to periodically scan the external environment, internal structures that can be quickly reconfigured, a means to distribute information to target audiences quickly, and people trained and motivated to quickly reconfigure, react to, and create desirable changes.

Balanced Scorecard   *Used as a noun:* a set of multiple measurements, typically grouped in the areas of financial, customer, internal process, and learning and innovation, that target areas for reporting and improving performance at a team, group, division, or company level. Balanced Scorecards at all levels are aligned with each other and based on the company's strategy. *Considered as a methodology:* a comprehensive approach to rolling out strategy through a linked network of cause-and-effect measurements that establish and monitor goals. Based on feedback and goal attainment, information from the Balanced Scorecard can also be used to alter strategy.

Black Belt   A person trained in simple and advanced improvement techniques such as problem solving, advanced statistical analyses, and change management. Black Belts receive about four weeks of training spread out over four months. They are considered a company's internal experts in process improvement and have a full-time commitment to being a Black Belt for about eighteen months as they provide leadership to improvement teams in their areas of expertise. (Compare with Green Belt, Master Black Belt.)

Bottoms   The organizational space responsible for producing products and services. Bottoms have a unique set of organizational conditions, common traps, and ways out of those traps based on thirty-five years of research by Barry Oshry.

Burning Platform for Change   A compelling set of logical and emotional reasons for the organization to abandon the status quo. A burning platform message from top management typically also emphasizes, and where possible demonstrates, top management's resolve to proceed with the new effort.

Business Literacy   A fundamental understanding of the way an organization makes money, the key products/services it provides to customers, how it fits into its industry, and emerging industry trends and patterns. In an LSS/HPO, it is important that all organizational levels have a basic level of business literacy so they can see the big picture and how they fit in and think strategically when required.

Change Leader   A person, usually with some level of informal or formal power or influence, who is instrumental in planning and implementing new practices and new ways of thinking and acting.

Change Management Profile   A common breakdown of people who will actively support a proposed change (20 percent), actively resist it (20 percent), or wait on the fence to see which way to go (60 percent).

Circle of Participation The total number of people involved in transformation activities and in the new ways of thinking and acting. Ideally, this circle grows as the organization proceeds from one stage to another of the LSS/HPO transformation.

Common Cause Variation Fluctuations in a process that are completely natural based on the capabilities of the machine or person performing the process. Such variations fall within an acceptable range of values. Management should not convene special process improvement teams or otherwise try to "fix" common cause variations. For example, let's say chemical reaction XYZ typically operates between 40 degrees and 60 degrees Fahrenheit. If one reaction is at 41 degrees, the next is at 59 and the next is at 50, these fluctuations would not require any process improvement, as they fall within the natural variation. (See Special Cause Variation, Tampering.)

Communication Plan A time-phased listing of key transformation messages, target audiences, communication channels, and measurements of effectiveness over the course of the transformation.

Community of Practice People who share interests, problems, best practices, and knowledge. They greatly help disseminate learning and create an environment for continuous improvement. Early communities of practice in an LSS/HPO are the Black Belts and the Initial Restructuring Team that leads the initial restructuring into HPTs.

Control Chart A visual representation of a variable over time. These charts help operators continually watch for critical changes in the variation or the average of a set of data.

Critical to Quality A characteristic of a product or service that is extremely important for a customer.

Culture The shared beliefs and assumptions that help determine behavior in the workplace.

Customer Drumbeat That rate at which customers order products, usually stated in units per time period. For example, two units per hour.

Customer Profile Key information about a customer or customer group that includes items such as customer characteristics, expectations, challenges customers face, purchasing patterns, and customer behaviors.

Dashboard   A set of eight to twelve critical metrics that show the general health of an organization, division, major process, or department. Each dashboard metric will have green, yellow, or red status to indicate respectively whether that measurement is satisfactory, if there are potential problems, or if there are serious problems.

DMAIC   The process of Define-Measure-Analyze-Improve-Control used by teams to improve processes.

Energizing Core   The three fundamental elements—know how, want to, and pay for—that fuel the improvement process and make it sustainable. The Energizing Core, together with the Performance Bases, make up the elements of the Performance Framework over which an organization has control.

Entitlement Mentality   A feeling by workers that they do not have to put forth effort to earn rewards or keep their jobs. Contributing factors to such feelings typically include (1) long periods of management failing to hold people accountable for results and (2) wildly successful products that require little or no extraordinary efforts by the majority of the workforce (such as the introduction of a new drug that addresses a profitable market niche where there is no competition). To move from a culture of entitlement, leaders need to value performance and skills over status and position.

"Everybody in the Pool"   A misguided philosophy of inviting every person who may be affected by the decision to a decision-making meeting. A better philosophy is to determine the purpose of a meeting, the people who could contribute, the most effective way to create buy-in for the decision, and a manageable size for a meeting that accommodates those factors.

Extrinsic Motivation   Engaging in an activity to receive promised outside rewards, such as a bonus, or to avoid punishment, such as being required to work a weekend. Extrinsic motivation is not inherently better or worse than intrinsic motivation in an LSS/HPO. Both are necessary. (Compare Intrinsic Motivation.)

Failure Mode and Effects Analysis (FMEA)   A method that helps identify potential failures of process components and their impacts on other process components and what should be done to address high priority and high likelihood problems.

Feedback Loop   The transmission of information about an action to the originating or controlling source. In LSS/HPOs establishing feedback loops is essential because both processes and people require information about their actions if they are to continuously improve.

Focus Group   A process in which a group of six to twelve people is posed a series of four to fifteen questions by a neutral party to obtain their views on a particular topic. In an LSS/HPO, managers often listen to the focus group data and trends (provided by the facilitator without attribution to individuals in the focus group session) and then prepare action items to respond to issues raised. A feedback loop is usually designed in to ensure that both management and front-line worker have lived up to any commitments made.

Forum   A gathering of people with a common interest, usually to share or obtain knowledge about a specific topic.

Gain Sharing   A plan that distributes bonuses based on groups meeting local performance targets. The gain sharing bonus distribution differs from a profit sharing plan that distributes bonuses based on corporation profits.

Green Belt (GB)   A person trained in simple improvement techniques who participates in process improvement projects. Green Belts receive about nine to twelve days of training. They provide detailed process knowledge in process improvement projects on a part-time basis as they continue their current job responsibilities. (Compare with Black Belt, Master Black Belt.)

Grid   Short for "Transformation Grid."

Guiding Coalition   A core group of people with formal positional power who enthusiastically embrace the proposed change and have the required knowledge and influence relationships with key workforce members to initiate, energize, and sustain the transformation.

High-Performance Organization (HPO)   A discipline that focuses on building organizational structures composed principally of high-performance teams (HPTs) whose members work interdependently to address specific performance challenges. This structure results in high performance because of the high levels of intrinsic motivation resulting from decisions, information, and rewards being pushed to the lowest possible level so that planning, error detection, and correction occur close to the source.

High-Performance Team (HPT)   A group of individuals whose work is interdependent, who set goals and are collectively held accountable for them. In addition to performing technical task work, HPTs also take on managerial tasks such as work scheduling, control and coordination of their work, and budgeting. Evolved HPTs are also trained to hire, fire, and discipline team members. HPTs are typically "standing teams," that is, they tend to have the same membership over time. Members of HPTs will sometimes participate, on a part-time basis, on an improvement team with a Black Belt who provides improvement guidance and expertise in statistical methods.

Improvement Teams   Groups of people who assemble for the specific purpose of improving a process. Sample target improvement areas include cycle time reduction, cost reduction, revenue enhancement, flexibility enhancement, and defect removal. Improvement teams will typically have people from HPTs participate on a part-time basis until the problem is solved.

Initial Restructuring Team   A group that facilitates the redesign workshops that convert the existing organizational structure into one consisting primarily of High-Performance Teams. This group, which also provides coaching to leaders after the redesign, is typically trained by external consultants or recent hires who have extensive experience in such redesign and coaching sessions. Once the redesigns have been completed and coaching occurs for about six months, this team usually disbands because most of what they know has been disseminated to the entire organization.

Integrated Work Plan   The overall plan for the LSS/HPO transformation that includes key activities, individuals or groups responsible for those activities, targeted start dates, and targeted completion dates. This one plan addresses all Lean, Six Sigma, HPO, and change management activities so that separate plans are not required for each. This is a "living plan" that is updated at the start of each stage based on information learned from the previous stage. In addition, at the start of each stage the plan is updated to include more detail for the upcoming stage, while future stages still remain at a higher level of detail.

Intelligent Empowerment   The systematic relocation of decisions to lower levels of the organization with accompanying information, skills training, authority, and rewards.

Intrinsic Motivation   Engaging in an activity for its own sake (instead of for monetary or other external rewards) to obtain a feeling of personal satisfaction. In an LSS/HPO, intrinsic motivation would come from feelings of personal competence, self-esteem, confidence, a degree of control over one's local work environment, and achievement. Intrinsic motivation is not inherently better or worse than extrinsic motivation in an LSS/HPO. Both are necessary. (Compare Extrinsic Motivation.)

Leader's Integrated Work Plan Shaping and Quality Assurance (QA) Guide   A set of questions leaders ask to ensure that high quality transformation plans exist, the right people are involved but not overloaded, and the right things are scheduled at the right times. This tool, which focuses on project management of the transformation, is one of the three basic tools leaders used in each LSS/HPO stage.

Lean Manufacturing   (Sometimes referred to as "Lean.") A discipline that uses a set of tools and principles to shorten cycle time, reduce inventory, and eliminate waste in the products and services that customers desire.

Low Hanging Fruit   A colloquial term denoting a process improvement that can be quickly implemented and that will return significant return on the time and money invested.

Macro Design   A high-level grouping of organizational units or other strategic organizational structuring design decision that top management decides is necessary and that will not be open for managers and front-line workers to redesign. Examples include the decision to combine the Information Technology and Internal Process Consulting Departments into one and the decision to organize European operations into customer-based teams that span country boundaries, instead of around geographic units.

Maslow's Hierarchy of Needs   A progression of needs that must be satisfied before a person reaches the top need of self-actualization, where he or she realizes personal potential, personal growth, and self-fulfillment. The progression, from lowest order needs to highest, is physiological, safety and security, love and belonging, esteem, self-actualization ("the desire to become more and more what one is, to become everything that one is capable of becoming").

Master Black Belt (MBB)   An experienced Black Belt who continues learning, assists in process improvement efforts, mentors new Black Belts, fosters learning among Black Belts, and promotes LSS/HPO within the organization. (Compare with Green Belt, Black Belt.)

Middles   The people in an organizational system who are between the Tops (who have ultimate responsibility) and Bottoms (who produce products and services). Middles have a unique set of organizational conditions, common traps, and ways out of those traps. The concept is based on thirty-five years of research by Barry Oshry.

Minimum Critical Specs   Guidelines, boundary conditions, and constraints for the workshops in which the organization designs itself into a structure composed principally of High-Performance Teams (HPTs). Examples include (1) increase client base by 15 percent within two years, (2) cost-effective processes and structures, (3) no penetration into Middle East markets, and (4) no increases in operating costs for one year.

Open and Direct Communication   An important cultural norm in an LSS/HPO that manifests itself as individuals speaking what is on their minds in a very frank manner. No topic is "off limits," even if it may prove potentially embarrassing or threatening for one of the parties involved. Initially many open and direct communications will likely be practiced mostly in one-on-one situations or small groups. However, as leaders model the new behavior and people become more comfortable with this practice, people do it in larger group meetings. This helps compress decision-making time and enables a questioning of old assumptions that may need to be changed.

Open Systems Theory   A body of knowledge and practice that assumes that an organizational "system," such as a corporation, joint venture, division, government agency, community, or trade association, has a set of objectives and intentions about how it will interact with the environment outside it. For such a system to be viable over time, it needs to constantly scan the environment for relevant changes and actively adapt to this information. Open systems theory asserts that a system and its environment work together to help shape and determine the future of both; do not evolve independent of one another, but rather co-evolve; and are governed by laws that can be articulated.[1] The open systems concept is important for LSS/HPO in the initial Direction Setting stage because it sets the stage for the joint evolution of the system and its environment and, on an ongoing basis, as it highlights the need for continual scanning of the environment and rapid adaptation to changes encountered.

Operating Norms   Generally accepted, often tacit, rules for interaction among organizational members. Examples include starting meetings ten minutes after the announced start time and senior management overriding middle management decisions irrespective of the quality of the middle management decision (a decision-making structure based solely on formal organization position and power). Calling specific attention to old and desired new norms can help pave the way for successful adoption of the new norms.

Organizational Space   One of the three conditions—Top, Middle, or Bottom—presented in this book that has typical condition characteristics, common traps, and ways out of the traps to enhance enterprise performance. The concept of organizational spaces is based on over thirty-five years of research by Barry Oshry.[2]

Pay for Skills Pay System   See Skill-Based Pay.

Performance Framework   A visual map of high leverage performance factors that helps LSS/HPO leaders develop plans, monitor progress, debate alternative courses of action, and conduct lessons-learned analyses in the context of a set of interrelated performance factors. This tool, which focuses on the interaction of key performance factors, is one of the three basic tools leaders use in each LSS/HPO stage.

Performance Bases   The nine interrelated, high-leverage factors that work together to influence organizational performance. These factors, which are part of the Performance Framework, are strategy, process, information and learning, HR practices, culture, and structure and relationships.

Plan-Do-Study-Act (PDSA)   An improvement cycle introduced by W. Edwards Deming that seeks to (1) determine goals and required changes to achieve them, (2) implement proposed changes, (3) evaluate the results obtained, and (4) take appropriate action (such as starting the cycle again, standardizing, or stabilizing the change). In an LSS/HPO this cycle is helpful for both process improvements and improvements in leadership skills. Deming had initially coined the phrase Plan-Do-Study-Act, but many organizations have changed this to Plan-Do-Check-Act.

Process   A collection of activities and decisions that produce an output for an internal or external customer. Processes often span departmental or group boundaries. Examples include new product development and order fulfillment that each require collaboration among multiple functional disciplines.

Process Fair   An event in which teams that have improved processes showcase their results, methods, tools, and approach for improvement. Typically, a process fair will showcase from three to ten processes at a time.

Process Improvement Team   A team that assembles to address a specific improvement issue and then disbands after the solution is designed, and sometimes after it has been implemented. A Process Improvement Team may contain members who are dedicated full-time to the team, but most often draw members from standing teams that are HPTs within the formal organizational structure. (Compare with Standing Team.)

Process Map   A visual depiction of the flow of activities and decisions that occur to produce an output for a customer. Process maps may also show department boundaries, time required for key activities, delays, and an indication of whether an activity adds values to the customer or not.

Product Family   A grouping of like products, usually by similarities in production and core features.

Productive Conflict   A perceived or real incompatibility of ideas, goals, or approaches that is instrumental in helping the organization reach higher levels of performance and build better working relationships. Leaders need to seek out opportunities to introduce and manage these incompatibilities and move them from the realm of destructive conflict to productive conflict. Productive conflict offers people an opportunity to become engaged in an issue, be heard, debate, and commit to the new way of doing things. Without such productive conflict, people may either internally resent the new ways or simply comply with them.

Profit Sharing   A plan that distributes bonuses based on corporate profits.

Pull System   A method of production in which a downstream operation signals its needs for materials from an upstream operation. Because the upstream operations can only produce when they receive a signal, overall inventory in the production process is kept low and average time for raw material to move from receiving to shipping is reduced.

Requisite Variety   A system (such as an organization, division, or HPT in an LSS/HPO) needs to incorporate internal variety so that it can cope with external variety. The term originates from cybernetics theory. One of the first examples provided by W. Ross Ashby, who coined the term, was related to national defense. He stated that if missiles that had a certain velocity and altitude were aimed at the United States, that the U.S. defense system needed to have the "requisite variety" capable of addressing both the speed and altitude of the incoming missiles. In short, it takes internal variety to address external variety. Requisite variety is important for two reasons in an LSS/HPO. First, teams or other grouping of organizational units need to have the requisite variety to address the performance challenge facing them. Second, if sufficient requisite variety does not exist, then it is highly likely that some sort of conflict will arise. It is important the leaders involved view this—and manage it—as "productive conflict."

Scope Creep   An expansion of the originally defined project boundaries and objectives. Such expansions are dangerous because they require additional time and resources, although most often the expectation is that the project will be delivered within the originally promised time and budget.

Service Family   A grouping of like services, usually by common characteristics or similarities in production methods.

Service Level Agreement   A formal arrangement between two parties about what the provider and supplier will give to each other. Such an arrangement typically includes targets for time, cost, and quality. Many also include reporting requirements and a process for resolving disputes. These agreements may be made between internal groups or between an internal group and an external group, such as customers or suppliers.

Six Criteria for Productive Work   Factors that, when present, lead to employees producing more output within a given period of time. These six factors, originally articulated by Fred Emery and Einar Thorsrud, have more than thirty-five years of research and data to support the claim for higher performance. The criteria are (1) autonomy in decision making; (2) continual learning, for which there must be the ability to (a) set goals and (b) receive accurate and timely feedback; (3) variety; (4) mutual support and respect; (5) meaningfulness, which consists of (a) doing something with social value and (b) seeing the whole product or service; and (6) a desirable future, either inside or outside the organization.[3]

Six Sigma   A discipline for improving processes that focuses on reducing variation through statistical methods and formal ties to an organization's management system.

Skills-Based Pay   A payment method that compensates employees for demonstrated skills or knowledge they possess. This is an alternative to traditional pay systems that compensate employees based on the jobs that they hold. It is also called "pay for knowledge," "competency-based pay," and "pay-for-skills."

Special Cause Variation   Fluctuations in a process that happen as a result of a special circumstance. These fluctuations are not the natural variation of the machine or person performing the process. Such variations fall outside the acceptable range of values. Management should convene special process improvement teams or take other corrective measures to address special cause variation. For example, let's say chemical reaction XYZ typically operates between 40 degrees and 60 degrees Fahrenheit. If one reaction is at 62 degrees, the next is at 63, and the next is at 62, these fluctuations would require process improvement as they do not fall within the natural variation. (See Common Cause Variation, Tampering.)

Standing Teams   Teams that retain the same membership and stay together to reach the same goals they have had before. Standing teams normally produce a product or service, instead of being assembled, performing work, and then disbanding like a Process Improvement Team or a special project team.

Strategic Focal Point   Clear, compelling, time-bound articulation of a strategic plan.

Tamper, Tampering   Taking action based on a perceived problem or variation when in fact no action should be taken because the variation was a common cause variation, meaning that it was within the acceptable natural variation limits of the process. This term was coined by quality pioneer Dr. W. Edwards Deming. (See Common Cause Variation, Special Cause Variation.)

Team   A group of people who share a common goal and must work collaboratively to achieve it. Two special types of teams are Process Improvement Teams (which assemble to address a performance challenge and then disband) and Standing Teams (which are parts of the organization's team-based structure).

360-Degree Evaluations   Feedback on performance from a boss, peers, project team members, and direct reports. Patterns and trends from such feedback are typically consolidated and presented to the feedback recipient by a facilitator trained in 360-degree feedback. For large populations undergoing 360-degree evaluations, an automated compilation mechanism is highly recommended.

Top/Middle/Bottom Space Analysis   A tool that helps leaders develop powerful change actions and communications based on an understanding of how various groups within the organization will experience the proposed actions and communications. In addition, the tool helps leaders better understand their own "organizational space" and plan for high leverage actions. This tool, which focuses on human interactions within and among organizational levels and groups, is one of the three basic tools leaders use in each LSS/HPO stage. (See Organizational Space.)

Tops   The people in an organizational system who are ultimately responsible for its output, survival, and development. Tops have a unique set of organizational conditions, common traps, and ways out of those traps.

Top Team   The way many people often refer to the two or three highest levels of the organization. In reality, sometimes this group of people does function as a team, and sometimes they function as individuals. They are a team when their work requires an interdependent effort to achieve a shared goal. At other times they perform as individuals who head up major organizational units.

Town Hall Meeting   A gathering of the entire organization or major unit of the organization in which top leaders provide information to the large gathering. Typically there is also a question-and-answer period that allows for a two-way exchange of information between top leaders and the workforce.

Transformation Grid   A matrix of high leverage action categories mapped to stages of a large-scale change effort. In an LSS/HPO, leaders use this tool to develop high level Leader To Do Lists that focus leader energy on high-impact actions for the transformation.[4]

Transformation Coordination Team (TCT)   A multidisciplinary group that acts as the initial driving force and coordination center for LSS/HPO transformation activities. The TCT acts as the project management arm of top management while top management provides the necessary direction for and visible commitment to LSS/HPO.

Transformation Technology Team   A group of information technology specialists, business analysts, and sometimes external resources that provides rapid automated solutions for LSS/HPO activities. To provide fast solution turnaround, this team typically operates outside the normal information technology department queue of existing system development requests.

Value Stream (for Product or Service Delivery)   The flow of activities and decisions required to provide a product or service "family" to a customer. This type of value stream typically starts with a customer order (for make-to-order production) or demand forecast (for make-to-stock production) and finishes with delivery.

Value Stream (for Product or Service Design)   The flow of activities and decisions required to develop new offerings within a product or service "family." This type of value stream typically starts with the concept and ends with the launch.

Value Stream Mapping™   A diagram showing major steps and information required to bring a product or service from order to delivery. Typically, groups of middle managers develop these maps for the current state and for the future state. In addition, for each major operation the map contains data such as cycle time, up time, change over time, available time, and value-added and non-value-added time throughout the process.[5]

Voice of the Customer   Requirements customers have articulated for products or services they receive.

Notes

1. Adapted from Emery, M., and Devane, T. (1999). Search conference. In P. Holman and T. Devane (Eds.), *The change handbook: Group methods for shaping the future.* San Francisco: Berrett-Koehler.

2. Oshry's research also includes a "customer" space, although this space was not presented in this book as a part of the LSS/HPO transformation. For more information on all the organizational spaces, refer to B. Oshry (1986), *The possibilities of organization.* Boston, MA: Power & Systems.

3. Adapted from Emery, M., and Devane, T. (1999). Search conference. In P. Holman and T. Devane (Eds.), *The change handbook: Group methods for shaping the future.* San Francisco: Berrett-Koehler.

4. For more information on the Transformation Grid and updates to content of the Grid, please refer to TransformationGrid.com.

5. For an excellent description of how to construct Value Stream Maps, see M. Rother and J. Shook (1988), *Learning to see.* Brookline, MA: Lean Enterprise Institute.

Large-Group Interventions

L ARGE-GROUP INTERVENTIONS (LGIs) are methods for engaging groups of people to collectively explore current reality, conduct a meaningful dialogue about a situation, and co-develop a path forward based on public conversations in which people typically commit to one or more actions. They are called "large-group interventions" because they typically involve more than twenty people, a number that is too high to utilize traditional rules of meeting management. This section provides some background information on LGIs, provides a list of types of LGIs and examples, and provides a sample agenda for two popular LGIs.

Background Information

LGIs can run from two hours to three days, depending on purpose and participant interaction requirements. Each LGI has a distinctive "design backbone," consisting of principles for success with the intervention and an agenda that can be tailored slightly to accommodate local organizational needs. The combined principles for design and conduct of the LGI combined with the LGI's agenda help large groups of people become productive very quickly and help the facilitator manage the group dynamics and generate high quality outputs in a short period of time.

LGIs are extremely important elements in an LSS/HPO conversion. They accomplish two purposes. First, they produce valuable work products for the transformation, such as strategic plans and organizational redesigns. Second, they fuel the important "energizing core" component of the Performance Framework (see Chapter 7), the "want to" component. It can be difficult for people who have not participated in an LGI to understand what a powerful motivator such an experience can be for participants. In fact, LGIs provide such power and such an intense focus on a particular issue for a short time that they can create a bit of a problem for leaders. The problem is that people think that the only time transformation is occurring is in an LGI. Transformation, as good leaders know, occurs in between the large-group events as well as during them. Leaders must make people aware of the fact that transformation activities are continual.

LGI standard agendas, or templates, can be grouped into major categories such as planning, restructuring, process awareness and high level definition, culture change, and a variety of other special purposes. It is not the intent of this book to go into details about LGIs. Other books provide overviews of various LGIs.[1] Rather, this book seeks to make leaders aware of these powerful methods that can be used to generate energy around the move to an LSS/HPO, dramatically reduce resistance, and improve the quality of transition and operating work products beyond what would normally be possible without an LGI. A starter list of LGIs that may be useful in an LSS/HPO transition appears in Table A.1.

At least thirty standard templates for LGIs exist, and, of course, there is always the option to design a custom LGI from scratch to suit one's own unique purposes. Although standard LGI's often provide a greater degree of safety and are excellent shapers of group success based on previous continual learning and refinement of the intervention, there are unique situations in which an organization may want to design and conduct their own.

Types of LGIs and Examples

Although LGIs are typically designed for groups of more than twenty people, some can be used with smaller groups. Table A.1 presents general categories of LGIs, some sample LGIs for each category, and where each sample might be used in an LSS/HPO transformation.

Table A.1. Types of LGIs and Examples of Each

General LGI Category	Method Name	Description and Example of Use	Useful in Stages
Participative Planning	Search Conference	A participative planning process in which people create a well-articulated, desirable, achievable future with action plans for implementing it that include a definite timetable, people who will do it, and who know how to do it. Used for strategic planning, transformation planning, process redesign and other plans where people collaboratively plan a future based on common interests.	2: Direction Setting 5: Operations and Continuous Improvement
	Future Search	A participative planning process designed to evolve a common-ground future for an organization or community and develop self-managed plans to move toward it. Used for strategic planning, transformation planning, process redesign and other plans in which groups of people collaboratively plan a future based on common interests.	2: Direction Setting 5: Operations and Continuous Improvement
Participative Design	Participative Design Workshop	A workshop in which participants redesign their current organization into one of high-performance teams that then establish goals, develop vertical and lateral team interfaces with other teams, and launch into a new logic of organizational interactions based on teams as the fundamental unit of performance, instead of individuals.	3: Design
	Fast Cycle Full Participation	A workshop in which participants redesign the structural, work process, work content, role, and support systems for an organization.	3: Design
Process Awareness	Process Mapping	A participative analysis process in which a group develops diagrams depicting both the current and ideal flows of activities and decisions as they act together to produce an output for a customer. Process maps can be at a high level (as they are used at the start of a LSS/HPO project to identify the first round of improvement projects) or a more detailed level (as they are later in an organization's process evolution to conduct the improvement projects). Most process maps also show interdepartment handoffs and time durations for key parts of the process.	2: Direction Setting 3: Design 4: Implementation 5: Operations and Continuous Improvement
	Value Stream Mapping™	A pictorial representation that shows the value-added and non-value-added high-level tasks currently required to bring a product family from suppliers to end customers. These maps also include cycle time durations, uptime, available time for production, key information flow, and points where inventory accumulates.	3: Design 4: Implementation 5: Operations and Continuous Improvement

Table A.1. Types of LGIs and Examples of Each, Cont'd

General LGI Category	Method Name	Description and Example of Use	Useful in Stages
Methods for Various Other High Leverage Objectives	Open Space	A participative session that enables high levels of group interaction and productivity, providing a basis for enhanced organizational functioning over time. This is helpful for teams—and entire organizations—to explore complex issues, disseminate information, create commitment to new directions, and develop action plans for the future.	5: Operations and Continuous Improvement
	Appreciative Inquiry	A participative session designed to enable full-voice appreciative participation that taps the organization's positive change core and inspires collaborative action that serves the whole system. These sessions are useful for creating positive energy and creating culture change.	5: Operations and Continuous Improvement
	Dialogue	A group session designed to build capacity to think together, to surface group assumptions, and to create shared meaning while taking into account the "big picture" perspective. These sessions are useful to explore complex issues, remove organizational barriers, and bring out all facts, opinions, and assumptions before taking any group action. Dialogue is a conversation bringing together multiple perspectives and enabling the group to go beyond deeply held individual and collective views and create new meaning that goes beyond any individual's previous understanding. Peter Senge has stressed the importance of dialogue for high order learning, particularly at the collective level.[i]	All
	Organization Workshop	An experience-based, principle-driven learning and action planning session in which participants discover common traps, reflex actions, and high leverage ways out of the Top, Middle, and Bottom organizational spaces. These sessions are used for developing awareness of the power that can be exercised at various levels of the organization. Most often organizations make time for these sessions during the Implementation stage, although they can also be helpful in Stage 3: Design and Stage 5: Operations and Continuous Improvement.	4: Implementation, or other stages where organizational space distinctions are useful

Sources: Rother, M., and Shook, J. (1999). *Learning to see.* Brookline, MA: Lean Enterprise Institute, Inc. *Learning to See,* for Value Stream Mapping, and for the remaining methods, adapted from P. Holman and T. Devane (Eds.), *The change handbook: Group methods for shaping the future.*

[i]Senge, P.M. (1990). *The fifth discipline: The art and practice of the learning organization.* New York: Doubleday/Currency.

Sample LGI Agendas

Exhibit A.1. presents a sample agenda for a Search Conference, an LGI used for planning and setting strategic direction. The design shown is typically a two-and-one-half-day process conducted for ten to thirty-five people within a session. Multiple sessions can be conducted and their results later integrated if more people have to be involved in the planning process. It is best if a Search Conference is conducted off-site to get away from day-to-day work pressures.

Exhibit A.1. Sample Search Conference Agenda

Segment	Tasks
Environmental understanding and analysis	Changes outside the organizational system Most desirable and probable futures of the environment outside the system
Organizational system understanding and analysis	Historical events and forces that shaped the organizational system Brief analysis of the current organization Most desirable future for the organization
Integration of the organizational system and the environment	Constraints and how to deal with them Most desirable and achievable organization Action plans to achieve desirable future
Diffusion planning	Strategy and structure to diffuse information with the workshop to the rest of the organization
Diffusion	Circle of engagement grows as goals and plans are diffused and implemented

Source: Reprinted with permission of the publisher. From *The Change Handbook: Group Methods for Shaping the Future*, copyright © 1999, by M. Emery and T. Devane, Berrett-Koehler Publishers, Inc, San Francisco, CA. All rights reserved. www.bkconnection.com

Exhibit A.2 shows a sample agenda for a Participative Design Workshop, an LGI used to restructure organizations into High-Performance Teams. The design shown is typically a one-to-three-day process conducted for a segment of the organization ranging in size from fifteen to two hundred people per workshop. To demonstrate that the organization is serious about the redesign to High-Performance Teams, it is helpful to have senior management kick off as many sessions as possible. It is most helpful for them to indicate they support the effort, say they trust people to come up with a great result, and then leave to let the people get to work.

Exhibit A.2. Sample Participative Design Workshop Agenda

Segment	Tasks
Analysis of the Current Structure	Introduction and presentation of design guidelines and boundaries established by top management
	Briefing 1: Traps and performance detractors that exist in traditional organization designs
	Participants score themselves on the six criteria for productive work
	Participants identify skills held and their distribution through the section
	Participants prepare reports and analyses of trends and patterns discovered in the above two activities
Structural Redesign	Briefing 2: Principles and methods for designing high-performance organizations
	Participants draw the workflow and current organizational structure.
	Participants then redesign the structure into high-performance teams (Process redesign is not a major objective here, although sometimes process boundaries and flow do shift because of new team boundaries. Large structural redesign projects based on process considerations may come later with Black Belt inputs)
	Participants report work flow and the new organizational structure of high performance teams
Other Practicalities of the Design	Briefing 3: Conditions and work products required to make the design work
	Participants draft a comprehensive set of measurable goals for each team and the work section
	Participants develop training requirements (based on the skills held analysis in the first workshop segment)
	Participants draft career paths for their "organizational chunk" based on people's skills
	Participants decide what else is required to make the design work (for example, mechanisms for coordination or technological or physical layout changes such as meeting rooms).
	Participants state how the redesign will improve their scores on the six criteria for productive work (developed in the first workshop segment)

Source: Reprinted with permission of the publisher. From *The Change Handbook: Group Methods for Shaping the Future*, copyright © 1999, by M. Emery and T. Devane, Berrett-Koehler Publishers, Inc, San Francisco, CA. All rights reserved. www.bkconnection.com

Note

1. Holman, P., and Devane, T. (1999). *The change handbook: Group methods for shaping the future.* San Francisco: Berrett-Koehler; Bunker, B., and Alban, B. (1997). *Large group interventions: Engaging the whole system for rapid change.* San Francisco: Jossey-Bass.

Reference Material

I'm astounded by people who want to know the universe, when it's
hard enough to find your way around Chinatown.

Woody Allen

A SINGLE BOOK COULD NEVER COVER all the important
information for leaders for implementing LSS/HPO. So this section
provides places to go for more information.

Table A.2 provides a list of books that can provide support for LSS/HPO
leaders and Table A.3 lists websites that support their endeavors.

General topics are listed across the top of each table representing factors
from the Performance Framework and some additional useful topics for
LSS/HPO leaders. The key is as follows:

- ● Excellent support for LSS/HPO leaders for the indicated topic;
- ☉ Very good support for LSS/HPO leaders for the indicated topic; and
- ○ Good support for LSS/HPO leaders for the indicated topic.

Within each category (such as Strategy or Process), the references are in order, starting with what I believe to be the most useful for an LSS/HPO and then placing the rest in descending order of relevance. All are *very* relevant for LSS/HPO or they wouldn't be on the list. It's just that some seem more relevant than others.

The amount of material presented may at first appear daunting. It should not be. Study teams can tackle different topics and different team members can read different books under that topic. They can then get together and synthesize the information they have learned and tailor it their specific organization's situation.

Table A.2. Books That Support LSS/HPO Leaders

	Author	Strategy	Process	Information and Learning	HR Practices	Culture	Structure & Relationships	Leadership	Human Interaction	Six Sigma	Lean	Change Mgt	HPO
Leading the Revolution	Hamel	●						●					
The Rise and Fall of Strategic Planning	Mintzberg	●											
Competitive Advantage	Porter	●											
Competing for the Future	Hamel & Prahalad	●						⊙					
The Balanced Scorecard	Kaplan & Norton	●	○	⊙									
Winning Through Innovation	O'Reilly III & Tushman	●				⊙	⊙	○					
The Profit Zone	Slywotzky et al.	●	○			○							
Search Conference	Emery & Purser	⊙		○		⊙	⊙	○	⊙				
Futures That Work	Rehm et al.	⊙		○		⊙	⊙	○	⊙			○	⊙
Future Search	Janoff & Weisbord	⊙		○		⊙	⊙	○	⊙				
Process Innovation	Davenport		●	⊙									
Improving Performance	Rummler & Brache		●	○									
The Process Edge	Keen	○	●					○					
If We Only Know What We Knew	O'Dell et al.		○	●									
The Knowledge Creating Company	Nonaka & Takeuchi			●		⊙		○	○				
Intelligent Enterprise	Quinn	○		●		○	⊙		○				
Wellsprings of Knowledge	Leonard-Barton			●					○				

Table A.2. Books That Support LSS/HPO Leaders, Cont'd

Book	Author	Strategy	Process	Information and Learning	HR Practices	Culture	Structure & Relationships	Leadership	Human Interaction	Six Sigma	Lean	Change Mgt	HPO
Working Knowledge	Davenport & Prusak		○	●		○		○					
Unleashing the Killer App	Downes et al.			●									
Human Resource Champions	Ulrich	○			●			○					
Best Practices in Organization Development and Change	Carter et al.				●	⊙		⊙				⊙	
Human Equation	Pfeffer				●	⊙		⊙					
Organizational Culture and Leadership	Schein					●		●					
Built to Last	Collins & Porras	⊙				●		⊙					
Overcoming Organizational Defenses	Argyris					●		○					
Managing on the Edge	Pascale	⊙				●		⊙					⊙
The Discipline of Teams	Katzenbach & Smith						●	⊙	⊙			○	⊙
Designing Team-Based Organizations	Mohrman et al.						●	⊙	⊙			○	●
Designing Organizations	Galbraith						●	⊙					⊙
Participative Design for Participative Democracy	Emery						●	⊙					
The Self-Managing Organization	Purser						●	⊙				○	⊙
Changing by Design	Zell	⊙				○	●					⊙	●
The Leadership Challenge	Kouzes & Posner					⊙		●	⊙			⊙	
Maslow on Management	Maslow					⊙		●	⊙			⊙	
Leadership Without Easy Answers	Heifitz							●	⊙			⊙	

Title	Author
Results-Based Leadership	Ulrich et al.
The Leadership Engine	Tichy
Credibility	Kouzes & Posner
Leading in a Time of Great Change	Drucker
Possibilities of Organization	Oshry
No More Teams	Schrage
PeopleSmart	Silberman, Hansburg
The Collaborative Work Systems Fieldbook	Beyerlein et al.
Productive Workplaces	Weisbord
Knowledge for Action	Argyris
People Skills	Bolton
Managing Six Sigma	Breyfogle et al.
What is Six Sigma?	Pande
Rath & Strong's Six Sigma Leadership Handbook	Rath & Strong
Lean Six Sigma	George
Lean Thinking	Womack & Jones
Learning to See	Rother & Shook
Lean Transformation	Henderson & Larco
Leading Change	Kotter
The Change Handbook	Holman & Devane
The Dance of Change	Senge et al.
The Ultimate Advantage	Lawler
People in Charge	Rehm
High-Involvement Management	Lawler

Table A.3. Websites That Support LSS/HPO Leaders

The following are web resources that provide useful information for the categories listed across the top of the table. As of the printing this book, these are the websites I found helpful for these categories. Updates to this list can be found on LeanSixSigmaHPO.com.

	Strategy	Process	Information and Learning	HR Practices	Culture	Structure & Relationships	Leadership	Human Interaction	Six Sigma	Lean	Change Mgt	HPO
Strategy-business.com	●						⊙				○	
hammerandco.com: some useful background and training offerings of Michael Hammer		●										
www.brint.com/papers/bpr.htm: myths, process redesign background, and future directions		●										
bus.utexas.edu/kman/kmprin.htm: basic principles of knowledge management as articulated by Thomas Davenport, a respected researcher and practitioner			●									
gsm.ucdavis.edu/Courses/Winter2003/224/mgp_br/ulrich_hr_champions.pdf: a good synopsis of Ulrich's book Human Resource Champions				●								
www.tmellen.com/ted/tc/schein.html: Schein's description of cultural leadership implications					●							
cpocma.army.mil/TMD/Organ%20Design/Ch9.doc: concise steps of how to design a team-based structure, based on an army unit redesign						●						
pfdf.org/leaderbooks/l2l/complete-text.html: selected Leader to Leader articles by luminaries like Bennis, DePree, Hamel, and Grove are available							●					
pfdf.org: formerly the Drucker Foundation, this Leader to Leader Institute membership entitles members to a large leadership library							●					

	TopMiddleBottomLSSHPO.com	Powerandsystems.com	PeopleSmartLSSHPO.com	isixsigma.com	lean.org	TransformationGrid.com	hbsp.com	LeanSixSigmaHPO.com
	⊙					⊙		●
	⊙	○	⊙			●	●	●
	⊙				●	⊙		●
	⊙			●		⊙		●
	●	●	●			⊙	○	
	⊙	⊙	⊙			●	●	
	⊙		⊙			○	●	
	⊙		⊙			●	●	
						○	○	
	⊙					●	○	
						●	○	
						●	⊙	

TopMiddleBottomLSSHPO.com: a website that presents customized high leverage actions for Tops, Middles, and Bottoms in an LSS/HPO

Powerandsystems.com: a website dedicated to organizational spaces that was developed by Barry Oshry, developer of the concept of organizational spaces

PeopleSmartLSSHPO.com: a website that contains tips for personal interactions like communication, negotiation, and conflict management. Courses are also available

isixsigma.com: In my view, this is the premier Six Sigma website. It provides a wealth of information through articles and also has "discussion threads" that allow people to post questions, answers, and have conversations for others to see and learn from

lean.org: In my view, this is the premier Lean website. Like isixsigma.com, it provides a wealth of information through articles and also has "discussion threads" that allow people to post questions, answers, and have conversations for others to see and learn from

TransformationGrid.com: a website that shows high leverage leadership actions in each stage of an LSS/HPO transformation

hbsp.com: The Harvard Business School press catalog is searchable by topic, author, or title. HBR articles cost about $7/article

LeanSixSigmaHPO.com: a website dedicated to helping leaders successfully lead from one LSS/HPO stage to the next. Free articles, late-breaking information related to topics in this book, and upcoming seminars are posted

MICHAEL M. BEYERLEIN, PH.D., is director of the Center for the Study of Work Teams (www.workteams.unt.edu) and professor of industrial/organizational psychology at the University of North Texas. His research interests include all aspects of collaborative work systems, organization transformation, work stress, creativity/innovation, knowledge management and the learning organization, and complex adaptive systems. He has published in a number of research journals and has been a member of the editorial boards for *TEAM Magazine, Team Performance Management Journal,* and *Quality Management Journal.* Currently, he is senior editor of the JAI Press/Elsevier annual series of books, *Advances in Interdisciplinary Studies of Work Teams,* as well as this new series of books on collaborative work systems. In addition, he has been co-editor with Steve Jones on two ASTD case books about teams and edited a book on the global history of teams, *Work Teams: Past, Present and Future.* He has been involved in change projects at the Center for the Study of Work Teams with such companies as Boeing, Shell, NCH, Advanced Micro Devices, Westinghouse, and Xerox and with government agencies such as the Bureau of Veterans' Affairs, Defense

Contract Management Agency, the Environmental Protection Agency, and the City of Denton, Texas.

JAMES R. BARKER, PH.D., is director of research and professor of organizational theory and strategy in the Department of Management at the U.S. Air Force Academy. His research interests focus on the development and analysis of collaborative control practices in technological and knowledge-based organizations. His research projects include collaborations with scientists at the Los Alamos and Sandia National Laboratories and with scholars at the University of Melbourne and the University of Western Australia. Dr. Barker's work has appeared in a number of professional journals, including *Administrative Science Quarterly, Journal of Organizational and Occupational Psychology,* and *Communication Monographs.* His new book, *The Discipline of Teamwork,* is now available from Sage Publications. He won the 1993 Outstanding Publication in Organizational Behavior award from the Academy of Management and the 1999 *Administrative Science Quarterly* Scholarly Contribution Award for his research on self-managing teams. He has lectured on teamwork in organizations at many universities and organizations, including the Sloan School of Management at the Massachusetts Institute of Technology and the University of Western Australia. He served as associate editor of the *Western Journal of Communication* and on the editorial boards of *Administrative Science Quarterly, Journal of Organizational Change Management,* and *Management Communication Quarterly.*

SUSAN TULL BEYERLEIN, PH.D., holds a B.A. in English from the University of Oregon, an M.S. in general psychology from Fort Hays State University, and a Ph.D. in organization theory and policy with a minor in education research from the University of North Texas, Denton. Since 1988, she has taught a variety of management courses as an adjunct faculty member at several universities in the Dallas metroplex, with a particular focus on strategic management at both the undergraduate and MBA levels. Dr. Beyerlein has served as a research scientist/project manager with the Center for the Study of Work Teams at the University of North Texas and has been a recipient of research grant awards from the Association for Quality and Participation, the National Science Foundation, and corporate donors. Since 1995, she has co-edited the Elsevier/JAI Imprint annual book series, entitled *Advances in Interdisciplinary Studies of Work Teams,* and during the same period has served as an *ad hoc* reviewer for *The Academy of Management Review.* She has published book reviews on contemporary business offerings in *Business and the Contemporary World,* and her work has also appeared in *Structural Equation Modeling: A Multidisciplinary Journal, Teams: The Magazine for High Performance Organizations* (UK), *Journal of Management Education, Empirical Studies of the Arts,* and *Multiple Linear Regression Viewpoints.* She is a member of the Academy of Management, Beta Gamma Sigma—the honor society for collegiate schools of business—and Phi Kappa Phi National Honor Society.

TOM DEVANE is an internationally known consultant, author, and workshop leader. He specializes in dramatic, sustainable performance improvements. Such improvements require a careful blending of improvement principles, simple and advanced tools, change management practices, and effective leadership. Prior to starting his own firm in 1988, Tom worked for two Big Six consulting firms and a refining and oil shale company.

Representative clients include Microsoft, General Electric, Hewlett-Packard, Johnson & Johnson, Honeywell, AT&T, the United States Federal Judicial Court System, StorageTek, Westin Hotel–Denver, Porter Memorial Hospital, the U.S. Forest Service, and the South African government. Mr. Devane considers himself fortunate to have participated in a number of large-scale, paradigm-shifting future changing improvement efforts. One was the breakup of AT&T that required people to rapidly shift from a monopolistic to a market-driven mindset. In another, he helped a South African government agency after the dismantling of apartheid. Within an eighteen-month period this agency successfully changed its customer base, business processes, organizational structure, culture, information systems, and product offerings in response to dramatic political, economic, and societal changes. Mr. Devane began integrating Lean, Six Sigma, and HPO disciplines in 1995 at StorageTek, a $2 billion electronic information storage company.

Devane is also a guest lecturer and adjunct faculty member at Cornell University, the University of Denver, and Sonoma State University. He is co-author and co-editor for *The Change Handbook: Group Methods for Shaping the Future.* In addition, he has contributed to books, magazines, and websites on the topics of team-based strategic planning, designing high-performance organizations, the Balanced Scorecard for planning and management, organizational transformation, and deploying Six Sigma in non-manufacturing environments. He holds B.S. and M.S. degrees in finance from the University of Illinois. He can be reached at tomd@tomdevane.com or 303.898.6172. Devane maintains a website that contains additional LSS/HPO tips and information sources at LeanSixSigmaHPO.com.

About Pfeiffer

Pfeiffer serves the professional development and hands-on resource needs of training and human resource practitioners and gives them products to do their jobs better. We deliver proven ideas and solutions from experts in HR development and HR management, and we offer effective and customizable tools to improve workplace performance. From novice to seasoned professional, Pfeiffer is the source you can trust to make yourself and your organization more successful.

Essential Knowledge Pfeiffer produces insightful, practical, and comprehensive materials on topics that matter the most to training and HR professionals. Our Essential Knowledge resources translate the expertise of seasoned professionals into practical, how-to guidance on critical workplace issues and problems. These resources are supported by case studies, worksheets, and job aids and are frequently supplemented with CD-ROMs, websites, and other means of making the content easier to read, understand, and use.

Essential Tools Pfeiffer's Essential Tools resources save time and expense by offering proven, ready-to-use materials—including exercises, activities, games, instruments, and assessments—for use during a training or team-learning event. These resources are frequently offered in looseleaf or CD-ROM format to facilitate copying and customization of the material.

Pfeiffer also recognizes the remarkable power of new technologies in expanding the reach and effectiveness of training. While e-hype has often created whizbang solutions in search of a problem, we are dedicated to bringing convenience and enhancements to proven training solutions. All our e-tools comply with rigorous functionality standards. The most appropriate technology wrapped around essential content yields the perfect solution for today's on-the-go trainers and human resource professionals.

Essential resources for training and HR professionals

Pfeiffer Publications Guide

This guide is designed to familiarize you with the various types of Pfeiffer publications. The formats section describes the various types of products that we publish; the methodologies section describes the many different ways that content might be provided within a product. We also provide a list of the topic areas in which we publish.

FORMATS

In addition to its extensive book-publishing program, Pfeiffer offers content in an array of formats, from fieldbooks for the practitioner to complete, ready-to-use training packages that support group learning.

FIELDBOOK Designed to provide information and guidance to practitioners in the midst of action. Most fieldbooks are companions to another, sometimes earlier, work, from which its ideas are derived; the fieldbook makes practical what was theoretical in the original text. Fieldbooks can certainly be read from cover to cover. More likely, though, you'll find yourself bouncing around following a particular theme, or dipping in as the mood, and the situation, dictate.

HANDBOOK A contributed volume of work on a single topic, comprising an eclectic mix of ideas, case studies, and best practices sourced by practitioners and experts in the field.

An editor or team of editors usually is appointed to seek out contributors and to evaluate content for relevance to the topic. Think of a handbook not as a ready-to-eat meal, but as a cookbook of ingredients that enables you to create the most fitting experience for the occasion.

RESOURCE Materials designed to support group learning. They come in many forms: a complete, ready-to-use exercise (such as a game); a comprehensive resource on one topic (such as conflict management) containing a variety of methods and approaches; or a collection of like-minded activities (such as icebreakers) on multiple subjects and situations.

TRAINING PACKAGE An entire, ready-to-use learning program that focuses on a particular topic or skill. All packages comprise a guide for the facilitator/trainer and a workbook for the participants. Some packages are supported with additional media—such as video—or learning aids, instruments, or other devices to help participants understand concepts or practice and develop skills.

- *Facilitator/trainer's guide* Contains an introduction to the program, advice on how to organize and facilitate the learning event, and step-by-step instructor notes. The guide also contains copies of presentation materials—handouts, presentations, and overhead designs, for example—used in the program.

• *Participant's workbook* Contains exercises and reading materials that support the learning goal and serves as a valuable reference and support guide for participants in the weeks and months that follow the learning event. Typically, each participant will require his or her own workbook.

ELECTRONIC CD-ROMs and web-based products transform static Pfeiffer content into dynamic, interactive experiences. Designed to take advantage of the searchability, automation, and ease-of-use that technology provides, our e-products bring convenience and immediate accessibility to your workspace.

METHODOLOGIES

CASE STUDY A presentation, in narrative form, of an actual event that has occurred inside an organization. Case studies are not prescriptive, nor are they used to prove a point; they are designed to develop critical analysis and decision-making skills. A case study has a specific time frame, specifies a sequence of events, is narrative in structure, and contains a plot structure—an issue (what should be/have been done?). Use case studies when the goal is to enable participants to apply previously learned theories to the circumstances in the case, decide what is pertinent, identify the real issues, decide what should have been done, and develop a plan of action.

ENERGIZER A short activity that develops readiness for the next session or learning event. Energizers are most commonly used after a break or lunch to stimulate or refocus the group. Many involve some form of physical activity, so they are a useful way to counter post-lunch lethargy. Other uses include transitioning from one topic to another, where "mental" distancing is important.

EXPERIENTIAL LEARNING ACTIVITY (ELA) A facilitator-led intervention that moves participants through the learning cycle from experience to application (also known as a Structured Experience). ELAs are carefully thought-out designs in which there is a definite learning purpose and intended outcome. Each step—everything that participants do during the activity—facilitates the accomplishment of the stated goal. Each ELA includes complete instructions for facilitating the intervention and a clear statement of goals, suggested group size and timing, materials required, an explanation of the process, and, where appropriate, possible variations to the activity. (For more detail on Experiential Learning Activities, see the Introduction to the *Reference Guide to Handbooks and Annuals*, 1999 edition, Pfeiffer, San Francisco.)

GAME A group activity that has the purpose of fostering team spirit and togetherness in addition to the achievement of a pre-stated goal. Usually contrived—undertaking a desert expedition, for example—this type of learning method offers an engaging means for participants to demonstrate and practice business and interpersonal skills. Games are effective for team building and personal development mainly because the goal is subordinate to the process—the means through which participants reach decisions, collaborate, communicate, and generate trust and understanding. Games often engage teams in "friendly" competition.

ICEBREAKER A (usually) short activity designed to help participants overcome initial anxiety in a training session and/or to acquaint the participants with one another. An icebreaker can be a fun activity or can be tied to specific topics or training goals. While a useful tool in itself, the icebreaker comes into its own in situations where tension or resistance exists within a group.

INSTRUMENT A device used to assess, appraise, evaluate, describe, classify, and summarize various aspects of human behavior. The term used to describe an instrument depends primarily on its format and purpose. These terms include survey, questionnaire, inventory, diagnostic, survey, and poll. Some uses of instruments include providing instrumental feedback to group members, studying here-and-now processes or functioning within a group, manipulating group composition, and evaluating outcomes of training and other interventions.

Instruments are popular in the training and HR field because, in general, more growth can occur if an individual is provided with a method for focusing specifically on his or her own behavior. Instruments also are used to obtain information that will serve as a basis for change and to assist in workforce planning efforts.

Paper-and-pencil tests still dominate the instrument landscape with a typical package comprising a facilitator's guide, which offers advice on administering the instrument and interpreting the collected data, and an initial set of instruments. Additional instruments are available separately. Pfeiffer, though, is investing heavily in e-instruments. Electronic instrumentation provides effortless distribution and, for larger groups particularly, offers advantages over paper-and-pencil tests in the time it takes to analyze data and provide feedback.

LECTURETTE A short talk that provides an explanation of a principle, model, or process that is pertinent to the participants' current learning needs. A lecturette is intended to establish a common language bond between the trainer and the participants by providing a mutual frame of reference. Use a lecturette as an introduction to a group activity or event, as an interjection during an event, or as a handout.

MODEL A graphic depiction of a system or process and the relationship among its elements. Models provide a frame of reference and something more tangible, and more easily remembered, than a verbal explanation. They also give participants something to "go on," enabling them to track their own progress as they experience the dynamics, processes, and relationships being depicted in the model.

ROLE PLAY A technique in which people assume a role in a situation/scenario: a customer service rep in an angry-customer exchange, for example. The way in which the role is approached is then discussed and feedback is offered. The role play is often repeated using a different approach and/or incorporating changes made based on feedback received. In other words, role playing is a spontaneous interaction involving realistic behavior under artificial (and safe) conditions.

SIMULATION A methodology for understanding the interrelationships among components of a system or process. Simulations differ from games in that they test or use a model that depicts or mirrors some aspect of reality in form, if not necessarily in content. Learning occurs by studying the effects of change on one or more factors of the model. Simulations are commonly used to test hypotheses about what happens in a system—often referred to as "what if?" analysis—or to examine best-case/worst-case scenarios.

THEORY A presentation of an idea from a conjectural perspective. Theories are useful because they encourage us to examine behavior and phenomena through a different lens.

TOPICS

The twin goals of providing effective and practical solutions for workforce training and organization development and meeting the educational needs of training and human resource professionals shape Pfeiffer's publishing program. Core topics include the following:

Leadership & Management

Communication & Presentation

Coaching & Mentoring

Training & Development

e-Learning

Teams & Collaboration

OD & Strategic Planning

Human Resources

Consulting

What will you find on pfeiffer.com?

- The best in workplace performance solutions for training and HR professionals

- Downloadable training tools, exercises, and content

- Web-exclusive offers

- Training tips, articles, and news

- Seamless online ordering

- Author guidelines, information on becoming a Pfeiffer affiliate, and much more

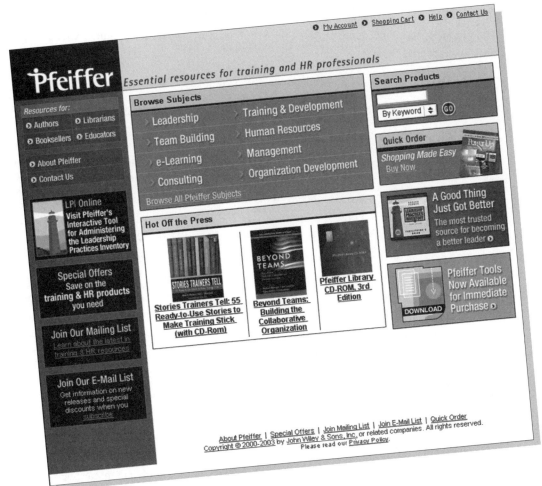

Discover more at www.pfeiffer.com

Customer Care

Have a question, comment, or suggestion? Contact us! We value your feedback and we want to hear from you.

For questions about this or other Pfeiffer products, you may contact us by:

E-mail: **customer@wiley.com**

Mail: **Customer Care Wiley/Pfeiffer**
        10475 Crosspoint Blvd.
        Indianapolis, IN 46256

Phone: **(US) 800-274-4434** (Outside the US: 317-572-3985)

Fax: **(US) 800-569-0443** (Outside the US: 317-572-4002)

To order additional copies of this title or to browse other Pfeiffer products, visit us online at **www.pfeiffer.com**.

For **Technical Support** questions call **(800) 274-4434.**

For author guidelines, log on to www.pfeiffer.com and click on "Resources for Authors."

If you are . . .

A **college bookstore, a professor, an instructor, or work in higher education** and you'd like to place an order or request an exam copy, please contact jbreview@wiley.com.

A **general retail bookseller** and you'd like to establish an account or speak to a local sales representative, contact Melissa Grecco at 201-748-6267 or mgrecco@wiley.com.

An **exclusively online bookseller**, contact Amy Blanchard at 530-756-9456 or ablanchard @wiley.com or Jennifer Johnson at 206-568-3883 or jjohnson@wiley.com, both of our Online Sales department.

A **librarian or library representative**, contact John Chambers in our Library Sales department at 201-748-6291 or jchamber@wiley.com.

A **reseller, training company/consultant, or corporate trainer**, contact Charles Regan in our Special Sales department at 201-748-6553 or cregan@wiley.com.

A **specialty retail distributor** (includes specialty gift stores, museum shops, and corporate bulk sales), contact Kim Hendrickson in our Special Sales department at 201-748-6037 or khendric@wiley.com.

Purchasing for the **Federal government**, contact Ron Cunningham in our Special Sales department at 317-572-3053 or rcunning@wiley.com.

Purchasing for a **State or Local government**, contact Charles Regan in our Special Sales department at 201-748-6553 or cregan@wiley.com.